GREAT BRITAIN SPECIALISED STAMP CATALOGUE

Queen Elizabeth II
Decimal Definitive Issues

Volume 4 Part 2

Machin portrait

Stanley Gibbons
Great Britain Specialised
Stamp Catalogue

Volume 4 Part 2

Queen Elizabeth II
Decimal Definitive Issues

10th Edition

STANLEY GIBBONS LTD
London and Ringwood

By Appointment to Her Majesty The Queen
Stanley Gibbons Ltd, London
Philatelists

Published by Stanley Gibbons Ltd
Editorial, Publications Sales Offices
and Distribution Centre:
7 Parkside, Christchurch Road, Ringwood,
Hants BH24 3SH

© Stanley Gibbons Ltd 2010

Copyright Notice

The contents of this Catalogue, including the numbering system and illustrations, are fully protected by copyright. No part of this publication may be reproduced, stored in a retrieval system, or transmitted in any form or by any means, electronic, mechanical, photocopying, recording or otherwise, without the prior permission of Stanley Gibbons Limited. Requests for such permission should be addressed to the Catalogue Editor. This Catalogue is sold on condition that it is not, by way of trade or otherwise, lent, re-sold, hired out, circulated or otherwise disposed of other than in its complete, original and unaltered form and without a similar condition including this condition being imposed on the subsequent purchaser.

1st edition – October 1976
Reprinted – November 1977, July 1978
2nd edition – April 1979
3rd edition – November 1981
4th edition – May 1985
5th edition – March 1988
6th edition – July 1991
7th edition – June 1994
8th edition – October 1996
9th edition – May 2008
10th edition – Part 1 April 2008
Part 2 August 2010

British Library Cataloguing in
Publication Data.
A catalogue record for this book is available from the British Library.

Errors and omissions excepted. The colour
reproduction of stamps is only as accurate as
the printing process will allow.

ISBN-10: 0-85259-738-X
ISBN-13: 978-0-85259-738-6

Item No. R2821-10

Printed by Latimer Trend & Company Ltd, Plymouth

Contents

Preface vii
Introductory Notes ix

Section UI   Machin No Value Indicated Issues (PVA gum) 1
     Checklist 2
     Single stamps 4
     Booklet panes 20
     Prestige Booklet panes 39

Section UJ   Decimal Self-adhesive Issues 44
     PSA gum single stamps 45
     SA gum single stamps 49
     Booklet panes 52
     Business sheets 64

Section UK   Decimal Castles Issues 67

Section UL   Britannia High Value 73

Section UM   Greetings stamps 74

Section UN   Dorothy Wilding Portrait stamps 94

Section XB   Regional Machin Issues – Gravure 98
     Isle of Man 99
     Northern Ireland 100
     Scotland 108
     Wales 115

Section XC   Regional Machin Issues – Lithography ... 124
     Northern Ireland 125
     Scotland 133
     Wales 143

Section XD   Regional Machin Prestige Booklet Panes ... 153

Section XE   Regional Pictorial Issues Gravure 156
     England 156
     Northern Ireland 162
     Scotland 163
     Wales 169

Section XF   Regional Pictorial Issues Lithography 175
     England 175
     Northern Ireland 176
     Scotland 181
     Wales 182

Section XG   Regional Pictorial Booklet Panes 182
     England 183
     Northern Ireland 183
     Scotland 184
     Wales 184

Section Y   Royal Mail Postage Labels 185
     Royal Mail Fast Stamps 186

Section ZB   Postage Due Stamps 187

Appendix J   Stamp Booklets 191
     Folded Booklets 191
     Barcode Booklets 191
     Barcode Penny Black Anniversary Booklets ... 206
     Barcode Greetings Stamps Booklets 207
     Self-adhesive Barcode Booklets 210

NEW

look for our 399 Strand store!

Come and experience it for yourself

STANLEY GIBBONS — Est 1856

The NEW 399 Strand
More space
Better displays
Interactive information
A better shop for you!

The new look home of stamp collecting

Following months of renovations in advance of the London 2010 show, the new look 399 Strand has officially re-opened its doors to provide you with an exciting new shopping and browsing experience.

The retail area has been expanded to allow you much more space, better, clearer displays and to allow dedicated seating areas for stamp viewing and helpful, interactive information points. **The famous stamp counter will remain** and the shop will continue to offer an unrivalled range of philatelic items, coupled with the expertise you expect from our dedicated team of philatelic specialists.

399 Strand - *The only choice for valuations, auctions, investments, gifts and a range of premium collectibles.*

We look forward to seeing you!

399 Strand, London, WC2R 0LX
+44 (0)20 7836 8444
orders@stanleygibbons.co.uk
www.stanleygibbons.com

Preface

When the last complete, single-volume edition of Volume 4 of the Stanley Gibbons Great Britain Specialised Catalogue, covering Queen Elizabeth Decimal Definitive Issues was published in 2000, it comprised almost 900 loose-leaf pages. Unfortunately, the loose-leaf format was not widely welcomed, however, and it was decided to return to a fast-bound publication for the 10th edition, although this would require the book to be split into two parts.

Part 1 was published in April 2008 and listed all the Machin head stamps with specific values, apart from self-adhesives, together with the booklet panes and stamp booklets in which they appeared.

Part 2, which is presented in this volume, lists all other Decimal Definitive issues: self-adhesive stamps, No Value Indicated (NVI) stamps, non-Machin definitives (high values), Regionals, Greetings stamps, Royal Mail Postage Labels and Postage Dues, including relevant booklet panes and booklets.

The catalogue has been re-styled since publication of Part 1, with a larger page size and two-column format allowing more information to be presented on a page, while the return to case binding improves durability and allows the book to lie flat on the desk in use. The reduced use of upper-case lettering in the text and the addition of a second colour also bring greater clarity to the listings.

The past ten years have seen numerous developments in British stamps. Happily, the now annual increases in postage rates have a limited effect on this catalogue as, apart from the regionals, most denominated stamps are in Part 1.

The continuing demand for self-adhesive stamps by the British public has resulted in increasing availability of stamp booklets, including those containing a combination of definitive and special issues; while sheet stamps of higher values are also now available in this form.

Another development has resulted from the increasing need on the part of Royal Mail to prevent re-use of uncancelled stamps. February 2009 saw the arrival of a completely new group of Machin definitives incorporating self-adhesive gum, U-shaped slits (to prevent removal from envelopes without damage) and an iridescent multiple "Royal Mail" overlay. This overlay incorporates a code to allow the source of a particular stamp to be identified.

Significant developments have taken place in the Regionals section, with the arrival of the first England stamps and the change over from Machin to "Pictorial" types. In Section 7 the new "Fast Stamps" have been added.

Rather less desirable in the eyes of many has been the proliferation of so-called "Prestige" stamp booklets, output of which has doubled over the past ten years. Postally unnecessary they may be, but they continue to be well produced and interesting and frequently contain stamps not available from other sources.

All of these developments are reflected in the listings in this catalogue.

Another unfortunate development has been the neglect by Royal Mail (and some specialist dealers and catalogue publishers) of collectors of used stamps; yet we know that such collecting remains popular. Accordingly, this catalogue continues to give prices for used single stamps, although, given the difficulty one has in obtaining fine used examples in these days of "Horizon" labels and pen-cancellation of adhesives, we wonder whether there should not be a greater premium placed on used examples in future editions.

In this respect, it should be noted that since the issue of the "Security" Machins in 2009 there is no longer a water-soluble layer of gum in the self-adhesive stamps, making it impossible to "soak" them in the traditional way. We therefore recommend that they be collected "on piece".

Publishing a catalogue that lists only recent issues would appear a simple undertaking but this is not the case. We do rely on help from specialists in their field. We thank Peter Shaw for his work on the Castle issues, John Deering on Machins in general and Jim Bond for his advice especially on the Regionals. To Mike Holt and Paul Skinner for advising us of new discoveries and special thanks to John Holman, former editor of the British Philatelic Bulletin. Collectors following Machins regularly are reminded that John Deering's "Machin Watch" articles appear each month in Gibbons Stamp Monthly, where the monthly supplement to this catalogue will also be found.

Hugh Jefferies
Robert Oliver

August 2010

About Us

Our History
Edward Stanley Gibbons started trading postage stamps in his father's chemist shop in 1856. Since then we have been at the forefront of stamp collecting for over 150 years. We hold the Royal Warrant, offer unsurpassed expertise and quality and provide collectors with the peace of mind of a certificate of authenticity on all of our stamps. If you think of stamp collecting, you think of Stanley Gibbons and we are proud to uphold that tradition for you.

399 Strand
Our world famous stamp shop is a collector's paradise, with all of our latest catalogues, albums and accessories and, of course, our unrivalled stockholding of postage stamps.
www.stanleygibbons.com   shop@stanleygibbons.co.uk   +44 (0)20 7836 8444

Specialist Stamp Sales
For the collector that appreciates the value of collecting the highest quality examples, Stanley Gibbons is the only choice. Our extensive range is unrivalled in terms of quality and quantity, with specialist stamps available from all over the world.
www.stanleygibbons.com/stamps   shop@stanleygibbons.co.uk   +44 (0)20 7836 8444

Stanley Gibbons Auctions and Valuations
Sell your collection or individual rare items through our prestigious public auctions or our regular postal auctions and benefit from the excellent prices being realised at auction currently. We also provide an unparalleled valuation service.
www.stanleygibbons.com/auctions   auctions@stanleygibbons.co.uk   +44 (0)20 7836 8444

Stanley Gibbons Publications
The world's first stamp catalogue was printed by Stanley Gibbons in 1865 and we haven't looked back since! Our catalogues are trusted worldwide as the industry standard and we print countless titles each year. We also publish consumer and trade magazines, Gibbons Stamp Monthly and Philatelic Exporter to bring you news, views and insights into all things philatelic. Never miss an issue by subscribing today and benefit from exclusive subscriber offers each month.
www.stanleygibbons.com/shop   orders@stanleygibbons.co.uk   +44 (0)1425 472 363

Stanley Gibbons Investments
The Stanley Gibbons Investment Department offers a unique range of investment propositions that have consistently outperformed more traditional forms of investment, from capital protected products with unlimited upside to portfolios made up of the world's rarest stamps and autographs.
www.stanleygibbons.com/investment   investment@stanleygibbons.co.uk   +44 (0)1481 708 270

Fraser's Autographs
Autographs, manuscripts and memorabilia from Henry VIII to current day. We have over 60,000 items in stock, including movie stars, musicians, sport stars, historical figures and royalty. Fraser's is the UK's market leading autograph dealer and has been dealing in high quality autographed material since 1978.
www.frasersautographs.com   sales@frasersautographs.co.uk   +44 (0)20 7557 4404

stanleygibbons.com
Our website offers the complete philatelic service. Whether you are looking to buy stamps, invest, read news articles, browse our online stamp catalogue or find new issues, you are just one click away from anything you desire in the world of stamp collecting at stanleygibbons.com. Happy browsing!
www.stanleygibbons.com

Introductory Notes

Detailed Introductory Notes
Before using the catalogue it is most important to study the General Notes as these detail the technical background of the issues in question. These General Notes will be found at the beginning of each section and also indicate some of the areas which are beyond the scope of this work.

Arrangement of Lists
In most cases, stamps are listed value by value, but in sections UI and UJ, because all, or the majority of stamps are No Value Indicated, this is not practicable. The format of these sections is given in their introductions. Within each section the order of listing is as follows:
  A. Basic listing of single stamps from sheets, booklets and coils according to paper and gum with errors and varieties.
  B. List of cylinder or plate blocks according to paper and gum combinations quoting ink and phosphor cylinder numbers and priced according to perforation types.
  C. List of Warrant Numbers and Dates of Printing.
  D. Illustrations of the listed cylinder varieties.
  E. Details of constant minor sheet flaws without illustrations and prices but quoting positions on stamps.
  F. Information relating to coils.
  G. Withdrawal dates. If there is a deliberate change in the number of phosphor bands this is treated as a separate issue which is then listed in the same order shown above. Booklet Panes are listed separately in Sections UI and UJ under the illustrations of complete panes and according to paper and gum.

Catalogue Numbering
Basic catalogue numbers bear the prefix letter which denotes its section of the catalogue. This is followed by the related number in the 2010 edition of the Great Britain Concise Catalogue. Shades, where there is more than one, are denoted by bracketed numbers, e.g. (1) Ultramarine, (2) Pale ultramarine. Varieties have a letter identification, e.g. a. Phosphor omitted, b. (short description of cylinder variety) and related varieties to item b, will be listed as ba., bb., etc. In Appendix J the booklets have the same numbers and prefix letters as are used in the G.B. Concise Catalogue.

Prices
Prices quoted in this Catalogue are those which Stanley Gibbons Ltd. estimate will be their selling prices at the time of publication. They are for stamps of fine condition for the particular issue, unless otherwise indicated; those of lesser quality may be offered at lower prices. In the case of unused stamps, our prices are for unmounted mint. Prices for used stamps refer to fine postally used examples. All prices are subject to change without prior notice and Stanley Gibbons Ltd. may from time to time offer stamps below catalogue price in consequence of special purchases or particular promotions. Subscribers to new issues are asked to note that the prices charged for them contain an element for the service rendered and so may exceed the prices shown when the stamps are subsequently catalogued. No guarantee is given to supply all stamps priced, since it is not possible to keep every catalogued item in stock. Individual low value stamps sold at 399 Strand are liable to an additional handling charge. Postage and packing charges are extra.

If a variety exists on more than one shade, the price quoted is for the most common shade; it will be worth correspondingly more for a scarcer shade. Cases can exist where a particular stamp shows more than one of the listed varieties. It might, for example, have a cylinder flaw as well as abroad phosphor band, both of which are listed but priced separately. It is not practical to cover every possible combination but the value of such items may be established by adding the difference between the price of the basic stamp and the dearest variety to the catalogue price of the cheapest variety. Cylinder blocks are priced according to the type of perforator used. This takes account of the state of the perforations on all four sides of the sheet, not just the corner where the cylinder number appears. Note that a full specification of a cylinder block should quote the basic number of the stamp; cylinder number; phosphor cylinder number and displacement if any; with or without dot; perforation type; and type of paper and gum wherever such alternatives exist. Prices for cylinder flaws are for single stamps and extra stamps required to make up positional blocks would be charged as normals. However all cylinder flaws and other varieties listed under booklet panes are priced for the complete pane. Prices for cylinder blocks containing listed varieties are indicated by an asterisk and include the cost of the variety. The prices quoted for booklet panes are for panes with good perforations and complete with the binding margin.

Items Excluded
In dealing with varieties and minor constant flaws we record only those for which we can vouch, namely items we have seen and verified for ourselves. It should be recognised, however, that some flaws described as constant may be transient: they may develop in size to be sufficiently noticeable to be worth retouching. To qualify for listing, imperforate errors must show no sign of indentation, i.e. blind perforations, on any side of a pair. Such part-perforated varieties can occur in Jumelle printings after re-starting the press during a run and are caused by the pins on the perforating drum only gradually coming into contact with the female cylinder so that some rows will show signs of indentation. Varieties caused by paper creases are listed but with a footnote. Colour shifts due to faulty registration range from minor shifts to quite spectacular varieties. As it is very difficult to draw a line between major and minor shifts we have not listed any. We likewise exclude: doctor blade flaws; partially omitted colours; and misplaced perforations. We do not quote for traffic light blocks, gutter margins or positional blocks showing various sheet markings other than cylinder blocks or Warrant number blocks, but when available they will be supplied at appropriate prices. Zero Value Stamps. Produced for trial purposes by Royal Mail are the property of Royal Mail and should not be in the public domain. Key News, Dec. 2007. Finally, we make no mention whatever of unusual items in a form not issued by the Post Office. In recent years many philatelic items have been prepared privately, with or without Post Office authority, some having postal validity. Many are made for laudable purposes, such as for the promotion of philatelic events, exhibitions and society anniversaries, or for charitable causes, but others have been purely commercial productions. They can be such things as legitimate postal issues with overprints in the margins, black prints, specially prepared packs and booklets made up

Stanley Gibbons Mail Order Department

Stanley Gibbons Mail Order Department provide the perfect support for those starting or furthering their collection, particularly for more modern issues. We produce regular brochures listing our available Great Britain, Channel Islands and Isle of Man material, as well as mailings for many Commonwealth countries.

Our friendly, personal service is built on the traditions of Stanley Gibbons and we are keen to help you fill your supplement pages. If you're looking for particular stamps, send your wants list to Mrs. Lesley Mourne at the address below or telephone us to discuss your needs.

Contact us today for any of the following:

- Mint and used Great Britain stamps
- Presentation Packs
- First Day Covers
- Regional Issues
- Postage Dues
- Booklets
- Smilers Sheets
- Channel Islands and Isle of Man issues
- Commonwealth stamps

For your free copy of the latest Great Britain Mail Order List call us on **020 7557 4460**

Did you know...
we also offer a mail order service for Commonwealth material.
Contact us on the details below for further information.

Stanley Gibbons Mail Order Department
399 Strand, London, WC2R 0LX Tel: +44 (0)20 7557 4460 Fax: +44 (0)20 7557 4499
Email: lmourne@stanleygibbons.co.uk

from sheet stock. Their variety seems endless and their status is arguable.

Correspondence

Letters should be addressed to the Catalogue Editor, Stanley Gibbons Publications, Parkside. Christchurch Road, Ringwood, Hants BH24 3SH, and return postage is appreciated when a reply is sought. New information and unlisted items for consideration are welcomed. Please note we do not give opinions as to the genuineness of stamps, nor do we identify stamps or number them by our Catalogue.

To order from this Catalogue, always quote the Specialised Catalogue number, mentioning Volume 4, 10th Edition and where necessary specify additionally the precise item wanted.

Guarantee

All stamps supplied by Stanley Gibbons Ltd., are guaranteed originals in the following terms: If not as described, and returned by the purchaser, we undertake to refund the price paid to us in the original transaction. If any stamp is certified as genuine by the Expert Committee of the Royal Philatelic Society, London, or by B.P.A. Expertising Ltd., the purchaser shall not be entitled to make any claim against us for any error, omission or mistake in such certificate. Consumers' statutory rights are not affected by the above guarantee.

Expertisation

We do not give opinions as to the genuineness of stamps. Expert Committees exist for this purpose and enquiry can be made of the Royal Philatelic Society, 41 Devonshire Place, London W1N 1PE or B.P.A. Expertising Ltd., P.O. Box 1141, Guildford, Surrey GU5 0WR. They do not undertake valuations under any circumstances and fees are payable for their services.

Symbols and Abbreviations

†	(in price column) does not exist
—	(in price column) exists or may exist, but no market price is known (a blank conveys the same meaning)
*	(against price of a cylinder block) price includes a listed variety
ACP	Advanced coated paper
BS	Business sheet
(E)	Elliptical perforation with size **15** × 14 or 14 as stated
FCP	Fluorescent coated paper
GA	Gum arabic
mm.	millimetres
No.	number
NVI	No Value Indicated
OCP	Original coated paper
Phos	Phosphor
PSA	PVA/Self-adhesive
Ptg	Printing
PVA	Polyvinyl alcohol (gum)
PVAD	Polyvinyl alcohol (gum) with dextrin added
R	Row (thus R. 6/4 indicates the fourth stamp from the left in the sixth horizontal row from the top of a sheet of stamps).
SA	Self-adhesive (without water soluble layer of gum)
Th	S.G. Thirkell Position Finder. The letters and figures which follow (e.g. Th E5) pinpoint the position of the flaw on the stamp according to the grid engraved on the Finder.
Type I	Usually refers to value size/shape, types I, II or III

How can Stanley Gibbons help you?

Our History

Stanley Gibbons started trading in 1856 and we have been at the forefront of stamp collecting for more than 150 years, making us the world's oldest philatelic company. We can help you build your collection in a wide variety of ways – all with the backing of our unrivalled expertise.

399 Strand, London, UK - **Recently Refurbished!**

'...I only wish I could visit more often...' JB, December 09

Our world famous stamp shop is a collector's paradise. As well as stamps, the shop stocks albums, accessories and specialist philatelic books. Plan a visit now!

Specialist Stamp Departments

When purchasing high value items you should definitely contact our specialist departments for advice and guarantees on the items purchased. Consult the experts to ensure you make the right purchase. For example, when buying early Victorian stamps our specialists will guide you through the prices – a penny red SG 43 has many plate numbers which vary in value. We can explain what to look for and where, and help you plan your future collection.

Stanley Gibbons Publications

Our catalogues are trusted worldwide as the industry standard, see the facing page for details on our current range. Keep up to date with new issues in our magazine, Gibbons Stamp Monthly, a must-read for all collectors and dealers. It contains news, views and insights into all things philatelic, from beginner to specialist.

Completing the set

When is it cheaper to complete your collection by buying a whole set rather than item by item? Use the prices in your catalogue, which lists single item values and a complete set value, to check if it is better to buy the odd missing item, or a complete set.

Auctions and Valuations

Buying at auction can be great fun. You can buy collections and merge them with your own - not forgetting to check your catalogue for gaps. But do make sure the condition of the collection you are buying is comparable to your own.

Stanley Gibbons Auctions have been running since the 1900's. They offer a range of auctions to suit both novice and advanced collectors and dealers. You can of course also sell your collection or individual rare items through our public auctions and regular postal auctions. Contact the auction department directly to find out more - email auctions@stanleygibbons.co.uk or telephone 020 7836 8444.

Condition

Condition can make a big difference on the price you pay for an item. When building your collection you must keep condition in mind and always buy the best condition you can find and afford. For example, ensure the condition of the gum is the same as issued from the Post Office. If the gum is disturbed or has had an adhesion it can be classed as mounted. When buying issues prior to 1936 you should always look for the least amount of disturbance and adhesion. You do have to keep in mind the age of the issue when looking at the condition.

The prices quoted in our catalogues are for a complete item in good condition so make sure you check this.

Ask the Experts

If you need help or guidance, you are welcome to come along to Stanley Gibbons in the Strand and ask for assistance. If you would like to have your collection appraised, you can arrange for a verbal evaluation Monday to Friday 9.00am – 4.30pm. We also provide insurance valuations should you require. Of course an up-to-date catalogue listing can also assist with the valuation and may be presented to an insurance agent or company.

Stanley Gibbons Publications
7 Parkside, Christchurch Road, Ringwood, Hants. BH24 3SH Tel: +44 (0)1425 472363 Fax: +44 (0)1425 470247
Email: orders@stanleygibbons.co.uk

Stanley Gibbons Stamp Catalogue
Complete list of parts

1 Commonwealth & British Empire Stamps 1840–1970
(112th edition, 2009)

Commonwealth Country Catalogues
Australia and Dependencies (6th edition, 2010)
Bangladesh, Pakistan & Sri Lanka
 (1st edition, 2004)
Belize, Guyana, Trinidad & Tobago
 (1st edition, 2009)
Brunei, Malaysia & Singapore (3rd edition, 2009)
Canada (3rd edition, 2008)
Central Africa (2nd edition, 2008)
Cyprus, Gibraltar & Malta (2nd edition, 2008)
East Africa with Egypt and Sudan (2nd edition, 2010)
Eastern Pacific (1st edition, 2007)
Falkland Islands (4th edition, 2010)
Hong Kong (3rd edition, 2010)
India (including Convention and Feudatory States)
 (3rd edition, 2009)
Indian Ocean (1st edition, 2006)
Ireland (4th edition, 2008)
Leeward Islands (1st edition, 2007)
New Zealand (3rd edition, 2009)
Northern Caribbean, Bahamas & Bermuda
 (2nd edition, 2009)
St. Helena & Dependencies (3rd edition, 2007)
Southern Africa (2nd edition, 2007)
West Africa (1st edition, 2009)
Western Pacific (2nd edition, 2009)
Windward Islands and Barbados (1st edition, 2007)

Foreign Countries
2 **Austria & Hungary** (7th edition, 2009)
3 **Balkans** (5th edition, 2009)
4 **Benelux** (6th edition, 2010)
5 **Czechoslovakia & Poland** (6th edition, 2002)
6 **France** (7th edition, 2010)
7 **Germany** (8th edition, 2007)
8 **Italy & Switzerland** (7th edition, 2010)
9 **Portugal & Spain** (5th edition, 2004)
10 **Russia** (6th edition, 2008)
11 **Scandinavia** (6th edition, 2008)
12 **Africa since Independence A-E** (2nd edition, 1983)
13 **Africa since Independence F-M** (1st edition, 1981)
14 **Africa since Independence N-Z** (1st edition, 1981)
15 **Central America** (3rd edition, 2007)
16 **Central Asia** (4th edition, 2006)
17 **China** (7th edition, 2006)
18 **Japan & Korea** (5th edition, 2008)
19 **Middle East** (7th edition, 2009)
20 **South America** (4th edition, 2008)
21 **South-East Asia** (4th edition, 2004)
22 **United States of America** (7th edition, 2010)

Great Britain Specialised Catalogues
Volume 1   Queen Victoria (15th edition, 2008)
Volume 2   King Edward VII to King George VI
           (13th edition, 2009)
Volume 3   Queen Elizabeth II Pre-decimal issues
           (11th edition, 2006)
Volume 4   Queen Elizabeth II Decimal Definitive
           Issues – Part 1 (10th edition, 2008)
           Queen Elizabeth II Decimal Definitive
           Issues – Part 2 (10th edition, 2010)
Volume 5   Queen Elizabeth II Decimal Special
           Issues (3rd edition, 1998 with 1998-99
           and 2000/1 Supplements)

Thematic Catalogues
Stanley Gibbons Catalogues for use with *Stamps of the World*.
Collect Aircraft on Stamps (2nd edition, 2009)
Collect Birds on Stamps (5th edition, 2003)
Collect Chess on Stamps (2nd edition, 1999)
Collect Fish on Stamps (1st edition, 1999)
Collect Fungi on Stamps (2nd edition, 1997)
Collect Motor Vehicles on Stamps
 (1st edition 2004)

Other Publications
Philatelic Terms Illustrated (4th edition, 2003)
Collect British Stamps (61st edition, 2010)
Great Britain Concise Stamp Catalogue
 (25th edition, 2010)
How to Identify Stamps (4th edition, 2007)
Collect Channel Islands and Isle of Man Stamps
 (26th edition, 2010)
Great Britain Numbers Issued (3rd edition, 2008)
Enjoy Stamp Collecting (7th edition, 2006)
*Antarctica (including Australian and
 British Antarctic Territories, French Southern
 and Antarctic Territories and
 Ross Dependency)* (1st edition, 2010)
*United Nations (also including International
 Organizations based in Switzerland and
 UNESCO)* (1st edition, 2010)

For other titles, and further details on the above,
please see *www.stanleygibbons.com*

Stanley Gibbons Auctions
Leading Philatelic Auctioneers since 1901

Thinking of selling all or part of your collection?

Contact us today in order to make the most of strong auction realisations in the current market

- Reach over 200,000 potential buyers
- The largest philatelic audience in the UK
- Unrivalled expertise in the field of philately
- 100% exceptional clearance rate
- Download each catalogue for FREE

- We can offer featured write-ups about any auction in GSM
- Confidence and trust make Stanley Gibbons Auctions the first port of call for people selling their collections
- Auctions hosted on www.stanleygibbons.com, offering massive worldwide exposure

Contact us today to consign your material to auction

Postal auction lots from £5 - £5,000

All World, specialised and one vendor sales

Mixed lots, boxes and One Country Albums

Stanley Gibbons Auctions Department, 399 Strand, London, WC2R 0LX, UK
Contact: Ryan Epps or Steve Matthews on
Tel: +44 (0)20 7557 4416 Fax: +44 (0)20 7836 7342 Email: repps@stanleygibbons.co.uk

www.stanleygibbons.com/auctions

The world of stamp collecting in your hands

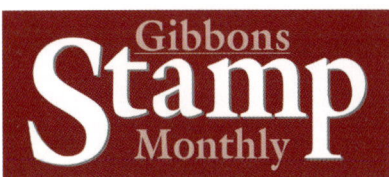

The Ultimate Stamp Magazine

- The UK's biggest selling stamp magazine
- Consistently over 150 pages per issue
- Written by stamp collectors for stamp collectors
- Monthly colour catalogue supplement
- Philatelic news from around the world
- Dedicated GB stamp section
- Regular offers exclusively for subscribers

FREE SAMPLE

For your **FREE** sample, contact us by:

Tel: +44(0)1425 472 363
Email: orders@stanleygibbons.co.uk
Post: Stanley Gibbons Limited, 7 Parkside, Christchurch Road, Ringwood, Hampshire, BH24 3SH

For more information, please visit
www.gibbonsstampmonthly.com

Est 1856

STANLEY GIBBONS

For the first time ever...

The Gibbons Stamp Monthly Digital Archive

You can have access to over 40,000 pages of the most useful and interesting philatelic material available.

All delivered to you in searchable digital format consisting of 5 DVDs plus a bonus disk.

Covering all articles, features, editorial and other content from the first issue of the Monthly Journal, Gibbons Stamp Weekly and Gibbons Stamp Monthly from 1890 up to the December 2009 issue of GSM.

Want to know more?

Email gsmarchive@stanleygibbons.co.uk if you have any questions about the archive or visit stanleygibbons.com/archive for a full demonstration.

The complete archive of Gibbons Stamp Monthly, offering you 120 years of articles at your fingertips.

- The complete archive of Gibbons Stamp Monthly from 1890 – 2009
- Search & browse by author, keyword, category, issue and/or type of article
- Easily find features on your favourite topic & create your own digital library
- Print any article as many times as you like

JUST £199.95
Code RGSMARC

Order yours today
0800 611 622

International +44 1425 472 363
orders@stanleygibbons.co.uk
www.stanleygibbons.com

SECTION UI

Machin No Value Indicated Issues
1989-2009. Stamps inscribed 1st, 2nd
and E from Sheets, Booklets, Coils
and "Boots" panes

General Notes

No Value Indicated Stamps. From 22 August 1989 various definitive and special stamps appeared inscribed "2nd", "1st" or "E" instead of a face value. These were sold at current minimum rates for these services, as follows:

Inland Postage Rate	2nd Class	1st Class
5 September 1988	14p.	19p.
2 October 1989	15p.	20p.
17 September 1990	17p.	22p.
16 September 1991	18p.	24p.
1 November 1993	19p.	25p.
8 July 1996	20p.	26p.
26 April 1999	19p.	26p.
17 April 2000	19p.	27p.
8 May 2003	20p.	28p.
1 April 2004	21p.	28p.
7 April 2005	21p.	30p.
3 April 2006	23p.	32p.
2 April 2007	24p.	34p.
7 April 2008	27p.	36p.
6 April 2009	30p.	39p.
6 April 2010	32p.	41p.

European Airmail Rate	
26 April 1999	30p.
25 October 1999	34p.
27 April 2000	36p.
2 July 2001	37p.
27 March 2003	38p.
1 April 2004	40p.

From June 2004, European Airmail rate stamps reverted to showing a face value.

From 21 August 2006 "Large" letters were charged at a higher rate following the introduction of "Pricing in Proportion". Rates as follows:

Inland Postage Rate	2nd Class Large	1st Class Large
21 August 2006	37p.	44p.
2 April 2007	40p.	48p.
7 April 2008	42p.	52p.
6 April 2009	47p.	61p.
6 April 2010	51p.	66p.

Booklet panes. Many of the panes come from booklets which had two or even three different selling prices as postage rates rose. This information is given in the booklet pane section so that dates of first issue are followed by the change of tariff value when the new, and changed postal charge came into effect. Four printers were involved—Enschedé, Harrisons/De La Rue, Questa and Walsall.

European Airmail. On 19 January 1999 the Post Office issued, in booklet form, the first no value indicated stamp printed by Walsall for European airmail.

Prestige Booklet DX22. This exceptional booklet contained recess, embossed and typographed NVI (1st) stamps from the Profile on Print prestige booklet issued on 16 February 1999 and listed as Nos. UY1/3.

Printers and primary sheet arrangements. The essential information on the printer's uncut booklet sheet, known as the primary sheet, is given after the pane listing. The work of each of the four printers is different and the earlier lithographed issues can be easily identified, before the introduction of elliptical perforations, as Questa used 15×14 perforations and Walsall 14. Questa used phosphor bands which were short, but Walsall bands were continuous over the horizontal perforations.

Phosphorised paper. After the introduction of advanced coated paper (ACP) the amount of optical brightening agent varied, with the result that some panes give a markedly dull response under ultraviolet light.

Phosphor bands. Harrison and Walsall used bands that went across the horizontal perfs. Questa employed short bands which tended to be misplaced.

Phosphor band layout. (1st) class stamps printed by Walsall from 1994 used the phosphor pane layouts as described.

Long wave phosphor. From 1997 both Questa and Walsall used long wave phosphor which gave a violet response when irradiated under ultraviolet light. This replaced short wave only phosphor and the two inks exist on some printings of booklet panes.

Fluor. Under ultraviolet light the fluor reacts blue to violet with varying brightness. Most stamps have blue fluor but the following stamps had a bright yellowish fluor designed to show up well—Nos. UHA4, UHB5, UQA4/6, UQB6/9, UWA4, UWB6/7.

The Boots pane printed by Questa is listed with both yellow and blue fluor (UQB9, 9A).

Imperforate edges. Single stamps with imperforate edges are not listed separately but are covered by footnotes. It is helpful to note that the Questa printings are perforated on all sides and that those stamps imperforate on adjacent sides only came from the panes of four.

Straight edges could be manufactured, but only by reducing the size of the stamp so that careful comparison with a normal example would reveal if a stamp had been trimmed.

With the introduction of elliptical perforation holes imperforate edges were abandoned and panes once again have trimmed perforations when the pane is misplaced inside the booklet cover.

"Boots" panes. For Boots panes printed by Questa, see No. UQB9 and for those printed by Enschedé, see No. UEB1 in the single stamp listing.

Checklist arrangement. The single stamp listings are in the order of (2nd), (1st) and (E) but of the latter there are only four examples and these were printed by Questa, Walsall, De La Rue and Enschedé. The (2nd) class stamps are designated "A", (1st) class with letter "B" and the (E) stamps are "C". The listings are in the alphabetical order of the printers and then chronological.

UI Machin no value indicated issues — General Notes

S.G.Spec Number	S.G.Standard Number	Date of Issue	Page
Printed in gravure by De La Rue (2nd) class.			
Bright blue. Machin			
UDA1	–	4.7.2001	4
UDA2	–	26.9.2003	4
Priced in proportion			
UDA3	2650	1.8.2006	4
UDA4	2652	1.8.2006	4
Printed in gravure by De La Rue (1st) class.			
Olive-brown. New Millennium p.15×14 (E)			
UDB1	2124	6.1.2000	5
Bright orange-red Machin			
UDB2	–	4.7.2001	5
Gold. Machin			
UDB3	–	28.5.2003	5
UDB4	–	16.3.2004	6
Priced in proportion			
UDB5	2651	1.8.2006	6
UDB6	2653	1.8.2006	6
Printed in lithography by De La Rue (1st) class.			
Gold. Machin			
UDB7	1672	8.1.2008	7
Printed in gravure by De La Rue (E)			
Deep blue. Machin			
European Air Mail.			
UDC1	1669	5.10.1999	7
Printed in gravure by Enschedé (2nd) class.			
Bright blue. Machin			
UEA1	–	6.2.2002	7
UEA2	–	15.10.2002	7
Printed in lithography by Enschedé (1st) class.			
Bright orange-red. Boots pane			
UEB1	1671mb	20.2.1997	7
Printed in gravure by Enschedé (1st) class.			
Gold. Machin			
UEB2	–	5.10.2002	8
UEB3	–	25.2.2003	8
UEB4	–	25.5.2004	8
UEB5	–	23.2.2006	8
UEB6	–	21.9.2006	8
Printed in gravure by Enschedé (E) class.			
Deep blue. Machin European Air Mail.			
UEC1	–	6.2.2002	9
Printed in gravure by Harrison (2nd) class.			
Bright blue. Machin			
UHA1	1445	22.8.1989	9
UHA2	1446	20.3.1990	9
Deep blue. Machin			
UHA3	1511	7.8.1990	9
Bright blue. Machin			
UHA4	–	7.9.1993	9
UHA5	1664	18.7.1995	9
UHA6	–	8.7.1996	9
UHA6A	–	–.4.1997	9
UHA7	–	8.7.1996	9
UHA8	–	29.4.1997	9
Printed in gravure by Harrison (1st) class.			
Brownish black. Machin			
UHB1	1447	22.8.1989	10
UHB2	1448	20.3.1990	10
Bright orange-red. Machin			
UHB3	1512	7.8.1990	10
UHB4	1666	6.4.1993	10
UHB5	1667	4.4.1995	10
UHB6	–	18.7.1995	10
UHB7	–	8.7.1996	10
UHB8	–	–.4.1997	10
Gold. Machin			
UHB9	1668	21.4.1997	10
Bright orange-red. Machin			
UHB10	–	29.4.1997	10
Printed in lithography by Questa (2nd) class.			
Bright blue. Machin			
UQA1	1451	19.9.1989	11
Deep blue. Machin			
UQA2	1513	7.8.1990	11
Bright blue. Machin			
UQA3	1451a	25.2.1992	11
UQA4	–	6.4.1993	11
UQA5	1451aEb	10.8.1993	11
UQA6	–	19.5.1994	11
UQA7	–	18.7.1995	11
UQA8	–	14.11.1995	11
UQA9	1670	3.12.1996	11
Printed in gravure by Questa (2nd) class.			
Bright blue. Machin			
UQA10	1664a	1.12.1998	12
UQA11	–	27.4.2000	12
Printed in lithography by Questa (1st) class.			
Brownish black. Machin			
UQB1	1452	19.9.1989	12
Bright orange-red. Machin			
UQB2	1514	7.8.1990	12
UQB3	–	6.8.1991	12
UQB4	1514a	25.2.1992	12
UQB5	–	27.10.1992	12
UQB6	–	10.8.1993	12
UQB7	–	6.9.1993	12
UQB8	–	1.11.1993	13
Bright orange-red. Boots promotion pane			
UQB9	1671m	17.8.1994	
UQB9B	1671ma	11.9.1995	13
Bright orange-red. Machin			
UQB10	1671	18.7.1995	13
Printed in gravure by Questa (1st) class.			
Bright orange-red. Machin			
UQB11	1667a	1.12.1998	14
UQB12	–	16.2.1999	14
Olive-brown. New Millennium p.14			
UQB13	2124d	6.1.2000	14
Bright orange-red. Machin			
UQB14	–	27.4.2000	14
Olive-brown. New Millennium p.15×14 (E)			
UQB15	–	4.8.2000	14
Gold. Machin			
UQB16	–	24.9.2002	14
Printed in gravure by Questa (E).			
Deep blue. Machin European Air Mail.			
UQC1	–	24.9.2002	14

Machin no value indicated issues *General Notes* **UI**

S.G.Spec Number	S.G.Standard Number	Date of Issue	Page
Printed in lithography by Walsall (2nd) class.			
Bright blue. Machin			
UWA1	1449	22.8.1989	14
Deep blue. Machin			
UWA2	1515	7.8.1990	14
Bright blue. Machin			
UWA3	–	16.3.1993	14
UWA4	–	6.4.1993	15
UWA5	–	12.12.1995	15
Printed in gravure by Walsall (2nd) class.			
Bright blue. Machin			
UWA6	–	29.4.1997	15
UWA7	1665	13.10.1998	15
UWA8	1665Ec	13.10.1998	15
UWA9	–	2.6.2003	15
UWA10	1670	18.9.2008	15
Printed in lithography by Walsall (1st) class.			
Blackish brown. Machin			
UWB1	1450	22.8.1989	16
Bright orange-red. Machin			
UWB2	1516	7.8.1990	16
UWB3	1516c	–.10.1990	16
UWB4	–	9.2.1993	16
UWB5	–	6.4.1993	16
UWB6	–	22.4.1994	16
UWB7	–	1.7.1994	16
UWB8	–	18.7.1995	16
UWB9	–	6.2.1996	16
Printed in gravure by Walsall (1st) class.			
Gold. Machin			
UWB10	1668	21.4.1997	16
Bright orange-red. Machin			
UWB11	–	26.8.1997	17
Olive-brown. New Millennium p.15x14(E)			
UWB12	–	6.1.2000	17
New Millennium p. 14(E)			
UWB13	–	15.2.2000	17
UWB14	–	21.3.2000	18
Gold. Machin			
UWB15	–	2.6.2003	18
UWB16	–	18.10.2005	18
Printed in lithography by Walsall (1st) class.			
Gold. Machin			
UWB17	1672	18.9.2008	18
Printed in gravure by Walsall (E).			
Deep blue. Machin European Air Mail.			
UWC1	–	19.1.1999	18
Large Format Machin Type UI 3 (1st).			
From Prestige Booklet DX22			
Self-adhesive and embossed printed by Walsall			
UY1	2077	16.2.1999	18
Recess printed by Enschedé			
UY2	2078	16.2.1999	18
Printed in Typography by Harrison			
UY3	2079	16.2.1999	18

UI Machin no value indicated issues

UI1 Queen Elizabeth II
(Des. after plaster cast by Arnold Machin)

Type UI1

De La Rue (2nd) Class Stamps in Gravure (2001-06)

(2nd) Bright blue (2001)

2001 (4 July). Perf. 15 × 14(E). One 4·5 mm centre band long wave (blue fluor). Non-fluorescent coated paper. PVA gum (bluish).

Sideways Coil

UDA1	(2nd) Bright blue	65	40

Coil
No. UDA1 one 4·5 mm centre phosphor band (blue fluor). Printed in continuous reels.

Issued	Number in roll	Face value sideways delivery	Gum	Cyl. Nos. used
4.7.01	1000	£190	PVA (bluish)	R5 (R21)

(2nd) Bright blue (2001) Gravure

2003 (26 September). Perf. 15 × 14(E). One 4·5 mm centre band long/short wave (blue fluor). Non-fluorescent coated paper. PVA gum

From Vertical coil, sheets (5.6.07)
UDA2

UDA2	(2nd) Bright blue	65	30

Originally due for realease with the (1st) class value, this value was delayed as stocks of the Enschedé coil it replaced were sufficient to meet demand.

Coils
No UDA2 one 4·5 mm centre phosphor band (blue fluor). Printed in continuous reels

Issued	Number in roll	Face value Vertical delivery	Gum	Cyl. Nos. used
26.9.03	500	£100	PVA	–

Barcode leader of 500 stamps 5 014721 104010
Rolls of 10,000 stamps were later produced.

UI2

(Des. Jeffery Matthews)
"Pricing in Proportion"

Type UI2

(2nd) Bright blue (2006)

2006 (1 August). Perf. 15 × 14(E). One 4·5 mm centre band long/short wave (blue fluor). Non-fluorescent coated paper. PVA gum

From Sheets and vertical coil (15.8.06)
UDA3 (=SG 2650)

UDA3	(2nd) Bright blue	65	40

Cylinder Numbers (Blocks of Six)
Perforation Type RE

Cyl. No.	Phos. No.	No dot	Dot
D1	D1	3·50	3·50

Dates of Printing (Blocks of Eight)

Date	Margin at left or right
28/04/06	7·00
15/09/06	7·00
15/01/07	8·00
16/01/07	8·00

Coils
No. UDA3 one 4·5 mm centre phosphor band (blue fluor). Printed in continuous reels.

Issued	Number in roll	Face value Vertical delivery	Gum	Cyl. Nos. used
15.8.06	500	£120	PVA	–
3.10.06	1000	£240	PVA	–

Barcode leader of 500 stamps 5 014721 104010
Barcode leader of 1000 stamps 5 014721 104027

UI3

Type UI3

(2nd) Bright blue inscribed "Large" (2006)

2006 (1 August). Perf. 15 × 14(E). Two bands long wave (blue fluor). Non-fluorescent coated paper. PVA gum

UDA4 (=SG 2652)

UDA4	(2nd Large) Bright blue	1·00	60

No. UDA4 was initially sold at 37p., which was increased to 40p. from 2.4.07.

Cylinder Numbers (Blocks of Six)

Perforation Type RE

Cyl. No.	Phos. No.	No dot	Dot
D1	D1	6·50	6·50

Machin no value indicated issues UI

Dates of Printing (Blocks of Eight)

Date	Margin at left or right
15/5/06	8·00
16/5/06	8·50
6/9/09	8·50
7/9/06	10·00
1/11/06	8·50
12/9/06	10·00
5/12/06	8·00
13/3/07	10·00
27/2/08	10·00

De La Rue (1st) Class Stamps in Gravure (2000-04)

UI4
Queen Elizabeth II
(Des. after plaster cast by Arnold Machin. Adapted by Richard Scholey)

2000. Type UI4

Printed in sheets by computer engraved cylinders

Type I

Type I. The centre cross is almost closed at the top left and right with a spot of hair visible through the right side of the cross (Type I). Used for De La Rue and Questa printings, this differs from the diadem on Walsall stamps issued on 6 January 2000 which is open without any spot of the Queen's hair visible through the centre cross.

Type UI4

(1st) Olive-brown (2000)

2000 (6 January). Perf 15 × 14(E). Two 9mm bands (blue fluor). Type I. Non-fluorescent coated paper. PVA gum (bluish)

UDB1 (=SG 2124)

UDB1	(1st) Olive-brown	1·00	1·00

No. UDB1 was initially sold at 26p. which was increased to 27p. from 27.4.00.

Cylinder Numbers (Blocks of Six)

Perforation Type RE

Cyl. Nos.	Phos. No.	No dot	Dot
1	47	7·00	7·00
2	47	7·00	7·00

Secure Stock Operations Numbers and Dates of Printing (Blocks of Eight)

SSO No.	Date	Margin at left or right
739	27/09/99	10·00
	26/10/99	10·00
	27/10/99	10·00
	28/10/99	10·00
753	03/12/99	–
	06/12/99	10·00
	18/12/99	10·00
	19/12/99	10·00
	20/12/99	10·00
	23/12/99	10·00
	04/01/00	–
	05/01/00	10·00
781	19/04/00	10·00
	26/04/00	10·00
	27/04/00	10·00
	28/04/00	10·00
	03/05/00	10·00
	08/05/00	10·00
	09/05/00	10·00
	11/05/00	10·00
	16/05/00	10·00

UI5

Type UI5

(1st) Bright orange-red (2001)

2001 (4 July). Perf 15 × 14(E). Two bands (long wave fluor). Non-fluorescent coated paper. PVA gum (bluish)

Horizontal coil

UDB2	(1st) Bright orange-red	1·00

Coil
No. UDB2 printed in continuous reels

Issued	Number in roll	Face value sideways delivery	Gum	Cyl. Nos. Used
4.7.01	1000	£270	PVA (bluish)	R7 (R20)

(1st) Gold (2003)

2003 (28 May). Perf. 15 × 14(E). Two bands long/short wave (blue fluor). Non-fluorescent coated paper. PVA gum

Vertical coil, sheets 1 July 2003. Sheets (5.6.07)

UDB3

UDB3	(1st) Gold	75

The fluor is very bright under ultraviolet compared to the yellowish blue response of the Harrison issue No. W1129 (21.4.97). This stamp was first issued to celebrate the Royal Golden Wedding but later became the standard colour for the first class rate.

No. UDB3 has the separate jewels behind the front cross on the Crown unlike the Questa (1st) in gold ink which merges.

UI Machin no value indicated issues

This is a Byfleet printing but with the Harrison characteristics used in 1997.

Cylinder Numbers (Blocks of Six)

Perforation Type RE

Cyl. No.	Phos. No.	No dot	Dot
D1	D1	5·00	5·00

Dates of Printing (Blocks of Eight)

Date	Margin at left or right	Source
02/04/03	9·00	Cyl. D1 pd1
18/09/03	10·00	
25/03/04	10·00	
20/04/04	10·00	
18/08/05	12·00	
10/11/05	12·00	
10/01/06	12·00	
21/03/06	12·00	
22/03/06	12·00	
29/03/07	9·00	Cyl. D2 pd1

Coils

No. UDB3 two phosphor bands (blue fluor). Printed in continuous reels

Issued	Number in roll	Face value Vertical delivery	Gum	Cyl. Nos. used
28.5.03	500	£140	PVA	–
30.11.04	1000	£280	PVA	–

Barcode leader of 500 stamps 5 014721 104041

▌ (1st) Gold (2004) Gravure

2004 (16 March). Screen change. Perf. 15 × 14(E). Two bands long/short wave (blue fluor). Non-fluorescent coated paper. PVA gum

From £7·44 "Letters by Night" se-tenant pane UEP41

UDB4

UDB4	(1st) Gold	75	70

No. UDB4 has a diamond dot screeen arranged horizontally not vertically on UDB3 from sheet and coil sources. This is difficult to identify, therefore check the pale area of the inside band of the Crown and shoulder.

UI6

(Des. Jeffery Matthews)
"Pricing in Proportion"

Type UI6

De La Rue (1st) Class Stamps in Gravure (2006)

▌ (1st) Gold (2006)

2006 (1 August). Perf. 15 × 14(E). Two bands long wave (blue fluor). Non-fluorescent coated paper. PVA gum

From Sheets and vertical coil (3.10.06)

UDB5 (=SG 2651)

UDB5	(1st) Gold	75	50

Cylinder Numbers (Blocks of Six)

Perforation Type RE

Cyl. No.	Phos. No.	No dot	Dot
D1	D1	5·50	5·50

Dates of Printing (Blocks of Eight)

Date	Margin at left or right
02/05/06	10.00
16/09/06	15.00
22/01/07	10.00

Coil

No. UDB5 two phosphor bands (blue fluor). Printed in continuous reels.

Issued	Number in roll	Face value Vertical delivery	Gum	Cyl. Nos. used
3.10.06	1000	£320	PVA	–
14.11.06	500	£160	PVA	–

Face values as stated when first issued.
Barcode leader of 1000 stamps 5 014721 104058
500 stamps 5 014721 104041

UI7

Type UI7

▌ (1st) Gold inscribed "Large" (2006)

2006 (1 August). Perf. 15 × 14 (E). Two bands long wave (blue fluor). Non-fluorescent coated paper. PVA gum

UDB6 (=SG 2653)

UDB6	(1st) Gold	1·50	70

No. UDB6 was initially sold at 44p., which was increased to 48p. from 2.4.07.

Cylinder Numbers (Blocks of Six)

Perforation Type RE

Cyl. No.	Phos. No.	No dot	Dot
D1	D1	10·00	10·00

Dates of Printing (Blocks of Eight)

Date	Margin at left or right
11/05/06	12·00
12/05/06	12·00
07/09/06	12·00
08/09/06	12·00
31/10/06	12·00

Machin no value indicated issues **UI**

01/11/06		12·00
04/12/06		12·00
05/12/06		12·00
08/03/06		12·00
09/03/07		12·00
12/03/07		12·00
16/04/07		12·00
20/09/07		12·00
21/09/07		12·00
12/11/07		12·00
25/02/08		12·00
26/02/08		12·00

Type U15

(1st) Gold printed in Lithography (2008)

Printed in lithography. Gold as Type UDB1
2008 (8 January). Perf. 15 × 14 (E). Two 9 mm Bands (blue fluor). Non-fluorescent coated paper. PVA

From £7·40 "Ian Fleming's James Bond" Prestige Booklet pane UIPP14 (8.1.08)
UDB7 (=SG 1672)

UDB7	(1st) Gold	1·75	1·75

UI8 Queen Elizabeth II
(Des. after plaster cast by Arnold Machin)

Type U18

(E) Deep blue (1999)

1999 (5 October). Perf. 15 × 14(E). Two 9 mm phosphor bands (blue fluor). Non-fluorescent coated paper. PVA gum (bluish).

UDC1 (=SG 1669)

UDC1	(E) Deep blue	1·25	1·00

Cylinder Numbers (Blocks of Six)
Perforation Type RE

Cyl. No.	Phos. No.	No dot	Dot
1	47	6·75	6·75

Warrant Numbers and Dates of Printing (Blocks of Eight)

Warrant No.	Source	Date	Margin at left or right
737	Cyl. 1 p47	10/08/99	9·00
737		11/08/99	9·00
738		21/09/99	9·00
738		22/09/99	9·00
778		25/02/00	9·00
778		25/02/00	14·00
778		28/02/00	9·00
778		28/02/00	–
778		28/02/00	–
791		24/05/00	9·00
791		26/05/00	9·00
791		30/05/00	9·00
791		31/05/00	9·00

Warrant No.	Source	Date	Margin at left or right
791		01/06/00	9·00
778		25/05/00	15·00
778		30/05/00	15·00

Enschedé (2nd) Class Stamp in Gravure (2002)

Perforation. 15 × 14 (E)

(2nd) Bright blue (2002)

2002 (6 February). Perf. 15 × 14(E). One 4·5 mm centre band (blue fluor). Non-fluorescent coated paper. PVA gum (bluish)

From £7·29 "A Gracious Accession" Booklet pane UIPP9

UEA1	(2nd) Bright blue	65	50

This stamp is identical to the De La Rue No. UHA8 although the Enschedé printing is dull under ultraviolet light. Another difference that includes the (E) value is the 0·5 mm between crown and frame at right. Enschedé (2nd) and (E) from pane UIPP9 show 1 mm at right. Walsall printings also have the 0·5 mm gap.

(2nd) Bright blue (2002)

2002 (15 October).* Perf. 15 × 14(E). One 4·5 mm centre band (blue fluor). Non-fluorescent coated paper. PVA gum (bluish). Thicker value

From Vertical coil

UEA2	(2nd) Bright blue	65	

The value, particularly "ND" is similar to Walsall but No. UEA2 shows bluish PVA. The base of the bust is distinctly separated from the background unlike booklet stamps which tend to merge.
*Date of Issue. The date 15 October 2002 was postponed but stocks were distributed to retail outlets. The later official date was 21 January 2003 from the Bureau.

Coils
No. UEA2 one 4·5 mm centre band (blue fluor). Printed in continuous reels.
Barcode: 5014721104010

Issued	Number in roll	Face value Vertical delivery	Gum	Cyl. Nos. used
15.10.02	500	£95	PVA (bluish)	(?)

Enschedé (1st) Class Stamp in Lithography (1997)

Perforation 15 × 14(E)

UEB1 (roulette arrowed)

UI Machin no value indicated issues

(1st) Pane. in Lithography (1997)

Boots the Chemist stationery promotion

Pane containing one (1st) class stamp sold at 26p. Roulette 10 across top corners of pane.

1997 (20 February*). Perf. 15 × 14(E). Two bands (blue fluor). Non-fluorescent coated paper. PVA gum

From 26p. Boots pane UIPE1
UEB1 (=SG 1671mb)

UEB1	(1st) Bright orange-red	1·40

*The date quoted is the earliest known from pre-packed greetings cards. The Philatelic Bureau sold the pane from 29 April 1997.

No. UEB1 can be distinguished from the same stamp printed by Questa by the finer detail on the portrait. Questa printings have a scar flaw on the Queen's jawline which does not occur on No. UEB1. The distance between the two phosphor bands is 11 mm on UEB1 and 12 mm on UQB9. The base of the bust is convex on the Enschedé printing but slightly concave on both Questa and Walsall (1st) class litho printings.

No. UIPE1 printed by Enschedé is rouletted 10 whereas the Questa pane No. UQB9 is roulette 8. The "1995" is larger on the Enschedé pane.

*These panes were provided by the Royal Mail for inclusion in single prepacked greetings cards sold by Boots. The examples included with greetings cards are folded but the Philatelic Bureau supplied unfolded panes of No. UEB1 I from 29 April 1997.

Sheet Make-up. Not known
Sold out: April 1999

Enschedé (1st) Class Stamps in Gravure (2002–06)

Type UI5

(1st) Gold (2002)

2002 (5 October)* Perf. 15 × 14(E). Two 9 mm bands (blue flour). Non-fluorescent coated paper. PVA gum (bluish)

From Vertical coil

UEB2	(1st) Gold	75	45

The base of the bust is separated from the background unlike the booklet stamps which tend to merge. The (1st) class shows the gap between "1" and "ST", common to Enschedé printings.

*Date of issue. The date 5 October 2002, was from stock distributed to retail outlets although originally planned for 15 October. The later official date was 21 January 2003 from the Bureau.

Coils

No. UEB2 two phosphor bands (blue flour) Printed in continuous reels.
Barcode: 5014721104041

Issued	Number in roll	Face value vertical delivery	Gum	Cyl. No. used
5.10.02	500	£135	PVA (bluish)	(?)

Type UI5

(1st) Gold (2003)

2003 (25 February). Perf 15 × 14(E). Two 9 mm bands (blue flour). Non-fluorescent coated paper. PVA gum (bluish).

From £6.99 (£7.24 from 8.5.03) "Microcosmos" booklet se-tenant pane UIPP11

UEB3	(1st) Gold	75

Similar to the coil issue, No. UEB2 also in gold ink, No. UEB3 is a booklet stamp with "ST" spaced away from "1".

Type UI5

(1st) Gold (2004)

2004 (25 May). Perf. 15 × 14(E). Two bands long/short wave (blue flour).Non-fluorescent coated paper. PVA gum

From £7.23 "The Glory of the Garden" prestige pane No. UEP42

UEB4	(1st) Gold	1·00	1·00

The main difference between the above and No. UEB3 (25.2.03) is the gum which lacks the bluish appearance. Again the De La Rue and Wallsall printings in gold ink have the same Crown but the Enschedé stamp has the "st" set further from the "1".

(1st) Gold (2006)

Screened area

2006 (23 February). Perf 15 × 14(E). Two bands long/short wave (blue fluor). Non-fluorescent coated paper. PVA gum

From £7·40 "Birth Bicentenary of Isambard Kingdom Brunel" Prestige pane No. UIPP17

UEB5	(1st) Gold	1·00	1·00

The main difference between the above and No. UEB4 (25.5.04) (both with PVA gum) is the shaded area to the right of the jewelled cross on the crown which is screened on No.UEB5 as it was on No. UEB3 (25.2.03). On No. UEB4 this area is mottled and the Queen's portrait is deeper and less sharp than on Nos UEB3 and 5. The three stamps Nos. UEB3/5 all differ in shade but are still within the shade band.

Again the De La Rue and Walsall printings in gold ink have the same Crown but the Enschedé stamp has the "st" set further from the "1".

Enschedé (1st) Class Stamps in Gravure (2006)

Type UI6

(1st) Gold (2006)

2006 (21 September). Perf. 15 × 14(E). Two 9 mm bands (blue fluor). Nonfluorescent coated paper. PVA gum

From £7·44 "150th Anniversary of the Victoria Cross" Prestige pane No. UIPP18

UEB6	(1st) Gold	1·00	1·00

No. UEB6 has dull fluor under ultraviolet light compared to the De La Rue printing.

Enschedé (E) Airmail Stamp in Gravure

Type U18

(E) Deep Blue (2002)

Machin no value indicated issues UI

2002 (6 February). Perf. 15×14(E). **Two 4·5 mm band (blue fluor).** Non-fluorescent coated paper. PVA gum (bluish)

From £7·29 "A Gracious Accession" Booklet pane UIPP9
UEC1

UEC1	(E) Deep blue	1·25	

No. UEC1 from booklet No. DX28 was for the basic European airmail rate of 37p. See note below No. UEA1 on how to identify the printing from the De La Rue No. UDC1. No. UWC1 differs in shade and the PVA gum without bluish dye

Harrison (2nd) Class Stamps in Gravure (1989–97)

Type UI1

(2nd) Bright blue (1989)

1989 (22 August). Perf 15×14. One 4·5 mm centre band. Fluorescent coated paper. PVAD gum

From £1·40 and 60p. Barcode booklet panes UIPH1, UIPH3
UHA1 (=SG 1445)

UHA1	(2nd) Bright blue	1·00	1·00

Imperforate edges: No. UHA1 exists with imperforate edges at top or bottom from pane UIPH1 or at top, top and right, bottom, or bottom and right from pane UIPH3

(2nd) Bright blue (1990)

1990 (20 March). Perf 15×14. One side band at right. Fluorescent coated paper. PVAD gum

From £5 "London Life" booklet *se-tenant* pane UEP33
UHA2 (=SG 1446)

UHA2	(2nd) Bright blue	3·00	3·25

(2nd) Deep blue (1990)

1990 (7 August). Perf 15×14. One 4·5 mm centre band. Fluorescent coated paper. PVAD gum

From £1·50 Barcode booklet pane UIPH5
UHA3 (= S.G.1511)

UHA3	(2nd) Deep blue	1·50	1·50

Imperforate edges: No. UHA3 exists with imperforate edges at top or bottom

(2nd) Bright Blue (1993)

1993 (7 September). Perf 15×14(E). One 4 mm centre phosphor band (yellow fluor). Non-fluorescent coated paper. PVAD gum

From 72p. Barcode booklet pane UIPH9

UHA4	(2nd) Bright blue	1·40	1·40

(2nd) Bright blue (1995)

1995 (18 July). Perf 15×14(E). Non-fluorescent coated paper. PVAD gum

UHA5 (=SG 1664)

A. One 4 mm centre phosphor band (blue fluor).
From 76p. Barcode booklet pane UIPH11

UHA5	(2nd) Bright blue	1·00	1·00
	a. One 4·75 mm band (ex. UIPH13, 11.11.95)		3·25

B. one 4·5 mm centre phosphor band (blue fluor).
From £1·90 Barcode booklet pane UIPH14 12.12.95, vertical coil 8.7.96

UHA6	(2nd) Bright blue	1·25	

C. One 4·5 mm centre phosphor band (blue fluor). PVA gum (bluish).
From £2 Barcode booklet pane UIPH14A (4.97)

UHA6A	(2nd) Bright blue	3·25	

No. UHA6A had PVA lay-flat gum and was printed by a chemically etched cylinder.

Coils

No. UHA6 one 4·5 mm centre band (blue fluor). Printed in continuous reels without code number from a chemically etched cylinder.

		Face value			
Issued	Number in roll	Vertical delivery	Gum	Screen	Cyl. No. used
8.7.96	500	£100	PVAD	150	R2 (R17)
8.7.96	1000	£200	PVAD	150	R2 (R17)

Printed from a computer engraved cylinder

No. UHA6 No. UHA7
Chemically etched Computer engraved

The distance between the crown and right-hand edge of the frame is ·4 mm on No. UHA6 and only ·2 mm on No. UHA7. The head is the same but the improved method used to create the UHA7 cylinder shows a higher degree of definition than seen on No. UHA6.

Type UI1

(2nd) Bright blue (1996)

1996 (8 July). Perf 15×14(E). One 4·5 mm centre phosphor band (blue fluor). Non-fluorescent coated paper

A. PVAD GUM. Vertical coil

UHA7	(2nd) Bright blue	3·00	

B. PVA GUM (bluish).
From £2 Barcode booklet pane UIPH15, coils (29.4.97), (4.7.01)

UHA8	(2nd) Bright blue	75	75

Nos. UHA7/8 were printed from computer engraved cylinders. No. UHA7 is identified by the PVAD gum.

Coils

No. UHA7 one 4·5 mm centre band (blue fluor). Printed on a Chambon press in continuous reels.

		Face value		
Issued	Number in roll	Vertical delivery	Gum	Cyl. Nos. used
8.7.96	1000	£200	PVAD	RI Phos (RI7)

It is believed that this coil was sold at the same time as other 1000 rolls containing stamps printed from chemically etched cylinders without prior announcement. Evidently the Chambon press was found unsuitable when used with computer engraved cylinders.

U1 Machin no value indicated issues

No. UHA8 one 4·5mm centre band (blue fluor). Printed on the Jumelle press in continuous reels.

Issued	Number in roll	Face value Vertical delivery	Gum	Cyl. Nos used
29.4.97	500	£100	PVA (bluish)	RI (R17)
	1000	£200	PVA (bluish)	RI (R17)
4.7.01	1000	£190	PVA (bluish)	

Withdrawn: No. UHA7, 1 September 1997. The 500 roll coils were withdrawn on 21 January 2004 and the 1000 roll on 31 October 2003.

Harrison (1st) Class Stamps in Gravure (1989–97)

Type U15

(1st) Brownish black (1989)

1989 (22 August). Perf 15×14. Phosphorised (advanced coated) paper. PVAD gum

UHB1 (=SG 1447)

From £1·90 and 80p. Barcode booklet panes UIPH2, UIPH4

UHB1	(1st) Brownish black	1·75	1·00

Imperforate edges: No. UHB1 exists with imperforate edges at top or bottom from pane UIPH2 or at top. top and right, bottom and right from pane UIPH4

(1st) Brownish black (1990)

1990 (20 March). Perf 15×14. Two 9·5mm phosphor bands. Fluorescent coated paper. PVAD GUM

UHB2 (=SG 1448)

From £5 London Life booklet *se-tenant* pane UEP33

UHB2	(1st) Brownish black	3·25	3·00

(1st) Bright orange-red (1990)

1990 (7 August). Perf 15×14. Phosphorised (advanced coated) paper. PVAD gum

UHB3 (=SG 1512)

From £2 Barcode booklet pane UIPH6

UHB3	(1st) Bright orange-red	1·50	1·50

Imperforate edges: No. UHB3 exists with imperforate edges at top or bottom

(1st) Bright orange-red (1993)

1993 (6 April). Perf 15×14(E). Phosphorised (non-fluorescent coated) paper. PVAD gum

UHB4 (=SG 1666)

From 96p. and £2·40 Barcode booklet panes UIPH7/8

UHB4	(1st) Bright orange-red	1·25	1·25

(1st) Bright orange-red (1995)

1995 (4 April). Perf 15×14(E). Two 9mm phosphor bands (yellow fluor). Non-fluorescent coated paper. PVAD gum

From £2·50 Barcode booklet pane UIPH10

UHB5	(1st) Bright orange-red	1·00	1·00

(1st) Bright Orange-red (1995)

1995 (18 July). Perf 15×14(E). Two 9 mm Phosphor bands (blue fluor). Non-fluorescent coated paper. PVAD gum

UHB6 (=SG 1664a)

From £2·50 Barcode booklet pane UIPH12

UHB6	(1st) Bright orange-red	75	45

1996 (8 July). Perf 15×14(E).Two phosphor bands (blue fluor). Nonfluorescent coated paper

Vertical coil

A. PVAD GUM

UHB7	(1st) Bright orange-red	75	50

No. UHB7 can be distinguished from No. UHB6 by the distance between the two phosphor bands which are 12·5mm apart on No. UHB7 and 11·5mm on No. UHB6.

B. PVA GUM (bluish).
From £2·60 Barcode booklet pane UIPH12A (4.97)

UHB8	(1st) Bright orange-red		2·50

Coils
No. UHB7 two phosphor bands (blue fluor). Printed in continuous reels without code number.

Issued	Number in roll	Face value Vertical delivery	Gum	Cyl. Nos. used
8.7.96	500	£130	PVAD	R4 (R16)
8.7.96	1000	£260	PVAD	R4 (R16)

Withdrawn: No. UHB7, 1 September 1997.

(1st) Gold (1997)

1997 (21 April). Perf 15×14(E). Two 9mm phosphor bands (blue fluor). Non-fluorescent coated paper. PVA (bluish).

UHB9 (=SG 1668)

From £2·60 Barcode booklet pane UIPH15, £6·15 "75 Years of BBC" *se-tenant* pane UEP34 (23.9.97)

UHB9	(1st) Gold	1·00	1·00

Printed by a computer engraved cylinder

(1st) Bright orange-red (1997)

1997 (29 April). One elliptical perf hole on each vertical edge. Two 9mm phosphor bands (blue fluor). Non-fluorescent coated paper. PVA gum (bluish)

From Vertical coil, £7·54 "Profile on Print" booklet pane UIPP1 (16.2.99), sideways coil (4.7.01)

UHB10	(1st) Bright orange-red	75	45

Coil
No. UHB10 two phosphor bands (blue fluor). Printed in continuous reels.

Issued	Number in roll	Face value Vertical delivery	Gum	Cyl. Nos. used
29.4.97	500	£130	PVA (bluish)	RI (R16)
	1000	£260	PVA (bluish)	RI (R16)

Withdrawn: No. UHB7, 1 September 1997. The 500 roll coils were withdrawn on 21 January 2004 and the 1000 roll on 31 October 2003.

Machin no value indicated issues — UI

Questa (2nd) Class Stamps in Lithography (1989–96)

NOTE. Under ultraviolet light the phosphor band can be found short at the top or bottom of the stamp due to fractional misplacement, but such variations are outside the scope of the catalogue.

Type UI1

(2nd) Bright blue (1989) Lithography

1989 (19 September). Perf 15×14. One centre 4 mm short phosphor band. Fluorescent coated paper. PVA gum

UQA1 (=SG 1451)

From £1·40 Barcode booklet pane UIPQ1

UQA1	(2nd) Bright blue	1·00	1·00

(2nd) Deep blue (1990) Lithography

1990 (7 August). Perf 15×14. One centre 4 mm short phosphor band. Fluorescent coated paper. PVA gum

UQA2 (=SG 1513)

From £1·50 Barcode booklet pane UIPQ3

UQA2	(2nd) Deep blue	2·50	2·50

(2nd) Bright blue (1992) Lithography

1992 (25 February). Perf 15×14. One side band at right. Fluorescent coated paper. PVA gum

UQA3 (=SG 1451a)

From £6 "Wales" and "Tolkien" booklet *se-tenant* panes UHP9 and UHP12

UQA3	(2nd) Bright blue	3·00	3·00
	a. Phosphor omitted	£600	

(2nd) Bright blue (1993) Lithography

1993 (6 April). Perf 15×14(E). One 4 mm centre short phosphor band (yellow fluor). Non-fluorescent coated paper. PVA gum

From £1·80 Barcode booklet pane UIPQ6, sheets (6.9.93 in trial areas and 5.10.93 Philatelic Bureau)

UQA4	(2nd) Bright blue	1·50	1·50
	a. Phosphor omitted		

For note on the forgery of No. UQA4 see below pane No. UIPQ6.

Plate Numbers (Blocks of Six)
Double Pane Plates
Perforation Type L(P)

Pl. No.	(P)
1, 1	11·00
2, 2	11·00
3, 3	18·00
4, 4	12·00

Sheet Markings
Plate Numbers: In left margin opposite row 18/I. There were no other markings.

Withdrawn: 29 March 1996

(2nd) Bright blue (1993) Lithography

1993 (10 August). Perf 15×14. One phosphor band (yellow fluor) at left. Non-fluorescent coated paper. PVA gum

UQA5 (=SG 1451aEb)

From £6 (£5·64) "Beatrix Potter" booklet *se-tenant* panes UHP14 and UIPP1

UQA5	(2nd) Bright blue	2·00	2·00
	a. Phosphor omitted	£325	

(2nd) Bright blue (1994) Lithography

1994 (19 May). Perf 15×14(E). One 4mm centre phosphor band (yellow fluor). Non-fluorescent coated paper. PVA gum

From £1·90 Barcode booklet pane UIPQ8

UQA6	(2nd) Bright blue	65	55

The phosphor band on No. UQA6 is continuous.

(2nd) Bright blue (1995) Lithography

1995 (18 July). Perf 15×14(E). One 4mm centre phosphor band (blue fluor). Non-fluorescent coated paper. PVA gum

From £1·90 Barcode booklet pane UIPQ14

UQA7	(2nd) Bright blue	65	45
	a. One centre long wave phosphor band (4.2.97)	65	45

(2nd) Bright blue (1995-96) Lithography

1995 (14 November). Perf 15×14(E). Non-fluorescent coated paper. PVA gum

A. One 4 mm short centre phosphor band (blue fluor)

UQA8	(2nd) Bright blue	90	90

Plate Numbers (Blocks of Six)
Double Pane Plates
Perforation Type L(P)

Pl. No.	(P)
3, 3	7·00
4, 4	7·00

B. One 4·5 mm centre phosphor band (blue fluor) (3.12.96)

UQA9 (=SG 1670)

UQA9	(2nd) Bright blue	1·00	1·00
	a. One centre long wave phosphor band (16.2.98)	12·00	

No. UQA9a was the "Novaglow" long wave phosphor, released on 16 February 1998 after the stamp had been withdrawn from the Bureau on 1 July 1997. It was sold at the same time as the Walsall (2nd) class in sheets from Bureau and Post Shops although it was not on the stock list.

Plate Numbers (Blocks of Six)
Double Pane Plates
Perforation Type L(P)

Pl. No.	(P)
5, 5 (No. UQA9)	7·00
6, 6 (No. UQA9)	7·00
7, 7 (No. UQA9a)	75·00
8, 8 (No. UQA9a)	75·00

Sheet Markings
Plate Numbers: In left margin opposite row 18/1.

Withdrawn: 1 July 1997

UI Machin no value indicated issues

(2nd) Bright blue (1998) Gravure

1998 (1 December). Perf 15×14(E). One 4·5 mm centre phosphor band (long wave phosphor) (blue fluor). Type I. Non-fluorescent coated paper. PVA gum

UQA10 (=SG 1664a)

From £2 Barcode booklet pane UIPQ16

UQA10	(2nd) Bright blue	1·10	1·10

Two Value Types on stamps with elliptical perfs.

Type I.
Thin value from £1·90 barcode booklet pane UIPQ16

Type II.
Thick value from machine booklets *se-tenant* panes UIPQ19/20

(2nd) Bright blue (2000) Gravure

2000 (27 April). One elliptical perf. hole on each vertical edge. One 4·5 mm centre phosphor band (blue fluor). Type II. Non-fluorescent coated paper. PVA gum

From £1 booklet pane UIPQ19, £2 booklet pane UIPQ20

UQA11	(2nd) Bright blue	1·00	1·00

Questa (1st) Class Stamps in Lithography (1989–95)

Type U15

(1st) Brownish black (1989) Lithography

1989 (19 September). Perf 15×14. Phosphorised (advanced coated) paper. PVA gum

UQB1 (=SG 1452)

From £1·90 Barcode booklet pane UIPQ2

UQB1	(1st) Brownish black	2·50	2·50

(1st) Bright orange-red (1990–91) Lithography

1990 (7 August). Perf 15×14. Phosphorised (advanced coated) paper

UQB2 (=SG 1514)

A. PVAD gum.
From £2 Barcode booklet pane UIPQ4

UQB2	(1st) Bright orange-red	1·00	1·00

B. PVA gum.
From £2·20 Barcode booklet pane UIPQ5 (6.8.91)

UQB3	(1st) Bright orange red	1·00	

(1st) Bright orange-red (1992) Lithography

1992 (25 February). Perf 15×14. Two phosphor bands. Fluorescent coated paper. PVA gum

UQB4 (=SG 1514a)

A. Two 4·5 mm Bands.
From £6 "Wales" booklet *se-tenant* pane UHP9

UQB4	(1st) Bright orange-red	2·25	2·25
	a. Phosphor omitted	£700	

B. Two 4 mm Bands.
From £6 "Tolkien" booklet *se-tenant* pane UHP12 (27.10.92)

UQB5	(1st) Bright orange-red	2·25	2·25

The distance between the phosphor bands on Nos. UQB4/5 is 11·5 and 12·5 mm respectively.

(1st) Bright orange-red (1993) Lithography

1993 (10 August). Perf 15×14. Two 8 mm phosphor bands (yellow fluor). Non-fluorescent coated paper. PVA gum

From £6 (£5·64) "Beatrix Potter" booklet *se-tenant* pane UIPP1

UQB6	(1st) Bright orange-red	3·25	3·25
	a. Phosphor omitted		

The band at left is 4 mm wide and at right 8 mm to overlap to the *se-tenant* No. UQA5.

Two Value Types on stamps with elliptical perfs.

Type I.
Thin value from sheets and panes

Type II.
Bold value from £2·50 barcode booklet pane UIPQ7, £1 Barcode booklet pane UIPQ9

(1st) Bright orange-red (1993) Lithography

1993 (6 September)*. Perf 15×14(E). Two 8 mm phosphor bands (yellow fluor). Non-fluorescent coated paper

A. Type I. PVA gum

UQB7	(1st) Bright orange-red	1·00	1·00
	a. Phosphor omitted		

*No. UQB7 in sheets was issued in four trial areas on 6.9.93 and at the Philatelic Bureau on 5.10.93. For No. UQB7 in Boots pane, see No. UQB9.

Plate Numbers (Blocks of Six)

Machin no value indicated issues **U1**

Three stages of phosphor two band layout for first class booklets from 6 April 1993, printed by Walsall

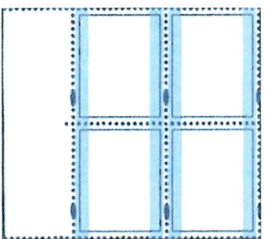

Layout A. (Inset left and right) Central split band and inset bands at each side

Layout B. (Inset left and right) Solid centre and inset bands at each side

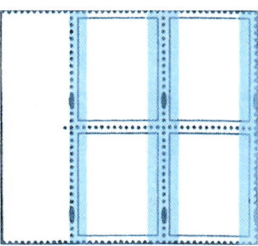

Layout C. (Inset left and right) Bands made wider at each outside edge

Double Pane Plates
Perforation Type L(P)

Pl. No.	(P)
1, 1	7·00
2, 2	7·00

The note on sheet markings below No. UQA4 applies here.
Withdrawn: 9 March 1996

B. Type II. PVA gum.
From £2·50 Barcode booklet pane UIPQ7 (1.11.93), £1 Barcode boolet panel UEPQ9.

UQB8	(1st) Bright orange-red	75	60
	a. Phosphor omitted .		

■ (1st) Pane in Lithography 1994.

Boots the Chemist stationery promotion

See also No UEB1 printed by Enschedé and without logo.

UQB9 (roulette arrowed)

Pane size 85x43mm, containing one (1st) class stamp sold at 25p. Roulette 8 across top corners of pane.

1994 (17 August). Perf 15×14(E). Two 4mm bands (yellow fluor). Non-fluorescent coated paper.

UQB9 (=SG 1671m)

UQB9	(containing No. UQB7) (17.8.94)	1·10
	a. Second ptg. size 85x42·5mm whiter gum	1·90
	ab. Phosphor omitted	£150
UQB9A	(containing No. UQB10) (9.95) folded only	5·50

No. UQB9A is known on cover postmarked 25 September 1995. It was not supplied by the Bureau and the price is for a folded pane.

UQB9B (=SG 1671ma)

As before but with two phosphor bands (blue fluor) and without Boots logo above stamp. Inscribed "The Post Office 1995".

UQB9B	(containing No. UQB10) (11.9.95)	1·25	
	a. Long wave phosphor bands (1.98)		12·00

These panes were provided by the Royal Mail for inclusion in single pre-packed greetings cards sold by Boots. The examples included with greetings cards are folded but the Philatelic Bureau supplied unfolded panes Nos. UQB9 and UQB9B and prices are for unfolded panes.
Sheet Make-up: The uncut sheet contained 55 panes in 5 columns and there were no plate numbers. A second printing was made and these panes were 42·5 mm as against 43 mm in height. They were supplied in packs of 100 panes with a label showing number 405. The second printing was number 434.
Withdrawn: 31 October 2003

Type U15

■ (1st) Bright orange-red (1995) Lithography

1995 (18 July). Perf 15×14(E). Two 7·5 mm phosphor bands (blue fluor). Type I. Non-fluorescent coated paper. PVA gum

UQB10 (=SG 1671)

From £2·50 Barcode booklet pane UIPQ15, sheets 14.11.95 and Boots pane

UQB10	(1st) Bright orange-red	1·00	1·00
	a. Two long wave phosphor bands (7.9.98)	1·50	1·50

No. QB10a is identical to the sheet stamp but singles, from sheets, ex. UIPQ15b can be identified with an attached margin i.e. top, bottom or right (Price £9 each mint). In addition the sheet examples show a 13mm gap between the bands instead of 12·5mm from booklets.

Plate Numbers (Blocks of Six)
Double Pane Plates Perforation Type L(P)

Pl. No.	(P)
3, 3 (No. UQBIO)	7·00
4, 4 (No. UQB10)	7·00
5, 5 (No. UQB10a)	80·00
6, 6 (No. UQB10a)	80·00

The note on sheet markings below No. UQA4 applies here.

Sold out: No: UQB10 in sheets, June 1998

UI — Machin no value indicated issues

(1st) Bright orange-red (1998) Gravure

1998 (1 December). Perf 15×14(E). Two 9mm phosphor bands (long wave phosphor) (blue fluor). Type I. Non-fluorescent coated paper. PVA gum

UQB11 (=SG 1667a)

From £2·60 Barcode booklet pane UIPQ17

UQB11	(1st) Bright orange-red	1·50	1·50

(1st) Bright orange-red (1999) Lithography

1999 (16 February). Perf. 15×14(E). Two 8mm phosphor bands (long wave phosphor) (blue fluor). Type I. Non-fluorescent coated paper. PVA gum

From £7·54 "Profile on Print" booklet pane UIPP5

UQB12	(1st) Bright orange-red	75	70

Questa (1st) Class Stamps in Gravure (1989–2000)

Type UI4

Printed by a computer engraved cylinder

(1st) Olive-brown (2000) Gravure

2000 (6 January). Perf 14(E). Two 9·5mm phosphor bands (blue fluor). Type I. Non-fluorescent coated paper. PVA gum

From £2·60 Barcode booklet pane UIPQ18
UQB13 (=SG 2124d)

UQB13	(1st) Olive-brown	1·00	1·00

No. UQB13 lacks the top serif to "S" of "ST". This present is on De La Rue and Walsall, Type U14.

Type III.
Thicker value from machine booklets *se-tenant* panes UIMP1/2

This value type follows types I and II of UQB7/8

Type U15

(1st) Bright orange-red (2000) Gravure

2000 (27 April). Perf 15×14(E). Two 9mm phosphor bands (blue fluor). Type III. non-fluorescent coated paper. PVA gum

From £1 booklet pane UIP19, £2 booklet pane UIPQ20

UQB14	(1st) Bright orange-red	75	45

Type UI4

(1st) Olive-brown (2000) Gravure

2000 (4 August). Perf 15×14(E). Two 9mm phosphor bands (blue fluor). Type I. Non-fluorescent coated paper. PVA gum

From £7·03 "The Life of the Century" booklet pane UIPP7

UQB15	(1st) Olive-brown	90	90

No. UQB15 differs in minor details from UQB13. A less fine screen and no repair line to the Queen's profile can be seen under magnification.

Type UI5

(1st) Gold (2002) Gravure

2002 (24 September). Perf 15×14(E). Two 9mm phosphor bands (blue fluor). Non-fluorescent coated paper. PVA gum. Head Type B3

From £6·83 "Across the Universe" booklet *se-tenant* pane UIPP10

UQB16	(1st) Gold	75	60

No. UQB16 shows the Head Type B3.

Printed by Questa in Gravure

Type UI8

(E) Deep blue (2002)

2002 (24 September). Perf 15×14(E). Two 9mm phosphor bands (blue fluor). Non-fluorescent coated paper. PVA gum. Head Type B3

From £6·83 "Across the Universe" booklet *se-tenant* pane UIPP10

UQC1	(E) Deep blue	1·25	70

No. UQC1 shows the Head Type B3.

Walsall (2nd) Class Stamps in Lithography or (1989–93)

Type UI1

(2nd) Bright blue (1989) Lithography

1989 (22 August). Perf 14. One 4mm centre band. Fluorescent coated paper. PVA gum

UWA1 (=SG 1449)

56p., 68p. and £1·70. Barcode booklet panes UIPW1, UIPW8/9

UWA1	(2nd) Bright blue	1·00	90

Imperforate edges: No. UWA1 exists with imperforate edges at top, top and right, bottom, or bottom and right
For No. UWA1 imperforate between vertical pair, see No. UIPW9a.

(2nd) Deep blue (1990) Lithography

1990 (7 August). Perf. 14. One 4mm centre band. Fluorescent coated paper. PVA gum

UWA2 (=SG 1515)

From 60p. and £1·50 Barcode booklet panes UIPW3, UIPW6

UWA2	(2nd) Deep blue	1·00	1·00

Imperforate edges: No. UWA2 exists with imperforate edges at top or bottom from both panes

(2nd) Bright blue (1993) Lithography

1993 (16 March). Perf. 14. One 4mm centre band. Fluorescent coated paper. PVAD gum

From £1·80 Barcode booklet pane UIPW12

UWA3	(2nd) Bright blue	1·25	1·25

Imperforate edges: No. UWA3 exists with imperforate edges at top or bottom
Printed on paper with reduced fluorescent additive, these stamps appear dull under ultraviolet light.

Machin no value indicated issues **UI**

(2nd) Bright blue (1993) Lithography

1993 (6 April). Perf 15×14(E). One 4mm phosphor band (yellow fluor). Non-fluorescent coated paper. PVA gum

From 72p. and £1·90 Barcode booklet panes UIPW13 and UIPW16 (1.11.93)

| UWA4 | (2nd) Bright blue | 1·75 | 1·75 |

No. UWA4 can be distinguished from No. UQA4 by the continuous phosphor band on the Walsall printing.

(2nd) Bright blue (1995) Lithography

1995 (12 December). Perf 15×14(E). One 4mm phosphor band (blue fluor). Non-fluorescent coated paper. PVA gum

From 76p. Barcode booklet pane UIPW23 (12.12.95)

| UWA5 | (2nd) Bright blue | 1·25 | 1·25 |
| | a. One long wave centre band (4.2.97) | 1·25 | 1·25 |

Walsall (2nd) Class Stamps in Gravure (1997–2003)

(2nd) Bright Blue (1997) Gravure

1997 (29 April). Perf 15×14(E). One 4·5mm phosphor band (blue fluor). Non-fluorescent coated paper. PVA gum

From Sheets (29.4.97) and 80p. Barcode booklet pane UIPW27 (26.8.97)

| UWA6 | (2nd) Bright blue | 65 | 60 |
| | a. Fine screen (Cyl. W5) | 70 | 70 |

Cylinder Numbers (Blocks of Six)
Perforation RE
Single pane

Cyl. No.	Phos. No.	No dot
W1	W1	4.00
W3	W1	18.00
W3	W2	8.00
W5	W2 above ink no.	5.00
W5	W2 below ink no.	7.00

The Walsall imprint was not etched on the cylinder block at left but was on the right margin.

Warrant Numbers and Dates of Printing (Blocks of Eight)

Warrant No.	Date	Margin at right	Source
WT390	none	5.00	W1
		Margin at left	
456	29/9/97	20.00	W3
	1/10/97	20.00	W3 (W2)
527	22/10/98	5.00	W5 (W2 below ink no.)
	23/10/98	5.00	
	26/10/98	5.00	
543	7/4/99	4.75	
548	6/5/99	4.75	
577	18/08/99	4.75	
	19/08/99	4.75	
	20/08/99	4.75	
636	12/07/00	4.75	
	13/07/00	4.75	
656	17/01/01	4.75	
664	20/03/01	4.75	
	21/03/01	4.75	
	22/03/01	4.75	
	23/03/01	4.75	
	24/04/01	4.75	W5 (W2 above ink no.)
	25/04/01	4.75	
	26/04/01	4.75	
	25/03/01	4.75	
	26/03/01	4.75	

For sheet markings see below No. UWB10.

Warrant Numbers and Dates of Printing (Blocks of Six)

Warrant No.	Date	Margin at right	Source
WT390	No date	4·25	Block of six

Warrant Numbers (Blocks of Eight)

SSO No.	Date	Margin at left	Source
527	22/10/98	6·00	W5
	23/10/98	6·00	
	26/10/98	6·00	
543	7/4/99		
577	19/08/99		

For sheet markings see below No. UWB10.

(2nd) Bright blue (1998) Gravure

1998 (13 October). Perf. 14(E). One side band at right (blue fluor). Non-fluorescent coated paper. PVA gum

UWA7 (=SG 1665)

From £6·16 Land Speed Prestige pane No. UEP36

| UWA7 | (2nd) Bright blue | 1·00 | 1·00 |

(2nd) Bright blue (1998) Gravure

1998 (13 October). Perf. 14(E). One side band at left (blue fluor). Non-fluorescent coated paper. PVA gum

UWA8 (=SG 1665bEc)

From £6·16 Land Speed Prestige pane No. UEP37

| UWA8 | (2nd) Bright blue | 75 | 75 |

Walsall (2nd) Class Stamps in Gravure (2003)
(2nd) Bright blue (2003) Gravure

2003 (2 June). Perf 15×14(E). One 4·5mm phosphor band long wave (blue fluor). Non-fluorescent coated paper. PVA gum

From £7·46 "A Perfect Coronation" Prestige pane No. UIPP12

| UWA9 | (2nd) Bright blue | 65 | |

Walsall (2nd) Class Stamps in Lithography (2008)

Type UI1

(2nd) Bright blue (2008) Lithography

2008 (18 September). Perf. 15×14(E). One 4·5mm centre band (blue fluor). Non-fluorescent coated paper. PVA

From £7·15 "Pilot to Plane" RAF Uniforms Prestige pane No. UIPP15 (18.9.08)

UWA10 (=SG 1670)

| UWA10 | (2nd) Bright blue | 90 | 90 |

The 1989/97 Walsall printings in lithography can be distinguished by the 4mm centre band. The improved portrait on No. UWA10 and the right frame is closer to the crown than before.

15

U1 Machin no value indicated issues

Walsall (1st) Class Stamps in Lithography (1989–97)

Type U15

(1st) Blackish brown (1989) Lithography

1989 (22 August). Perf. 14. Two phosphor bands. Fluorescent coated paper. PVA gum

UWB1 (=SG 1450)

From 76p. Barcode booklet pane UIPW2

UWB1	(1st) Blackish brown	2·50	2·40
	a. Phosphor omitted	£600	

Imperforate edges: No. UWB1 exists with imperforate edges at top, top and right, bottom, bottom and right.
Complete panes of four of pane UIPW2 without phosphor have not been seen.
Examples of No. UWB1 exist showing a clear edge of the phosphor band on one side due to slight misplacement. The side bands were 5 mm but between the horizontal pair the band was 9·5 mm wide.

(1st) Bright orange-red (1990–93) Lithography

1990 (7 August). Phosphorised (advanced coated) paper

UWB2 (=SG 1516)

A. Perf. 14. PVA gum
From 80p. and £2 Barcode booklet panes UIPW4, UIPW7

UWB2	(1st) Bright orange-red	1·25	1·25

In common with other contemporary Walsall printings of these designs No. UWB2 was produced from a sequence of three plates. Examples from the 80p. Barcode booklet exist on which the ink used for the first "W I" plate was in shades of ochre instead of the normal pale to deep orange. Stamps from such panes show a brownish portrait and this variety is listed as a plate number pane only.

B. Perf. 13. PVA gum.
From 80p. Barcode booklet pane UIPW5 (10.90)

UWB3 (=SG 1516c)

UWB3	(1st) Bright orange-red	2·75	3·00

C. Perf. 14. PVAD gum.
From £2·40 and 96p. Barcode booklet panes UIPW10 (9.2.93) and UIPW11 (16.3.93)

UWB4	(1st) Bright orange-red	1·25	

Imperforate edges: Nos. UWB2/3 exists with imperforate edges at top or bottom from both panes. No. UWB3 was first reported in October 1990 and was caused by the use, in error, of a smaller gauge comb perforator.

(1st) Bright orange-red (1993) Lithography

1993 (6 April). Perf. 15 × 14(E). Two 3·5 mm phosphor bands (yellow fluor) at each side. (Layout A). Non-fluorescent coated paper. PVA gum

From £2·40 and 96p. Barcode booklet panes UIPW14 and UIPW15 (17.8.93)

UWB5	(1st) Bright orange-red	90	90
	a. Phosphor omitted	£150	
	b. Two 3·5 mm split bands with 1 mm gap between		
	c. Single 3·5 mm band		

No. UWB5 was printed with 3·25 to 3·5 mm phosphor bands so that the phosphor just failed to cover the vertical perforations at each side. The gap was 1 mm or less between vertical rows 2/3 where the pane was folded into the booklet cover.

Nos. UWB5b/c were from panes with phosphor band misplacement to left.

(1st) Bright orange-red (1994) Lithography

1994 (22 April). Perf. 15×14(E). Non-fluorescent coated paper. PVA gum £1 Barcode booklet pane UIPW 17

A. One 3 mm Inset band at left and one side band at right (yellow fluor) (Layout B)

UWB6	(1st) Bright orange-red	80	80
	a. Inset band at right and side band at left	80	80

B. Two phosphor bands (yellow fluor) (layout C).

From £2·50 Barcode booklet panes UIPW18 (1.7.94), UIPW19 (7.10.94), UIPW20 (16.5.95)

UWB7	(1st) Bright orange-red	80	80
	b. One 7·5 mm broad band		
	c. One 4 mm band		

No. UWB7b came from panes on which the phosphor bands were misplaced showing one band on each stamp.
No. UWB7 shows both bands cover the edges of the stamp.

(1st) Bright orange-red (1995-96) Lithography

1995 (18 July). Perf. 15 × 14(E).Non-fluorescent coated paper. PVA gum

UWB8 (=SG 1666)

From £1 Barcode booklet panes UIPW21, UIPW29, £2·50 Barcode booklet pane UIPW22, UIPW25/6, UIPW31 (14.11.98)

A. Two phosphor bands (blue fluor) (Layout C)

UWB8	(1st) Bright orange-red	80	80
	b. Two long wave phosphor bands (4.2.97)	80	80

B. One 3 mm Inset band at left and one side band at right (blue fluor) (Layout B)
From £1 Barcode booklet pane UIPW24 (6.2.96)

UWB9	(1st) Bright orange-red	80	80
	a. Inset band at right and side band at left	80	80
	b. As UMB9 two long wave phosphor hands (4.2.97)	80	80
	c. As UMB9a but long wave (4.2.97)	80	80

(Walsall (1st) Class Stamps in Gravure (1997)

Type U15

(1st) Gold (1997) Gravure

1997 (21 April). perf. 15 × 14(E). two phosphor bands short wave (blue fluor). nonfluorescent coated paper. PVA gum white back

From Barcode booklet pane UIPW47, sheets
UWB10 (=SG 1668)

UWB10	(1st) Gold	1.00	1.00

This stamp was issued originally in celebration of HM the Queen and HRH the Duke of Edinburgh's golden wedding. Issued on Her Majesty's birthday. Subsequently the stamp printed in gold became the standard for first class stamps.

Machin no value indicated issues

Cylinder Numbers (Blocks of Six)
Perforation RE
Single pane

Cyl. No.	Phos. No.		No dot
W1	W1	W1	7.00

Warrant Numbers and Dates of Printing (Blocks of Six or Eight)

Warrant No.	Date	Margin at right	
WT389	none	10.00	Block of six
443	16/04/97	15.00	Block of eight

The phosphor reaction was poor from Warrant 389 and improved on the next printing.

Sheet Details

Sheet size: 200 (20 horizontal rows of ten stamps). Single pane reel-fed

Sheet markings:
Cylinder numbers: Opposite row 18, left margin with phosphor "W1" below the the ink number.
Colour register marks: In right margin opposite row 3, triangles opposite rows 5/6
Perforation guide marks: Thin bars opposite every perforation row, left margin
Warrant numbers and dates (where applicable): Opposite rows 13/15, warrant and sheet numbers and with date rows 12/15, right margin
Walsall imprint: Two-line imprint reading up opposite rows 17/18 with light cross in right margin
Traffic lights: Walsall segmented circles opposite rows 3/4, left margin

▌ (1st) Bright orange-red (1997) Gravure

1997 (26 August). Perf. 15 × 14(E). Two 9mm phosphor bands (blue fluor). Non-fluorescent coated paper. PVA gum

From £1·04 Barcode booklet panes UIPW28, UIPW32, UIPW34, £2·08 Barcode booklet pane UIPW33, £2·60 Barcode booklet pane pane UIPW30, sheets (18.11.97), "Profile on Print" booklet pane UIPP5 (16.2.99)

UWB11	(1st) Bright orange-red	75	45
	a. 6·5 mm band at left (with left margin) (18.11.97)	75	
	b. 6·5 mm band at right (with right margin)	75	

Cylinder Numbers (Blocks of Six)
Single Pane Cylinder Perforation Type RE

Cyl. No.	Phos. No.		
W1	W1		5·00
W1	W2		5·00
W2	W2		7·00

Warrant Numbers and Dates of Printing (Blocks of Eight)

Warrant No.	Date	Margin at left	Source
455	19/09/97	5·50	W1 (W1)
	22/9/97	5·50	

Secure Stock Operations Numbers and Dates of Printing (Blocks of Eight)

SSO No.	Date	Margin at left	Source
528	4/12/98	8·00	W1 (W2)
	08/12/98	8·00	W1 (W2)
	09/12/98	8·00	
	10/12/98	8·00	
544	6/5/99	8·00	
576	22/09/99	8·00	
	23/09/99	8·00	
663	19/04/01	8·00	
	20/04/01	8·00	
	21/04/01	8·00	
	24/04/01	8·00	

Sheet Markings: (2nd), W1
Cylinder numbers: In left margin opposite row 18/1
Walsall Eltromat Register Marks: Used for quality control, these appear in the right margin opposite row 3 and triangle opposite row 5
Coloured cross: In right margin opposite row 16 following the imprint
Segmented circle: Used for colour check this is in the left margin opposite row 4
Perforation register marks: Thin bars opposite each horizontal perforation row, left margin
Warrant number and date: In right margin opposite rows 13/15. The position does vary
Marginal arrows: Above and below vertical rows 5/6 and opposite rows 10/11 at both sides
Imprint: "Walsall Security Printers Ltd Walsall England" in right margin opposite rows 17/18

Later printings (2nd), W5 and (1st) exist with SSO. No at left with imprint opposite row 20 and no other markings except for marginal arrows.

Walsall (1st) Class Stamps in Gravure (2000)

Type II

Type II. The centre cross is open at both top left and right without the spot of hair on the right as seen on Type I printed by De La Rue and Questa.

Type UI4

▌ (1st) Olive-brown (2000) Gravure

2000 (6 January). Perf. 15 × 14(E). Two 9mm phosphor bands (blue fluor). Type II. Non-fluorescent coated paper. PVA gum

From £2·60 Barcode booklet pane UIPW35

UWB12	(1st) Olive-brown	75	45

▌ (1st) Olive-brown (2000) Gravure

2000 (15 February). Perf. 14(E). Two phosphor bands (blue fluor). Type II. Non-fluorescent coated paper. PVA gum

From £7·50 "Special by Design "booklet pane UIPP7

UWB13	(1st) Olive-brown	75	45

Walsall (1st) Class Stamps in Gravure (2000)

Type III

Type III. This type is a second Walsall version with a semi-closed centre cross but without the spot of hair which is visible in Type I. The three protruding jewels remain as in Type II and these are not so evident on either the De La Rue or Questa Type I.

U1 Machin no value indicated issues

■ (1st) Olive-brown (2000) Gravure

2000 (21 March). Perf. 15 × 14(E). Two phosphor bands (blue fluor). Type III. Non-fluorescent coated paper. PVA gum

From £1·04 Barcode booklet panes UIPW36/7
| UWB14 | (1st) Olive-brown | 75 | 45 |

Walsall (1st) Class Stamps in Gravure (2003)

Type U15

■ (1st) Gold (2003) Gravure

2003 (2 June). Change of phosphor ink. Perf. 15 × 14(E). Two phosphor bands long/short wave (blue fluor) Non-fluorescent coated paper. PVA gum

From £7·46 "A Perfect Coronation" Prestige pane No. UIPP12
| UWB15 | (1st) Gold | 90 |

■ (1st) Gold (2005) Gravure

2005 (18 October). Change to fine screen. Perf. 15 × 14(E). Two phosphor bands long/short wave (blue fluor). Non-fluorescent coated paper. PVA gum

From £7·26 "Bicentenary of the Battle of Trafalgar" Prestige pane No. UIPP16
| UWB16 | (1st) Gold | 90 |

The printed ink screen on No. UWB16 is fine rather than the heavy diamond dots seen on No. UWB15 from the pane UIPP12 (2.6.03).

De La Rue   Walsall

Type U15

■ (1st) Gold (2008) Lithography

2008 (18 September). Perf. 15 × 14(E). Two bands (blue fluor). NFCP/PVA

From £7·15 "Pilot to Plane" RAF Uniforms Prestige pane No. UIPP15 (18.9.08)
UWB17 (=SG 1672)
| UWB17 | (1st) Gold | 1·00 | 1·00 |

This was the first Walsall printing in gold by lithography which is distinguished from gravure by clear cut edges to the "1st". The horizontal parts of 1st are thin compared to De La Rue and the value is placed further to the right, away from the left frame

Printed by Walsall in gravure from a computer engraved cylinder

Type U18

■ (E) Deep blue (1999)

1999 (19 January). Perf. 15 × 14(E). Two 9 mm phosphor bands (blue fluor). Non-fluorescent coated paper. PVA gum

From £1·20 Barcode booklet pane UEAP1
| UWC1 | (E) Deep blue | 1·25 |

No. UWC1 was only issued in booklets and was valid for the basic European airmail rate, initially 30p., which was increased to 34p. from 25.10.99.

Large Format Machins from Prestige booklet DX22 (1999)

UY3 Queen Elizabeth II

(Des. after plaster cast by Arnold Machin)

A. Embossed and Lithographed by Walsall

Die-cut roulette 14 × 15

■ (1st) Queen's Head in Colourless Relief

1999 (16 February). Die-cut perf 14 × 15. Phosphor background (blue fluor). Self-adhesive

UY1 (=SG 2077)
From £7·54 "Profile on Print" booklet pane UIPP2
| UY1 | (1st) Grey (face value) | 3·00 | 2·50 |

B. Recess by Enschedé

Engraved by Czeslaw Slania.

■ (1st) Grey-black

1999 (16 February). Perf. 14 × 14½. Two phosphor bands (blue fluor). Non-fluorescent coated paper. PVA gum (bluish)

From £7·54 "Profile on Print" booklet pane UIPP3
UY2 (=SG 2078)
| UY2 | (1st) Grey-black | 3·00 | 2·50 |

C. Typographed by Harrison

Perforated 14 × 15

■ (1st) Black

1999 (16 February). Perf. 14 × 15. Two phosphor bands (blue fluor). Non-fluorescent coated paper. PVA gum (bluish)

UY3 (=SG 2079)
From £7·54 "Profile on Print" booklet pane UIPP4
| UY3 | (1st) Black | 3·00 | 2·50 |

Machin no value indicated issues

Miniature sheets, containing Non Value Indicated Machin Stamps

2000 (23 May). Stamp Show 2000 International Stamp Exhibition, London. "Her Majesty's Stamps"

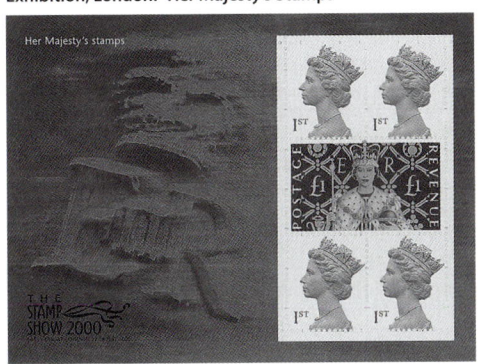

WMS1309

(Des. Delananey Design Consultants. Photogravure de La Rue)

WMS1309 (=SG**MS**2147)

Sheet size 121×89mm. Phosphorised paper (blue fluor) PVA (bluish) gum. Perf. 15×14

WMS1309	(23.5.00)	21·00	21·00

First Day Cover (WMS1390)	†	22·00
Presentation Pack		£100
PHQ Cards (set of 2)		16·00

The £1 value is an adaption of the 1953 Coronation 1s.3d. stamp originally designed by Edmund Dulac. It is shown on one of the PHQ cards with the other depicting the complete miniature sheet.

2005 (5 July). 60th Anniversary of End of the Second World War

Containing the 1995 Type W959 25p. St. Paul's Cathedral as a 1st class stamp, Machin (1st) (5) and sheet background as Type W957 British troops and French civilians celebrating. Non-fluorescent coated paper/PVA gum

WMS1755 Miniature Sheet
(Illustration reduced to half actual size)

(Des. Jeffery Matthews)
(Printed in Gravure by Enschedé)

WMS1755 (=SG **MS**2547)

Sheet size 115 × 105 mm Two phosphor bands Perf. 15 × 14(E) (1st gold) or 14½ × 14 (other)

WMS1755	(5.7.05)	6·00	6·00
First Day Cover			8·00

The (1st) printed in gold has PVA gum and would be listed but we do not allocate separate numbers for stamps issued in miniature sheets. The other Enschedé (1st) class in gold are Nos. UEB2/3 which have bluish gum and can be distinguished from the above when in mint condition.

First Day Covers

On official covers prepared and issued by the Post Office and the stamps cancelled with circular "FIRST DAY OF ISSUE" postmarks.

UIFD1 (22.8.89)	Nos. UHA1 (2nd), UHB1 (1st)	5·00
UIFD2 (7.8.90)	Nos. UHA2 (2nd). UHB2 (1st)	6·00
UFD42 (21.4.97)	26p (U302), (1st) (UHB9)	3·50
UIFD3 (19.1.99)	No. UX1 (E)	3·50
UIFD4 (16.2.99)	Nos. UY1/3 (1st) (3)	12·00
UIFD5 (6.1.00)	(1st) (UDB1)	1·50
UIFD6 (1.8.06)	12p., 14p., PiP (2nd) (2), (1st) (2)	5·00

Presentation Packs

UIPP1 No. 48 (6.1.00) (1st) (UDB1)	90
UIPP2 No. 74 (1.8.06) Six values	4·75

The contents of No. U1PP2, were 12p., 14p., De La Rue and pricing in proportion Walsall (2nd) ×2 and (1st) ×2 all printed in Gravure, perforated 15 × 14(E).

BOOKLET PANES

Checklist of Machin No Value Indicated Booklet Panes
The checklist gives date of issue and pane content arranged according to printer.
Note: Panes with an elliptical perf. hole on each vertical stamp edge were issued from 6 April 1993 (excl. Prestige booklet pane No. UIMP1). Computer engraved cyls. were first used by Harrison/De La Rue and Walsall in 1997 and Questa in 1998 (comp. eng.).
  Boots the Chemist single stamp panes are listed in Section UI under UQB9 (Questa and UIPEI (Enschedé).

Harrison/De La Rue NVI panes

SG Spec. No.	Date of issue	Description	No. of stamps	Page
UIPH1	22.8.89	2nd brt. blue	10	21
UIPH2	22.8.89	1st black	10	21
UIPH3	28.11.89	2nd brt. blue	4	21
UIPH4	5.12.89	1st black	4	21
UIPH5	7.8.90	2nd dp. blue	10	22
UIPH6	7.8.90	1st red	10	22
UIPH7	6.4.93	1st red	4	22
UIPH8	6.4.93	1st red	10	22
UIPH9	7.9.93	2nd brt. blue	4	22
UIPH10	4.4.95	1st red	10	23
UIPH11	18.7.95	2nd brt. blue	4	23
UIPH12	18.7.95	1st red	10	23
UIPH13	11.11.95	2nd brt. blue	10	23
UIPH14	12.12.95	2nd brt. blue PVAD gum	10	23
UIPH14A	—.4.97	2nd brt. blue PVA gum	10	23
UIPH15	21.4.97	1st gold	10	23
UIPH16	29.4.97	2nd brt. blue (comp. eng.)	10	24
UIPH17	8.11.97	1st red (comp. eng.)	10	24

Questa NVI panes

SG Spec. No.	Date of issue	Description	No. of stamps	Page
UIPQ1	19.9.89	2nd brt. blue	10	24
UIPQ2	19.9.89	1st black	10	24
UIPQ3	7.8.90	2nd dp. blue	10	25
UIPQ4	7.8.90	1st red PVAD gum	10	25
UIPQ5	6.8.91	1st red PVA gum	10	25
UIPQ6	6.4.93	2nd brt. blue	10	25
UIPQ7	1.11.93	1st red	10	25
UIPQ8	19.5.94	2nd brt. blue	10	26
UIPQ9	27.7.94	1st red and Bank of England label	4	26
UIPQ13	4.10.94	1st red	10	26
UIPQ14	18.7.95	2nd brt. blue	10	26
UIPQ15	18.7.95	1st red	10	27
UIPQ16	1.12.98	2nd brt. blue (comp. eng.)	10	27
UIPQ17	1.12.98	1st red (comp. eng.)	10	27
UIPQ18	6.1.00	1st Millennium	10	27
UIPQ19	27.4.00	2nd (1) & 1st (3)	4	27
UIPQ20	27.4.00	2nd (2) & 1st (6)	8	28
UIPQ20	17.4.01	2nd (1) & 1st (3)	4	28

Walsall NVI panes

SG Spec No.	Date of issue	Description	No. of Stamps	Page
UIPW1	22.8.89	2nd brt. blue	4	28
UIPW2	22.8.89	1st blk. brown	4	28
UIPW3	7.8.90	2nd dp. blue	4	29
UIPW4	7.8.90	1st red perf. 14	4	29
UIPW5	—.10.90	1st red perf. 13	4	30
UIPW6	7.8.90	2nd dp. blue	10	30
UIPW7	7.8.90	1st red	10	30
UIPW8	6.8.91	2nd brt. blue	4	30
UIPW9	6.8.91	2nd brt. blue	10	31
UIPW10	9.2.93	1st red	10	31
UIPW11	16.3.93	1st red	4	31
UIPW12	16.3.93	2nd brt. blue	10	31
UIPW13	6.4.93	2nd brt. blue	4	31
UIPW14	6.4.93	1st red	10	32
UIPW15	17.8.93	1st red	4	32
UIPW16	1.11.93	2nd brt. blue	10	32
UIPW17	22.4.94	1st red	4	33
UIPW18	1.7.94	1st red	10	33
UIPW19	7.10.94	1st red	4	33
UIPW20	16.5.95	1st red and Mitchell label	4	33
UIPW21	18.7.95	1st red	4	33
UIPW22	22.8.95	1st red	10	34
UIPW23	12.12.95	2nd brt. blue	4	34
UIPW24	6.2.96	1st red	4	34
UIPW25	16.4.96	1st red and Queen's Birthday label	4	35
UIPW26	12.2.97	1st red and Hong Kong '97 label	4	35
UIPW27	26.8.97	2nd brt. blue (comp. eng.)	4	35
UIPW27A	21.4.97	1st gold	10	35
UIPW28	26.8.97	1st red (comp. eng.)	4	36
UIPW29	21·10.97	1st red and Heads of Govt. label	4	36
UIPW30	8.11.97	1st red (comp. eng.)	10	36
UIPW31	14.11.98	1st red and Prince of Wales Birthday label	4	36
UIPW32	12.5.99	1st red and Berlin Airlift label	4	37
UIPW33	12.5.99	1st red	8	37
UIPW34	1·10.99	1st red and Rugby World Cup label	4	37
UIPW35	6.1.00	1st Millennium	10	37
UIPW36	26.5.00	1st Millennium	8	38
UIPW37	21.3.00	1st Millennium	4	38
UIPW38	4.4.00	1st Millennium	4	38

European Airmail

UEAP1	19.1.99	blue	4	38

Prestige booklet Panes containing No Value indicated stamps

SG Spec No.	Date of issue	Booklet Title	Page
UIPP1	10.8.93	Beatrix Potter	39
UIPP2	16.2.99	Profile on Print	39
UIPP3	16.2.99	Profile on Print	39
UIPP4	16.2.99	Profile on Print	39
UIPP5	16.2.99	Profile on Print	39
UIPP6	16.2.99	Profile on Print	40
UIPP7	15.2.00	Special by Design	40
UIPP8	4.8.00	Queen Elizabeth the Queen Mother	40
UIPP9	6.2.02	A Gracious Accession	40
UIPP10	24.9.02	Across the Universe	40
UIPP11	25.2.03	Microcosmos	41
UIPP12	2.6.03	A Perfect Coronation	41
UIPP13	5.6.07	Machin The Making of a Masterpiece	41

Machin no value indicated issues *Booklet panes* **U1**

UIPP14	8.1.08	Ian Fleming's James Bond	41
UIPP15	18.9.08	Pilot to Plane	41

Prestige Panes containing mixed Non Value Indicated and denominated stamps

SG Spec No.	Date of issue	Booklet Title	Page
UEPP33	20.3.90	London Life	41
UEPP34	23.9.97	75th Anniv of BBC	42
UEPP38	13.10.98	Breaking Barriers	42
UEPP41	16.3.04	Letters by Night	42
UEPP42	25.5.04	The Glory of the Garden	42
UEPP43	24.2.05	The Brontë Sisters	42
UEPP44	18.10.05	Battle of Trafalgar	43
UEPP45	23.2.06	Isambard Kingdom Brunel	43
UEPP46	21.9.06	150th anniv of Victoria Cross	43
UEPP47	1.3.07	World of Invention	43
UEPP48	12.2.09	Birth Bicentenary of Charles Darwin	43

Booklet Panes containing Machin No Value Indicated stamps

1. Printed by Harrison in Gravure (1989-97)

■ **(2nd) £1·40 Pane**

(£1·50 from 2.10.89, £1·80 from 16.9.91). From Barcode Booklets HC1a, HC10

UIPH1, UIPH5, UIPW6, UIPW9, UIPW12

Pane of ten (2nd) class stamps (bright blue) with one 4·5 mm centre phosphor band from Barcode Booklet Nos. HC1/a and HC10. The pane has imperforate horizontal edges

Pane UIPH1. Gravure. selvedge at left

UIPH1	(containing No. UHA1 × 10) (22.8.89)	8·00

Booklet Cylinder Numbers

Pane No.	Cyl. No.	Phos. No.	Perf. Type IEI No dot
UIPH1	B1	(B84)	15·00

Sheet Make-up. The printer's sheet from the Jumelle press and perforated by the APS machine was single pane containing four columns of ten booklet panes each. Gutter margins between vertical columns 2, 3 and 4 were trimmed to provide the binding margin at left. The right side margin was trimmed to the perforation edge, but the extent of trim varies. The columns were continuous and contained a cylinder pane every fifth pane. There were 8 cylinder and 32 ordinary panes in the printer's sheet. Horizontal trimming lines in the vertical margins at left indicated the cutting lines with cylinder numbers placed opposite row 1 in the pane.

■ **(1st) £1·90 Pane**

(£2 from 2.10.89). From Barcode Booklet HD1/a

UIPH2, UIPH6, UIPW7, UIPW10

Pane of ten (1st) class stamps (brownish black) on phosphorised (advanced coated) paper. The pane has imperforate horizontal edges

Pane UIPH2. Gravure, selvedge at left

UIPH2	(containing No. UHB1 × 10) (22.8.89)	10·00

Booklet Cylinder Number

Pane No.	Cyl. No.	Perf. Type IEI No dot
UIPH2	B3	15·00

Sheet Make-up. As Pane UIPH1

■ **(2nd) 60p. Pane**

From Barcode Booklet HA2

UIPH3, UIPW1, UIPH4, UIPW2

Pane of four (2nd) class stamps (bright blue) with one 4·5 mm centre phosphor band. Pane has three edges imperforate from Walsall cover

Pane UIPH3. Gravure, selvedge at left

UIPH3	(containing No. UHA1 × 4) (28.11.89)	24·00

Cylinder Numbers and Sheet Make-up. Printed on the Chambon press and perforated by the integral comb machine, the primary sheet contained a total of 18 booklet panes of four arranged in six vertical columns of three panes. Each pane was perforated across its centre, but otherwise left imperforate horizontally. Each pane was also imperforate vertically at right and each of the six columns was separated by a vertical gutter margin just over 15 mm wide. A single cylinder number in L right-angle was placed in the bottom margin but this was wide and always trimmed off. See Appendix I for illustration.

Those used were: B2, (B83).

■ **(1st) 80p. Pane**

From Barcode Booklet HB2

Pane of four (1st) class stamps (brownish black) on phosphorised (advanced coated) paper. Pane has three edges imperforate from Walsall cover

Pane UIPH4. Gravure, selvedge at left

UIPH4	(containing No. UHB1 × 4) (5.12.89)	30·00

UI Machin no value indicated issues *Booklet panes*

Cylinder Number and Sheet Make-up. As UIPH3. It is believed that B2 was the cylinder number.

(2nd) £1·50 Pane

(£1·70 from 17.9.90). From Barcode Booklet HC3

As pane No. UIPH1.
Pane of ten (2nd) class stamps (deep blue) with one 4·5 mm centre phosphor band. The pane has imperforate horizontal edges

Pane UIPH5. Gravure, selvedge at left

UIPH5 (containing No. UHA3 × 10) (7.8.90)   8·50

Booklet Cylinder Numbers

Pane No.	Cyl. No.	Phos. No.	Perf. Type IEI No dot
UIPH5	B1	(B84)	12·00

Sheet Make-up. As Pane UIPH 1.

(1st) £2 Pane

(£2·20 from 17.9.90, £2·40 from 16.9.91). From Barcode Booklets HD3/3b, HD6 As pane No. UIPH2

Pane of ten (1st) class stamps (bright orange-red) on phosphorised (advanced coated) paper. The pane has imperforate horizontal edges

Pane UIPH6. Gravure. selvedge at left

UIPH6 (containing No. UHB3 × 10) (7.8.90)   6·50

Booklet Cylinder Numbers
Perf. Type IEI

Pane No.	Cyl. Nos.	No dot
UIPH6	B3	9·00
	B5	12·00

Sheet Make-up. As Pane UIPH1

(1st) 96p. Pane

From Barcode Booklet HB5 (£1 from 1.11.93).

UIPH7

Pane of four (1st) class stamps (bright orange-red) on phosphorised (non-fluorescent coated) paper. Two elliptical perf. holes on each vertical edge.

Pane UIPH7. Gravure. selvedge at left

UIPH7 (containing No. UHB4 × 4) (6.4.93)   3·00

Booklet Cylinder Number

Pane No.	Cyl. No.	Perf. Type I No dot
UIPH7	B8	6·00

Sheet Make-up. The primary sheet of 70 panes. printed by the Jumelle, contained seven vertical columns made up of two cylinder and eight ordinary panes with left-hand gutter margins between each column.

(1st) £2·40 Pane

(£2·50 from 1.11.93)
From Barcode Booklets HD9/9a, HD20

UIPH8, UIPH10, UIPH12

Pane of ten (1st) class stamps (bright orange-red) on phosphorised (non-fluorescent coated) paper. Two elliptical perf. holes on each vertical edge.

Pane UIPH8. Gravure, selvedge at left

UIPH8 (containing No. UHB4 × 10) (6.4.93)   6·50

Booklet Cylinder Number

Pane No.	Cyl. No.	Perf. Type I No dot
UIPH8	B5	8·00

Sheet Make-up: This was a Jumelle printing with the APS rotary perforator as UIPH6 but perforated all round.

(2nd) 72p. Pane

(76p. from 1.11.93, 80p. from 8.7.96).
From Barcode Booklets HA7, HA8

UIPH9, UIPHI I, UIPHI3

Pane of four (2nd) class stamps (bright blue) with one 4 mm centre phosphor band (yellow fluor). Two elliptical perf. holes on each vertical edge.

Pane UIPH9. Gravure. selvedge at left

UIPH9 (containing UHA4 × 4) (7.9.93)   3·50

Booklet Cylinder Numbers

Pane No.	Cyl. Nos.	Phos. No.	Perf. Type I No dot
UIPH9	B4	(B95)	6·50
	B6	(B95)	6·50

Sheet Make-up: As UIPH7 this was printed on the Jumelle press and perforated by the APS rotary machine.

(1st) £2·50 Pane

From Barcode Booklet HD24

As pane No. UIPH8
Pane of ten (1st) class stamps (bright orange-red) with two 9mm phosphor bands (yellow fluor) on non-fluorescent coated paper. Two elliptical perf. holes on each vertical edge.

Pane UIPH 10. Gravure, selvedge at left

	Perf. Type I
UIPH10 (containing No. UHB5 × 10) (4.4.95)	6·50

Booklet Cylinder Numbers

Pane No.	Cyl. No.	Phos. No.	Perf. Type I No dot
UIPH10	B5	(B99)	12·00

Sheet Make-up: As pane No. UIPH8.

(2nd) 76p. Pane

(80p. from 8.7.96). From Barcode Booklet HA8a

As pane No. UIPH9
Pane of four (2nd) class stamps (bright blue) with one 4mm centre phosphor band (blue fluor) on non-fluorescent coated paper. Two elliptical perf. holes on each vertical edge.

Pane UIPH11. Gravure, selvedge at left

UIPH11 (containing No. UHA5 × 4) (18.7.95)	3·00

Booklet Cylinder Numbers

Pane No.	Cyl. No.	Phos. No.	Perf. Type I No dot
UIPH11	B6	(B95)	6·00

Sheet Make-up: As pane No. UIPH7.

(1st) £2·50 Pane

(£2·60 from 8.7.96). From Barcode Booklets HD24a, HD27, HD29/33, HD35, HD39/a

As pane No. UIPH8
Pane of ten (1st) class stamps (bright orange-red) with two 9mm phosphor bands (blue fluor) on non-fluorescent coated paper. Two elliptical perf. holes on each vertical edge.

Pane UIPH 12. Gravure, selvedge at left

UIPH12 (containing No. UHB6 × 10) (18.7.95)	6·50

As pane No. UIPH12 but with PVA gum (bluish) from booklet No. HD39a

UIPH12A (containing No. UHB8 × 10) (4.97)	25·00

Booklet Cylinder Numbers

Pane No.	Cyl. Nos.	Phos. No.	Perf. Type 1 No dot
UIPH12	B5	(B99)	9·00
	B11	(B99)	9·00
UIPH12A	B11	(B99)	32·00

Sheet Make-up: As pane No. UIPH8 from chemically etched cylinders.

(2nd) 76p. Pane

From Barcode Booklet HA8b (80p. from 8.7.96).

As pane No. UIPH9
Pane of four (2nd) class stamps (bright blue) with one 4·75mm centre phosphor band (blue fluor) on non-fluorescent coated paper. Two elliptical perf. holes on each vertical edge.

Pane UIPH13. Gravure, selvedge at left

UIPH13 (containing No. UHASa × 4) (11.11.95)	7·00

The 4·75 mm band was at the extreme of the tolerance allowed and derived from an old cylinder with an imperial rather than a metric band width.

Booklet Cylinder Numbers

Pane No.	Cyl. No.	Phos. No.	Perf. Type I No dot
UIPH13	B7	(B9)	15·00

Sheet Make-up: As pane No. UIPH9.

(2nd) £1·90 Pane

(£2 from 8.7.96) From Barcode Booklets HC14/15, HC17, HC19

UIPH14, UIPH14A

Pane of ten (2nd) class stamps (bright blue) with one 4·5mm, centre phosphor band (blue fluor) on non-fluorescent coated paper/PVAD gum. Two elliptical perf. holes on each vertical edge.

Pane UIPH14. Gravure, selvedge at left

UIPH14 (containing No. UHA6 × 10) (12.12.95)	6·00

As pane No. UIPH14 but with PVA gum (bluish) from booklet No. HC19a

UIPH14A (containing No. UHA6A × 10) (4.97)	25·00

Booklet Cylinder Numbers

Pane Nos.	Cyl. Nos.	Phos. No.	Perf. Type I No dot
UIPH14	B1	(B8)	11·00
	B3	(B8)	11·00
UIPH14A	B3	(B8)	32·00

Sheet Make-up: As pane No. UIPH8 from chemically etched cylinders.

(1st) £2·60 Pane

From Barcode Booklets HD41, HD43

Pane of ten (1st) class stamps (gold) with two 9mm bands (blue flour). Two elliptical perf. holes on each vertical edge.

Pane UIPH15. Gravure, selvedge at left

UIPH15 (containing No. UHB9 × 10)(21.4.97)	8·00
a. 3mm unvarnished phosphor strip in left margin	10·00

Pane No. UIPH15a came from column 1 where the varnish failed to cover the phosphor band in the binding margin.

Booklet Cylinder Numbers

Pane No.	Cyl. No.	Phos. No.	Perf. Type I
UIPH15	B13	(B12)	10·00
UIPH15	B14	(B12)	10·00
UIPH15a	B13	(B12)	15·00

The phosphor cylinder number occurs above or below the ink number opposite row 1 in both instances.

Sheet Make-up
Printed on the Jumelle press, the sheets were perforated by the rotary APS style machine. Primary sheets contained four columns each of ten panes including a cylinder pane.

UI Machin no value indicated issues *Booklet panes*

■ (2nd) £2 Pane

(£1·90 from 26.4.99).
From Barcode Booklets HC19b, HC21

As pane UIPH14/A but printed from computer engraved cylinders
  Pane of ten (2nd) class stamps (bright blue) with one 4·5 mm centre phosphor band on non-fluorescent coated paper. Printed from computer engraved cylinders. Two elliptical perf. holes on each vertical edge.

Pane UIPH16. Gravure from computer engraved cyls., selvedge at left

UIPH16 (containing No. UHA8 × 10) (29.4.97)		6·00

Booklet Cylinder Numbers

Pane No.	Cyl. Nos.	Phos. No.	Perf. Type I No dot
UIPH16	B10	(B13)	7·50
	B11	(B13)	7·50

Sheet Make-up: As pane No. UIPH8 but with a computer engraved cylinder.

■ (1st) £2·60 Pane

From Barcode Booklets HD39b, HD45/49

As pane UIPH12A but printed from computer engraved cylinders
  Pane of ten (1st) class stamps (bright orange-red) with two 9 mm phosphor bands (blue fluor) on non-fluorescent coated paper. PVA (bluish) gum. Two elliptical perf. holes on each vertical edge.

Pane UIPH16. Gravure from computer engraved cylinders, selvedge at left

UIPH17 (containing No. UHB9 × 10) (8.11.97)		6·50

Booklet Cylinder Numbers

Pane No.	Cyl. Nos.	Phos. No.	Perf. Type I No dot
UIPH17	B13	(B12)	9·00
	B14	(B12)	9·00

Sheet Make-up: Printed by computer engraved cylinder on the Jumelle press. Both cylinders were used for the Royal Golden Wedding issue.

2. Printed by Questa in Lithography and Gravure from 1998

For the Boots the Chemist loose panes printed by Questa see below No. UQB9.

■ (2nd) £1·40 Pane

(£1·50 from 2.10.89, £1·70 from 17.9.90,
£1·80 from 16.9.91).
From Barcode Booklets HC2, HC6/6a, HC9

UIPQ1, UIPQ3

Pane of ten (2nd) class stamps (bright blue) with one centre 4 mm short phosphor band.

Pane UIPQ1. Lithographed, selvedge at left

	Perf. Type	
	P	I
UIPQ1 (containing No. UQA1 × 10) (19.9.89)	6·50	£120

Booklet Plate Numbers

Pane No.	Pl. Nos	Phos. No.	Perf. Type P
UIPQ1	1, 1	1	10·00
	2, 2	1	12·00
	3, 3	1	12·00
	4, 4	1	10·00
	5, 5	1	15·00
	6, 6	1	12·00
	7, 7	1	10·00
	8, 8	1	15·00
	9, 9	1	12·00
	10, 10	1	10·00
	11, 11	1	10·00
	12, 12	1	10·00
	13, 13	1	10·00

Sheet Make-up (first format): The uncut printer's sheet contained 16 booklet panes arranged in four vertical columns of four panes in each. The panes were perforated all round and across the selvedge to give perf. Type P. Panes with perf. Type I came from a small part of the printing towards the end of November 1989. These were not distributed through the Philatelic Bureau but were available from some post offices and other retail outlets. Plate numbers do not appear on these panes as none were printed on the primary sheets. They were printed on a Heidelberg press and perforated by a Bickel machine. Changed sheet format with plate nos. 6 August 1991
  This pane was issued from 6 August 1991 in booklet No. HC6 when plate numbers were added. The sheet format was changed to one of four panes across and five panes in each vertical column. The plate number panes were ranged diagonally across the primary sheet starting, at left, with pane 2 and across to pane 5 in the bottom right-hand corner of the sheet. Panes exist with torn or cut perforations. The selvedge usually shows nine perforation holes but eight, or a combination of both, exist.

■ (1st) £1·90 Pane

(£2 from 2.10.89). From Barcode Booklet HD2

UIPQ2, UIPQ4, UIPQ5

Pane of ten (1st) class stamps (brownish black) on phosphorised (advanced coated) paper from Barcode Booklet No. HD2.

Pane UIPQ2. Lithographed, selvedge at left

	Perf. Type	
	P	I
UIPQ2 (containing No. UQB1 × 10) (19.9.89)	18·00	18·00

Pane UIPQ2 also exists with low optical brightening property in the coating.

Sheet Make-up: As Pane UIPQ1.

(2nd) £1·50 Pane

(£1·70 from 17.9.90). From Barcode Booklet HC4

As pane No. UIPQ1
Pane of ten (2nd) class stamps (deep blue) with one centre 4mm short phosphor band.

Pane UIPQ3. Lithographed. selvedge at left (Perf. Type P)

UIPQ3 (containing No. UQA2 × 10) (7.8.90)	15·00

No. UIPQ3 exists with either guillotined or torn edges.
Sheet Make-up: As Pane UIPQ1 but only perf. Type P.

(1st) £2 Pane

(£2·20 from 17.9.90, £2·40 from 16.9.91).
From Barcode Booklet HD4

As pane No. UIPQ2
Pane of ten (1st) class stamps (bright orange-red) on phosphorised (advanced coated) paper with PVAD gum.

Pane UIPQ4. Lithographed, selvedge at left (Perf. Type P)

UIPQ4 (containing No. UQB2 × 10) (7.8.90)	7·00

No. UIPQ4 exists with either guillotined or torn edges.
Sheet Make-up: As Pane UIPQ1 but only perf. Type P.

(1st) £2·20 Pane

(£2·40 from 16.9.91). From Barcode Booklets HD4a/b

As pane No. UIPQ2
Pane of ten (1st) class stamps (bright orange-red) on phosphorised (advanced coated) paper with PVA gum.

Pane UIPQ5. Lithographed. selvedge at left

UIPQ5 (containing No. UQB3 × 10) (6.8.91)	7·00

Booklet Plate Numbers

Pane No.	Pl. Nos.	Perf. Type P
UIPQ5	1, 1	9·00
	2, 2	10·00
	3, 3	10·00
	4, 4	10·00
	5, 5	12·00
	6, 6	28·00
	7, 7	10·00
	8, 8	10·00
	9, 9	11·00
	10, 10	15·00

Sheet Make-up: The primary sheet contained 20 booklet panes arranged in four vertical columns with 5 panes in each. Plate number panes were placed in each vertical column in positions row 1 pane 2, row 2 pane 3, row 3 pane 4 and row 4 pane 5 as seen from left to right. The notes describing torn or cut perforations and the selvedge of pane No. UIPQ 1 apply here.

(2nd) £1·80 Pane

(£1·90 from 1.11.93). From Barcode Booklets NCH /11a

UIPQ6, UIPQ8, UIPQ14

Pane of ten (2nd) class stamps (bright blue) with one short centre phosphor band (yellow fluor). Two elliptical perf. holes on each vertical edge.

Pane UIPQ6. Lithographed, selvedge at left

UIPQ6 (containing No. UQA4 × 10) (6.4.93)	6·00
a. Phosphor omitted	

Booklet Plate Numbers

Pane No.	Pl. Nos.	Phos. No.	Perf. Type P
UIPQ6	1, 1	1	7·00
	2, 2	I	7·50
	3, 3	1	7·50
	4, 4	1	7·50
	5, 5	1	10·00
	6, 6	1	10·00
	7, 7	1	7·50
	8, 8	1	7·50
	9, 9	1	2·00
	10, 10	1	11·00
	11, 11	1	15·00

Sheet Make-up: The primary sheet contained 20 panes.
Postal Forgery. Booklets containing ten (2nd) class stamps appeared in March 1994 intended to defraud the Royal Mail. The booklet cover is a copy of the 6 April 1993 issue. The stamps have a fluorescent (yellow fluor) band but no phosphor. The gum is matt PVA and the front of the paper has a high gloss unlike the genuine. The perf. type was PEP as used by Walsall but the imprint is Questa. Perforation resembles the genuine with an elliptical perf. hole.

(1st) £2·50 Pane

From Barcode Booklets HD11/a

UIPQ7 (Plate no. pane), UIPQ13, UIPQ15

Pane of ten (1st) class stamps (bright orange-red) Type II thick value with two 8mm phosphor bands (yellow fluor) on non-fluorescent coated paper. Two elliptical perf. holes on each vertical edge.

Pane UIPQ7. (1st) Type II. Lithographed. selvedge at left

UIPQ7 (containing No. UQB8 × 10) (1.11.93)	7·00

Booklet Plate Numbers

Pane No.	Pl. Nos.	Phos. No.	Perf. Type P
UIPQ7	1, 1	1	9·00
	2, 2	1	30·00
	3, 3	1	10·00

Sheet Make-up: Not known at the time of going to press. With the introduction of the elliptical perforation as a security feature plate numbers restarted at plate 1,1.

UI Machin no value indicated issues — Booklet panes

(2nd) £1·90 Pane

(£2 from 8.7.96).
From Barcode Booklets HC11b/c, HC13

As pane No. UIPQ6
Pane of ten (2nd) class stamps (bright blue) with continuous 4 mm centre phosphor band (yellow fluor). Two elliptical perf. holes on each vertical edge.

Pane UIPQ8. Lithographed, selvedge at left

		Perf. Type	
		P	I
UIPQ8	(containing No. UQA6 × 10) (19.5.94)	5·00	£850
a. Phosphor omitted			

Booklet Plate Numbers

Pane No.	Pl. No.	Phos. No.	Perf. Type I
UIPQ8	11, 11	1	

Pane No.	Pl. Nos.	Phos. No.	Perf. Type P
UIPQ8	11, 11	1	7·50
	12, 12	1	8·00
	14, 14	1	8·00
	15, 15	1	9·00
	16, 16	1	7·50
	17, 17	2	9·00
	18, 18	2	8·00
	19, 19	1	8·00
	19, 19	2	8·00
	20, 20	1	9·00
	21, 21	1	9·00

Sheet Make-up: The primary sheet contained 20 panes and 40 panes with the use of phosphor plate 2.

(1st) £1 Pane with attached commemorative label.

From Barcode Booklet HB7

UIPQ9 (Plate no. pane)
300th Anniversary of the Bank of England

Pane of four (1st) class stamps (bright orange-red) with two 8 mm phosphor bands (yellow fluor) on non-fluorescent coated paper *se-tenant* with label. Two elliptical perf. holes on each vertical edge.

Pane and *se-tenant* label UIPQ9. Lithographed, selvedge at left

UIPQ9	(containing No. UQB8 × 4) (27.7.94)	6·00
a. Phosphor omitted		

No. UIPQ9 was also supplied by the Philatelic Bureau, unfolded, without cover, price £2·75, plate nos. 1 (×7), £4·50.

Booklet Plate Numbers

Pane No.	Pl. No.	Phos. No.	Perf. Type I
UIPQ9	1 (×7)	I	10·00

Sheet Make-up: Pane UIPQ9 was printed on a Heidelberg press. It is understood that stocks of the unfolded panes were all sold by November 1994.

The seven colours employed were, deep blue, new blue, turquoise-green, bright emerald for the label and pale orange, orange and orange-red for the stamps.

For Boots the Chemist stationery promotion panes see below No. UQB9 (1st).

Nos. UIPQ10/12 are void.

(1st) £2·50 Pane

(£2·60 from 8.7.96). From Barcode Booklets HD11b, HD21, HD26

As pane No. UIPQ7
Pane of ten (1st) class stamps (bright orange-red) with two 8 mm phosphor bands (yellow fluor) on non-fluorescent coated paper. Type I thin value. Two elliptical perf. holes on each vertical edge.

Pane UIPQ13. Lithographed, selvedge at left

UIPQ13	(containing No. UQB7 × 10) (4.10.94)	7·00
a. Phosphor omitted		

Booklet Plate Numbers

Pane No.	Pl. No.	Phos. No.	Perf. Type P
UIPQ13	4, 4	2	9·00

Sheet Make-up: The primary sheet contained 40 panes arranged in five vertical columns of eight panes separated by the gutter margin trimmed to provide the binding margins. Position of plate numbers is not known.

(2nd) £1·90 Pane

(£2 from 8.7.96). From Barcode Booklets HC13a, HC16, HC18, HC20/a

As pane No. UIPQ6
Pane of ten (2nd) class stamps (bright blue) with one 4 mm centre phosphor band (blue fluor) on non-fluorescent coated paper. Two elliptical perf. holes on each vertical edge.

Pane UIPQ14. Lithographed, selvedge at left

UIPQ14	(containing No. UQA7 × 10) (18.7.95)	6·00
a. As UIPQ14 but long wave phosphor bands (4.2.97)		6·00

Booklet Plate Numbers

Pane No.	Pl. Nos.	Phos. Nos.	Perf. Type P
UIPQ14	21, 21	2	8·50
	22, 22	2	8·50
	23, 23	2	8·50
	24, 24	2	8·50
	25, 25	2	8·50
	26, 26	2	7·00
UIPQ14a	26, 26	2	7·00
	27, 27	2	7·00
	28, 28	2	7·00
	28, 28	3	7·00
	29, 29	2	7·00
	30, 30	3	7·00
	31, 31	3	7·00
	32, 32	3	7·00
	33, 33	3	7·00
	34, 34	3	7·00
	35, 35	3	7·00

Sheet Make-up: As pane No. UIPQ13.

Machin no value indicated issues Booklet panes UI

■ (1st) £2·50 Pane

(£2·60 from 7.9.98). From Barcode Booklets HD21a, HD50

As pane No. UIPQ7
Pane of ten (1st) class stamps (bright orange-red) with two 7·5 mm short wave phosphor bands (blue fluor) on non-fluorescent coated paper. Type I thin value. Two elliptical perf. holes on each vertical edge.

Pane UIPQ15 Lithographed, selvedge at left

UIPQ15.	(containing No. UQB9 × 10) (18.7.95)	7·00
	b. As pane UIPQ15 but long wave phos Bands (7.9.98)	7·00

Booklet Plate Numbers

Pane No.	Pl. Nos.	Phos. No.	Perf. Type P
UIPQ15	4, 4	2	8·00
UIPQ15b	5, 5	2	7·50
	6, 6	2	7·50
	6, 6	3	7·50

Sheet Make-up: As pane No. UIPQ13.

■ (2nd) £2 Pane

(£1·90 from 26.4.99). From Barcode Booklet HC22

UIPQ16 Type P/IEI

Pane of ten (2nd) class stamps (bright blue) with one 4·5 mm centre phosphor band (blue fluor) on non-fluorescent coated paper. Two elliptical perf. holes on each vertical edge.

Pane UIPQ16. Gravure. selvedge at left

UIPQ16 (containing No. UQAI0 x 10) (1.12.98)	6·00	†
UIPQ16A Miscut	†	7·00

Booklet Cylinder Numbers

Pane No.	Cyl. No.	Perf. Type P/IEI	P/EIE
UIPQ16	1 (row 1)	7·00	
UIPQ16A	1 (row 2)	8·00	

Sheet Make-up: The primary sheet contained four columns without interpanneau gutter.

■ (1st) £2·60 Pane

From Barcode Booklets HD51/a

UIPQ17 Type P/IEI

Pane of ten (1st) class stamps (bright orange-red) with two 9 mm phosphor bands (blue fluor), Type I thin value on non-fluorescent coated paper. Two elliptical perf. holes on each vertical edge.

Perf. Type

Pane UIPQ17. Gravure. selvedge at left

		Perf. Type	
		P/IE	P/EIE
UIPQ17	(containing No. UQB10 × 10) (1.12.98)	6·00	†
U1PQ17A	Miscut	†	25·00

Booklet Cylinder Numbers

Perf. Type	Pane No.	Cyl. No.	P/IEI	P/EIE
UIPQ17	1 (row 1)		7·00	†
UIPQ17A	1 (row 2)		†	90·00

Sheet Make-up: As pane UIPQ16.

■ (1st) £2·60 Pane.

From Barcode Booklet HD52

UIPQ18 Type P/IEI

Pane of ten (1st) class stamps (olive-brown) with two 9·5 mm phosphor bands (blue fluor) on non-fluorescent coated paper Type I central cross closed. Two elliptical perf. holes on each vertical edge.

Pane UIPQ18. Gravure, selvedge at left

UIPQ18 (containing No. UQB13 × 10) (6.1.00)	7·00

Booklet Cylinder Numbers

Pane No.	Cyl. No.	Perf. Type P/IEI
UIPQ18	1 (row 1)	8·00
	1 (row 2)	8·00

■ £1 Pane

From Crown and Royal Mail and Yellow Booklet FH44

UIPQ19 (inscribed "postcode" on top right label)   UIPQ20

UI Machin no value indicated issues *Booklet panes*

Pane UIPQ19. *Se-tenant* pane of (2nd) centre band and (1st) two bands (3) (blue flour). On the (2nd) the band stops both top and bottom of the stamp and there are no bands on the four printed labels. From £1 Red and yellow non-pictorial booklet No. FH44

UIPQ19 (containing Nos. UQA11 UQB14×3, (27.4.00)	4·50

Booklet Cylinder Numbers

Pane No.	Cyl Nos	Perf Type IPT
UIPQ19	1(×2)	6·00

Sheet make up: Printed on the Applications Technologies Nouvelles press but sheet make up is not confirmed. Some panes exist with a small ½v Cut at either right or left of the margin.
The perforations below the ½v Cut will be torn by hand.

▎£2 Pane

From Crown and Royal Mail and Yellow Booklet FW12

Pane UIPQ20. Pair of (2nd) (bright blue) and six (1st) (bright orange-red) centre band / two band stamps. Between the (2nd) and (1st) stamps the band stop at the perforations.

UIPQ20 (containing Nos. UQA11×2, UQB14×6, (27.4.00)	6·50

Booklet Cylinder Numbers

Pane No.	Cyl Nos	Perf Type IPT
UIPQ20	1(×2)above stamp1	8·00
	1(×2)above stamp2	8·00

Sheet make up: Printed on the Applications Technologies Nouvelles press but sheet make up is not confirmed. Some panes exist with a small ½v Cut at either right or left of the margin.
The perforations below the ½v Cut will be torn by hand.

▎£1 Pane

From Crown and Royal Mail and Yellow Booklet FH44a

UIPQ21
(Inscribed "postcodes" on top right label)

Pane UIPQ21. Pane of (2nd) (bright blue) centre band with three (1st) (bright orange-red) two band stamps (blue flour). No phosphor bands on four labels.

UIPQ21 (containing Nos. UQA11×2, UQB14×3, (17.4.01)	5·50

Booklet Cylinder Numbers

Pane No.	Cyl Nos	Perf Type IPT
UIPQ21	1(×2)	8·00
	1(×2)	8·00

3. Printed by Walsall in Lithography and Gravure from 1997

All stamps from UIPW1 to UIPW12 are perforated 14. except pane No. UIPW5 (perf. 13). From pane No. UIPW13 stamps are perf. 15×14(E).

▎(2nd) 56p. Pane

(60p. from 2.10.89). From Barcode Booklet HA1

As pane No. UIPH3
Pane of four (2nd) class stamps (bright blue) with one 4 mm centre phosphor band. The pane has three edges imperforate

Pane UIPW1. Lithographed, selvedge at left

	Perf. Type	
	IEI	IEIb
UIPW1 (containing No. UWAI×4) (22.8.89)	8·50	14·00

Booklet Plate Numbers

				Perf. Type
Pane No.	Pl. Nos.	IEI	IEIb	IEI + Bar
UIPW1	WI, W I	10·00	50·00	15·00

Sheet Make-up: Printed on a Roland Favorit press the uncut sheet contained 72 panes made up of eight vertical columns of nine panes each. The top selvedge was perforated through, but the bottom of the sheet was not and this gives a blind perforation to eight panes across the bottom of the sheet (perf. type IEIb). Plate number panes were in the first vertical column in positions 1/3 and 7/9 and this format was repeated in vertical column 8. A further 3 plate number panes were in the fifth column in positions 4/6 giving a total of 15 plate number panes. The pane in position 7 in column 1 had a plate number plus the trace of a bar on left edge on early printings. The Bickel perforator had a blind perforation at base. Eight panes were IEIb and two of these had plate numbers.

▎(1st) 76p. Pane

(80p. from 2.10.89). From Barcode Booklet HB1

As pane No. UIPH4
Pane of four (1st) class stamps (blackish brown) with 2 phosphor bands from Barcode Booklet No. HB1. Pane has three edges imperforate

Pane UIPW2. Lithographed, selvedge at left

	Perf. Type	
	IEI	IEIb
UIPW2 (containing No. UWB1×4) (22.8.89)	9·00	15·00

Booklet Plate Numbers

	Pl. Nos.	Perf. Type		
Pane No.	(No dot)	IEI	IEIb	IEI+ Bar
UIPW2	WI, W1	9·00	+	£100
	WI, W2	9·00	40·00	40·00
	W3	9·00	45·00	90·00
	W4	12·00	55·00	£200

Sheet Make-up: As Pane UIPW1.

(2nd) 60p. Pane

(68p. from 17.9.90, 72p. from 16.9.91).
From Barcode Booklets HA3/3a

UIPW3 (Plate no. pane)

UIPW4

Pane of four (2nd) class stamps (deep blue) with one 4 mm centre phosphor band from Barcode Booklet Nos. HA3/3a. The pane has imperforate horizontal edges

Pane UIPW3. Lithographed, selvedge at left

		Perf. Type	
		IEI	IEIb
UIPW3	(containing No. UWA2×4) (7.8.90)	3·50	5·00

Booklet Plate Numbers

Pane No.	Pl. Nos.	WI	Perf. Type IEIb	IEI + Bar
UIPW3	W1, W1, WI	5·00	8·00	12·00
	W2, WI, W2	5·00	8·00	12·00
	W2, W2, W2	5·00	10·00	14·00
	W3, W3, W3	5·00	8·00	†
	W3, W4, W3	5·00	12·00	

Sheet Make-up: As Pane UIPW1

(1st) 80p. Pane

(88p. from 17.9.90, 96p. from 16.9.91, £1 from 1.11.93).
From Barcode Booklets HB3, b/d, HB4

Pane of four (1st) class stamps (bright orange-red) on phosphorised (advanced coated) paper. The pane has imperforate horizontal edges

Pane UIPW4. Lithographed, selvedge at left

		Perf. Type	
		IEI	IEIb
UIPW4	(containing No. UWB2×4) (7.8.90)	3·50	7·00

Pane UIPW4 also exists with low optical brightening property in the coating.

Booklet Plate Numbers

Pane No.	Pl. Nos.	Perf. Type IEI	IEIb	IEI+Bar	Description
UIPW4	WI (pale/deep orange), WI, WI	7·00	10·00	14·00	
	WI (ochre), W1, W1	—	—	—	
	W I, W2, W2	15·00	20·00	20·00	
	W2, W3, W3	12·00	15·00		
	W2, W4, W3	40·00	90·00		
	W3, W4, W3	7·00	7·00	†	
	W3, W4, W4	£225	£450		- W4 top row
	W3, W4, W4	9·00	25·00	†	W4, W4 top row
	W3, W5, W4	8·00 12·00	†		W5. W4 top row
	W4, W5, W5	10·00	10·00		
	W4, W6, W6	9·00	10·00		
UIPW4	W4, W6, W6, W6	50·00	†		W6 doubled
	W4, W6, W6, (W6)	15·00	†		(W6) erased
	W4, W6, W7	9·00	12·00		W7 top row
	W4, W6, W7, (W6)	15·00	†		(W6) erased
	W4, W7, W6	8·00	10·00		See below
	W4, W8, W7	8·00	10·00	-	
	W5, W9, W8	8·00	12·00		
	W5, W10, W9	8·00	12·00		
	W5, W10, W9, W1	£250			
	W5, W11, W9, W1	£1400			
	W5, W11, W10, WI	8·00	10·00	†	
	W5, W12, W10, W2	9·00	18·00		
	W6, W14, W10, W3	8·00	12·00		
	W6, W15, W10, W3	8·00	12·00	†	
	W6, W16, W10, W3	8·00	15·00		
	W6, W16, W11, W3	10·00	15·00	†	
	W6, W16, W11, W4	8·00	10·00		
	W7, W16, W11	14·00	30·00		
	W7, W17, W11	8·00	12·00	†	
	W8, W18, W12	8·00	12·00		
	W9, W18, W12	8·00	15·00		
	W9, W19, W12	10·00	12·00		
	W9, W19, W13	10·00	14·00		
	W9, W20, W13	9·00	12·00		
	W10, W21, W14	8·50	12·00		

The (W6) erased shows upper tips of W and 6 only.
The following flaws affecting the plate numbers exist:
Flat back to 3—Plates W2, W3, W3, W3, W3, W3
Short centre bar 4—Plates W2, W4, W3, W3, W4, W3, W3, W4, W4 Flat curve to 5—Plates W4, W5, W5
Sliced 7 at top right—Plates W7, W16, W11, W7, W17, W11
Other varieties may exist. The broken figures which show straight right-hand sides, were caused by incorrect masking when the plate was made.

Sheet Make-up: As Pane UIPW1.

(1st) 88p. Pane perforated 13.

From Barcode Booklet HB3a

As pane No. UIPW4 but perforated 13 in error
Pane of four (1st) class stamps (bright orange-red) on phosphorised (advanced coated) paper from Barcode Booklet No. HB3a. The pane has imperforate horizontal edges

Pane UIPW5. Lithographed, selvedge at left

UIPW5 (containing No. UWB3 × 4) (10.90)   11·00

Booklet Plate Numbers

Pane No.	Pl. Nos.	Perf. Type	
		I	*I + Bar*
UIPW5	WI, W 1, W I	14·00	40·00

Sheet Make-up: As Pane UIPWI.

(2nd) £1.50 Pane

(£1·70 from 17.9.90, £1·80 from 16.9.91).
From Barcode Booklets HC5/5a

As pane No. UIPH1
Pane of ten (2nd) class stamps (deep blue) with one 4 mm centre phosphor band. The pane has imperforate horizontal edges

Pane UIPW6. Lithographed. selvedge at left

	Perf. Type	
	IEI	*IEIb*
UIPW6 (containing No. UWA2 × 10) (7.8.90)	6·50	9·00

Booklet Plate Numbers

Pane No.	Pl. Nos.	Perf. Type		
		IEI	*IEIb*	*IEI + Bar*
UIPW6	WI, WI, W1	8·50	11·00	12·00
	W2, WI, W1	9·50	18·00	20·00
	W2, WI, W2	25·00	40·00	£120
	W2	9·50	15·00	18·00
	W3, W3	8·50	11·00	12·00
	W3, W3	8·50	15·00	18·00
	W4, W3, W4	8·50	11·00	12·00
	W5, W3, W5	8·50	11·00	12·00
	W6, W3, W5	9·00	11·00	12·00
	W6, W4, W5	10·00	14·00	40·00
	W7, W4, W5	8·50	20·00	20·00

The W2, W2 printing had the third plate number (W3) trimmed off.
Sheet Make-up: Printed on the Roland Favorit press the uncut sheet contained 36 panes in a similar format to the panes of four. The sheet was made up of four vertical columns with nine panes in each. As in the panes of four the top selvedge was perforated through and the bottom of the sheet gave perf. type. IEIb. Plate number panes were in the first vertical column in positions 1/3 and 7/9 and this was repeated in the last column in the sheet In addition there were a further three plate number panes in the third column in positions 4/6. The plate number bar booklet was again in the first column, position 7 on early printings. The length of the bar varied according to the trim.

(1st) £2 Pane

(£2·20 from 17.9.90, £2·40 from 16.9.91).
From Barcode Booklets HD5/c, HD7

As pane No. UIPH2
Pane of ten (1st) class stamps (bright orange-red) on phosphorised (advanced coated) paper. The pane has imperforate horizontal edges
Pane UIPW7. Lithographed, selvedge at left

	Perf. Type	
	IEI	*IEIb*
UIPW7 (containing No. UWB2 × 10) (7.8.90)	7·00	7·50

Pane UIPW7 also exists with low optical brightening property in the coating.

Booklet Plate Numbers

Pane No.	Pl. Nos.	Perf. Type		
		IEI	*IEIb*	*IEI + Bar*
UIPW7	WI, WI	8·00	12·00	15·00
	WI, W1, WI	10·00	12·00	12·00
	W3, W3	12·00	18·00	35·00
	W4, W4	14·00	15·00	18·00
	W5, W4	9·00	11·00	14·00
	W5, W6, W5	9·00	11·00	14·00
	W5, W6, W6	9·00	14·00	16·00
	W6, W7	9·00	14·00	14·00
	W6, W7, W8	9·00	14·00	18·00
	W7, W8	9·00	12·00	14·00
	W7, W7, W9	9·00	12·00	15·00
	W8, W8, W10	9·00	12·00	14·00
	W8, W10	9·00	14·00	15·00
	W9, W11	8·00	14·00	15·00
	W9, W11	8·00	15·00	15·00
	W11, W10, W12	70·00	£200	£275
	W12, W10, W12	9·00	14·00	15·00
	W13, W10, W12	8·00	15·00	†
	W14, W10, W13	8·00	15·00	†

The following flaws affecting the letter in the plate number exist:
W sliced at left—Plates W6, W7, W8, W7, W7, W8, W7, W7, W9
W with angled centre point—Plates W8, W8, W10, W9, W8, W10
Sheet Make-up: As Pane UIPW6.

(2nd) 68p. Pane

(72p. from 16.9.91).
From Barcode Booklets HA4/4a, HA5

As pane UIPW3 but printed in bright blue
Pane of four (2nd) class stamps (bright blue) with one 4 mm centre phosphor band. The pane has imperforate horizontal edges

Pane UIPW8. Lithographed, selvedge at left

	Perf. Type	
	IEI	*IEIb*
UIPW8 (containing No. UWA1 × 4) (6.8.91)	4·00	7·00

Booklet Plate Numbers

Pane No.	Pl. Nos.	Perf. Type	
		IEI	*IEIb*
UIPW8	W4, W4	7·00	12·00
	W5, W5	7·50	9·00
	W6, W6	8·00	18·00
	W6, W7	8·00	10·00
	W8	8·00	18·00
	W9	8·00	16·00
	WI0	8·50	12·00

Sheet Make-up: As Pane UIPW1.

(2nd) £1·70 Pane

(£1·80 from 16.9.91).
From Barcode Booklets HC7/7a, HC8

As pane UIPH1
Pane of ten (2nd) class stamps (bright blue) with one 4 mm centre phosphor band. The pane has imperforate horizontal edges

Pane UIPW9. Lithographed. selvedge at left

		Perf. Type	
		IEI	IEIb
UIPW9	(containing No. UWA1 × 10) (6.8.91)	6·00	10·00
	a. Imperforate between vertical pair		

No. UIPW9a was caused by a paper fold and is unique. It appears as a pane of ten but with a vertical pair joined by the imperforate margin to stamp 10. Portions of two other stamps at left remain from the diagonal misfold.

Booklet Plate Numbers

		Perf. Type		
Pane No.	Pl. Nos.	IEI	IEIb	IEI + Bar
UIPW9	W6, W4	10·00	18·00	50·00
	W4	9·00	14·00	18·00
	W4	10·00	17·00	22·00
	W9, W5	9·00	14·00	18·00
	W6	10·00	18·00	22·00
	W7	10·00	15·00	18·00
	W12, W7	12·00	18·00	50·00
	W8	40·00	60·00	£130
	W8	10·00	15·00	22·00
	W9	10·00	15·00	18·00
	W10	20·00	£190	†

Plate numbers W11, W7 and W12. W7 exist with the W sliced at left flaw.
Sheet Make-up: As Pane UIPW6.

(1st) £2·40 Pane

From Barcode Booklet HD8

As pane UIPH2
Pane of ten (1st) class stamps (bright orange-red) on phosphorised (advanced coated) paper with PVAD gum. The pane has imperforate horizontal edges

Pane UIPW10. Lithographed, selvedge at left

		Perf. Type	
		IEI	IEIb
UIPW10	(containing No. UWB4 × 10) (9.2.93)	6·50	9·00

Booklet Plate Numbers

		Perf. Type		
Pane No.	Pl. Nos.	IEI	IEIb	IEI + Bar
UIPW10	W13, W10, W12	9·00	15·00	20·00
	W14, W10, W13	10·00	15·00	
	W15, W10, W13	10·00	18·00	†
	W11, W14	15·00	70·00	
	W11, W14	10·00	16·00	
	W12, W15	10·00	16·00	

Sheet Make-up: As Pane UIPW6.

(1st) 96p. Pane

From Barcode Booklet HB3e

As pane No. UIPW4 but with PVAD gum
Pane of four (1st) class stamps (bright orange-red) on phosphorised (advanced coated) paper with PVAD gum. The pane has imperforate horizontal edges

Pane UIPW11. Lithographed, selvedge at left

		Perf. Type	
		IEI	IEIb
UIPW11	(containing No. UWB4 × 4) (16.3.93)	3·50	6·00

Booklet Plate Numbers

		Perf. Type	
Pane No.	Pl. Nos.	IEI	IEIb
UIPW11	W10, W21, W14	7·00	10·00

Sheet Make-up: As Pane UIPW1.

(2nd) £1·80 Pane

From Barcode Booklet HC7b

As pane No. UIPHI
Pane of ten (2nd) class stamps (bright blue) with one 4 mm centre phosphor band on dull fluorescent coated paper with PVAD gum. The pane has imperforate horizontal edges

Pane UIPW12. Lithographed, selvedge at left

		Perf. Type	
		IEI	IEIb
UIPWI2	(containing No. UWA3 × 10) (16.3.93)	12·00	18·00

Booklet Plate Numbers

		Perf. Type	
Pane No.	Pl. Nos.	IEI	IEIb
UIPW12	W15, W10	15·00	20·00

Sheet Make-up: As Pane UIPW6.

(2nd) 72p. Pane.

(76p. from 1.11.93) From Barcode Booklet HA6/6a

UIPW13, UIPW23

Pane of four (2nd) class stamps (bright blue) with one 4 mm centre fluorescent phosphor band. Two elliptical perf. holes on each vertical edge.

Pane UIPW 13. Lithographed, selvedge at left

UIPW13 (containing No. UWA4 × 4) (6.4.93)	3·50

Booklet Plate Numbers

Pane No.	Pl. Nos.	Perf. Type PEP
UIPW13	W8, W10	7·50
	W9, W11	8·00
	W10, W12	7·50
	W11, W13	9·00

Sheet Make-up: Believed to he similar to Pane UIPW I.

UI Machin no value indicated issues — Booklet panes

■ (1st) £2·40 Pane

(£2·50 from 1.11.93).
From Barcode Booklets HD10/10a, HD12/13

For phosphor band layout see notes above No. UW8.

UIPW14 (Plate no. pane), UIPW18, UIPW22

Pane of ten (1st) class stamps (bright orange-red) with two 3·5 mm phosphor bands (yellow fluor). Two elliptical perf. holes on each vertical edge.

Pane UIPW14. Lithographed, selvedge at left

UIPW14 (containing No. UWB5 × 10) (6.4.93)	6·50
a. Phosphor omitted	
b. Phosphor band displaced to left by 13·5mm broad band on all £2000 except stamps 5 and 10 with side band (with pl. W20/W16)	
c. Phosphor band displaced 4 mm to left. Broad split band at right except stamps 5 and 10 with band at right (with p1. W29/W22)	£700

Booklet Plate Numbers

Pane Nos.	Pl. Nos.	Perf. Type PEP
UIPW14	W16, W11, W14	70·00
	W12, W15	7·00
	W12, W16	25·00
	W12, W16	8·00
	W21, W13, W17	11·00
	W22, W13, W17	14·00
	W23, W13, W17	9·00
	W23, W13, W18	8·00
	W24, W13, W18	£250
	W24, W14, W18	7·00
	W25, W14, W19	8·00
	W25, W14, W20	7·00
	W26, W14, W20	8·00
	W15, W21	8·00
	W15, W21	8·00
	W16, W21	11·00
	W28, W16, W22	8·00
	W17, W22	7·00
	W18, W23	8·00
	W30, W19, W23	9·00
	W19, W23	9·00
UIPW14A	W29, W17 only	

No. UIPW14A is a miscut variety and has not been seen with W22 or without plate nos.
Sheet Make-up: As Pane UIPW6.

■ (1st) 96p. Pane.

(£1 from 1.11.93) From Barcode Booklets HB6/6a

UIPW15, UIPW17, UIPW19, UIPW21, UIPW24

Pane of four (1st) class stamps (bright orange-red) with two 3·5 mm phosphor bands (yellow fluor). Two elliptical perf. holes on each vertical edge.

Pane UIPW15. Lithographed, selvedge at left

		Perf Type PEP
UIPW15 (containing No. UWB5 × 4) (17.8.93)		3·00
b. Bands displaced 6·5 mm to left		

No. UIPW15b shows two bands together on stamps 1 and 3. One band on margin and on stamps 2 and 4.

Booklet Plate Numbers

Pane No.	Pl. Nos.	Perf. Type PEP
UIPW15	W11, W22, W15	7·00
	W11, W22, W16	7·00
	W12, W22, W18	55·00
	W12, W23, W18	8·00
	W23, W19	9·00
	W13, W23, W20	10·00
	W24, W21	8·00

Sheet Make-up: As Pane UIPWI.

■ (2nd) £1·90 Pane

From Barcode Booklet HC12

UIPW16

Pane of ten (2nd) class stamps (bright blue) with one 4 mm centre phosphor band (yellow fluor). Two elliptical perf. holes on each vertical edge.

Pane UIPW16. Lithographed, selvedge at left

UIPW16 (containing No. UWA4 × 10) (1.11.93)	6·00

The Philatelic Bureau date of issue was 22 February 1994.

Booklet Plate Numbers

Pane No.	Pl. Nos.	Perf. Type PEP
UIPW16	WI, W1	8·00

Sheet Make-up: As Pane UIPW6.

(1st) £1 Pane

From Barcode Booklet HB6b

As pane No. UIPW15
Pane of four (1st) class stamps (bright orange-red) with 7·5 mm wide band between the stamps and two 3·5 mm inset side phosphor bands (yellow fluor). Two elliptical perf. holes on each vertical edge.

Pane UIPW17. Lithographed, selvedge at left

UIPW17 (containing Nos. UWB6×2, UWB6a×2) (22.4.94) 3·00

Booklet Plate Numbers

Pane. No.	Pl. Nos.	Perf. Type PEP
UIPW17	W15, W25, W22	5·00
	W16, W25, W23	5·00
	W17, W26, W24	6·50
	W18, W26, W24	6·00
	W18, W27, W25	6·25

Sheet Make-up: As pane No. UIPW1.

(1st) £2·50 Pane

(£2·60 from 8.7.96). From Barcode Booklets HD12a, HD14/19, HD22/23, HD25

As pane No. UIPW14
Pane of ten (1st) class stamps (bright orange-red) with 7·5 mm wide band between the stamps and a side band (yellow fluor) at left or right. Two elliptical perf. holes on each vertical edge.

Pane UIPW18. Lithographed, selvedge at left

UIPW18	(containing Nos. UWB6/a×2, UWB7×8) (1.7.94)	7·00
	a. Phosphor omitted	
	b. One band on each stamp	

No. UIPW18b was caused by phosphor band displacement.

Booklet Plate Numbers

Pane No.	Pl. Nos.	Perf. Type PEP
UIPW18	W32, W20, W24	12·00
	W33, W21, W25	12·00
	W34, W22, W26	12·00
	W34, W22, W27	12·00
	W35, W22, W27	12·00
	W22, W28	12·00
	W35, W23, W28	13·00
	W24, W29	14·00
	W36, W24, W30	12·00
	W36, W24, W31	14·00
	W37, W25, W32	13·00
	W38, W26, W33	12·00
	W39, W27, W34	15·00
	W28, W35	13·00
	W29, W35	15·00
	W41, W30, W35	13·00
	W41, W30, W36	12·00

Sheet Make-up: As pane No. UIPW6.

(1st) £1 Pane

From Barcode Booklets HB6c, HB8 As pane No. UIPW15

Pane of four (1st) class stamps (bright orange-red) with 7·5 mm central band and two side bands (yellow fluor). The bands overlap the perforations. Two elliptical perf. holes on each vertical edge.

Pane UIPW19. Lithographed, selvedge at left

		Perf. Type PEP
UIPW19 (containing No. UWB7×4) (7.10.94)		3·00
a. Phosphor omitted		
b. One band on each stamp		

Perf. Type EPE UIPW19A Miscut

Booklet Plate Numbers

Pane No.	Pl. Nos.	Perf. Type PEP
UIPW19	W18, W27, W26	7·00
	W19, W28, W26	4·00
	W20, W29, W27	12·00
	W20, W29, W28	5·50
	W29, W29	4·00
	W29, W29	5·00
	W21, W29, W30	5·00
	W30, W31	6·00
	W30, W31	8·00
	W23, W31, W32	6·00
	W23, W32, W32	
	W32, W32	5·00
	W26, W34, W34	5·00
	W36, W36	6·00
	W37, W37	10·00
	W29, W37, W38	22·00

Sheet Make-up: As pane No. UIPW1.

(1st) £1 Pane with attached commemorative label.

From Barcode Booklet HB9

UIPW20 Birth Centenary of R. J. Mitchell (designer of Spitfire)

Pane of four (1st) class stamps (bright orange-red) with se-tenant label at right. Two side and one central band between stamps (yellow fluor). Two elliptical perf. holes on each vertical edge.

Pane UIPW20. Lithographed, selvedge at left

UIPW20 (containing Nos. UBW6×2, UWB6a×2) (16.5.95) 6·00

No UIPW20 was also supplied by the Philatelic Bureau, unfolded, without cover, price £7. Plate nos. W25, W33, W33 price £12.

Booklet Plate Numbers

Pane. No.	Pl. Nos.	Perf. Type PIP
UIPW20	W25, W33, W33	7·00
	W27, W35, W35	8·00

Sheet Make-up: Details not known.

(1st) £1 Pane

(£1·04 from 8.7.96). From Barcode Booklet HB8a

As pane No. UIPW15
Pane of four (1st) class stamps (bright orange-red) with 7·5 mm central and two 4 mm side phosphor bands (blue fluor). Two elliptical perf. holes on each vertical edge.

Pane UIPW21. Lithographed, selvedge at left

Pane UIPW21 (containing No. UWB8×4) (18.7.95) 3·50

UI Machin no value indicated issues *Booklet panes*

Booklet Plate Numbers

Pane No.	Pl. Nos.	Perf. Type PEP
UIPW2I	W29, W38, W39	7·00
	W38, W39	15·00
	W39, W40	9·00
	W32, W40, W41	8·00
	W33, W41, W42	8·00
	W33, W41, W43	7·00
	W34, W42, W44	7·00
	W34, W42, W45	
	W35, W43, W46	8·00

Sheet Make-up: As pane No. UIPW1.

■ (1st) £2·50 Pane

(£2·60 from 8.7.96). From Barcode Booklets HD22a, HD28, HD34, HD36/37a, HD38, HD40

As pane No. UIPW14
Pane of ten (1st) class stamps (bright orange-red) with two 7·5 mm bands (blue fluor). Two elliptical perf. holes on each vertical edge.

Pane UIPW22. Lithographed, selvedge at left

UIPW22	(containing No. UWB8×10) (22.8.95)	6·50
	b. As UIPW22 but long wave phosphor bands (4.2.97)	6·50

Perf. Type EPE UIPW22A Miscut
Panes showing an inset of phosphor at left or right came from a phosphor misplacement and are outside the scope of the listings.

Booklet Plate Numbers

Pane No.	Pl. Nos.	Perf. Type PEP
UIPW22	W42, W31, W37	10·00
	W43, W32, W38	12·00
	W44, W32, W38	10·00
	W45, W33, W38	10·00
	W45, W33, W39	15·00
	W46, W33, W39	
	W34, W39	12·00
	W35, W40	12·00
	W47, W36, W40	12·00
	W48, W36, W40	12·00
	W48, W36, W41	
	W49, W36, W41	12·00
	W49, W37, W4I	12·00
	W50, W38, W41	10·00
	W50, W38, W42	10·00
	W51, W38, W42	10·00
	W52, W38, W42	10·00
	W52, W39, W42	10·00
	W53, W39, W42	10·00
	W53, W40, W42	10·00
	W53, W40, W43	8·00
	W53, W41, W44	8·00
	W54, W41, W44	8·00
	W42, W44	8·00
	W42, W44	8·00
UIPW22	W55, W42, W45	8·00
	W56, W43, W45	8·00
	W57, W44, W46	8·00

Sheet Make-up: As pane No. UIPW6.

■ (2nd) 76p. Pane

(80p. from 8.7.96). From Barcode Booklets HA9/11

As pane No. UIPW13
Pane of four (2nd) class stamps (bright blue) with one 4 mm centre phosphor band (blue fluor). Two elliptical perf. holes on each vertical edge.

Pane UIPW23. Lithographed, selvedge at left

UIPW23	(containing No. UWA5×4) (12.12.95)	3.00
	a. As pane UIPW23 but long wave phosphor bands (4.2.97)	3.00

Booklet Plate Numbers

Pane No.	Pl. Nos.	Perf. Type PEP
UIPW23	W11, W14	7·00
	W12, W15	7·00
	W12, W15	8·00
	W13, W16	7·00
	W14, W17	8·00
	W14, W18	7·00
	W14, W19	7·00
UIPW23a	W14, W19	7·00
	W20	7·00
	W21	7·00
	W17, W22	7·00

Sheet Make-up: Believed to be similar to Pane UIPW1.

■ (1st) £1 Pane

(£1·04 from 8.7.96). From Barcode Booklets HB10/10a, HB12

As pane No. UIPW15
Pane of four (1st) class stamps (bright orange-red) with 7·5 mm central and two 3 mm inset phosphor bands (blue fluor). Two elliptical perf. holes on each vertical edge.

Pane UIPW24. Lithographed. selvedge at left

UIPW24	(containing Nos. UWB9×2, UWB9a×2) (6.2.96)	3·50
	a. As pane UIPW24 but long wave phosphor bands (4.2.97)	3·50
	b. As pane UIPW24a but 4 mm bands at sides (layout C)	3·50

Booklet Plate Numbers

Pane No.	Pl. Nos.	Perf. Type PEP
UIPW24	W34, W42, W45	11·00
	W42, W46	40·00
	W43, W46	7·00
	W36, W44, W47	7·00
	W39, W46, W50	9·00
	W39, W46, W51	9·00
	W40, W46, W51	7·50
	W41, W47, W52	7·00
	W42, W47, W52	7·00
	W42, W48, W52	9·00
	W42, W48, W53	9·00
	W42, W49, W53	9·00
	W43, W49, W53	9·00
	W49, W54	9·00
	W49, W54	7·50
	W44, W49, W55	7·50
	W45, W49, W55	7·50

Machin no value indicated issues *Booklet panes* UI

Pane No.	Pl. Nos.	Perf. Type PEP
	W45, W49, W56	7·50
	W45, W50, W56	7·50
	W46, W50, W56	7·50
	W47, W50, W57	7·50
	W47, W51, W57	7·50
	W48, W51, W57	7·50
	W48, W51, W58	7·50
UIPW24a	W48, W51, W59	7·50
	W48, W51, W60	7·50
UIPW24b	W50, W53, W62	7·50
UIPW24a	W51, W53, W63	7·50
	W51, W54, W63	7·50
	W55, W64	7·50
	W52, W55, W64	7·50
	W55, W65	7·50
	W57, W67	7·50
	W58, W68	7·50

No. HB10a exists with plate nos. W42, W49, W53 (price £250); W43, W49, W53 and W43, W49, W54 (price £50 each).
Sheet Make-up.: As pane No. UIPW1.

(1st) £1 Pane with attached commemorative label

(£1·04 from 8.7.96). From Barcode Booklet HB11

UIPW25
70th Birthday of Queen Elizabeth II

Pane of four (1st) class stamps (bright orange-red) with *se-tenant* label at right. Two 3·5 mm side and one central phosphor band (blue fluor) between stamps and no phosphor on the label. Two elliptical perf. holes on each vertical edge.

Pane UIPW25. Lithographed, selvedge at left

UIPW25 (containing No. UWB8×4) (16.4.96)	6·00

No. UIPW25 was also supplied by the Philatelic Bureau, unfolded, without cover price £7. Plate nos. W37, W45. W48 and W38, W45. W59 price £9 each. Plate no. W38, W45, W48 was reported. These panes frequently include two examples of UWB9a inset band at right to prevent phosphor printing on the label.

Booklet Plate Numbers

Pane No.	Pl. Nos.	Perf. Type PIP
UIPW25	W37, W45, W48	8·00
	W38, W45, W48	10·00
	W38, W45, W49	7·00

Sheet Make-up: The primary sheet contained four columns of nine panes. It was printed on a Roland 306 press.

(1st) £1·04 Pane with attached commemorative label

From Barcode Booklet HB13

UIPW26
"Hong Kong '97" International Stamp Exhibition

Pane of four (1st) class stamps (bright orange-red) with *se-tenant* label at right. Two 3·5 mm side and one central phosphor band (blue fluor) between stamps and no phosphor on the label. Two elliptical perf. holes on each vertical edge.

Pane UIPW26. Lithographed, selvedge at left

UIPW26 (containing No. UWB8×4) (12.2.97)	6·00

No. UIPW26 was also supplied by the Philatelic Bureau, unfolded, without cover price £7. Plate nos. W49, W52, W61 price £10 each.

Booklet Plate Numbers

Pane No.	Pl. Nos.	Perf. Type PIP
UIPW26	W49, W52, W61	8·00

Sheet Make-up: As pane UIPW25.

(1st) £2·60 Pane

From Barcode Booklets HD42

As pane No. UIPW22 but printed in gold by gravure.
Pane of ten (1st) class stamps (gold) with two 9 mm bands (blue fluor). Two elliptical perf. holes on each vertical edge.

Pane UIPW27. Gravure, selvedge at left

UIPW27	(containing No. UWB10×10) (21.4.97)	8·00
	a. 6 mm wide band between stamps and left margin	10·00

On pane No. UIPW27a the band at left is 6 mm and overlaps the margin by about 1-2 mm.

Booklet Cylinder Numbers

Pane No.	Cyl. No.	Perf. Type PEP	
		Upper	Lower
UIPW27	W1, W1	12·00	10·00
	W2, W2	15·00	15·00

Sheet Make-up: The primary sheet contained three columns with ten panes in each. Intially a rotary machine was used but later the sheets were comb perforated, both were type PEP.

(2nd) 80p. Pane

(76p. from 26.4.99). From Barcode Booklets HA12/a

As pane No. UIPW13 but printed in Gravure
Pane of four (2nd) class stamps (bright blue) with one 4·5 mm centre phosphor band (blue fluor). Two elliptical perf. holes on each vertical edge.

Pane UIPW27. Gravure from computer engraved cyl., selvedge at left

UIPW27A (containing No. UWA6×4) (26.8.97)	2·25

The fluorescent phosphor band reacts from dull to bright under ultraviolet light.

35

UI Machin no value indicated issues — Booklet panes

Booklet Cylinder Numbers

Pane No.	Cyl. Nos.	Perf. Type PEP
UIPW27A	W1	4·00
	W2	4·00
	W4	3·50
	W5	3·50

Sheet Make-up: Printed on the Chesnut press using computer engraved cylinder with an APS and later a Bickel comb perforator. Sheet make-up unknown.

(1st) £1·04 Pane.

From Barcode Booklets HB14/b

As pane No. UIPW15 but printed in Gravure
Pane of four (1st) class stamps (bright orange-red) with two 9 mm phosphor bands (blue fluor). Two elliptical perf. holes on each vertical edge.

Pane UIPW28. Gravure from computer engraved cyl., selvedge at left

UIPW28	(containing No. UWB10×4) (26.8.97)	2·75
a.	As UIPW28 but 6·5 mm band at left	5·00
b.	Phosphor omitted	

Pane No. UIPW28a came from column 1 with thinner 6·5 mm band over stamps 1, 3 and margin.

Booklet Cylinder Numbers

Pane Nos.	Cyl. Nos.	Perf. Type PEP
UIPW28	W1	4·00
UIPW28a	W1	6·00
UIPW28	W2	4·00
UIPW28a	W2	6·00
UIPW28	W3 (row 1)	4·00
UIPW28a	W3	6·00
UIPW28	W3 (row 2)	4·00
UIPW28a	W3	6·00

Sheet Make-up: Not known.

(1st) £1.04 Pane with attached commemorative label.

From Barcode Booklet HB15

UIPW29
Commonwealth Heads of Government Meeting, Edinburgh

Pane of four (1st) class stamps (bright orange-red) with se-tenant label at right. Two 3·5 mm side and one central phosphor band (blue floor) between stamps and no phosphor on the label. Two elliptical perf. holes on each vertical edge.

Pane UIPW29. Lithographed, selvedge at left

UIPW29 (containing No. UWB8×4) (21·10.97)	6·00

No. UIPW29 was supplied by the Philatelic Bureau, unfolded, without cover price £7. Plate nos. W56, W59, W69 price £10 each.

Booklet Plate Numbers

Pane No.	Pl. Nos.	Perf. Type PIP
UIPW29	W56, 59, W69	8·00

Sheet Make-up: As pane UIPW25.

(1st) £2·60 Pane

From Barcode Booklets HD44/b

UIPW 30

Pane of ten (1st) class stamps (bright orange-red) with two 9 mm phosphor bands (blue fluor). Two elliptical perf. holes on each vertical edge and printed in Gravure from computer engraved cylinders.

Pane UIPW30. Gravure from a computer engraved cylinder, selvedge at left

UIPW30	(containing No. UWB10×10) (8.11.97)	7·00
a.	As UIPW30 but 6·5 mm band at left	8·00

Panes react from dull to bright under ultraviolet light.

Booklet Cylinder Numbers

Pane Nos.	Cyl. Nos.	Perf. TRype PEP
UIPW30	W1	8·00
UIPW30	W2	8·00
UIPW30a	W2	9·00
UIPW30	W3	8·00
UIPW30a	W3	9·00

Sheet Make-up: Perf. Type PEP exists comb and rotary with the latter being less common than the comb perf. The sheet make-up is not known.

(1st) £1.04 Pane with attached commemorative label.

From Barcode Booklet HB16

UIPW31
50th Birthday of Prince of Wales

Pane of four (1st) class stamps (bright orange-red) with se-tenant label at right. Two 3·5 mm side and one central phosphor band (blue fluor) between stamps and no phosphor on the label. Two elliptical perf. holes on each vertical edge.

Pane UIPW31. Lithographed, selvedge at left

UIPW31 (containing No. UWB8×4) (14.11.98)	6·00

No. UIPW31 was supplied by the Philatelic Bureau, unfolded, without booklet cover price £7. Plate nos. W56, W59, W69 price £10 each

Booklet Plate Numbers

Pane No.	Pl. Nos.	Perf. Type PIP
UIPW31	W56, W59, W69	8·00

Sheet Make-up: As pane UIPW25.

(1st) £1.04 Pane with attached commemorative label

From Barcode Booklet HB17

UIPW32
50th Anniversary of the Berlin Airlift

Pane of four (1st) class stamps (bright orange-red) with se-tenant label at right. Two 4·5 mm side and one 9 mm central phosphor band (blue fluor) between stamps and no phosphor on the label. Two elliptical perf. holes on each vertical edge.

Pane UIPW32. Gravure, selvedge at left

UIPW32 (containing No. UWB10×4) (12.5.99)	6·00

No. UIPW32 was supplied by the Philatelic Bureau, unfolded, without booklet cover price £7 Cylinder pane price £9 each.

Booklet Cylinder Numbers

Pane No.	Cyl. No.	Phos. No	Perf. Type PEP
UIPW32	W1 (×7)	WI	8·00

Sheet Make-up: Printed on the Chesnut press. The primary sheet contained three columns of nine panes.

(1st) £2·08 Pane

From Barcode Booklet HBA1/2

UIPW33

Pane of eight (1st) class stamps (bright orange-red) with two 9 mm phosphor bands (blue fluor). Two elliptical perf. holes on each vertical edge and printed in Gravure from computer engraved cylinders.

Pane UIPW33. Gravure from a computer engraved cylinder, selvedge at left

UIPW33	(containing No. UWB10×8) (12.5.99)	5·50
	a. As UIPW33 but 6·5 mm band at left	7·00

Booklet Cylinder Numbers

Pane No.	Cyl. Nos	Perf. Type PEP
UIPW33	W2	5·50
	W3	5·50

Sheet Make-up: Printed on the Chesnut press with nine instead of ten panes in each of three columns. Stamps 5 and 10 being burst, not guillotined off.

(1st) £1.04 Pane with attached commemorative label.

From Barcode Booklet HB18

UIPW34 Rugby World Cup 1999

Pane of four (1st) class stamps (bright orange-red) with se-tenant label at right. Two 4·5 mm side and one 9 mm central phosphor band (blue fluor) between stamps and no phosphor on the label. Two elliptical perf. holes on each vertical edge. From Barcode Booklet No. HB18.

Pane UIPW34. Gravure, selvedge at left

UIPW34 (containing No. UWB10×4) (1.10.99)	1·50

No. UIPW34 was supplied by the Philatelic Bureau, unfolded, without booklet cover price £7 Cylinder pane price £9 each.

Pane No.	Cyl. No.	Phos. No.	Pelf. Type PEP
UIPW34	W1 (×7)	WI	8·00

Sheet Make-up: As pane UIPW32.

(1st) £2·60 Pane.

From Barcode Booklet HD53

UIPW35

Pane of ten (1st) class stamps (olive-brown) with two 9 mm phosphor bands (blue fluor). Two elliptical perf. holes on each vertical edge.

Pane UIPW35. Gravure, selvedge at left

UIPW35 (containing No. UWB11×10) (6.1.00)	7·00
a. As UIPW36 but 6·5 mm band at left	7·50

Booklet Cylinder Numbers

Pane No.	Cyl. No.	Perf. Type PEP
UIPW35	W1	8·00
UIPW35a	W1	10·00

Sheet Make-up: Details of the sheet make-up are unknown but the Chesnut press was used with a computer engraved cylinder.

UI Machin no value indicated issues *Booklet panes*

(1st) £2·16 Pane.

From Barcode Booklet HBA3

UIPW36

Pane of eight (1st) class stamps (olive-brown) with two 9 mm phosphor bands (blue fluor). Two elliptical perf. holes on each vertical edge. from

Pane UIPW36. Gravure, selvedge at left

UIPW36 (containing No. UWB11 × 8) (26.5.00)	5·50
a. As UIPW36 but 6·5 mm band at left	6·00

Booklet Cylinder Numbers

Pane No.	Cyl. No.	Perf. Type PEP
UIPW36	W1	8·00
UIPW36a	W1	9·00

Sheet Make-up: The same cylinder was used for pane UIPW36 on the Chesnut press. Two stamps were torn away to create the pane of 8.

(1st) £1·04 Pane with attached commemorative label.

(£1·08 from 27.4.00) From Barcode Booklet HB19

UIPW37
The Stamp Show 2000, Earls Court, London 22–28 May 2000

Pane of four (1st) class Millennium stamps (olive-brown) with *se-tenant* label at right. Two 4·5 mm side and one 9 mm central phosphor band (blue fluor) between stamps and no phosphor on the label. Two elliptical perf. holes on each vertical edge.

Pane UIPW37. Gravure, selvedge at left

UIPW37 (containing No. UWB13 × 4) (21.3.00)	6·00

No. UIPW37 was supplied by Philatelic Bureau, unfolded, without booklet cover price £7. Cylinder pane price £9 each.

Booklet Cylinder Numbers

Pane No.	Cyl. Nos.	Phos. No.	Perf. Type PEP
UIPW37	W1 (×6)	W1	8·00

Sheet Make-up: As pane UIPW33.

(1st) £1·04 Pane with attached commemorative label

(£1·08 from 27.4.00). From Barcode Booklet HB20

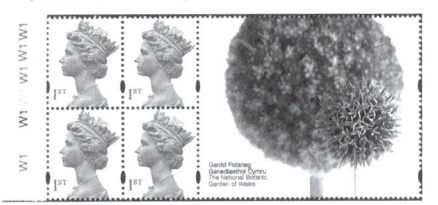

UIPW38 (Cyl. no. pane)
Opening of National Botanic Garden of Wales

Pane of four (1st) class Millennium stamps (olive-brown) with *se-tenant* label at right. Two 4·5 mm side and one 9 mm central phosphor band (blue fluor) between stamps and no phosphor on the label. Two elliptical perf. holes on each vertical edge.

Pane UIPW38. Gravure, selvedge at left

UIPW38 (containing No. UWB13 × 4) (4.4.00)	6·00

No. UIPW38 was supplied by Philatelic Bureau, unfolded, without booklet cover price £7. Cylinder pane price £9 each.

Booklet Cylinder Numbers

Pane No.	Cyl. Nos.	Phos. No.	Perf. Type PEP
UIPW38	W1 (×6)	W1	8·00

Sheet Make-up: As pane UIPW38.

European Air Mail "E" Pane (E) £1·20 Pane

(£1·36 from 25.10.99). From Barcode Booklet HF1

UEAP1

Pane of four (E) European air mail stamps with two 9 mm phosphor bands (blue fluor). Two elliptical pelf. holes on each vertical edge.

Pane UEAP1. Gravure from computer engraved cylinder, selvedge at left

UEAP1 (containing, No. UEA1 × 4) (19.1.99)	4·50
a. As UEAP1 but 6·5 mm hand at left	6·00

The distance between the bands is identical on both 6·5 mm and 9 mm panes. It is likely that the 6·5 mm panes were from column 1 of the sheets.

Booklet Cylinder Numbers

Pane Nos.	Cyl. Nos.	Perf. Type PEP
UEAP1	WI	7·00
UEAPIa	WI	8·00

Prestige Booklet panes containing No Value Indicated Stamps Only

Panes are listed by date of issue.
 The illustrations are reduced, the actual size being 162× 95mm.

From £6 (£5·64) "Beatrix Potter" Booklet No DX15 Printed by Questa in Lithography
Third pane comprising 3×(1st) with two 4mm bands and 3×(2nd) left band in fluorescent phosphor ink on non-fluorescent coated paper.

UIPP1

| UIPP1 (containing Nos. UQAS×3, UQB6×3) (10.8.93) | 10·50 |

Plate Numbers: No plate numbers occur on the issued panes. The primary sheet contained 3 columns each with four panes.

From £7·54 "Profile on Print" Booklet No. DX22 Printed by De La Rue in Gravure
The illustrations are reduced, the actual size being 162×95 mm
 First pane comprising 8×(1st) with two phosphor bands (blue fluor) on non-fluorescent coated paper. Printed label without phosphor and perforated 15×14 and one elliptical perf. hole on each vertical edge.

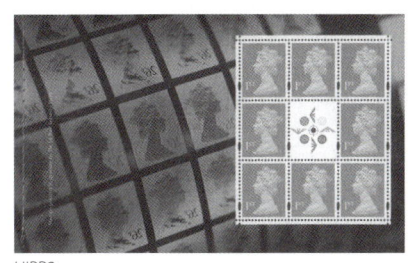

UIPP2

| UIPP2 (containing No. UHB9×8) (16.2.99) | 9·00 |

Sheet Make-up: Printed on the Jumelle press and perforated by a rotary APS machine. The primary sheet make-up is not known.

Printed by Walsall. Self-adhesive, Embossed
Second pane comprising 4×(1st) grey (face value) Queen's head in colourless relief. Phosphor background (blue fluor). Die-cut roulette 14×15.

UIPP3

| UIPP3 (containing No. UY1×4) (16.2.99) | 10·00 |

Sheet Make-up: The primary sheet contained two columns of four panes. A Roland four colour press was used for ink and phosphor background. The Queen's head was embossed and the perforations were die-cut on a Gietz FSA 700 press.

Printed by Enschedé in Recess
Third pane comprising 4×(1st) (grey-black) with two phosphor bands (blue fluor) on non-fluorescent coated paper. Perforated 14×14.

UIPP4

| UIPP4 (containing No. UY2×4) (16.2.99) | 10·00 |

Sheet Make-up: The primary sheet contained two columns of four panes. A Mitsubishi press was used for the text in lithography. The stamps were printed in recess on a Giori press. The sheets were then perforated on a Bickel comb machine.

Printed by Harrison in Typography
Fourth pane comprising 4×(1st) (black) with two phosphor bands (blue fluor) on non-fluorescent coated paper. Perforation 14×15.

UIPP5

| UIPP5 (containing No. UY3×4) (16.2.99) | 10·00 |

Sheet Make-up: The primary sheet contained two columns of four panes. The stub in litho was printed on a Heidelberg two colour press. Another Heidelberg cylinder press was used for the stamps in typography.

Printed by Questa in Lithography
Fifth pane comprising 9×(1st) (bright orange-red) with two 8mm phosphor bands (blue fluor) on non-fluorescent coated paper. Perforated 15×14 and one elliptical perf. hole on each vertical edge.

UIPP6

UIPP6 (containing No. UQB12×9) (16.2.99)   9·00

Cylinder Numbers
The cylinder and plate numbers did not appear on the issued panes. Pane No. UIPP5 is found with "age 21 WITH CHOKED KNOCKOUT PMS 3005 Silver Black" on the left-hand margin by the stitching holes.

Sheet Make-up: The primary sheet contained three columns of four panes. Printed on a six colour Mitsubishi press the stamps were perforated on a Bickel comb machine.

From £7·50 "Special by Design" No. DX24
Printed by Walsall in Gravure
First pane comprising 8×(1st) with two phosphor bands (blue fluor) on non-fluorescent coated paper. Printed label without phosphor. Perforated 14 and one elliptical perf. Hole on each vertical edge

UIPP7

UIPP7 (containing No. UWB12×8) (15.2.00)   8·00

From £7·03 "The Life of the Century, The Queen Mother"
Booklet No. DX25. Printed by Questa in Gravure
The other panes in the booklet are Nos. XSP1 (Section XE), WP1334 and WP1335 (Vol. 5).

Second pane comprising 9×(1st) two 9mm phosphor bands (blue fluor) on non-fluorescent coated paper. Perforated 15×14 and one elliptical perf. hole on each vertical edge and printed in gravure. Portrait rouletted at both sides.

UIPP8

UIPP8 (containing No. UQB15×9) (4.8.00)   9·00

Cylinder Numbers
No cylinder numbers occur on the pane which is inscribed in red "Page 7" at bottom left.

From £7·29 "A Gracious Accession" Prestige Stamp Booklet No. DX28 Printed by Enschedé in Gravure
The other panes in the booklet are Nos. UNW5 (Section UN), WP1448/9 (Vol 5).

First pane comprising 4×(2nd) 4×(E) two bands (blue fluor) on non-fluorescent coated paper. The are no bands on the Centre label showing the Head of King George VI printed in purple. Perforated 15×14 and one elliptical perf. hole on each vertical edge and printed text with vertical roulette at each side.

UIPP9

UIPP9 (containing No. UEA1×4) (6.2.02)   6·00

From £6·83 "Across the Universe" Prestige Stamp Booklet No. DX29 Printed by Questa in Gravure
The other panes in the booklet are Nos. XEP1 (Section XE), WP1501/02a(Vol 5).

Third pane pane comprising 4×(2nd) 4×(E) two bands (blue fluor) on non-fluorescent coated paper. The are no bands on the centre label showing Jodrell Bank and the constellation Cygnus (swan)

UIPP10

UIPP10 (containing No. UQB16×4) UX4×4 (24.9.02)   9·00

Cylinder Numbers
No cylinder numbers occur on the issued panes.

From £6·99 "Microcosmos" Prestige Stamp Booklet No. DX30. Printed by Enschedé in Gravure

Machin no value indicated issues *Prestige booklet panes* UI

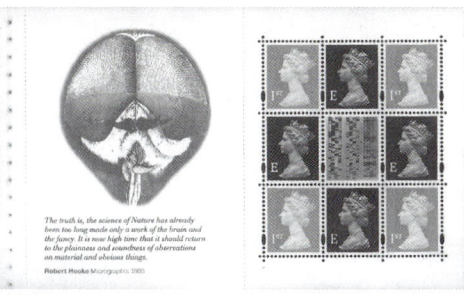

UIPP11

UIPP11 (containing No. UEB3 × 4, UX3 × 4) (25.2.03)　　9·00

Cylinder Numbers
No cylinder numbers occur on the issued panes.

From £7·46 "A Perfect Coronation" Prestige Stamp Booklet No. DX31. Printed by Walsall in Gravure
The other panes in the booklet are Nos. WP1573/4 and UNW6 (Section UN).

First pane comprising 4×(2nd) centre band and 4×(1st) gold two bands (blue fluor) on non-fluorescent coated paper. There are no bands on the centre label printed in gold showing crown, dates 1953 and 2003.

UIPP12

UIPP12 (containing No. UUWA9 × 4, UWB15 × 4) (2.6.03)　5·00

From £7·66 "The Machin. The Making of a Masterpiece". Prestige Stamp Booklet No. DX29. Printed by De La Rue in Gravure
The other panes in the booklet are Nos. UEP48/50 (Section UE),.

Fourth pane comprising PiP design (2nd) centre band, (1st) gold 2 × PiP "Large" (2nd) and 2 × PiP "Large" (1st) (blue fluor) on non-fluorescent coated paper. There are no bands on the centre label showing Sir Rowland Hill

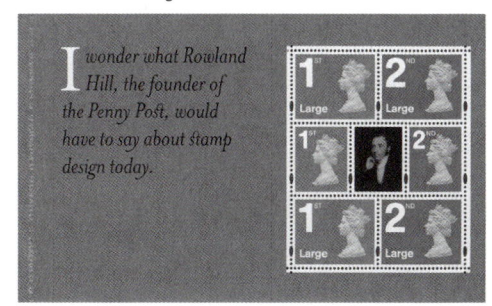

UIPP13

UIPP13 (containing Nos. UDA3/6, each × 2)　　5·25　　5·25

From £7·40 (£7·68 from 7.4.080 "Ian Fleming's James Bond" Prestige Stamp Booklet DX41

First pane printed in lithography comprising 8×(1st). two phosphor bands (blue fluor) with centre label showing typewriter all on non-fluorescent coated paper. Vertical roulettes between stamps and stub. Perforated 15×14(E). At right text begins "In his next adventure.

UIPP14

UIPP14 (containing No. UDB5 × 8) (8.1.08)　　12·00

From £7·15 (7·54 from 6.4.09) "Pilot to Plane" RAF Uniforms Prestige Stamp Booklet No. DX42 Printed by Cartor in Lithography
Fourth pane printed in lithography comprising 4 × (2nd) centre band 4 × (1st) two bands (blue fluor) with centre label showing RAF roundel all on non-fluorescent coated paper. The pane is rouletted twice between stitched margin and left of the *se-tenant* stamps Perforated 15 × 14(E).

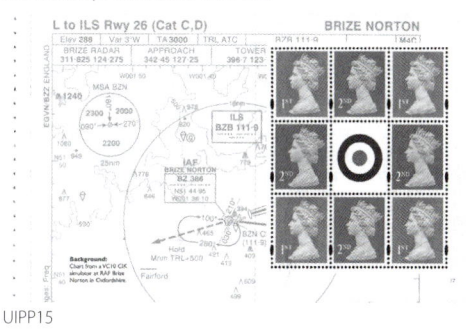

UIPP15

UIPP15 (containing No. UWA10, UWB17 × 4) (18.9.08)　5·75

Prestige Booklet Panes containing a combination of Denominated and No Value Indicated Stamps From £5 "London Life" Booklet No. DX11.

Third pane on fluorescent coated paper comprising (2nd), 15p., (1st), 20p., and 50p. Machin with 15p., 20p. and 29p. Penny Black Anniversary stamps in the bottom row. All with two phosphor bands except the three stamps in the first vertical row at left which have a side band at right.

UEP33

41

UEP33 (containing Nos. U234, U398, UHA2, UHB2,
W790, W792, W7966) (20.3.90) 20·00
  a. Third column with 5.5 mm band between
    stamps and right margin 24·00

Cylinder Numbers
The primary sheet contained three columns of four panes each. Printed on the Jumelle press, the cylinder numbers were trimmed off but those used were:
UEP33 1A, 1B (20p. W792), 1C (50p.), 1D (2nd., 15p. (2), W790), 1F (1st., 20p.), B56 (phosphor).

From £6·15 "Celebrating 75 years of the BBC" Booklet No. DX19. Printed in gravure from computer engraved cylinders.
Second pane on non-fluorescent coated paper comprising 4 × 26p. (gold) and 4 × (1st) (gold) with two 9mm bands (blue fluor).

UEP34

UEP34 (containing Nos. U302 × 4, W1129 × 4
(23.9.97) 9·00

From £6·16 "Breaking Barriers" Booklet No. DX21.
Fourth pane comprising 2 × 10p. (dull orange), 43p. (sepia) with two phosphor bands and 3 × (2nd) phosphor side band at left all with (blue fluor) on non-flourescent paper.

UEP38

UEP38 (containing Nos. U195D × 2, U379 × 3,
UWA8 × 3) (13.10.98) 12·00

Cylinder Numbers
Printed by Walsall on the reel-fed Chesnut press. The primary sheet contained two columns each of five panes. All markings were trimmed off.

UEP41

UEP41 (containing Nos. UDB2 × 40 (16.3.04) 8·50

From £7·23 "The Glory of the Garden" Prestige Stamp Booklet No. DX33
The other panes in the booklet are Nos. WP1664/66 and WP1669.
First pane comprising Machin 4 × (1st) Gold, 2 × 42p. (deep olive-grey) and 2 × 47p. (turquoise-green) two bands (blue fluor), centre label on non-fluorescent coated paper. There are no bands on the centre label. The pane is rouletted twice between stitched margin and left of the four *se-tenant* stamps

UEP42

UEPP42 (containing Nos. UEB4 × 4, U372A × 2)
(25.5.04) 9·25

The were no cylinder numbers or other marks on the issued panes.

From £7·43 "The Brontë Sisters" Prestige Stamp Booklet No. DX34
First pane comprising Machin 4 × (1st) Bright blue 2 × 39p. (grey) and 2 × 42p. (deep olive-grey) two bands (blue fluor), centre label on non-fluorescent coated paper. The pane is rouletted twice between stitched margin and left of the *se-tenant* stamps.

UEP43

UEP43 (containing Nos. UWA9 × 4, U372B × 2)
(24.4.05) 9·25

There were no cylinder numbers or other marks on the issued panes

From £7·26 "Bicentenary of the Battle of Trafalgar" Prestige Stamp Booklet No. DX35

The booklet contains panes WP1786 (White Ensign, see 2nd issue) and WP1783/4.

Second pane comprising Machin 4×(1st) gold, 2×50p. ochre and 2×68p. grey-brown two bands (blue fluor), centre label Without bands, showing the Lifemask of Nelson cast by Franz Thallerin, on non-fluorescent coated paper. The pane is rouletted twice between stitched margin and left of the *se-tenant* stamps.

UEP44

UEP44	(containing Nos. UWB16×4, U405×2, U432×2) (18.10.05)	6·50

There were no cylinder numbers or other marks on the issued panes

From £7·40 "Birth Bicentenary of Isambard Kingdom Brunel" Prestige Stamp Booklet No. DX36

The booklet contains panes WP1821/22, WP1824 and the Machin pane No UIPP17(Section UI).

Fourth pane printed in gravure comprising Machin 4×(1st) gold 2×35p. (yellow-olive) and 2×40p. (turquoise-blue) two bands (blue fluor), centre label without bands, showing a bust of Brunel on non-fluorescent coated paper. The margin at left depicts Brunel's last successful project, the Saltash Bridge across the Tamar. The pane is rouletted twice between stitched margin and left of the *se-tenant* stamps.

UEP45

UEP45	(containing Nos. UEB5×4, U341C×2, U362×2) (22.2.06)	6·50

From £7·44 "150th Anniversary of the Victoria Cross" Prestige Stamp Booklet No. DX37

The booklet contains panes WP1869/71, and the Machin pane No UIPP18 (Section UI).

Third pane printed in gravure comprising Machin 4×(1st PiP design) and 4×50p. (ochre) two bands (blue fluor), centre label without bands, showing the Victoria Cross on non-fluorescent coated paper. The margin at left features Alfred Joseph Knight who was the only Post Office Rifleman to have been awarded the Victoria Cross. The pane is rouletted twice between stitched margin and left of the *se-tenant* stamps

UEP46

UEP46	(containing Nos. UEB6×4, U406×4, (21.9.06)	7·50

From £7·49 "World of Invention" Prestige Stamp Booklet No. DX38

Second pane printed by De la Rue in gravure comprising Machin 4×(1st PiP design) gold 4×5p. (dull red-brown) two bands (blue fluor), centre label without bands, showing the originator of the Penny Post, Rowland Hill, all on non-fluorescent coated paper. The pane is rouletted twice between stitched margin and left of the *se-tenant* stamps.

UEP47

UEP47	(containing Nos. UDB5×4, U140G×4, (1.3.07)	3·50

From £7·75 Charles Darwin Prestige Stamp Booklet No. DX45

First pane printed by De La Rue in gravure comprising 2×5p., 2×10p., 2×(1st), 2×48p. all two bands except the centre label showing, Darwin, all on non-fluorescent coated paper. the pnae is rouletted twice between stitched margin and left of the *se-tennant* stamps

UEP48	(12.2.09)	4·50

SECTION UJ
Decimal Self-adhesive Issues 1993–2009

Introduction. After considerable research and tests Walsall was given the task of producing the first self-adhesive stamp booklet. Initially it was restricted to the Tyne-Tees area, but it was available from the Philatelic Bureau.

The gravure printings by Enschedé and Walsall (1998) were from computer engraved cylinders.

The self-adhesive 1st class stamp from the prestige booklet No. DX22 issued on 16.2.99 is listed in the UI section as UYI from pane UIPP2.

Paper. Initially, the stamps were printed on paper supplied by Coated Papers Limited and it was backed by a water soluble gum between the stamp paper and a self-adhesive layer with a backing paper. In 2009 the water soluble layer was replaced by a pressure sensitive adhesive which was resistant to water. These stamps cannot therefore be removed from the envelope or wrapping paper by immersion in water.

Paper and gum We use NFCP to describe non-fluorescent coated paper. The gum was polyvinyl self-adhesive or later self-adhesive abbreviated to PSA and SA. Both were pressure sensitive without moisture to affix the stamp.

Perforations. Special die-cut perforations were used to maintain security although the stamps were individually placed on their backing liner in the booklet. The perforation is 14 × 15 with an elliptical hole on each vertical stamp edge.

Matrix. Some stamps from business sheets, coils or booklets exist with matrix on later printings this was removed. We do not list with or without matrix where both conditions exist for stamps which are otherwise identical.

Backing Paper. We list single examples from booklets but we do not expand the listing to include the various different printed backings that are possible.

Stamps with U-shaped slits and security overprint

Self-adhesive Gum. The gum employed is without the soluble additive allowing stamps to be floated from backing paper. It is coded as SA meaning self-adhesive whereas the previous acrylic gum was PSA water soluble as in PVA.

U-shaped slits. The stamps from booklets had U-shaped die-cut slits with breaks at the top, base and both vertical sides to discourage the removal of used stamps for re-use.

Enlargement slowing position of breaks in U-shaped slits

"Royal Mail" Iridescent Overprint with Code letter. Stamps from booklets and business sheets were overprinted in iridescent ink with a simple code to enable the original source to be identified.

The code was in the spelling of "MAIL" in iridescent ink at the top right above the centre cross of the Crown. No. UJW19 has "MCIL" instead of "MAIL" on every stamp. The letter "C" refers to "Custom". Use a 2×lens or greater with the light source reflecting on the stamp surface. The Queen's head shows a jumble of letters and ignore these and inspect the surrounding wavy "ROYAL MAIL" inscription then check the top right corner. A normal spelling means the stamp was from a sheet source.

Sheets. The primary sheet comprised 300 stamps in six panes (5x5). The counter sheets comprise two panes (5×5) with horizontal a gutter margin. Cylinder blocks are from rows 8/10 bottom left corner showing the 6 box grid below the cylinder numbers. The numbers were D1 and D1 phosphor for all values issued in February 2009. The sheet is rouletted between each row and column to allow removal of single examples. The date of printing, shown sideways reading up is opposite horizontal row 8 in the right margin together with the sheet serial number opposite row 9.

Large format stamps. These were printed in primary sheets of 200 (10x20) divided into counter sheets of 50 comprising two panes (5x5). These have a 4 box grid below the cylinder numbers.

Arrangement of this section
Section J is divided into four parts:
1. PSA gum single stamps, 2. SA gum single stamps, 3. Booklet panes, 4. Business sheets. Within each part division is as shown below, while, within each sub-part it is according to alphabetical order by printer (apart from section 1A, which is chronological.

The second table is by printer and stamp type, listed chronologically.

1. PSA gum single stamps
A.	Stamps in horizontal format (UJW1, UJE1/2)
B.	Denominated stamps in vertical format (UJW8/9)
C.	NVI stamps, vertical format (UJD1, UJE3/5, UJQ1/4, UJW2/6,)
D.	Airmail stamps (UJW7, UJW10/14)
E.	'Pricing in Proportion' stamps (UJW17/18)
F.	'Pricing in Proportion' large stamps (UJW15/16)

2. SA gum single stamps (with security slits).
A.	Denominated stamps (UJD6/11)
B.	NVI stamps (UJD2/3, UJD12/13, UJW19/22)
C.	NVI Large stamps (UJD4/5, UJD14/15, UJW23/4)
D.	Recorded Delivery stamps (UJD16/17)

3. Booklet panes
A.	Panes of denominated stamps (UJWMP1/2)
B.	Panes from NVI booklets printed by Questa (UJPQ1/7)
C.	Panes from NVI booklets printed by Walsall (UJPW1/30)
D.	Panes from airmail booklets (UJWEP1/6)
E.	Commemorative / definitive panes

4. Business Sheets (BS1/24)

Decimal self-adhesive issues — UJ

Description	S.G. Spec. Number	Date of Issue	Source
Printed in lithography by Walsall			
(1st) Orange-red (horiz)	UJW1	19.10.1993	Booklet
Printed in gravure by Walsall			
(2nd) Bright blue	UJW2	22.6.1998	BS
(1st) Bright orange-red	UJW3	22.6.1998	BS
(2nd) Bright blue Type I	UJW4	4.9.2000	BS
(2nd) Bright blue Type II	UJW4a	29.1.2001	BS, Booklet
(1st) Bright orange-red	UJW5	29.1.2001	Booklet
(1st) Gold	UJW6	5.6.2002	BS, Booklet
(E) Deep blue	UJW7	4.7.2002	Booklet
42p. Deep olive-grey	UJW8	4.7.2002	Booklet
68p. Grey-brown	UJW9	4.7.2002	Booklet
"40g" Europe	UJW10	27.3.2003	Booklet
"40g" Worldwide	UJW11	27.3.2003	Booklet
Worldwide postcard	UJW12	1.4.2004	Booklet
"40" Europe	UJW13	15.6.2004	Booklet
"40" Worldwide	UJW14	15.6.2004	Booklet
(2nd) Bright blue Large PIP	UJW15	15.8.2006	BS, Booklet
(1st) Gold Large Pip	UJW16	15.8.2006	BS, Booklet
(2nd) Bright blue Pip	UJW17	12.9.2006	BS, Booklet
(1st) Gold Pip	UJW18	12.9.2006	BS, Booklet
U-shaped slits security overprint			
(1st) Gold code "C"	UJW19	10.3.2009	Booklet
(1st) Gold code "S"	UJW20	31.3.2009	Booklet
(2nd) Bright blue code "T2"	UJW21	31.3.2009	Booklet
(1st) Gold "T"	UJW22	31.3.2009	Booklet
As before but inscribed "LARGE"			
(2nd) Bright blue code "F"	UJW23	31.3.2009	Booklet
(1st) Gold code "F"	UJW24	31.3.2009	Booklet
Printed in gravure by Enschedé			
(2nd) Bright blue (horiz)	UJE1	18.3.1997	Coil
(1st) Orange-red (horiz)	UJE2	18.1997	Coil
(2nd) Bright blue	UJE3	6.4.1998	Coil
(2nd) Bright blue	UJE3a	9.5.2002	BS
(1st) Bright orange-red	UJE4	6.4.1998	Coil
(1st) Bright orange-red	UJE4a	9.5.2002	BS
(1st) Gold	UJE5	4.7.2002	BS
Printed in gravure by Questa			
(1st) Bright orange-red	UJQ1	4.9.2000	BS, Booklet
(2nd) Bright blue	UJQ2	29.1.2001	Booklet
(1st) Gold	UJQ3	5.6.2002	Booklet
(2nd) Bright blue	UJQ4	4.7.2002	Booklet
Printed in gravure by De La Rue			
(1st) Gold	UJD1	29.4.2003	Booklet
U-shaped slits security overprint			
(2nd) Bright blue	UJD2	17.2.2009	Sheet
(1st) Gold	UJD3	17.2.2009	Sheet
(2nd) Bright blue Large	UJD4	17.2.2009	Sheet
(1st) Gold large	UJD5	17.2.2009	Sheet
U-shaped slits security overprint with face values			
50p Grey	UJD6	17.2.2009	Sheet
£1 Magenta	UJD7	17.2.2009	Sheet
£1·50 Brown-red	UJD8	17.2.2009	Sheet
£2 Deep blue-green	UJD9	17.2.2009	Sheet
£3 Deep Mauve	UJD10	17.2.2009	Sheet
£5 Azure	UJD11	17.2.2009	Sheet
U-shaped slits security overprint			
(2nd) Bright blue code "B"	UJD12	31.3.2009	BS
(1st) Gold code "B"	UJD13	31.3.2009	BS
Before but inscribed "LARGE"			
(2nd) Bright blue code "B"	UJD14	31.3.2009	BS
(1st) Gold code "B"	UJD15	31.3.2009	BS
"Recorded Signed For" stamps. U-shaped slits security overprint			
(1st) Bright orange-red and lemon	UJD16	17.11.2009	Sheet
(1st) Bright orange-red and lemon	UJD17	17.11.2009	Sheet

1. PSA gum single stamps

A. NVI Stamps in horizontal format

Type SA1

Des. Jeffery Matthews.

Printed in lithography by Walsall

Type SA1

(1st) Orange-red (1993)

1993 (19 October). Two bands. Non-fluorescent paper. Acrylic gum

UJW1 (= S.G.1789)

From £4·80 Self-adhesive booklet pane UJPW1

UJW1	(1st) Orange-red	1·25	1·40
	a. Phosphor omitted	£200	
	b. Phosphor bands double		

Each stamp was printed with two phosphor bands (yellow fluor) at each side. Stamps at the sides had a 5 mm band and the stamps in the vertical rows 2 and 5 had 12 mm bands which overlapped the margin between and formed the side bands of adjacent stamps. The bands stopped short of the horizontal edges of the booklet cover.

No. UJW1 was initially sold at 24p. which was increased to 25p. from 1 November 1993.

Examples of No. UJW1 with two bands but inset on one side exist from panes where the phosphor was misplaced sideways.

UJ Decimal self-adhesive issues

Printed by Enschedé in rolls

SA2

SA3

(Des. Jeffery Matthews)

(Printed in gravure by Enschedé)

Type SA2

(2nd) Bright blue (1997)

1997 (18 March). Perf. 15 × 14(E). One 4·5 mm. Phosphor band (blue fluor). Non-fluorescent coated paper. PSA gum

UJE1 (S.G. 1976)

From Vertical coil

UJE1	(2nd) Bright blue	2·75	2·50

Type SA3

(1st) Bright orange-red (1997)

1997 (18 March). Perf. 15 × 14(E). Two phosphor bands (blue fluor). Non-fluorescent coated paper. PSA gum

UJE2 (= S.G.1977)

From Vertical coil

UJE2	(1st) Bright orange-red	2·75	2·75

Nos. UJ2/3 were initially priced at 20p. and 26p. and sold in boxed rolls of 100 with the stamps separate on the backing paper. Every seventh box showed an ink-jet printed serial number on the backing paper of every tenth stamp in the roll. **Short Phosphor Bands.** Examples showing short bands came from misplaced phosphor printing but the number of bands on the stamp remained the same and are outside the scope of this catalogue.

Although this was a continuous printing, the primary sheet was of 210 stamps arranged in seven vertical columns with 30 stamps in each.

Sold out: October 1998

B. Denominated stamps in vertical format

SA4

42p. Deep olive-grey (2002)

2002 (4 July). Die-cut Perf. 15 × 14(E). Two phosphor bands (blue fluor). A non-fluorescent coated paper. PSA gum.

From £2·52 Barcode booklet pane UJWMP1
UJW8 (=SG. 2297)

UJW8	42p. Deep olive-grey	3·00	3·00

68p. Grey-brown (2002)

2002 (4 July). Die-cut Perf. 15 × 14(E). Two phosphor bands (blue fluor). Non-fluorescent coated paper. PSA gum

From £4·08 Barcode booklet pane UJWMP2
UJW9 (=S.G. 2298)

UJW9	68p. Grey-brown	4·00	4·00

C. NVI stamps in vertical format

SA5

SA6

Type SA5

(1st) Gold (2003-04)

2003 (29 April). Head B. Die-cut Perf. 15 × 14(E). Two phosphor bands (blue fluor) Non-fluorescent coated paper. PSA gum

From barcode booklets PM9 to PM14

UJD1	(1st) Gold	1·00	1·00

Very similar to No. UJQ3 Head B3 but with a different screen. The crown at right is closer to the frame on No. UJD1.

ENSCHEDÉ Rounded   WALSALL Square cut

Types SA4 and SA5. The gravure 2nd and 1st class printings of Enschedé and Walsall can be distinguished by the perforation tips. The Enschedé stamps (6.4.98) from coils have rounded die-cut perf. tips and the stamps from sheets printed by Walsall have perforation tips that are square cut.

Type SA5

(2nd) Bright blue (1998)

1998 (6 April). Die-cut perf. 15 × 14(E). One 4·5 mm phosphor band (blue fluor). Non-fluorescent coated paper. PSA gum

From vertical coil with bluish-grey backing paper

~~UJE3~~	(2nd) Bright blue	5·00	
	a. Plain backing paper (9.5.02)	75·00	

UJE3a came from business sheets

Type SA6

(1st) Bright orange-red (1998)

1998 (6 April). Die-cut Perf. 15 × 14(E). Two phosphor bands (blue fluor). Non-fluorescent coated paper. PSA gum

From Vertical coil with bluish-grey backing paper

~~UJE4~~	(1st) Bright orange-red	5·00	1·50
	a. plain backing paper (9.5.02)	75·00	

UJE4a came from business sheets.
Nos UJE4 and UJE5 were initially priced at 20p. and 26p., and were available in coils of 200.

Decimal self-adhesive issues UJ

Sheet make up The primary sheet contained nine columns and twenty five horizontal rows. The Walsall colour control marks appeared in the right margin opposite rows 2/6 and repeated opposite rows 21/25. These were trimmed off.

Withdrawn: 1 February 2001

(1st) Gold (2002)

2002 (4 July). Die-cut Perf. 15 × 14(E). Two phosphor bands (blue fluor). Non-fluorescent coated paper. PSA gum

From Business sheets of 100 BS8

UJE5	(1st) Gold	75	70

No. UJE5 is similar to No. UJQ3 (5 June 2002). The coarse screen used for the Enschedé printing gives an excellent photo negative effect which is sufficient to distinguish this printing from the first Questa and Walsall printings from booklets.

Printed by Questa in sheets

Type SA5

(1st) Bright orange-red (2000)

2000 (4 September). Rounded die-cut Perf. 15 × 14(E). Two phosphor bands (blue fluor). Non-fluorescent coated paper. PSA gum

From Sheets of 100 BS4 Booklet panes UJPQ3/4

UJQ1	(2nd) Bright orange-red	1·00	1·00
	a. Imperforate pair	75·00	

No. UJQI has a thick value compared to No. UJE4 (Enschedé) with round perforation tips. The Head B3 was used as illustrated on page 15 of GB Spec. Vol. 4.

Printed by Questa in booklets

Type SA4

(2nd) Bright blue (2001)

2001 (29 January). Rounded die-cut Perf. 15 × 14(E). One 5 mm phosphor band (blue fluor). Non-fluorescent coated paper. PSA gum

From £1·90 Barcode booklet pane UJPQ1 £2·28 Barcode booklet pane UJPQ2

UJQ2	(2nd) Bright blue	1·25	1·25
	a. Imperforate pair	75·00	

Printed by Questa in booklets

Type SA5

(1st) Gold (2002)

2002 (5 June). Die-cut Perf. 15 × 14(E). Two phosphor bands (blue fluor). Non-fluorescent coated paper. PSA gum

From £1·62 Barcode booklet pane UJPQ5

UJQ3	(1st) Gold	1·00	1·00

The distance between the two phosphor bands is 11 mm. The head type is B3.

Printed by Questa in booklets

TYPE SA4

(2nd) Bright Blue (2000–02)

2002 (4 July). Die-cut perf. 15 × 14(E). One 4 mm phosphor band (blue fluor). Non-fluorescent coated paper. PSA gum

From £2·28 Barcode booklet pane UJPQ7

UJQ4	(2nd) Bright blue	1·00	1·00

This is as No. UJQ2 (3.02 supp) but with 4 mm band from panes without matrix.

Printed by Walsall in sheets

Type SA5

(2nd) Bright blue (1998)

1998 (22 June). Die-cut Perf. 15 × 14(E). One 4·5 mm. Phosphor band (blue fluor). Non-fluorescent coated paper. PSA gum

UJW2 (= S.G.2039)

UJW2	(2nd) Bright blue..	1·00	1·00
	a. Perf 14½ × 14	£150	

Type SA6

(1st) Bright orange-red (1998)

1998 (22 June). Die-cut Perf. 15 × 14(E). Two phosphor bands (blue fluor). Non-fluorescent coated paper. PSA gum

UJW3 (= S.G.2040)

UJW3	(1st) Bright orange-red	1·50	1·50
	a. Perf 14½ × 14	£150	

Nos. UJW2 and UJW3 were initially priced at 20p. and 26p. available in sheets of 100 individual examples on backing paper (BS1/2)

On the (1st) class value the horizontal distance between the bands is 11·5 mm on No. UJE4 and 13·5 mm on No. UJW3.

Nos. UJW2a and UJW3a come from initial stocks of these Walsall sheet printings sent to the Philatelic Bureau and supplied to collectors requiring single stamps.

They can be indentified by the pointed perforation tips in the corners of the stamp, as illustrated below.

Nos. UJW2/3   UJW2a/3a

Sold out: December 1999

Type SA6

(2nd) Bright blue (2000)

2000 (4 September). Rounded die-cut Perf. 15 × 14(E). One 4·5 mm phosphor band (blue fluor). Type I Non-fluorescent coated paper. PSA gum

From sheets of 100 BS3

UJW4	(2nd) Bright blue	1·00	1·00
	a. Type II (pane UJPW2, 29.1.01)	1·00	1·00

This stamp has thinner "ND" than No. UJW2.

UJ Decimal self-adhesive issues

Printed by Walsall in booklets

Type SA5

(1st) Bright orange-red (2001)

2001 (29 January). Rounded die-cut Perf. 15 × 14(E). Two phosphor bands (blue fluor). Non-fluorescent coated paper. PSA gum

From £1·62 Barcode booklet panes UJPW3/4 , £3·24 Barcode booklet pane UJPW5

UJW5	(1st) Bright orange-red	1·50	1·50
	a. Two gradated bands 13·5 mm between (ex. PM1, 13.2.01)	1·50	1·50
	b. Phosphor omitted	£125	

The distance between the phosphor bands is 11·5 mm and 13·5 mm on No. UJW5a. This is as Questa No. UJQ1 which has head type B3.

(1st) Gold (2002)

2002 (5 June). Die-cut Perf. 15 × 14(E). Two phosphor bands (blue fluor). Non-fluorescent coated paper. PSA gum

From barcode booklet panes £1·62 UJPW6, £3·24 UJPW7

UJW6	(1st) Gold	1·00	1·00

The distance between the two phosphor bands is 11·5 mm. The serifs on the figure "1" are flat compared to those in No. UJQ3

D. Airmail stamps

Type SA4

SA7

(E) Deep blue (2002)

2002 (4 July). Die-cut Perf. 15 × 14(E). Two phosphor bands (blue fluor). Non-fluorescent coated paper. PSA gum

From £2·22 Barcode booklet pane UJWEP1
UJW7 (= S.G. 2296)

UJW7	(E) Deep blue	2·00	2·00

This was initially sold at 37p.

OVERSEAS BOOKLET STAMPS

Printed by Walsall in booklets

SA8   SA9

European Air Mail Stamp (2003)

2003 (27 March). Die-cut Perf. 15 × 14(E). Two phosphor bands (blue fluor). Non-fluorescent coated paper. PSA gum

From £2·08 Barcode booklet pane UJWEP2
UJW10 (=S.G.2358)

UJW10	(Europe) New blue and rosine	1·40	1·40
	a. Bureau example with white backing paper		1·40

Worldwide Airmail Stamp (2003)

2003 (27 March). Die-cut Perf. 15 × 14(E). Two phosphor bands (blue fluor). Non-fluorescent coated paper. PSA gum

From £4·48 Barcode booklet pane UJWEP3
UJW11 (=S.C. 2359)

UJW11	(Worldwide) Rosine and new blue	2·50	2·50
	a. Bureau example with white backing paper		2·50

The Philatelic Bureau sold these stamps with backing because individual stamps cut from booklets were not available to clients requesting single stamps.

SA10

Worldwide Postcard Air Mail Stamp (2004)

2004 (1 April). Die-cut Perf. 15 × 14(E). Two phosphor bands (blue fluor). Non-fluorescent coated paper. PSA gum

From £1·72 Barcode booklet pane UJWEP4
UJW12 (=S.G. 2357a)

UJW12	(Worldwide postcard) Grey-black, rosine and ultramarine	1·20	1·20
	a. Bureau example with white backing paper		1·20

No. UWE4a was also from the presentation pack No. UPP28 listed in the Section UD Machin (Gravure).

As Type UJWE210 inscribed "Europe up to 40 grams"
Second stamp shows a diamond screen with top of central cross incomplete (Worldwide stamp shown)

Decimal self-adhesive issues

Type SA10

European Air Mail Stamp (2004)

2004 (15 June). Die-cut Perf. 15 × 14(E). Two phosphor bands (blue fluor). Non-fluorescent coated paper. PSA gum

From £2·08 Barcode booklet pane UJWEP5
UJW13 (=S.G. 2358)

| UJW13 | (Europe) New blue and rosine | 1·40 | 1·40 |

Printed in a brighter shade of new blue than No. UJW10 (27.3.03) the inscription shows a dotted edge under 10 × magnification.

As Type UJWE3 inscribed "Worldwide up to 40 grams"
This stamp shows a diamond screen with top of central cross incomplete

Type SA11

Worldwide Air Mail Stamp (2004)

2004 (15 June). Die-cut Perf. 15 × 14(E). Two phosphor bands (blue fluor). Non-fluorescent coated paper. PSA gum

From £4·48 Barcode booklet pane UJWEP6
UJW14 (=S.G. 2359)

| UJW14 | (Worldwide) Rosine and new blue | 2·50 | 2·50 |

Printed in a brighter shade of rosine than No. UJW11 (27.3.03) the inscription shows a dotted edge under 10 × magnification.

E. "Pricing in Proportion" stamps small format

SA11

Type SA11

(2nd) Bright blue (2006)

2006 (12 September). Die-cut Perf. 15 × 14(E). One 4·5 mm phosphor band (blue fluor). Non-fluorescent coated paper. Acrylic gum

Business sheet BS15, £2·88 Self-adhesive booklet pane UJPW12
UJW17 (=S.G.2654)

| UJW17 | (2nd) Bright blue | 65 | 60 |

Self-adhesive stamps printed by Enschedé

(2nd) Bright blue (2006)

2006 (November). As No. UJW17 Vertical coil

Created for use by a large mail company, complete rolls were not sold by Royal Mail to the public. Single examples are as No. UJW17.

Coil

Issued	Number in roll	Face value Vertical delivery	Gum
4·05	10,000	£2300	Acrylic

The yellowish backing paper was printed with an inkjet number in reverse. Looking through the printed stamp side the number is in five digits reading from left.

(1st) Gold (2006)

2006 (12 September). Die-cut Perf. 15 × 14(E). Two phosphor bands (blue fluor). Non-fluorescent coated paper. PSA gum

From business sheet BS16, £2·04, £4·08 Self-adhesive booklet panes
UJW18 (=S.G.2655)

| UJW18 | (1st) Gold | 80 | 80 |

F. "Pricing in Proportion" stamps, large format

SA12

Type SA12

(2nd) Bright blue inscribed "Large" (2006)

2006 (15 August). Die-cut Perf. 15 × 14(E). Two phosphor bands (blue fluor). Non-fluorescent coated paper. PSA gum

From £1·60 Self-adhesive booklet pane UJPW15
UJW15 (=S.G. 2656)

| UJW15 | (2nd Large) Bright blue | 1·00 | 60 |

(1st) Gold inscribed "Large" (2006)

2006 (15 August). Die-cut Perf. 15 × 14(E). Two phosphor bands (blue fluor). Non-fluorescent coated paper. PSA gum

From £1·92 Self-adhesive booklet pane UJPW16
UJW16 (=S.C. 2657)

| UJW16 | (1st Large) Gold | 1·40 | 70 |

2. SA gum single stamps

Printed by De La Rue in sheets

SA13

Type SA13

50p. Grey (2009)

2009 (17 February). Die cut perf. 15 × 14 (E). two bands (blue fluor). U-shaped slits. Iridescent overprint. Non-fluorescent coated paper. SA gum

UJD6 (=S.G.U2915)

| UJD6 50p. Grey | 1·10 | 1·10 |

Cylinder Numbers (Blocks of Six)

Cyl. No	Phosphor No.	
D1	D1	6.50

UJ Decimal self-adhesive issues

Date of Printing (Blocks of Six)

Date	Right margin
08/12/08	6.50

£1 Magenta (2009)

2009 (17 February). die cut perf. 15 × 14 (E). two bands (blue fluor). U-shaped slits. Iridescent overprint. Non-fluorescent coated paper. SA gum

UJD7 (=S.G.U2916)

UJD7 £1 Magenta	2.25	2.25

Cylinder Numbers (Blocks of Six)

Cyl. No.	Phosphor No.	
D1	D1	12·00

Date of Printing (Blocks of Six)

Date	Right margin
08/12/08	8·00

£1.50 Brown-red (2009)

2009 (17 February). die cut perf. 15 × 14 (E). two bands (blue fluor). U-shaped slits. Iridescent overprint. Non-fluorescent coated paper. SA gum

UJD8 (=S.G.U2917)

UJD8 £1.50 Brown-red	3.25	3.25

Cylinder Numbers (Blocks of Six)

Cyl. No.	Phosphor No.	
D1	D1	15·00

Date of Printing (Blocks of Six)

Date	Right margin
20/01/09	15·00

£2 Deep Blue-green (2009)

2009 (17 February). Die cut perf. 15 × 14(E). two bands (blue fluor). U-shaped slits. Iridescent overprint. Non-fluorescent coated paper. SA gum

UJD9 (=S.G.U2918)

UJD9 £2 Deep blue-green	4.25	4.25

Cylinder Numbers (Blocks of Six)

Cyl. No.	Phosphor No.	
D1	D1	20·00

Date of Printing (Blocks of Six)

Date	Right margin
20/01/09	20·00

£3 Deep Mauve (2009)

2009 (17 February). die cut perf. 15 × 14 (E). two bands (blue fluor). U-shaped slits. Iridescent overprint. Non-fluorescent coated paper. SA gum

UJD10 (=S.G.U2919)

UJD10 £3 Deep mauve	6.25	6.25

Cylinder Numbers (Blocks of Six)

Cyl. No.	Phosphor No.	
D1	D1	27·00

Date of Printing (Blocks of Six)

Date	Right margin
20/01/09	27·00

£5 Azure (2009)

2009 (17 February). die cut perf. 15 × 14 (E). two bands (blue fluor). U-shaped slits. Iridescent overprint. Non-fluorescent coated paper. SA gum

UJD11 (=S.G.U2920)

UJD11 £5 Azure	10.50	10.50

Cylinder Numbers (Blocks of Six)

Cyl. No.	Phosphor No.	
D1	D1	50·00

Date	Right margin
20/01/09	50·00

2009 (17 February). Die cut perf. 15 × 14 (E). One centre band (blue fluor). Non-fluorescent coated paper. SA gum

Type SA11

UJD2 (=S.G.U2911)

UJD2 (2nd) Bright blue	65	60

Cylinder Numbers (Blocks of Six)

Cyl. No.	Phosphor No.	
D1	D1	4·00

Date of Printing (Blocks of Six)

Date	Right margin
04/12/08	4·00

Type SA6

2009 (17 February). Die cut perf. 15 × 14 (E). Two bands (blue fluor). Non-fluorescent coated paper. SA gum

UJD3 (=S.G.U2912)

UJD3 (1st) Gold	80	80

Cylinder Numbers (Blocks of Six)

Cyl. No.	Phosphor No.	
D1	D1	5·00

Date of Printing (Blocks of Six)

Date	Right margin
03/12/08	5·00

UJ Decimal self-adhesive issues

Type SA5

Printed in Gravure with U-shaped slits and iridescent overprint code "B" (ROYAL MBIL)

2009 (31 March). Die cut perf. 15 × 14(E). One 4·5mm centre band (blue fluor). Non-fluorescent coated paper. SA gum

From Business sheet of 100 initially sold at £27

UJD12	(2nd) Bright blue	65	60

Printed in Gravure with U-shaped slits and iridescent overprint code "B" (ROYAL MBIL)

2009 (31 March). die cut perf. 15 × 14(E). two bands (blue fluor). Non-fluorescent coated paper. SA gum

From Business sheet of 100 initially sold at £36

UJD13	(1st) Gold	80	80

Type SA12

Printed in Gravure with U-shaped slits and iridescent overprint code "C"

2009 (10 March). Die cut perf. 15 × 14(E). Two bands (blue fluor). U-shaped slits. Iridescent overprint. Non-fluorescent coated paper. SA gum

From £2·16 Barcode booket pane WP2129

UJW19	(1st) Gold	80	80

Printed in Gravure with U-shaped slits and iridescent overprint "S"

2009 (31 March). Die-cut perf. 15 × 14(E). Two bands (blue fluor). U-shaped slits iridescent overprint. Non-fluorescent coated paper. SA gum

From £2·16 Barcode booklet UJPW26

UJW20	(1st) Gold	85	85

Printed in Gravure with U-shaped slits and iridescent overprint code "T"

2009 (31 March). Die-cut Perf. 15 × 14(E). One 4·5mm centre band (blue fluor) U-shaped slits, iridescent overprint, non-fluorescent coated paper. SA gum.

From £3·24 Barcode booklet pane UJPW27

UJW21	(2nd) Bright blue	80	80

2009 (31 March). Die-cut Perf. 15 × 14(E). Two bands (blue fluor). U-shaped slits, iridescent overprint, non-fluorescent coated paper. SA gum

From £4·32 Barcode booklet pane UJPW28

UJW22	(1st) Gold	85	85

Type SA6

(2nd) Bright blue inscribed "Large" (2009)

Printed in Gravure with U-shaped slits and iridescent overprint

2009 (17 February). Die cut perf. 15 × 14 (E). Two bands (blue fluor). Non-fluorescent coated paper. SA gum

UJD4 (=S.G. U2913)

UJD4	(2nd) Bright blue	90	90

Cylinder Numbers (Blocks of Six)

Cyl. No.	Phosphor No.	
D1	D1	6·00

Cylinder Numbers (Blocks of Six)

Date	Right margin
10/12/08	6·00

(1st) Gold inscribed "Large" (2009)

Printed in Gravure with U-shaped slits and iridescent overprint

2009 (17 February). Die cut perf. 15 × 14 (E). Two bands (blue fluor). Non-fluorescent coated paper. SA gum

UJD5 (=S.G.U2914)

UJD5	(1st) Bright blue	1·10	1·10

Cylinder Numbers (Blocks of Six)

Cyl. No.	Phosphor No.	
D1	D1	6·00

Date of Printing (Blocks of Six)

Date	Right margin
09/12/08	6·00

Type SA12

(2nd) Bright Blue inscribed "Large" (2009)

Printed in Gravure with U-shaped slits and iridescent overprint code "B" (ROYBL MAIL)

2009 (31 March). die cut perf. 15 × 14(E). two bands (blue fluor). Non-fluorescent coated paper. SA gum

From Business sheet of 50 initially sold at £21

UJD14	(2nd) Bright blue	90	90

(1st) Gold inscribed "Large" (2009)

Printed in Gravure with U-shaped slits and iridescent overprint code "B" (ROYBL MAIL)

2009 (31 March). Die cut perf. 15 × 14(E). Two bands (blue fluor). Non-fluorescent coated paper. SA gum

From Business sheet of 50 initially sold at £26

UJD15	(1st) Gold	1·10	1·10

Recorded Delivery

2009 (17 November). Die-cut perf. 15 × 14(E). Two bands (blue fluor). Iridescent overprint. Non-fluorescent coated paper. SA gum

UJ Decimal self-adhesive issues — Booklet panes

Type SA6

(2nd) Bright Blue inscribed "Large" (2009)

Printed in Gravure with U-shaped slits and iridescent overprint code "F" (FOYAL MAIL)

2009 (31 March). Die cut perf. 15 × 14 (E). Two bands (blue fluor). Non-fluorescent coated paper. SA gum

From £1.68 Barcode booklet pane UJPW29

UJW23	(2nd) Bright blue	90	90

(1st) Gold inscribed "Large" (2009)

Printed in Gravure with U-shaped slits and iridescent overprint code "F" (FOYAL MAIL)

2009 (31 March). Die cut perf. 15 × 14(E). Two bands (blue fluor). Non-fluorescent coated paper. SA gum

From £2.08 Barcode booklet pane UJPW30

UJW24	(1st) Gold	1·10	1·10

"Recorded Signed For" stamps

Type SA14

UJD16 = U2916a

UJD16	(Recorded Signed for 1st) Bright orange-red and lemon	2·25	2·25

2009 (17 November). Die-cut Perf. 15 × 14(E). Two bands (blue fluor). Iridescent overprint. Non-fluorescent coated paper. SA Gum

Type SA15

UJD17 = U2916B

UJD17	(Recorded signed for 1st large) Bright orange-red and lemon	2·75	2·75

First Day Covers

UJFD1	(19.10.93)(No. UJW1)	4·50
UJFD2	(18.3.97) (Nos. UJE1/2)	5·50
UJFD3	(27.3.03) (Nos. UJW10/11)	5·25
UJFD4	(1.8.06) (Nos. UJW15/8, +U211A and U230A	5·00
UJFD5	(17.2.09) (Nos. UJD2/7)	9·00
UJFD6	(17.2.09) (Nos. UJD8/11)	30·00

Presentation Packs

UJPP1	(19.10.93) (No. UJW1)	25·00
UJPP2	(18.3.97) (Nos. UJE1/2)	4·75
UJPP3	(27.3.03) (Nos. UJW10/11)	6·00
UJPP4	(1.8.06) (Nos. UJW15/18, U211A and U230A	4·75
UJPP5	(17.2.69) (Nos. UJD2/7)	8·00
UJPP6	(17.2.09) (Nos. UJD8/11)	30·00

PHQ cards

UJPQ1	(19.10.93)(No. UJW1)	4·00	8·00
UJPQ2	(4.7.02) (No. UJW7)	60	3·50
UJPQ3	(27.3.03) (No. UJW10)	45	3·50

Booklet Panes containing self-adhesive denominated stamps

£2·52 Pane

From Barcode Booklet NA1

UJWMP1

Pane of six 42p. (deep olive-grey) stamps with two phosphor bands (blue fluor) on non-fluorescent coated paper. Two elliptical perf. holes on each vertical edge.
Pane UJWMP1. Gravure, self-adhesive without matrix

UJWMP1 (containing No. UJW8 × 6) (4.7.02)	25·00

Booklet Cylinder Numbers

Pane No.	Cyl. No.	Phos. No.	Die-cut perf.
UJWMP1	W1	W1	28·00

£4·08 Pane

From Barcode Booklet NB1

As pane No. UJWMP1 but 68p. values
Pane of six 68p. (grey-brown) stamps with two phosphor bands (blue fluor) on non-fluorescent coated paper. Two elliptical perf. holes on each vertical edge.
Pane UJWMP2. Gravure, self-adhesive without matrix

UJWMP2 (containing No. UJW9 × 6) (4.7.02)	28·00

Booklet Cylinder Numbers

Pane No.	Cyl. No.	Phos. No.	Die-cut perf.
UJWMP2	W1	W1	27·00

Booklet Panes containing self-adhesive No Value Indicated stamps

I. Printed by Questa in Gravure

(2nd) £1·90 Pane

From Barcode Booklet MC1

UJPQ1

Pane of ten (2nd) class stamps (bright blue) with one 5mm centre phosphor band.
Pane UJPQ1. Gravure, self-adhesive

UJPQ1 (containing No. UJQ2 × 10) (29.1.01)	7·50

Booklet Cylinder Numbers

Pane No.	Cyl. No.	Phos. No.	Die-cut perf.
UJPQ1	1	1	10·00

(2nd) £2·28 Pane

From Barcode Booklet ME1

UJPQ2

Pane or twelve (2nd) class stamps (bright blue) with one 5 mm centre phosphor band.
Pane UJPQ2. Gravure, self-adhesive

UJPQ2 (containing No. UJQ2 ×12) (29.1.01) 8·00

Booklet Cylinder Numbers

Pane No.	Cyl. No.	Phos. No.	Die-cut perf.
UJPQ2	1	1	10·00

(1st) £2·70 Pane

From Barcode Booklet MD1

UJPQ3

Pane of ten (1st) class stamps (bright orange-red) with two phosphor bands
Pane UJPQ3. Gravure, self-adhesive

UJPQ3 (containing No. UJQ1 ×10) (29.1.01) 10·00

Booklet Cylinder Numbers

Pane No.	Cyl. No.	Phos. No.	Die-cut perf.
UJPQ3	1	1	13·00

(1st) £3·24 Pane

From Barcode Booklet MF1

UJPQ4

Pane of twelve (1st) class stamps (bright orange-red) with two phosphor bands
Pane UJPQ4. Gravure, self-adhesive

UJPQ4 (containing No.UJQ1 ×12) (29.1.01) 12·00

Booklet Cylinder Numbers

Pane No.	Cyl. No.	Phos. No.	Die-cut perf.
UJPQ4	1	1	14·00

(1st) £1·62 Pane

From Barcode Booklet MB3

As Pane No. UJPW3 but with one notch at top right
Pane of six (1st) class stamps (gold) with two phosphor bands
Pane UJPQ5. Gravure, self-adhesive

UJPQ5 (containing No. UJQ3 ×6) (5.6.02) 5·00

Booklet Cylinder Numbers

Pane No.	Cyl. No.	Phos. No.	Die-cut perf.
UJPQ5	1	1	7·00

(1st) £1·62 Pane

From Barcode Booklet MB5

As Pane No. UJW3 but with one notch at top right
Pane of six (1st) class stamps (bright orange-red) with two phosphor bands
Pane UJPQ6. Gravure, self-adhesive with matrix

UJPQ6 (containing No. UJQ1 ×6) (4.7.02) 5·00

Booklet Cylinder Numbers

Pane No.	Cyl. No.	Phos. No.	Die-cut perf.
UJPQ6	1	1	7·00

(2nd) £2·28 Pane

From Barcode Booklet ME2 (£2·40 from 8.5.03).

As Pane No. UJPQ2 but with two notches at top right
Pane of twelve (2nd) class stamps (bright blue) with one 4 mm centre phosphor band
Pane UJPQ7. Gravure, self-adhesive

UJPQ7 (containing No. UJQ4 ×12) (4.7.02) 8·00

Booklet Cylinder Numbers

Pane No.	Cyl. No.	Phos. No.	Die-cut perf.
UJPQ7	1	1	10·00

II Printed by Walsall in Lithography

(1st) Orange-red (1993)

From Barcode Booklet MG1

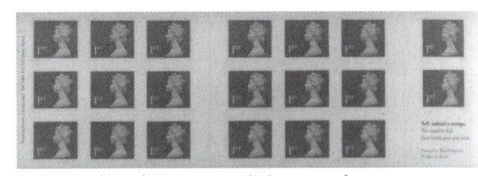

UJPW1 Booklet of 20 stamps with die-cut perforations
(Actual size 23½ × 76 mm)

1993 (19 October). Two bands. Non-fluorescent paper. PSA gum

UJPW1	(Barcode booklet No. HE1 containing No. UJ1 × 20 sold at £4·80)	20·00
	a. Phosphor omitted	
	b. Phosphor bands double	

Sheet Make-up: The primary sheet contained two columns each of five booklets. There were no markings apart from trimming lines. Consisting of three layers, the sheet was unusual as both sides were printed and folded between vertical rows 3/4 and 6/7.

Withdrawn: 28 April 1995

UJ Decimal self-adhesive issues — Booklet panes

III Printed by Walsall in Gravure

(2nd) £1·14 Pane

From Barcode Booklet MA1

UJPW2 (cylinder pane)

Pane of six (2nd) class stamps (bright blue) with one phosphor band
Pane UJPW2. Gravure, self-adhesive

UJPW2 (containing No. UJW4a × 6) (29.1.01)   4·00

Booklet Cylinder Numbers

Pane No.	Cyl. No.	Phos. No.	Die-cut perf.
UJPW2	W1	W1	6·00

(1st) £1·62 Pane

From Barcode Booklet MB1

UJPW3 (cylinder pane)

Pane of six (1st) class stamps (bright orange-red) with two phosphor bands
Pane UJPW3. Gravure, self-adhesive

UJPW3 (containing No. UJW5 × 6) (29.1.01)   6·00

Booklet Cylinder Numbers

Pane No.	Cyl. No.	Phos. No.	Die-cut perf.
UJPW3	W2	W1	8·00

(1st) £1·62 Pane with Queen Victoria commemorative label at left.

From Barcode Booklet MB2

UJPW4 (cylinder pane)
Death Centenary of Queen Victoria

Pane of six (1st) class stamps (bright orange-red) with two phosphor bands with die-cut perforated label (65 × 50 mm) at left.
Pane UJPW4. Gravure, self-adhesive

UJPW4 (containing No. UJW5 × 6) (29.1.01)   14·00

Booklet Cylinder Numbers

Pane No.	Cyl. No.	Phos. No.	Die-cut perf.
UJPW4	W1 (× 4)	W1	16·00

Booklet Cylinder Numbers

The cylinder numbers are opposite stamp 4 at bottom left. Reading up the margin the colours are bright orange-red, phosphor, gold, grey and black.

(1st) £3·24 Pane

From Barcode Booklet MF2

UJPW5

(1st) £3·24 Pane

From Barcode Booklet MF2

Pane of twelve (1st) class stamps (bright orange-red) with two phosphor bands
Pane UJPW5. Gravure, self-adhesive

UJPW5 (containing No. UJW5 × 12) (29.1.01)   12·00

Booklet Cylinder Numbers

Pane No.	Cyl. No.	Phos. No.	Die-cut perf.
UJPW5	W1	W1	14·00

(1st) £1·62 Pane

From Barcode Booklet MB4

As Pane UJPQ5 but printed by Walsall
Pane of six (1st) class stamps (gold) with two phosphor bands
Pane UJPW6. Gravure, self-adhesive

UJPW6 (containing No. UJW6 × 6) (5.6.02)   5·00

Booklet Cylinder Numbers

Pane No.	Cyl. No.	Phos. No.	Die-cut perf.
UJPW6	W1	W1	7·50

The initial printing did not show the cylinder numbers.

(1st) £3·24 Pane

From Barcode Booklet MF3

UJPW7

Pane of twelve (1st) class stamps (gold) with two phosphor bands
Pane UJPW7. Gravure, self-adhesive

UJPW7 (containing No. UJW6 × 12) (5.6.02)   12·00

Booklet Cylinder Numbers

Pane No.	Cyl. No.	Phos. No.	Die-cut perf.
UJPW7	W1	W1	14·00

The initial printing did not show the cylinder numbers.

■ (2nd) £2·28 Pane

(£2·40 from 8.5.03, £2·52 from 1.4.04). From Barcode Booklet ME3

UJPW8

Pane of twelve (2nd) class stamps (bright blue) with one 4·5 mm centre phosphor band From barcode Booklet No. ME3 Pane UJPW8. Gravure, self-adhesive

	Die-cut perf.
UJPW8 (containing No. UJW4a × 12) (27.3.03)	8·00

Although outside the scope this pane exists with minor phosphor misplacement which results in some examples with short bands at top or bottom.

Booklet Cylinder Numbers

Pane No.	Cyl. No.	Phos. No.	Die-cut perf.
UJPW8	W1	W1	10·00

■ (1st) £1·68 Pane

(£1·80 from 7.4.05). From Barcode Booklet MB7

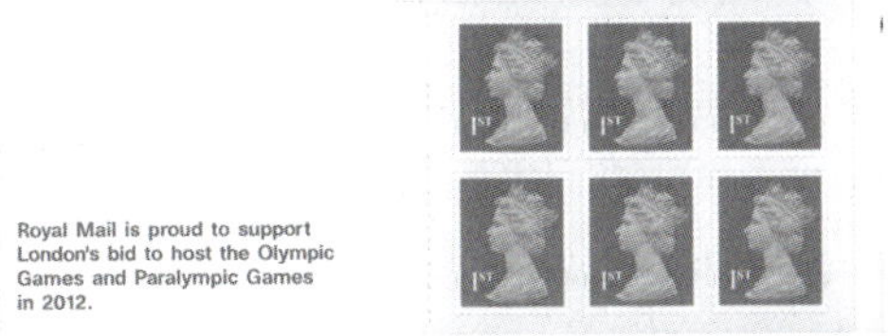

UJPW9

Pane of six (1st) class stamps (gold) with two phosphor bands From barcode Booklet No. MB7 (Supporting London 2012) Pane UJPW9. Gravure, self-adhesive

	Die-cut perf.
UJPW9 (containing No. UJW6 × 6) (15.6.04)	9·00

Booklet Cylinder Numbers

Pane No.	Cyl. No.	Phos. No.	Die-cut perf.
UJPW9	W3	W2	12·00

■ 1(st) £1·68 Pane

(£1·80 from 7.4.05). From Barcode Booklet MB4a

UJPW10

Pane of six (1st) class stamps (gold) with two phosphor bands From barcode Booklet No. MB4a. Self-adhesive Smilers advertisement at left
Pane UJPW10. Gravure, self-adhesive

	Die-cut perf.
UJPW10 (containing No. UJW6 × 6) (27.1.05)	4·25

This pane was first available from Tallents House on 27 January 2005 and later from the post offices from 22 March 2005.

Booklet Cylinder Numbers

Pane No.	Cyl. No.	Phos. No.	Die-cut perf.
UJPW10	W2	W2	20·00
	W3	—	7·50
	W3	W2	7·50

The first printing of W3 did not show the phosphor number.

■ (1st) £1·80 Pane

(£1·92 from 3.4.06). From Barcode Booklet MB4a

UJPW11

Pane of six (1st) class stamps (gold) with two phosphor bands From barcode Booklet No. MB4a. Self-adhesive "Love" Smilers advertisement at left
Pane UJPW10. Gravure, self-adhesive

	Die-cut perf.
UJPW11 (containing No. UJW6 × 6) (26.7.05)	5·00

The advertisement shows Type UM 135 and bride.

Booklet Cylinder Numbers

Pane No.	Cyl. No.	Phos. No.	Die-cut perf.
UJPW11	W3	W2	7·00

■ (2nd) £2·76 Pane

(£2·88 from 2.4.07). From Barcode Booklet RD1

UJPW12

Pane of twelve (2nd) class stamps (bright blue) with one 4·5 mm centre phosphor band
Pane UJPW12. Gravure, self-adhesive

	Die-cut perf.
UJPW12 (containing No. UJW17 × 12) (12.9.06)	8·00

Booklet Cylinder Numbers

Pane No.	Cyl. No.	Phos. No.	Die-cut perf.
UJPW12	W1	W1	10·00
	W2	W1	11·00

UJ Decimal self-adhesive issues — Booklet panes

(1st) £1·92 Pane

(£2·04 from 2.4.07). From Barcode Booklet RC1

UJPW13

Pane of six (1st) class stamps (gold) with two phosphor bands
Pane UJPW13. Gravure, self-adhesive

UJPW13 (containing No. UJW8 × 6)(12.9.06)   7·00

Booklet Cylinder Numbers

Pane No.	Cyl. No.	Phos. No.	Die-cut perf.
UJPW13	W1	W1	9·00

(1st) 3·84 Pane

(£4·08 from 2.4.07). From Barcode Booklet RE1

UJPW14

Pane of twelve (1st) class stamps (gold) with two phosphor bands
Pane UJPW14. Gravure, self-adhesive

UJPW14 (containing No. UJW8 × 12) (12.9.06)   12·00

Booklet Cylinder Numbers

Pane No.	Cyl. No.	Phos. No.	Die-cut perf.
UJPW14	W1	W1	14·00

(2nd) class stamps inscribed "Large".

£1·48 Pane (£1·60 from 2.4.07)
From Barcode Booklet RA1

UJPW15

Pane of four (2nd) class stamps (bright blue) with two phosphor bands
Pane UJPW15. Gravure, self-adhesive

UJPW15 (containing No. UJW15 × 4)(15.8.06)   6·00

Booklet Cylinder Numbers

Pane No.	Cyl. No.	Phos. No.	Die-cut perf.
UJPW15	W1	W1	7·00

(1st) class stamps inscribed "Large".

From Barcode Booklet RB1 £1·76 Pane
(£1·92 from 2.4.07).

UJPW16

Pane of four (1st) class stamps (gold) with two phosphor bands
Pane UJPW16. Gravure, self-adhesive

UJPW16 (containing No. UJW16 × 4) (15.8.06)   6·50

Booklet Cylinder Numbers

Pane No.	Cyl. No.	Phos. No.	Die-cut perf.
UJPW16	W1	W1 above ink cylinder	8·00
	W1	W1 below ink cylinder	8·00

(1st) £1·92 Pane

From Barcode Booklet RC1a (£2·04 from 2.4.07)

UJPW17

Pane of six (1st) class stamps (gold) with two phosphor bands
Pane UJPW17. Gravure, self-adhesive

UJPW17 (containing No. UJW8 × 6) (2·10.06)   7·00

Booklet Cylinder Numbers

Pane No.	Cyl. No.	Phos. No.	Die-cut perf.
UJPW17	W1	W1	8·00

(1st) £1·92 Pane

(£2·04 from 2.4.07). From Barcode Booklet SA1

UJPW18

Pane of six containing 5 × (1st) class stamps (gold) and UM166 with two phosphor bands
Pane UJPW18. Gravure, self-adhesive

UJPW18 (containing No. UJW8 × 5, UM166) (16.1.07)   30·00

The strip at right shows hearts printed in red. There were no cylinder numbers.

(1st) £1·92 Pane

(£2·04 from 2.4.07). From Barcode Booklet RC1b

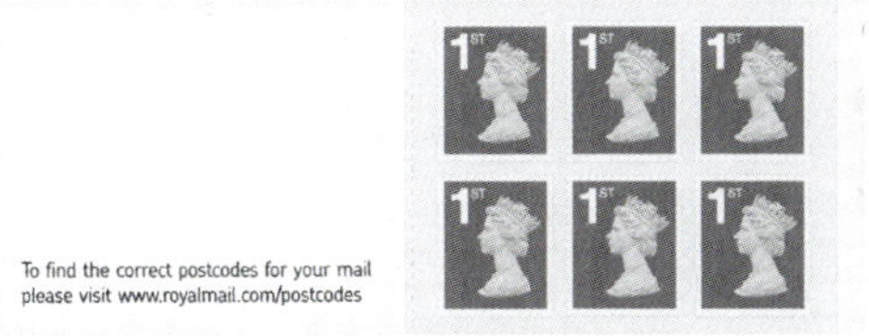

UJPW19

Pane of six (1st) class stamps (gold) with two phosphor bands
Pane UJPW19. Gravure, self-adhesive

UJPW 19 (containing No. UJW8 × 6) (1.2.07)		7·00

Booklet Cylinder Numbers

Pane No.	Cyl. No.	Phos. No.	Die-cut perf.
UJPW19	W1	W1	8·00

Withdrawn: 31 January 2008

(1st) £2·04 Pane

(£2·16 from 7.4.08). From Barcode Booklet MB4c

UJPW20

Pane of six (1st) class stamps (gold) with two phosphor bands
From barcode Booklet No. MB4c.
Pane UJPW20. Gravure, self-adhesive

UJPW20 (containing No. UJW6 × 6) (5.6.07)		4·25

Booklet Cylinder Numbers

Pane No.	Cyl. No.	Phos. No.	Die-cut perf.
UJPW20	W4	W1	5·00

(1st) £2·04 Pane

From Barcode Booklet MB4d (£2·16 from 7.4.08).

UJPW21

Pane of six (1st) class stamps (gold) with two phosphor bands
From barcode Booklet No. MB4d. Self-adhesive Machin Fortieth Anniversary at left
Pane UJPW21. Gravure, self-adhesive

UJPW21 (containing No. UJW6 × 6) (5.6.07)		4·25

There were no cylinder numbers on the pane.

(1st) £2·04 Pane

From Barcode Booklet MB4e (£2·16 from 7.4.08).

UJPW22

Pane of six (1st) class stamps (gold) with two phosphor bands
From barcode Booklet No. MB4e. Self-adhesive Harry Potter advert "STAMPS MAKE MAGICAL GIFTS" at left
Pane UJPW22. Gravure, self-adhesive

UJPW22 (containing No. UJW6 × 6) (28.8.07)		4·25

There were no cylinder numbers on the pane.
Withdrawn: 27 August 2008

(1st) £2·04 Pane

From Barcode Booklet MB4f (£2·16 from 7.4.08).

UJPW23

Pane of six (1st) class stamps (gold) with two phosphor bands
From barcode Booklet No. MB4f. Self-adhesive with inside cover postcode addresses in English and Welsh
Pane UJPW23. Gravure, self-adhesive

UJPW23 (containing No. UJW6 × 6) (20.9.07)		4·25

Booklet Cylinder Numbers

Pane No.	Cyl. No.	Phos. No.	Die-cut perf.
UJPW23	W4	W1	5·00

Withdrawn: 19 September 2008

(1st) £2·04 Pane

From Barcode Booklet SA2 (£2·16 from 7.4.08).

UJPW24

Pane of six containing 2 × UM167 with labels and 4 × (1st) class stamps (gold). Stamps with two phosphor bands
Pane UJPW24. Gravure, self-adhesive

UJPW24 (containing No. UM167 × 2, UJW6 × 4) (15.1.08)		20·00

The strip at right shows hearts printed in gold. There were no cylinder numbers.

In order to hold together the labels and the stamps once removed from the cover the three perforations at top, midway and bottom of the "Love" stamps were intact.

(1st) £2·16 Pane

From Barcode Booklet MB4g (£2·34 from 6.4.09).

UJPW25

Pane of six (1st) class stamps (gold) with two phosphor bands From barcode Booklet No. MB4g. Self-adhesive with label showing "Carry on Sergeant" facsimile of the 1st class special issue stamp and website address.
Pane UJPW25. Gravure, self-adhesive

| UJPW25 (containing No. UJW6×6) (10.6.08) | 4·25 |

There were no cylinder numbers.

(1st) £2·16 Pane

From Barcode Booklet MB8 (£2·34 from 6.4.09).

UJPW26
Pane of six (1st) class stamps (gold) with U-shaped slits and two phosphor bands From barcode Booklet No. MB8. Self-adhesive with inside cover postcode addresses in English and Welsh.
Pane UJPW26. Code "S" (MSIL). Gravure, self-adhesive

| UJPW26 (containing No. UJW12 ×6) (31.3.09) | 5·00 |

Booklet Cylinder Numbers

Pane No.	Cyl. Nos.	Phos. No.	Die-cut perf.
UJPW26	W5, W1	W2	6·00

Iridescent ink was cylinder W1 in sequence W5,W2,W1 reading up the margin.

(2nd) £3·24 Pane

From Barcode Booklet ME5 (£3·60 from 6.4.09).

UJPW27
Pane of twelve (2nd) class stamps (bright blue) with U-shaped slits and two 4·5 mm. centre phosphor band
Pane UJPW27L. Code "T" (MTIL). Gravure, self-adhesive

| UJPW27 (containing No. UJW13×12) (31.3.09) | 7·00 |

Booklet Cylinder Numbers

Pane No.	Cyl. Nos.	Phos. No.	Die-cut perf.
UJPW27	W4, W1	W2	8·00

Iridescent ink was cylinder W1 in sequence W4,W2,W1 reading up the margin.

(1st) £4·32 Pane

From Barcode Booklet MF5 (£4·68 from 6.4.09).

UJPW28
Pane of twelve (1st) class stamps (gold) with U-shaped slits and two phosphor bands
Pane UJPW28. Code "T" (MTIL). Gravure, self-adhesive

| UJPW28 (containing No. UJW14×12) (31.3.09) | 9·50 |

Booklet Cylinder Numbers

Pane No.	Cyl. Nos.	Phos. No.	Die-cut perf.
UJPW28	W5, W1	W2	12·00

Iridescent ink was cylinder W1 in sequence W5,W2,W1 reading up the margin. The phosphor cylinder number is partially printed on some examples.

(2nd) class stamps inscribed "Large". £1·68 Pane

From Barcode Booklet RA2 (£1·88 from 6.4.09).

UJPW29

Pane of four (2nd) class stamps (bright blue) with U-shaped slits and two phosphor bands Pane UJPW29. Code "F" (FOYAL). Gravure, self-adhesive

| UJPW29 (containing No. UJW15×4) (31.3.09) | 3·75 |

Booklet Cylinder Numbers

Pane No.	Cyl. Nos.	Phos. No.	Die-cut perf.
UJPW29	W1, W1	W1	4·50

Iridescent ink was cylinder W1 in sequence W1,W1,W1 reading up the margin. The phosphor cylinder number is partially printed on some examples.

(1st) class stamps inscribed "Large". £2·08 Pane

From Barcode Booklet RB2 (£2·44 from 6.4.09).

UJPW30
Pane of four (1st) class stamps (gold) with U-shaped slits and two phosphor bands
Pane UJPW30. Code "F" (FOYAL). Gravure, self-adhesive

| UJPW30 (containing No. UJW16×4) (31.3.09) | 5·00 |

Booklet Cylinder Numbers

Pane No.	Cyl. Nos.	Phos. No.	Die-cut perf.
UJPW30	W1, W1	W1	6·00

Iridescent ink was cylinder W1 in sequence W1,W1,W1 reading up the margin. The phosphor cylinder number is partially printed on some examples.

European Air Mail "E" Pane

(E) £2·22 Pane

From Barcode Booklet MH1 (£2·28 from 8.5.03).

UJWEP1

Pane of six (E) European air mail stamps with two phosphor bands (blue fluor). Two elliptical perf. holes on each vertical edge.
Pane UJWEP1 Gravure, self-adhesive without matrix
UJWEP1 (containing No. UJW7 × 6) (4.7.02) 12·00

Booklet Cylinder Numbers

Pane No.	Cyl. No.	Phos. No.	Die-cut perf.
UJWEP1	W1	W1	16·00

European Air Mail Pane

£2·08 Pane

Barcode Booklet MI1

UJWEP2

Pane of four European air mail stamps with two phosphor bands (blue fluor). Two elliptical perf. holes on each vertical edge.
Pane UJWEP2. Gravure, self-adhesive without matrix
UJWEP2 (containing No. UJW10 × 4) (27.3.03) 8·50

Booklet Cylinder Numbers

Pane No.	Cyl. No.	Phos. No.	Die-cut perf.
UJWEP2	W1, W1	W1	11·00

Worldwide Air Mail Pane

£4·48 Pane

From Barcode Booklet MJ1

UJWEP3

Pane of four Worldwide air mail stamps with two phosphor bands (blue fluor). Two elliptical perf holes on each vertical edge.
Pane UJWEP3. Gravure, self-adhesive without matrix
UJWEP3 (containing No. UJW11 × 4) (27.3.03) 12·00

Booklet Cylinder Numbers

Pane No.	Cyl. No.	Phos. No.	Die-cut perf
UJWEP3	W1, W1	W1	14·00

Worldwide Postcard Air Mail Pane

£1·72 Pane.

From Barcode Booklet MJA1

UJWEP4 (cylinder pane)

Pane of four Worldwide Postcard air mail stamps with two phosphor bands (blue fluor). Two elliptical perf. holes on each vertical edge. From barcode Booklet No. MJA1
Pane UJWEP4. Gravure, self-adhesive without matrix
UJWEP4 (containing No. UJW12 × 4) (1.4.04) 5·00

Booklet Cylinder Numbers

Pane No.	Cyl. No.	Phos. No.	Die-cut perf.
UJWEP4	W1(× 3)	W1	7·00

European Air Mail Pane

£2·08 Pane

From Barcode Booklet MI2

As Type UJWE2 inscribed "Europe up to 40 grams". This pane contains stamps showing a diamond screen with top of central cross incomplete
Pane of four European air mail stamps with two phosphor bands (blue fluor). Two elliptical perf. holes on each vertical edge.
Pane UJWEP5. Gravure, self-adhesive without matrix
UJWEP5 (containing No. UJW13 × 4) (15.6.04) 9·00

Booklet Cylinder Numbers

Pane No.	Cyl. No.	Phos. No.	Die-cut perf.
UJWEP5	W2, W2	W1	11·00

Worldwide Air Mail Pane

£4·48 Pane

From Barcode Booklet MJ2

As Pane No. UJWEP5 but with Worldwide stamps. This pane contains stamps showing a diamond screen with top of central cross incomplete
Pane of four Worldwide air mail stamps with two phosphor bands (blue fluor). Two elliptical perf. holes on each vertical edge.
Pane UJWEP6. Gravure, self-adhesive without matrix
UJWEP6 (containing No. UJW14 × 4) (15.6.04) 16·00

UJ Decimal self-adhesive issues *Booklet panes*

Booklet Cylinder Numbers

Pane No.	Cyl. No.	Phos. No.	Die-cut perf.
UJWEP6	W2, W2	W1	18·00

Booklet Panes containing a mixed self-adhesive No Value Indicated and commemorative stamps

2001 Cats and Dogs

From Cats and Dogs PM1

WP1369

Pane comprising £3.24 "Cats and Dogs" Barcode booklet PM1 10×(1st) Cats and Dogs stamps and 2×(1st) Bright orange-red. Two bands (blue fluor). Printed in gravure by Walsall.

WP1369 (containing Nos. W1359/68, (1st)×2 (10.2.01) 35·00

No. PM1 was initially sold at £3·24. Stamps from WP1369 have gradated bands whereas those from the sheetlet have straight edge bands

2001 Royal Navy Submarine Service

From £1·62 Barcode Booklet PM2

Pane comprising 2×(1st) W1369 printed in gravure with two bands (blue fluor) and 4×(1st) 2 bands Machin bright orange-red. No. UJQ1 die-cut perf 15×14(E). Self adhesive. No. W1379 die cut perf 15½×14.

WP1384 (Actual size 154x56 mm.)

WP1384 (containing Nos. W1379×2.UJQ1×4) (17.4.01) £100

No. PM2 was initially sold at £2·16, £2·34 from 17.4.01. A notch at top right of the cover, when closed, was to facilitate identification by the blind.

Booklet Cylinder Numbers

Pane No.	Cyl. No.	Phos. No.	Die-cut perf.
WP1384	1(×5)	1	£125

2003 Punch and Judy Puppets

From £1·62 Barcode Booklet PM3

Pane comprising 2×(1st) W1412/3 printed in gravure with two bands (blue fluor) and 4×(1st) 2 bands, Machin No UJQ1. die-cut perf. 15×14 (E), self-adhesive. Nos. W1412/3 die-cut perforation 14×15½.

WP1414 (Actual size 154x56 mm.)

WP1414 (containing Nos. W1412/3, UJQ1×4) (4.9.01) 20·00

No. PM3 was initially sold at £1·62 from 4.9.01. A notch at top right of the cover, when closed, was to facilitate identification by the blind.

Booklet Cylinder Numbers

Pane No.	Cyl. No.	Phos. No.	Die-cut perf.
WP1414	1(×7)	1	24·00

2001 Flags and Ensigns

From £1.62 Barcode Booklet PM4

Pane comprising 2×(1st) W1389/90 printed in gravure with two bands (blue fluor) and 4×(1st) 2 bands, Machin No. UJQ1 die-cut perf. 15×14 (E), self-adhesive. Nos. W1389/90 die-cut perforation 14½.

WP1391 (Actual size 154x56 mm.)

WP1391 (containing Nos. W1389/90, UJQ1×4) (22.10.01) 24·00

No. PM16 was initially sold at £1·62. A notch at top right of the cover, when closed, was to facilitate identification by the blind.

Booklet Cylinder Numbers

Pane No.	Cyl. No.	Phos. No.	Die-cut perf.
WP1391	1(×6)	1	28·00

2002 Passenger Jet Aviation

From £1·62 Barcode Booklet PM5

Pane comprising 2×(1st) W1475 printed in gravure with two bands (blue fluor) and 4×(1st) 2 bands, Machin bright orange-red No. UJQ1 die-cut perf. 15×14 (E), self-adhesive. No. W1475 die-cut perforation 14½.

WP1476 (Actual size 154x56 mm.)

WP1476 (containing Nos.1475×2, UJQ1x4) (2.5.02)   15·00

No. PM5 was initially sold at £1·62. A notch at top right of the cover, when closed, was to facilitate identification by the blind.

Booklet Cylinder Numbers

Pane No.	Cyl. No.	Phos. No.	Die-cut perf.
WP1476	1(×6)	1	18·00

2002 World Cup Football Championship

From £2.16 Barcode Booklet PM6

Pane comprising 2×(1st) W1479/80 printed in gravure with two bands (blue fluor) and 4×(1st) 2 bands, Machin bright orange-red No. UQ1 die-cut perf. 15×14 (E), self-adhesive. Nos. W1479/80 die-cut perforation 14½.

WP2129 (Actual size 154x56mm.)

WP1481	(containing Nos. W1479/80, UJW6x4) (21.5.02)	15·00

No. PM6 was initially sold at £1·62. A notch at top right of the cover, when closed, was to facilitate identification by the blind.

Booklet Cylinder Numbers

Pane No.	Cyl. No.	Phos. No.	Die-cut perf.
WP1481	W1(×6)	None	18·00

2002 Bridges of London

From £1.62 Barcode Booklet PM7

Pane comprising 2×(1st) W1497 printed in gravure with two bands (blue fluor) and 4×(1st) 2 bands, Machin (gold). No. UJQ3 die-cut perf. 15×14 (E), self-adhesive. No. W1497 die-cut perforation 15×14.

WP1498 (Actual size 154x56mm.)

WP1498	(containing Nos. W1497×2, UJQ3x4) (10.9.02)	15·00

No. PM7 was initially sold at £1·62. A notch at top right of the cover, when closed, was to facilitate identification by the blind.

Booklet Cylinder Numbers

Pane No.	Cyl. No.	Phos. No.	Die-cut perf.
WP1498	1(×5)	1	18·00

2003 "Occasions" Greetings stamps

From £1.62 Barcode Booklet PM8

Pane comprising 2×(1st) UM139 printed in gravure with two bands (blue fluor) and 4×(1st) 2 bands, Machin (gold). No. UJQ3 die-cut perf. 15×14 (E), self-adhesive. Nos. UM139 die-cut perforation 15×14.

UMP140 (Actual size 154x56mm.)

UMP140	(containing Nos. UM139×2, UJQ3x4) (4.3.03)	16·00

No. PM9 was initially sold at £1·62. A notch at top right of the cover, when closed, was to facilitate identification by the blind.

Booklet Cylinder Numbers

Pane No.	Cyl. No.	Phos. No.	Die-cut perf.
UMP140	1(×5)	1	20·00

2003 Extreme Endeavours

From £1.68 Barcode Booklet PM9

Pane comprising 2×(1st) printed in gravure with two bands (blue fluor) and 4×(1st) 2 bands, Machin (gold). No. UJD1 die-cut perf. 15×14 (E), self-adhesive. No. W1553 die-cut perforation 14½.

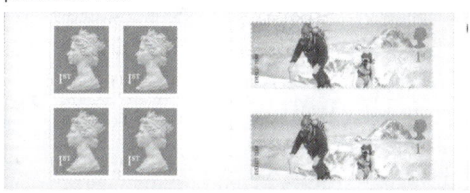

WP1554 (Actual size 154x56mm.)

WP1554	(containing Nos. W1553×2, UJD1x4) (2.4.03)	15·00

No. PM9 was initially sold at £1·62, £1·68 From 8.5.03. A notch at top right of the cover, when closed, was to facilitate identification by the blind.

Booklet Cylinder Numbers

Pane No.	Cyl. No.	Phos. No.	Die-cut perf.
WP1554	D1(×5)	D1	18·00

2003 A British Journey: Scotland

From £1.68 Barcode Booklet PM10

Pane comprising 2×(1st) W1585 printed in gravure with two bands (blue fluor) and 4×(1st) 2 bands, Machin (gold). No. UJQ3 die-cut perf. 15×14 (E), self-adhesive. No. W1585 die-cut perforation 14½.

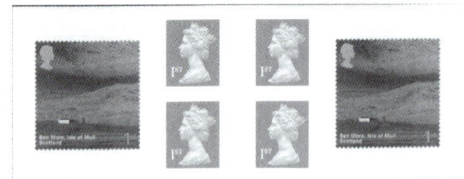

UJ Decimal self-adhesive issues *Booklet panes*

WP1586 (Actual size 154x56 mm.)

WP1586	(containing Nos. W1585×2, UJQ3x4)	
	(15.7.03)	15·00

No. PM10 was initially sold at £1·68. A notch at top right of the cover, when closed, was to facilitate identification by the blind.

Booklet Cylinder Numbers

Pane No.	Cyl. No.	Phos. No.	Die-cut perf.
WP1586	D1(×6)	D1	18·00

2003 Classic Transport Toys

From £1.68 Barcode Booklet PM11

Pane comprising 2×(1st) W1600 printed in gravure with two bands (blue fluor) and 4×(1st) 2 bands, Machin (gold). No. UJQ3 die-cut perf. 15×14 (E), self-adhesive. Nos. W1600 die-cut perforation 14½×14.

WP1601 (Actual size 154x56 mm.)

WP1601	(containing Nos. W1600×2, UJQ3x4) (18.9.03)	5·00

No. PM11 was initially sold at £1·68. A notch at top right of the cover, when closed, was to facilitate identification by the blind.

Booklet Cylinder Numbers

Pane No.	Cyl. No.	Phos. No.	Die-cut perf.
WP1601	D1(×6)	D1	18·00

2004 A British Journey: Northern Ireland

From £1.68 Barcode Booklet PM12

Pane comprising 2×(1st) W1644 printed in gravure with two bands (blue fluor) and 4×(1st) 2 bands, Machin (gold). No. UJQ3 die-cut perf. 15×14 (E), self-adhesive. No. W1644 die-cut perforation 14½.

WP1645 (Actual size 154x56 mm.)

WP1645	(containing Nos. W1644×2, UJQ3x4)	
	(16.3.04)	15·00

No. PM12 was initially sold at £1·68. A notch at top right of the cover, when closed, was to facilitate identification by the blind.

Booklet Cylinder Numbers

Pane No.	Cyl. No.	Phos. No.	Die-cut perf.
WP1645	D1(×6)	D1	18·00

2004 Ocean Liners

From £1.68 Barcode Booklet PM13

Pane comprising 2×(1st) W1655 printed in gravure with two bands (blue fluor) and 4×(1st) 2 bands, Machin (gold). No. UJD1 die-cut perf. 15×14 (E), self-adhesive. Nos. W1655 die-cut perforation 14½×14.

WP1656 (Actual size 154x56 mm.)

WP1656	(containing Nos. 1655×2, UJD1x4) (13.4.04)	15·00

No. PM13 was initially sold at £1·68. A notch at top right of the cover, when closed, was to facilitate identification by the blind.

Booklet Cylinder Numbers

Pane No.	Cyl. No.	Phos. No.	Die-cut perf.
WP1677	D1(×6)	D1	18·00

The gold Machin stamp and gold booklet cover was printed from two separate cylinders

2004 A British Journey: Wales

From £1.68 Barcode Booklet PM14

Pane comprising 2×(1st) W1676 printed in gravure "all over" phosphor (blue fluor) and 4×(1st) 2 bands, Machin (gold). No. UJD1 die-cut perf. 15×14 (E), self-adhesive. Nos. W1676 die-cut perforation 14½.

WP1677 (Actual size 154x56 mm.)

WP1677	(containing Nos. W1676×2, UJD1x4) (15.6.04)	15·00

No. PM14 was initially sold at £1·68. A notch at top right of the cover, when closed, was to facilitate identification by the blind.

Booklet Cylinder Numbers

Pane No.	Cyl. No.	Phos. No.	Die-cut perf.
WP1677	D1(×6)	D1	18·00

The gold Machin stamp and gold booklet cover was printed from two separate cylinders

2008 Beside the Seaside

From £2.16 Barcode Booklet PM15

Pane comprising 2×(1st) W2044 printed in gravure with phosphor bands (blue fluor) and 4×(1st) 2 bands, Machin (gold). Machin (1st) No. UJW8 die-cut perf. 15×14 (E) self-adhesive. No. W2044 die-cut perforation 14½.

Decimal self-adhesive issues *Booklet panes* **UJ**

WP2045 (Actual size 154x56mm.)

WP2045 (containing Nos. W2044×2, UJW8x4) (13.5.08)   5·00

No. PM15 was initially sold at £2·16. A notch at top right of the cover, when closed, was to facilitate identification by the blind.

Shade variations which do not affect the stamps, exist in the ochre background at the bottom left and right corners of the opened booklet. There were no cylinder numbers

2009 Design Classics (1st Issue)

From £2.16 Barcode Booklet PM16

Pane comprising 2×(1st) W2127/8 printed in gravure with phosphor background (blue fluor) and 4×(1st) 2 bands, Machin (gold). Machin (1st) No. UJW11 die-cut perf. 15×14 (E), U-shaped cuts, iridescent overprint and self-adhesive. Nos. W2127/8 die-cut perforation 14½.

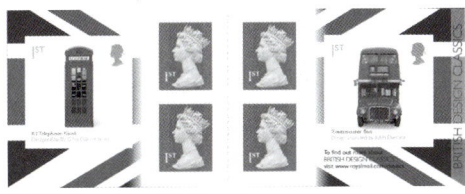

WP2129 (Actual size 154x56mm.)

WP2129 (containing Nos. W2127/28, UJW11x4) (10.3.09)   5·00

No. PM16 was initially sold at £2·16, £2·34 from 6.4.09. A notch at top right of the cover, when closed, was to facilitate identification by the blind.

Booklet Cylinder Numbers

Pane No.	Cyl. No.	Phos. No.	Die-cut perf.
WP2129	W1(×7)	W1	7·00

The cylinder numbers were printed reading left to right, below the three lines of text on the inside right panel.

2009 Design Classics (2nd issue)

From £2.34 Barcode Booklet PM17

Pane comprising 2×(1st) W2132 printed in gravure with phosphor background (blue fluor) and 4×(1st) 2 bands, Machin (gold). Machin (1st) No. UJW11 die-cut perf. 15×14 (E), U-shaped cuts, iridescent overprint and self-adhesive. No. W2130 die-cut perforation 14½.

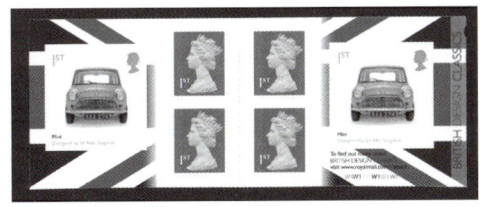

WP2131 (Actual size 154x56mm.)

WP2131 (containing No. W2132x2, UJW11x4) (21.4.09)   5·00

No. PM17 was initially sold at £2·34. A notch at top right of the cover, when closed, was to facilitate identification by the blind.

Booklet Cylinder Numbers

Pane No.	Cyl. No.	Phos. No.	Die-cut perf.
WP2131	W1(×7)	W1	7·00

The cylinder numbers were printed reading left to right, below the three lines of text on the inside right panel.

2009 50th Anniversary of NAFAS

From £2.34 Barcode Booklet PM18

Pane comprising 2×(1st) UM175/6 printed in gravure with phosphor background (blue fluor) and 4×(1st) 2 bands, Machin (gold). Machin (1st) No. UJW11 die-cut perf. 15×14 (E), U-shaped cuts, iridescent overprint and self-adhesive. Nos. UM175/6 die-cut perforation 14(E).

UMP177 (Actual size 154x56mm.)

WP2129 (containing Nos. W2127/28, UJW11x4) (10.3.09)   5·00

No. PM18 was initially sold at £2·34. A notch at top right of the cover, when closed, was to facilitate identification by the blind.

Booklet Cylinder Numbers

Pane No.	Cyl. No.	Phos. No.	Die-cut perf.
UMP177	W1(×7)	W1	7·00

The cylinder numbers were printed reading left to right, below the three lines of text on the inside right panel below No. UM176.

2009 Design Classics (3rd issue)

From £2.34 Barcode Booklet PM19

Pane comprising 2×(1st) W2167 printed in gravure with phosphor background (blue fluor) and 4×(1st) 2 bands, Machin (gold). Machin (1st) No. UJW11 die-cut perf. 15×14 (E), U-shaped cuts, iridescent overprint and self-adhesive. No. W2167 die-cut perforation 14½.

WP2168 (Actual size 154x56mm.)

WP2168 (containing Nos. W2167×2, UJW11x4) (18.8.09)   5·00

No. PM19 was initially sold at £2·34. A notch at top right of the cover, when closed, was to facilitate identification by the blind.

Booklet Cylinder Numbers

Pane No.	Cyl. No.	Phos. No.	Die-cut perf.
WP2168	W1(×7)	W1	7·00

The cylinder numbers were printed reading left to right, below the three lines of text on the inside right panel below No. W2167.

2009 Design Classics (4th issue)

Printed by WALSALL

From £2.34 Barcode Booklet PM20

Pane comprising 2×(1st) W2186 printed in gravure with phosphor background (blue fluor) and 4×(1st) 2 bands, Machin (gold). Machin (1st) No. UJW11 die-cut perf. 15×14 (E), U-shaped cuts, iridescent overprint and self-adhesive. No. W2186 die-cut perforation 14½.

WP2187	(containing Nos. W2186/×2, UJW11x4)	
	(17.9.09)	5·00

No. PM20 was initially sold at £2·34. A notch at top right of the cover, when closed, was to facilitate identification by the blind.

Booklet Cylinder Numbers

Pane No.	Cyl. No.	Phos. No.	Die-cut perf.
WP2187	W1(×7)	W1	7·00

The cylinder numbers were printed reading left to right, below the three lines of text on the inside right panel below No. 2186.

Business Sheets

Spec. No	Date of Issue	Value	Printer	Source Spec. No.
BS1	22.6.98	2nd	Walsall	UJW2
BS2	22.6.98	1st	Walsall	UJW3
BS3	4.9.00	2nd	Walsall	UJW4
BS4	4.9.00	1st	Questa	UJQ1
BS5	9.5.02	2nd	Enschedé	UJE3
BS6	9.5.02	1st	Enschedé	UJE4
BS7	4.7.02	2nd	Enschedé	UJE3
BS8	4.7.02	1st	Enschedé	UJE5
BS9	18.3.03	2nd	Walsall	UJW4a
BS10	18.3.03	1st	Walsall	UJW6
BS11	15.6.04	2nd	Walsall	UJW4a
BS12	15.6.04	1st	Walsall	UJW6
BS13	16.5.06	2nd	Walsall	UJW4a
BS14	16.5.06	1st	Walsall	UJW6
BS15	12.9.06	2nd	Walsall PiP	UJW15
BS16	12.9.06	1st	Walsall PiP	UJW16
BS17	27.3.07	2nd L	Walsall PiP	UJW13
BS18	27.3.07	1st L	Walsall PiP	UJW14
BS19	5.6.07	2nd	Walsall	UJW4a
BS20	5.6.07	1st	Walsall	UJW6
BS21	31.3.09	2nd	De La Rue	UJD6
BS22	31.3.09	1st	De La Rue	UJD7
BS23	31.3.09	2nd L	De La Rue	UJD8
BS24	31.3.09	1st L	De La Rue	UJD9

Nos. BS1/8 had the matrix intact but from 2003 the matrix was removed.

Sheet of 100 1st class stamps printed by Walsall

The 2nd and 1st class self-adhesive stamps were supplied folded between each horizontal row of three stamps and the top row. This was developed from a prototype sheet which had the Walsall imprint and W I (x 3) at bottom left and may have been trimmed off the issued sheets.

This was a double pane printing on the Chesnut press. There were four colour cylinders for the Royal Mail logo at the top, another cylinder for the stamps, 2nd or Ist class plus a cylinder applying the phosphor bands. The centre of the web was rouletted which meant that sheets of 100 (above) with left side cut smooth would have been from the left (no dot) and those with a right-hand side cut smooth would be the dot pane.

Dates of printing. In addition to printing dates Nos. BS5 had warrant numbers 261, 268 and BS6 had warrants 260 and 267. These occur on the bottom panels of 24 stamps. price 2nd class £15 and 1st class £18 each block of 24 stamps.

Top panels. From February 2002, Nos. BS5/6 the top face panels had the inkjet date of printing. We do not price these individually and give the earliest recorded date known to us.

2nd class	1st class
BS5 from 07/02/02	BS6 from 15/02/02
BS7 from 14/05/02	BS8 from 21/05/02
BS9 from 8/02/03	BS10 from 12/02/03
BS11 from 30/03/04	BS12 from 24/05/04
BS13 from 16/03/06	BS14 from 21/03/06
BS15 from 18/07/06	BS16 from 20/07/06
BS17 from 24/01/07	BS18 from 22/01/07
BS19 from 17/04/07	BS20 from 17/04/07
BS21 from 13/01/09	BS22 from 11/12/08
BS23 from 18/01/09	BS24 from 19/01/09

Matrix intact undated

Spec No.	Date of issue	Value	Printer	Source Spec. No.	Top panel
BS1	22.6.98	2nd	Walsall	UJW2	50·00
BS2	22.6.98	1st	Walsall	UJW3	50·00

Sold out 12.99

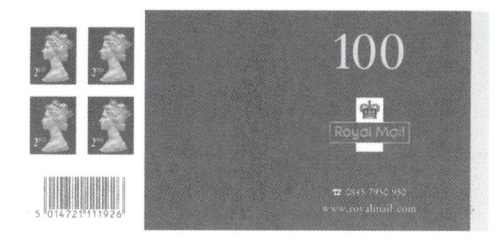

Matrix intact undated

Spec No.	Date of issue	Value	Printer	Source Spec. No.	Top panel
BS3	4.9.00	2nd	Walsall	UJW4	25·00
BS4	4.9.00	1st	Questa	UJQ1	40·00

Matrix intact undated

Spec No.	Date of issue	Value	Printer	Source Spec. No.	Top panel
BS5	9.5.02	2nd	Enschedé	UJE3	17·00
BS6	9.5.02	1st	Enschedé	UJE4	17·00

Matrix intact undated

Spec No.	Date of issue	Value	Printer	Source Spec. No.	Top panel
BS7	4.7.02	2nd	Enschedé	UJE3	15·00
BS8	4.7.02	1st	Enschedé	UJE5	15·00

Matrix removed dated

Spec No.	Date of issue	Value	Printer	Source Spec. No.	Top panel
BS9	18.3.03	2nd	Walsall	UJW5	10·00
BS10	18.3.03	1st	Walsall	UJW6	12·00

Matrix removed dated

Spec No.	Date of issue	Value	Printer	Source Spec. No.	Top panel
BS11	15.6.04	2nd	Walsall	UJW4a	10·00
BS12	15.6.04	1st	Walsall	UJW6	12·00

A single sheet of BS11 was discovered with the bright blue colour omitted, resulting in a blank top panel (apart from the Royal Mail logo) and blank labels in place of the stamps. The phosphor was present, but displaced approximately 8mm to the right, resulting in some labels having a single band at right and others having two thin bands. The Royal Mail logo and barcode were also shifted to the right, eith an incomplete barcode appearing in the top-panel label.

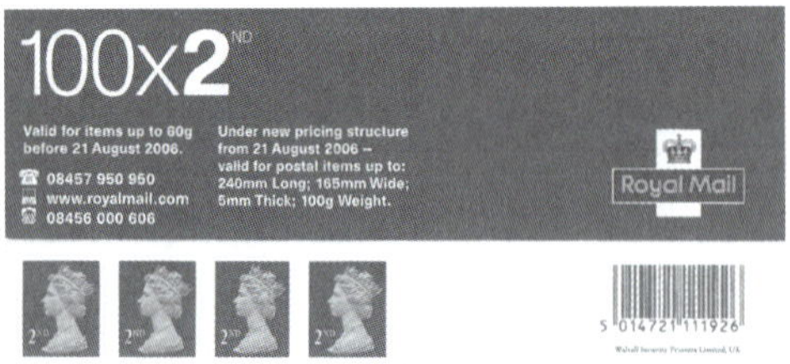

UJ Decimal self-adhesive issues *Business sheets*

Matrix removed dated

Spec No.	Date of issue	Value	Printer	Source Spec. No.	Top panel
BS13	16.5.04	2nd	Walsall	UJW4a	10·00
BS14	16.5.04	1st	Walsall	UJW6	12·00

Matrix removed dated

Spec No.	Date of issue	Value	Printer	Source Spec. No.	Top panel
BS15	12.9.06	2nd	Walsall Pip	UJW15	10·00
BS16	12.9.06	1st	Walsall PiP	UJW16	12·00

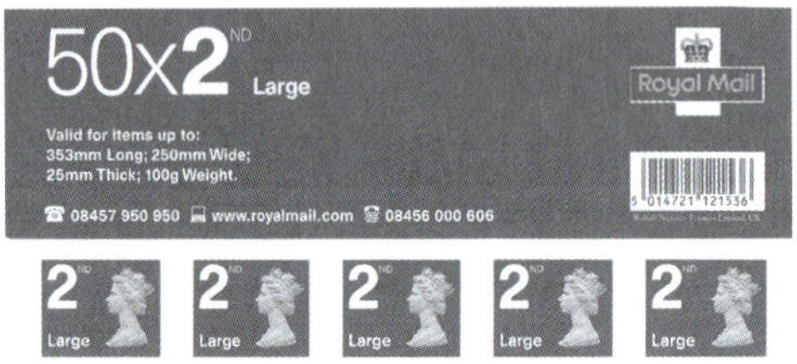

Matrix removed dated

Spec No.	Date of issue	Value	Printer	Source Spec. No.	Top panel
BS17	27.3.07	2nd	Walsall	UJW13	10·00
BS18	27.3.07	1st	Walsall	UJW14	12·00

Matrix removed dated

Spec No.	Date of issue	Value	Printer	Source Spec. No.	Top panel
BS19	5.6.07	2nd	Walsall	UJW4a	10·00
BS20	5.6.07	1st	Walsall	UJW6	12·00

Security issue code "B"

Matrix removed dated

Spec No.	Date of issue	Value	Printer	Source Spec. No.	Top panel
BS21	31.3.09	2nd	De La Rue	UJD6	10·00
BS22	31.3.09	1st	De La Rue	UJD7	12·00

Security issue code "B" inscribed "Large"

Matrix removed dated

Spec No.	Date of issue	Value	Printer	Source Spec. No.	Top panel
BS23	31.3.09	2nd	De La Rue	UJD8	12·00
BS24	31.3.09	1st	De La Rue	UJD9	15·00

SECTION UK
Decimal Castles Issues
1988-97. High Values. Recess-printed

General Notes

Introduction. This issue was adapted from photographs taken by H.R.H. The Duke of York. The dies were engraved by Chris Matthews and the stamps were printed by Harrison & Sons Limited on their Giori press.

Printers. When it was decided to change from the large high value Machins in 1987 Harrison retained the contract until it expired in 1997. Enschedé were asked to keep the same designs, but they made small changes which are described before numbers UK18/21. The series was finally withdrawn in August 2000 when Machins, printed in recess, had replaced them.

Paper and fluorescent ink. Prior to 1992 the stamps were all on fluorescent coated paper without watermark. Variations in the amount of fluorescent or brightening agent are apparent, but this is within standards and varieties of this kind are not listed. A glossy surface on printings of the £1·50 and £2 values has been recorded in combination with weak fluorescent reaction.

The second issue of 24 March 1992 was printed on non-fluorescent coated paper but with fluorescent ink which, under ultraviolet light appears as green to lemon. The Queen's head was printed in optically variable ink which changes colour from gold to green when viewed from different angles.

Perforation. All stamps in this Section are perforated 15 × 14. Top and bottom margins are perforated through and side margins have a single extension hole opposite each horizontal row. The vertical and horizontal gutter margins separating the four panes of 25 stamps are perforated across their width.

The perforation gauge remained at 15 × 14 when an elliptical perforation hole was introduced in the centre of each vertical edge. On the Enschedé issue the elliptical hole was moved up by a single perforation. Harrison show 9 holes up and Enschedé 10.

Elliptical perforation and extension hole at left 9 holes from bottom

Gum. PVAD with greenish dye additive was used at first, but PVA (white back) was gradually introduced from March 1996.

Sheet layout. All values were issued in sheets of 100 (4 panes of 5 × 5) with `TOTAL SHEET VALUE' inscriptions repeated four times in the horizontal margins reading left to right at top and right to left (upside down) at base. A colour band printed in the colour of the stamp is printed horizontally on the central gutter as these are stamp-size. A boxed guide hole which is unpunched appears opposite row 2 in the right-hand vertical margin.

Plates. A master die was used to make a 5 × 5 pane of 25 impressions. This produced a master sheet plate of 100. Any flaws and retouch marks introduced on the pane of 25 was repeated in identical positions on all four panes. Printing plates were made from it and each was lettered sequentially. Any re-entries or flaws made on the master plate sheet will therefore only be found once in the printed sheet of 100 impressions. Plate numbers missing from the issued series were probably prepared but were found unsuitable for printing and rejected. Plate numbers are added to the plates and this explains the positional variations and the different style from solid colour to a dot pattern. Plate number blocks of four including the Harrison logo are from the bottom left-hand corner of the sheet.

The issue with the Queen's head printed in optically variable ink was first issued on 24 March 1992. The following enlarged illustration shows the Queen's head was changed when the re-etched printings were introduced.

Original   Re-etched

Re-Etched Printings. In August 1994 the £5 re-etched printing appeared and was followed by three other values by the end of the year. The Queen's head on the original stamps shows heavy horizontal lines and the diamond-shaped holes appear to be on their sides in horizontal rows. The re-etched printings show no clearly defined lines in the gold shading and the diamond-shaped holes are vertical on one point. On the re-etched stamps it appears that the pattern was starting to break as shown in the enlarged illustration above.

Individual Values

£1 The first boat at the left shows a very faint split windscreen on the original, but the re-etched stamp shows this as a very clear line.

£1·50. The window on the first floor above "C" of "CAERNARFON" is shown as six windows above two vertical openings. These are formed by three vertical lines. In the re-etched stamp all these windows are blobs of colour.

£2 In the centre of the stamp the sloping bank below the castle is shown as oblique lines which are broken only by a row of vertical lines. The re-etched stamp shows the oblique lines broken and patchy.

£5 The trees in the bottom left corner have 45 degree shading on the original stamp. This shading is not apparent in the re-etched version as the trees obscure these fine lines altogether. The point above the "L" of "CASTLE" is another place to check this difference.

UK Decimal Castles issues

Dates of Issue. We have used the dates as they appeared on the Philatelic Bureau stock lists. We are aware that earlier dates may be known from used examples.

UK1. Carrickfergus Castle
UK2. Caernarfon Castle 
UK3. Edinburgh Castle 
UK4. Windsor Castle 

(Des. from photographs by Prince Andrew. Duke of York. Eng. Chris Matthews and recess-printed by Harrison)

£1 Type UK1 (1988)

1988 (18 October). FCP/PVAD gum

UK1 (=SG 1410)

UK1	Deep green	4·25	0·60

Plate Numbers (Blocks of Four)

Pl. No.	
1B	35·00
1C	35·00
1D	22·00
1E	22·00
1F	22·00
1G	18·00
1H	£150
1I	18·00
1J	18·00
1K	30·00
1M	18·00
1N	18·00
1O	32·00
1P	18·00
1Q	2400
1R	20·00
1S	24·00
1T	27·00

Minor Constant Flaws: Some of the following varieties are repeated within the sheet of 100 impressions. The same flaw may also occur on succeeding plates but the list is not complete and we have noted only those varieties which appear to be constant.
 £1 Plate 1C
 3/3 Diagonal scratch above third R in CARRICKFERGUS
 3/8 As R. 3/3
 8/3 As R. 3/3
 8/8 As R. 3/3
 5/4 Thin vertical scratch above T in CASTLE
 5/9 As R. 5/4
 10/4 As R. 5/4

Plates 1C, ID, 1E
9/2 Small thickness at the inner centre of C of CASTLE

£1.50 Type UK2 (1988)

1988 (18 October). FCP/PVAD gum

UK2 (=SG 1411)

UK2	Maroon	4·50	1·25

Examples of No. UK2 from plates 2F and 2G exist on paper with a glossy or glazed surface. *Price £10, mint.*

Plate Numbers (Blocks of Four)

Pl. No.	
2A	18·00
2B	22·00
2D	18·00
2E	18·00
2F	18·00
2G	18·00
2H	20·00
2I	20·00
2J	18·00
3A	22·00
4A	18·00
4B	18·00

£2 Type UK3 (1988)

1988 (18 October). FCP/PVAD gum

UK3 (=SG 1412)

UK3	Indigo	8·00	1·50

Examples of No. UK3 from plates 1G and 1H exist with a weak fluorescent reaction and a glossy surface to the paper. *Price £175, mint.* Plate blocks of four price 1G £800, 1H £1250 each

Plate Numbers (Blocks of Four)

Pl. No.	
1C	50·00
1D	32·00
1E	32·00
1F	32·00
1G	55·00
1H	55·00
1I	£125
2M	35·00
2N	32·00
2O	32·00
2P	32·00
2Q	32·00
2R	32·00
2S	32·00
2T	32·00
2U	35·00
2V	50·00

£5 Type UK4 (1988)

1988 (18 October). FCP/PVAD gum

UK4 (=SG 1413)

UK4	Deep brown	21·00	5·50

Plate Numbers (Blocks of Four)

Decimal Castles issues UK

Pl. No.	
1C	80·00
1D	80·00
1E	80·00
1F	80·00
1G	80·00

Quantities Sold: £1 101,259,400; £1·50 50,467,200; £2 80,303,200; £5 34,181,500

Withdrawn: 23 March 1992

UK5. Carrickfergus Castle
UK6. Caernarfon Castle

UK7. Edinburgh Castle
UK8. Windsor Castle

(Des. from photographs by Prince Andrew, Duke of York. Eng Chris Matthews and recess-printed by Harrison)

Note: The following all have the Queen's head printed in optically variable ink which changes colour from gold to green when viewed from different angles.
Nos. UK5/14 are perf. 15×14 with one elliptical perf. hole on each vertical edge

£1 Type UK5 (1992-94)

1992 (24 March). Non-fluorescent coated paper. PVAD gum

UK5 (=SG 1611)

UK5	Bottle green and gold	5·50	1·00
	b. Inverted perforation		

Plate 2A was perforated with nine holes above the ellipse instead of the normal ten. One sheet is known. This was the way Enschedé perforated their sheets but they did not print the £1 value.

Plate Numbers (Blocks of Four)

Pl. No.	
1A	22·00
1B	24·00
1C	22·00
1D	
1E	
1H	
1I	
1J	26·00
1K	
1L	
1M	26·00
1O	28·00
1P	22·00
1Q	22·00
1R	24·00
1S	24·00
1T	24·00
1U	26·00
2A	26·00
2B	85·00
2C	
2D	27·00
2E	27·00
2F	26·00
2G	26·00
2H	
2I	22·00
2K	
2L	22·00

Later printings of Plate 1B show remains of "2A" engraved in error (same price). A dot appeared after plate 1C.
One example pf plate 1E is in the Royal Collection.

1994 (6 December). Re-etched printing. Non-fluorescent paper//PVAD gum

UK6	Bottle green and gold	10·00	3·50

Plate Numbers (Blocks of Four)

Pl. No.	
3A	£130
3B	80·00
3C	40·00
3E	40·00
3F	40·00
3G	40·00
3H	40·00
3I	40·00
3J	40·00
3K	40·00

Withdrawn: 30 August 1996

£1.50 Type UK6 (1992–96)

1992 (24 March). Non-fluorescent coated paper. PVAD gum

UK7 (=SG 1612)

UK7	Maroon and gold	6·00	1·20

Plate Numbers (Blocks of Four)

Pl. No.	
2A	24·00
2B	24·00
2C	24·00
2D	24·00
2H	28·00
2I	24·00
2J	26·00
2K	24·00
2L	50·00
2M	24·00
2N	24·00
2O	35·00
2P	28·00
2Q	24·00
2R	24·00

UK Decimal Castles issues

Pl. No.	Price
2S	50·00
2T	72·00
2U	£225
2V	24·00
2X	28·00
2Y	26·00
2Z	24·00
2AA	30·00

1994 (1 November). Re-etched printing. Non-fluorescent coated paper.

A. PVAD gum

UK8	Maroon and gold		8·00	1·50

Plate Numbers (Blocks of Four)

Pl. No.	Price
2DD	32·00
2EE	32·00
2FF	42·00
2GG	42·00
2II	£300
2LL	£300
4A	£100
4B	32·00
4C	40·00
4D	32·00
4E	32·00
4F	32·00
4G	£225
4H	32·00
4I	
4J	32·00
4K	35·00
4L	32·00
4M	38·00

B. PVA GUM (5 March 1996)

UK9	Maroon and gold		8·00

Plate Numbers (Blocks of Four)

Pl. No.	Price
4J	£100
4L	£100
4M	£100
4N	32·00
4O	32·00
4P	32·00

Withdrawn: No. UK7. 30 August 1996; Nos. UK8/9, 1 December 1997

£2 Type UK7 (1992–96)

1992 (24 March). Non-fluorescent coated paper. PVAD gum

UK10 (=SG 1613)

UK10	Indigo and gold		8·00	1·20

Plate Numbers (Blocks of Four)

Pl. No.	Price
2A	32·00
2B	35·00
2C	32·00
2D	32·00
2E	£900
2I	40·00
2L	40·00
2M	24·00
2N	32·00
2O	42·00
2P	38·00
2Q	55·00
2R	32·00
2S	32·00
2T	35·00
2U	40·00
2V	35·00
2W	40·00
2X	48·00
2Z	35·00
2BB	38·00
2CC	32·00
2DD	32·00
2EE	32·00

1994 (25 November). Re-etched printing. Non-fluorescent coated paper..

A. PVAD gum

UK11	Indigo and gold		10·00	2·00

Plate Numbers (Blocks of Four)

Pl. No.	Price
3A	£375
3B	75·00
3C	£2500
3D	£110
3E	40·00
3F	40·00
3H	£250
3I	50·00
3J	42·00
3K	80·00
3L	40·00
4A	£275
4C	45·00
4D	42·00
4E	42·00
4F	42·00

B. PVA gum (2 May 1996)

UK12	Indigo and gold		10·00

Plate Numbers (Blocks of Four)

Pl. No.	Price
4C	75·00
4F	40·00
4G	40·00
4I	45·00
4J	40·00
4K	50·00

Withdrawn: No. UK10, 30 October 1996; Nos. UK11/12, 1 December 1997

£3 Type UK5 (1995)

1995 (22 August). Non-fluorescent coated paper.

UK13 (=SG 1613a)

A. PVAD gum

UK13	Reddish violet and gold	19·00	3·00

Plate Numbers (Blocks of Four)

Pl. No.	
1A	75·00
1B	£100
1C	£125
1D	75·00
1E	80·00
1G	80·00
1H	85·00
1I	85·00
1J	75·00
1K	75·00
1L	75·00
1M	75·00

B. PVA gum (2.97)

UK14	Reddish violet and gold	50·00

No. UK14 was first reported in February 1997 and did not appear on Bureau stock lists.

Plate Numbers (Blocks of Four)

Pl. No.	
1L	£200
1M	£200

Withdrawn: 1 December 1997

£5 Type UK8 (1992–94)

1992 (24 March). Non-fluorescent coated paper. PVAD gum

UK15 (=SG 1614)

UK15	Deep brown and gold	18·00	3·00
	a. Gold (Queen's head) omitted	£450	

No. UK15a was from plate 2A.

Plate Numbers (Blocks of Four)

Pl. No.	
2A	75·00
2B	75·00
2C	72·00
2D	72·00
4B	
4D	75·00
4E	75·00
4F	80·00
4G	£325

Plates 2A and 2B both show "1" below A and "11" BELOW 2B.
Minor Constant Flaw: 6/5 Blob to left of third window below battlements of castle. This flaw was later removed.

1994 (August). Re-etched printing. Non-fluorescent coated paper.

A. PVAD gum

UK16	Deep brown and gold	18·00	3·00

Plate Numbers (Blocks of Four)

Pl. No.	
5B	£600
5C	£600
5F	75.00
5G	75.00
5O	75.00
5P	75.00
7B	75.00
7C	75.00
7D	75.00
7E	£225

B. PVA gum (17.9.96)

UK17	Deep brown and gold	18·00

Plate Numbers (Blocks of Four)

Pl. No.	
7D	75·00
7E	75·00

Withdrawn: No. UK15, 28 February 1997; Nos. UK16/17, 1 December 1997

Presentation Packs

UKPP1 No. 17 (18.10.88) £1., £1·50., £2., £5	35·00
UKPP2 No. 27 (24.3.92) £1,. £1·50., £2., £5	38·00
UKPP3 No. 33 (22.8.95) £3	30·00

Withdrawn: No. UKPP1. 23 March 1992; Nos. UKPP2/3, 31 December 1998

First Day Covers

On official cover prepared and issued by the Post Office and stamps franked with a commemorative postmark.

UKFD1 (18.10.88) £1., £1·50., £2., £5	35·00
UKFD2 (24.3.92) £1., £1·50., £2., £5	35·00
UKFD3 (22.8.95) £3	10·00

PHQ Cards

UKC1 (Nos. UK5. 7, 10, 14)	15·00	15·00
UKC2 (No. UK13)	10·00	25·00

The cards of No. UKC1 were released on 16 February 1993 and therefore do not exist used on the first day of issue of the stamps depicted. There was a "First Day of Sale" handstamp available at Windsor for these cards.

Printed by Enschedé

UK9. Caernarfon Castle   UK10. Edinburgh Castle

UK Decimal Castles issues

UK11. Carrickfergus Castle UK12. Windsor Castle

(Des. from photographs by Prince Andrew, Duke of York. Eng. Inge Madlé. Recess (Queen's head by silk screen process) by Enschedé)

Note: Types UK9/12 have the Queen's head printed in optically variable ink which changes colour from gold to green when viewed from different angles

Nos. UK18/21 are perf. 15 × 14 with one elliptical perf. hole on each vertical edge. As Nos. UK5/17 but the elliptical hole is a single perforation higher

Differences between Harrison and Enschedé: Harrison "C" has top serif and tail of letter points to right. "A" has flat top. "S" has top and bottom serifs

Enschedé "C" has no top serif and tail of letter points upwards. "A" has pointed top. "S" has no serifs

CASTLE
Harrison Plates (Nos. UK5/17)

CASTLE
Enschedé Plates (Nos. UK 18/20)

Sheet layout and markings. Similar to Harrison with 100 stamps arranged in 4 panes (5 × 5) separated by a horizontal and vertical gutter margin. The horizontal gutter was printed with a 2 mm. wide band in the colour of the stamps. The "Total Sheet Value" inscription was repeated four times on the sheet reading from left to right above and below vertical rows 2/4 and 7/9.

Small traffic light colour dots were printed in the right margin opposite horizontal row 2, showing the design colour first and the head plate colour below. Plate numbers were in the left margin opposite row 9 with the metallic colour above. The imprint, reading up, was opposite row 10 "Joh. Enschedé Stamps" in one line. Therefore the sheets resemble those of Harrison but the "Total Sheet Value" inscription in the bottom margin was upright instead of inverted. The plate blocks occupied the same position for both printers.

■ £1.50 Type UK9 (1997)

Printed by Enschedé'

1997 (29 July). Re-engraved. Non-fluorescent coated paper. PVA gum

UK18 (=SG 1993)

UK18	Deep claret and gold	12·00	6·00
	a. Gold (Queen's head) omitted	—	£1850

Plate Numbers (Blocks of Four)
Pl. No.
1A, 1A   50·00

Withdrawn: 4 August 2000

■ £2 Type UK10 (1997)

Printed by Enschedé

1997 (29 July). Re-engraved. Non-fluorescent coated paper. PVA gum

UK19 (=SG 1994)

UK19	Indigo and gold ..	14·00	2·25
	a. Gold (Queen's head) omitted	£750	

Plate Numbers (Blocks of Four)
Pl. No.
1A, 1A   55·00

Withdrawn: 4 August 2000

■ £3 Type UK11 (1997)

Printed by Enschedé

1997 (29 July). Re-engraved. Non-fluorescent coated paper. PVA gum

UK20 (=SG 1995)

UK20	Violet and gold ..	4·50	4·75
	a. Gold (Queen's head) omitted £2500		

Plate Numbers (Blocks of Four)
Pl. No
1A, 1A   £120

Withdrawn: 4 August 2000

■ £5 Type UK12 (1997)

Printed by Enschedé

1997 (29 July). Re-engraved. Non-fluorescent coated paper. PVA gum

UK21 (=SG 1996)

UK21	Deep brown and gold ..	36·00	10·00
	a. Gold (Queen's head) omitted £5000		

No. UK20a occurred on R. 5/8 and 6/8 from several sheets with foreign matter preventing the gold ink from being printed.

Plate Numbers (Blocks of Four)
Pl. No.
1A, 1A   £140

It is believed that sheets were made available as stocks of the Harrison printing became sold out and an early use date is likely.

Withdrawn: 4 August 2000

Presentation Pack

UKPP4 No. 40 (11.8.98) £1·50., £2., £3., £5	£150

Withdrawn: 4 August 2000

Post Office first day covers were not prepared as the Enschedé values were not treated as a new issue.

SECTION UL
Britannia High Value 1993

General Notes
This stamp was issued primarily for overseas mail. It was the first design to use braille with an embossed figure ten. Other features to counteract imitation and forgery were used, including coloured fibres in the paper, two elliptical perforation holes in the horizontal perforation rows and metallic ink.

Paper. The stamp is printed on paper free of brightening agents, but with fluorescent fibres. The braille ten at right is below the Queen's head.

Perforation. The stamps are perforated (14 x 14½) with two elliptical perforation holes in each horizontal perforation row placed above and below Britannia.

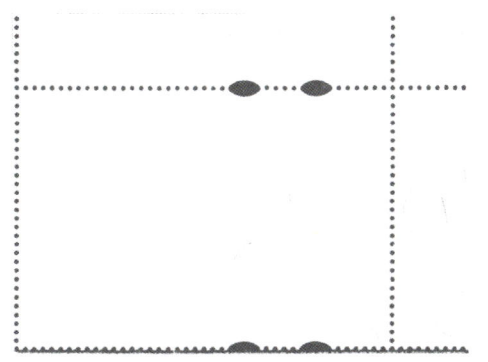

Reverse side showing the two elliptical perforation holes in each row of horizontal perforations

Printing. Printed in lithography and embossed with the Queen's head and 25 stars in silver. Under ultraviolet light the shield is shown printed in fluorescent ink.

Sheet Details
Sheet size: 25 (5 x 5). Single pane sheet-fed

Sheet markings:
Plate numbers: In top margin above vertical columns 1/2
Sheet values: Opposite rows 2/4 reading up at left and down at right
Imprint: In top margin above R. 1/1

Imprint and Plate Numbers

Type UL1

(Des. Barry Craddock, adapted by the Roundel Design Group. Printed by The House of Questa in lithography with the Queen's head and stars die-stamped in silver and braille embossed)

£10 Type UL1 (1993)

1993 (2 March). Granite paper. Perf. 14 × 14½E. PVA gum

UL1 (= S.G.1658)

UL1	Greenish grey, rosine, yellow, new blue, reddish violet, vermilion, violet, bright green and silver	40·00	12·00
	a. Silver omitted		£3700
	b. Braille symbol for "10" omitted		
	c. Fluorescent value (plate 2A)	32·00	

Examples from plate 2A show "Ten Pounds" under ultraviolet light at the bottom right-hand corner.

Plate Numbers (Blocks of Four)

1A (x 10)	60·00
2A (x 10)	£100
3A (x 10)	60·00
4A (x 10)	60·00
5A (x 10)	60·00

Withdrawn: 29 December 2000

Presentation Pack
ULP1 No. 28 (2.3.93) £10   45·00

First Day Cover
On official cover prepared and issued by the Post Office and the stamp franked with a commemorative postmark.
ULFD1 (2.3.93)   25·00

PHQ Card
ULC1 (UL1)8   8·00   60·00

This card was available from 16 February along with a set of cards for Castle High Values issued on 24 March 1992.

UM

SECTION UM
Greetings Stamps

General Notes

Introduction. The basic idea of these issues was to use the stamp with the label on the envelope containing a card or letter. The labels were selected after consultation with greeting card producers; the subjects chosen being the most popular designs for greetings cards. The first issue on 31 January 1989 was in the form of a folded booklet with label panel attached to the stamp pane. This was followed by similar issues all from Greetings Stamp booklets. Since 5 February 1991 the stamps have been inscribed "1st" and are in panes of ten different designs with labels. Stamps with elliptical perforation holes in the vertical edge appeared on 2 February 1993.

During 1997 Walsall changed the formulation from short to long wave phosphor ink.

1989 Greetings stamps

From £1.90 Greetings Booklet FX10

UM1 Rose
UM2 Cupid 
UM3 Yachts 
UM4 Fruit 
UM5 Teddy Bear 

Types UM1/5 were printed horizontally *se-tenant* within the booklet pane

(Des. Philip Sutton)

1989 (31 January). Types UM1/5. Phosphorised (advanced coated) paper. PVAD Gum. Printed in gravure by Harrison. Perf. 15 × 14, reel-fed

UM1 (= SG 1423)

UM1	19p. black, greenish yellow, bright rose, red, new blue, light green and gold..	60	50
	a. Strip of 5. Nos. UM1/5 ..	25·00	25·00

UM2 (= SG 1424)

UM2	19p. black, greenish yellow, bright rose, red, new blue, light green and gold..	60	50

UM3 (= SG 1425)

UM3	19p. black, greenish yellow, bright rose, red, new blue, lightgreen and gold..	60	50

UM4 (= SG 1426)

UM4	19p. black, greenish yellow, bright rose, red, new blue, light green and gold..	60	50

UM5 (= SG 1427)

UM5	19p. black, greenish yellow, bright rose, red, new blue,. light green and gold..	60	50
	First Day Cover (UM1/5)		25·00

Folded *se-tenant* Booklet Pane of Ten 19p.

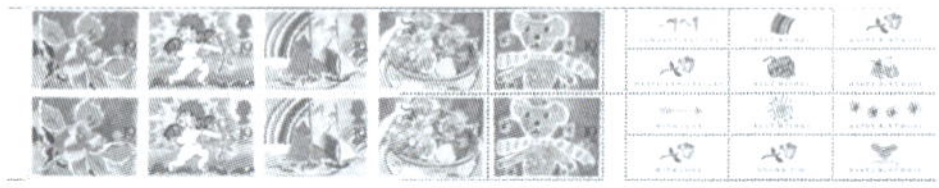

UMP6 Se-tenant pane of 10 with binding margin at left and 12 labels at right (Actual size 331 × 60 mm.)

	Perforation Type E
UMP6 (containing Nos. UM 1/5 × 2) (31.1.89)..	50·00
UMP6A Gutter perforated through (as illustrated)	55·00

These panes have black cutting lines and are folded three times between vertical rows 3/4, 5/6 and 7/8.

No. UMP6 includes the label panel with a gutter margin perforated horizontally at the top and bottom and not across the centre as in the case of No. UMP6A. Both panes are perf. type E with an extension hole in the binding margin opposite each row of stamps.

No. UMP6 exists with half of each design above and below a centre row of complete stamps due to cutting a half stamp width below the trim line.

Booklet Cylinder Numbers

Pane No.	Cyl. Nos. (No dot)	Perforation Type E
UMP6	B1A (black)-B1B (greenish yellow)-B1C (bright rose)-B1D (red)-B1E (new blue)-B1F (light green)-B1G (gold)	55·00
UMP6A	Gutter perforated through (as illustrated)	60·00

Booklet Cylinder Numbers and Sheet Make-up: The stamps and labels were printed by Harrison on the Jumelle press. The printer's uncut sheet contained 11 booklet panes with labels. There were two cylinder numbers (upright) in the left margin opposite panes 5 and 11. The pane opposite position 5 had a short "1" in "B1D". This figure is normal height opposite pane 11.

Prices are the same.
Withdrawn: 30 January 1990

1990 Greetings stamps

From Greetings Booklet KX1

UM7 Teddy Bear
UM8 Dennis the Menace 
UM9 Punch 
UM10 Cheshire Cat 
UM11 Man in the Moon 
UM12 Laughing Policeman 
UM13 Clown 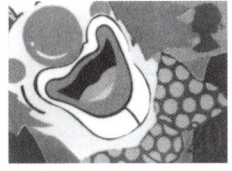
UM14 Mona Lisa 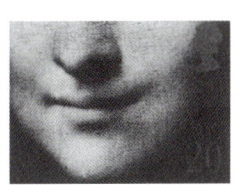
UM15 Queen of Hearts 
UM16 Stan Laurel (comedian) 

Types UM7/16 were printed *se-tenant* in a booklet pane with margins all round. The designs of Type Nos. UM7, 9/11, 13 and 16 extend onto the pane margin.

(Des. Michael Peters and Partners Ltd.)

1990 (6 February). Types UM7/16. "Smiles". Two 4 mm. Phosphor bands. Fluorescent coated paper. PVAD gum

UM7 (= SG 1483)

Printed in gravure by Harrison. Perf. 15 × 14, reel-fed

UM7	20p. gold, greenish yellow, bright rose-red, new blue and grey-black	70	60

UM8 (= SG 1484)

UM8	20p. gold. greenish yellow, bright rose-red, new blue, deep blue and grey-black	70	60

UM9 (SG 1485)

UM9	20p. gold, greenish yellow, bright rose-red, new blue, deep blue and grey-black	70	60

UM10 (= SG 1486)

UM10	20p. gold, greenish yellow, bright rose-red, new blue and grey-black	70	60

UM11 (= SG 1487)

UM 11	20p. gold, greenish yellow, bright rose-red, new blue and grey-black .	70	60

UM12 (= SG 1488)

UM12	20p. gold, greenish yellow, bright rose-red, new blue and gold,	70	60

UM13 (= SG 1489)

UM13	20p. gold, greenish yellow, bright rose-red, new blue and grey-black	70	60

UM14 (= SG 1490)

UM14	20p. gold, greenish yellow, bright rose-red and grey- black	70	60

UM15 (= SG 1491)

UM15	20p. gold. greenish yellow, bright rose-red, new blue and grey-black	70	60

UM16 (= SG 1492)

UM16	20p gold and grey-black	70	60
First Day Cover (UM7/16)			28·00

Folded *se-tenant* Booklet Pane of Ten 20p.

UMP17 *Se-tenant* pane of 10 with margins all round (Actual size 223 × 80 mm.)

Perforation Type P

UMP17 (containing Nos. UM7/16) (6.2.90)	30·00	26·00

These panes are folded once between rows 3/4 in order that they would fit inside the booklet.

Booklet Cylinder Numbers and Sheet Make-up. There were no markings on the margins of the pane. The printer's sheet contained two columns of six panes with cylinder numbers in the left-hand vertical margin opposite pane 4. Crossed lines were set below opposite panes 4/6 which were repeated in the right-hand vertical margin of the sheet. The central gutter margin had traffic light markings between horizontal rows 1 and 4. All markings were placed so that they were removed when the individual panes were guillotined. The traffic light colour dabs were (from top to bottom) greenish yellow, bright rose-red, new blue, deep blue, grey-black and gold. The

UM Greetings Stamps

cylinder numbers were upright in the vertical margin opposite the third pane in the first of the two columns of the sheet. It is understood that those used were: 2A (gold), 1B (greenish yellow), 1C (bright rose-red), ID (new blue), 1E (deep blue), 1F (grey-black), P93 (phosphor). These numbers were trimmed off in production and do not appear on the issued panes.

THE LABELS

Sheet of 12 greetings labels (Actual size 132 × 80 mm.)

The labels were printed by offset-lithography and were loose in the folder. Instances are known where more than one of these sheets were supplied in error. The paper used was Harrison's HS8 clay-coated litho paper with PVAD gum on reverse. Printed on the Roland sheet-fed machine the uncut printer's sheet contained 16 panes (4 × 4). Each pane of 12 labels (4 rows of 3) is inscribed in gold which on pale colours is very distinct; less so on the darker backgrounds. Perforation was by a sheet-fed Grover machine with margins fully perforated through at top and bottom and single extension holes at each side. There were no marginal markings.

Withdrawn: 5 February 1991

1991 Greetings Stamps

From Greetings Barcode Booklet KX2 (£2·40 from 16.9.91). 1991

UM18 Thrush's Nest

UM19 Shooting Star and Rainbow

UM20 Magpies and Charm Bracelet

UM21 Black Cat

UM22 Common Kingfisher with Key

UM23 Mallard and Frog

UM24 Four-leaf Clover in Boot Match Box

UM25 Pot of Gold at End of and Rainbow

UM26 Heart-shaped Butterflies

UM27 Wishing Well and Sixpence

Types UM18/27 were printed *se-tenant* in a booklet pane with margins all round. The backgrounds of the stamps form a composite design.

(Des. Tony Meeuwissen)

1991 (5 February). Types UM18/27. "Good Luck". Two 4 mm. Phosphor bands. Fluorescent coated paper. PVAD gum Printed in gravure by Harrison. Perf. 15 × 14. reel fed

UM18 (= SG 1536)

| UM18 | (1st) silver, greenish yellow, magenta, new blue, olive-brown and black | 75 | 60 |

UM19 (= SG 1537)

| UM19 | (1st) silver, greenish yellow, magenta, new blue, olive-brown and black | 75 | 60 |

UM20 (= SG 1538)

| UM20 | (1st) silver, greenish yellow, magenta, new blue, olive-brown and black | 75 | 60 |

UM21 (= SG 1539)

| UM21 | (1st) silver, greenish yellow, magenta, new blue, olive-brown and black | 75 | 60 |

UM22 (= SG 1540)

| UM22 | (1st) silver, greenish yellow, magenta, new blue, olive-brown and black | 75 | 60 |

UM23 (= SG 1541)

| UM23 | (1st) silver, greenish yellow, magenta, new blue, olive-brown and black | 75 | 60 |

UM24 (= SG 1542)

| UM24 | (1st) silver, greenish yellow, magenta, new blue, olive-brown and black | 75 | 60 |

UM25 (= SG 1543)

| UM25 | (1st) silver, greenish yellow, magenta, new blue, olive-brown and black | 75 | 60 |

Greetings Stamps UM

UM26 (= SG 1544)

UM26	(1st) silver, greenish yellow, magenta, new blue, olive-brown and black	75	60

UM27 (= SG 1545)

UM27	(1st) silver, greenish yellow, magenta, new blue, olive- brown and black	75	60
First Day Cover (UM18/27)			19·00

Folded *se-tenant* booklet pane of ten (1st)

UMP28 *Se-tenant* pane of 10 with binding margin at left and 12 labels at right (Actual size 331 × 69 mm.)

Perforation Type E

UMP28 (containing Nos. UM18/27) (5.2.91)	15·00

These panes are folded four times between vertical rows 1/2, 3/4, 5/6 and 7/8.

Booklet Cylinder Numbers

Pane No.	Cyl. Nos. (No dot)	Perforation Type E
UMP28	B1A (silver)-B1B (greenish yellow)-B2C (magenta)-B1D (new blue)-B1E (olive-brown)-B1F (black)-B90 (phosphor)	20·00

Booklet Cylinder Numbers and Sheet Make-up: The stamps were printed by Harrison on the Jumelle press. The uncut sheet contained 9 booklet panes with labels. The cylinder pane was the fourth pane in the sheet and cutting bars were opposite the gutter margins. The right margin of the sheet was trimmed off. This had crossed lines, cross in circle and autotron marks (1A, 1F, 1E, 1D, 2C, 1B). "W" shaped central mark and perforation register bar.

Withdrawn: 4 February 1992

1991 Greetings Stamps

From Greetings Barcode Booklet Nos. KX3/3a (£2.40 from 16.9.91 and £2.50 from 1.11.93). 1991

UM29 Teddy Bear

UM30 Dennis the Menace

UM31 Punch

UM32 Cheshire Cat

UM33 Man in the Moon

UM34 Laughing Policeman

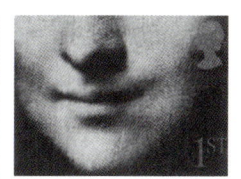

UM35 Clown

UM36 Mona Lisa

UM37 Queen of Hearts

UM38 Stan Laurel (comedian)

Types UM29/38 were printed *se-tenant* in a booklet pane with margins all round. The designs of Type Nos. UM29, 31/3. 35 and 38 extend onto the pane margin

(Des. Michael Peters and Partners Ltd.)

1991 (26 March). Types UM29/38. "Smiles" as Nos. UM7/16, but inscribed (1st). two 4 mm. phosphor bands. Fluorescent coated paper. PVAD gum. Printed in gravure by Harrison. Perf. 15 × 14, reel-fed

UM29 (= SG 1550)

UM29	(1st) gold, greenish yellow, bright rose-red, new blue and grey-black	75	60

UM30 (= SG 1551)

UM30	(1st) gold, greenish yellow, bright rose-red. new blue: deep blue and grey-black..	75	60

UM31 (= SG 1552)

UM31	(1st) gold, greenish yellow, bright rose-red, new blue, deep gold, and grey-black ..	75	60

UM32 (= SG 1553)

UM32	(1st) gold, greenish yellow, bright rose-red, new blue and grey-black	75	60

UM33 (= SG 1554)

UM33	(1st) gold, greenish yellow, bright rose-red, new blue and grey-black	75	60

UM34 (SG 1555)

UM34	(1st) gold, greenish yellow, bright rose-red, new blue and grey-black	75	60

UM Greetings Stamps

UM35 (= SG 1556)

UM35	(1st) gold, greenish yellow, bright rose-red, new blue and grey-black	75	60

UM36 (= SG 1557)

UM36	(1st) gold, greenish yellow, bright rose-red, new blue and grey-black	75	60

UM37 (= SG 1558)

UM37	(1st) gold, greenish yellow, bright rose-red, new blue and grey-black	75	60

UM38 (= SG 1559)

UM38	(1st) gold and grey-black..	75	60
First Day Cover (UK29/38) ..		13·00	

Folded *se-tenant* booklet pane of ten (1st)

UMP39 *Se-tenant* pane of 10 with binding margin at left and 12 labels at right (Actual size 331 × 69 mm.)

Perforation Type E

UMP39 (containing Nos. UM29/38) (26.3.91)	12·00	13·00

These panes are folded four times between vertical rows 1/2, 3/4, 5/6 and 7/8.

Booklet Cylinder Numbers

Pane No.	Cyl. Nos. (No dot)	Perforation Type E
UMP39	B1A (gold)-B1B (greenish yellow)-B1C (bright-rose-red)-B1D (new blue)-B1E (deep blue)-B1F (grey-black)-B91 (phosphor)	16·00

Booklet Cylinder Numbers and Sheet Make-up: The stamps and labels were printed in gravure by Harrison on the Jumelle press. The make-up of the uncut sheet is similar to No. UMP28. Cylinder numbers were placed opposite the fourth pane and the right margin was trimmed off. This showed crossed lines (1 and 9). cross in circle (3) autotron marks 1A, 1F, 1E, 1D, 1C, 1B (4/6), perforation register bar (7), "W" shaped arrow (8). Numbers in brackets refer to the pane order reading from the top of the sheet. The left binding margin showed crossed lines (trimmed off) and cutting lines opposite the gutter margins.
Withdrawn: 29 March 1996

1992 Greetings stamps

From Greetings Barcode Booklet KX4 (£2.50 from 1.11.93 and £2.60 from 8.7.96).

UM40 Flower Spray

UM4I Double Locket

UM42 Key

UM43 Model Car and Cigarette Cards

UM44 Compass and Map

UM45 Pocket Watch

UM46 1854 1d. Red Stamp and Pen

UM47 Pearl Necklace

UM48 Marbles

UM49 Bucket, Spade and Starfish

Types UM40/49 were printed *se-tenant* in a booklet pane with margins all round. The backgrounds of the stamps form a composite design.

(Des. Trickett and Webb Ltd.)

1992 (28 January). Types UM40/49. "Memories" (1st). Two 4 mm. phosphor bands. Fluorescent coated paper. PVAD gum Printed in gravure by Harrison. Perf. 15 × 14, reel-fed

UM40 (= SG 1592)

UM40	(1st) gold, greenish yellow, magenta, ochre, light blue and grey-black	75	60

UM41 (= SG 1593)

UM41	(1st) gold, greenish yellow, magenta, ochre, light blue and grey-black	75	60

UM42 (= SG 1594)

UM42	(1st) gold, greenish yellow, magenta, ochre, light blue and grey-black	75	60

UM43 (= SG 1595)

UM43	(1st) gold, greenish yellow, magenta, ochre, light blue and grey-black	75	60

Greetings Stamps **UM**

UM44 (= SG 1596)

UM44	(1st) gold, greenish yellow, magenta, ochre, light blue and grey-black	75	60

UM45 (= SG 1597)

UM45	(1st) gold, greenish yellow, magenta, ochre, light blue and grey-black	75	60

UM46 (= SG 1598)

UM46	(1st) gold, greenish yellow, magenta, ochre. light blue and grey-black.	75	60

UM47 (= SG 1599)

UM47	(1st) gold, greenish yellow, magenta, ochre, light blue and grey-black	75	60

UM48 (= SG 1600)

UM48	(1st) gold, greenish yellow, magenta, ochre, light blue and grey-black	75	60

UM49 (= SG 601)

UM49	(1st) gold, greenish yellow, magenta, ochre, light blue and grey-black	75	60
First Day Cover (UM40/49)		†	13·00
Presentation Pack (UM40/49) ..		17.00	†

Folded *se-tenant* booklet pane of ten (1st)

UMP50 *Se-tenant* pane of 10 with binding margin at left and 12 labels at right (Actual size 335×69 mm.)

Perforation Type E

UMP50 (containing Nos. UM40/49) (28.1.92)	13·00	13·00

These panes are folded four times between vertical rows 1/2, 3/4, 5/6 and 7/8.

Booklet Cylinder Numbers

Pane No.	Cyl. Nos. (No dot)	Perforation Type E
UMP50	B1A (gold)-B1B (greenish yellow)-B1C (magenta)-B1D (ochre)-B1E (light blue)-B1F (grey-black)-B90 (phosphor)	15·00

Phosphor number B90 occurs opposite row 1 at various measurements above B1A (gold).

Booklet Cylinder Numbers and Sheet Make-up: The stamps and labels were printed by Harrison in gravure on the Jumelle and perforated by an APS machine. There was one column of 9 panes in the uncut sheet including pane 4 with cylinder numbers in the left margin. Panes in booklets had the right margin trimmed off whereas panes in presentation packs had the left margin removed and the right margin was retained. Markings in the margins include crossed lines at both sides (panes 1 and 9), cross in circle (pane 3, right margin), autotron marks (panes 4/6, right margin), perforation register bar (pane 7, right margin) and "W" shaped arrow (pane 8, right margin). Cutting lines in the gutter margins at left occur but were usually trimmed off.

Sold out : Presentation pack February 1995
Withdrawn: 30 June 1997

1993 Greetings Stamp

From Greetings Barcode Booklet Nos. KX5/5b (£2.40 from 1.11.93).

UM51 Long John Silver and Parrot (*Treasure Island*)

UM52 Tweedledum and Tweedledee (*Alice Through the Looking-Glass*)

UM53 William (*William* books)

UM54 Mole and Toad (*The Wind in the Willows*)

UM55 Teacher and Wilfrid ("*The Bash Street Kids*")

UM56 Peter Rabbit and Mrs. Rabbit (*The Tale of Peter Rabbit*)

UM57 Snowman (*The Snowman*) and Father Christmas (*Father Christmas*)

UM58 The Big Friendly Giant and Sophie (*The BFG*)

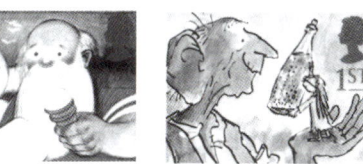

UM59 Bill Badger and Rupert Bear

UM60 Aladdin and the Genie

Types UM51/60 were printed in a pane of ten designs together with a pane of 20 half stamp-sized labels

(Des. Newell and Sorrell)

1993 (2 February). Types UM51/60. "Gift Giving" (1st). One elliptical perf. hole on each vertical stamp edge. Two phosphor bands. Non-fluorescent coated paper. PVAD gum Printed in gravure by Harrison. Perf. 15×14, reel-fed

UM51 (= SG 1644)

UM51	(1st) gold. greenish yellow, magenta, pale brown, light blue and black ..	75	50

UM Greetings Stamps

UM52 (= SG 1645)		
UM52 (1st) gold, cream and black	75	50

UM53 (= SG 1646)		
UM53 (1st) gold, greenish yellow, magenta, cream, new blue and black	75	50

UM54 (= SG 1647)		
UM54 (1st) gold, greenish yellow, magenta, cream, new blue and black	75	50

UM55 (= SG .1648)		
UM55 (1st) gold, greenish yellow, magenta, cream, new blue and black	75	50

UM56 (= SG 1649)		
UM56 (1st) gold, greenish yellow, magenta, cream, new blue and black	75	50

UM57 (= SG 1650)		
UM57 (1st) gold, greenish yellow, magenta, cream, new blue and black	75	50

UM58 (= SG 1651)		
UM58 (1st) gold, greenish yellow, magenta, cream, new blue and black	75	50

UM59 (= SG 652)		
UM59 (1st) gold, greenish yellow, magenta, cream, new blue and black	75	50

UM60 (= SG 1653)		
UM60 (1st) gold, greenish yellow, magenta, cream, new blue and black	75	50
First Day Cover (UM51/60)	†	12·00
Presentation Pack (UM51/60)	16·00	†
PHQ Cards Set of 10 (UM51/60)	16·00	30·00

No. UM59 depicting Rupert, is known postmarked 22 January 1993 at Cardiff.

Folded *se-tenant* booklet pane of ten (1st)

UMP61. *Se-tenant* pane of 10 with binding margin in centre and 20 (5 × 4) labels at right (Actual size 407 × 60 mm.)

UMP61 (containing Nos. UM51/60) (2.2.93)	11·00	12·00

These panes are folded five times between vertical rows 1/2, 3/4, 5/binding margin, 7/8 and 9/10.

Booklet Cylinder Numbers

Pane No.	Cyl. Nos. (No dot)	
UMP61	B1A (gold)-B1B (greenish yellow)-B2C (magenta)- B1D (cream)-B1E (new blue)-B1F (black)-B92 (phosphor)	15·00

Phosphor number B92 occurs above B1A (gold). Between the stamps the phosphor bands are 13 mm. wide and on stamps 5 and 10 the band at right is only 11 mm. in order to leave the binding margin and labels without phosphor.

Booklet Cylinder Numbers and Sheet Make-up: The stamps and labels were printed in gravure by Harrison on the Jumelle press and perforated by the APS machine. There was a single column of ten panes giving a cylinder pane with numbers placed on the binding margin. All other margins were trimmed off and to allow for 8 mm. wide margin the first two columns of labels are 36.5 mm. wide instead of the usual stamp width.

Sold out: Presentation Pack April 1995
Withdrawn: 29 March 1996

Stitched booklet pane of four (1st) 10.8.93

From £6 (£5.64) Booklet "The Story of Beatrix Potter" No. DX15 First pane comprising 4 × (1st) with two phosphor bands on Non-fluorescent coated paper. Two elliptical holes on each vertical edge.

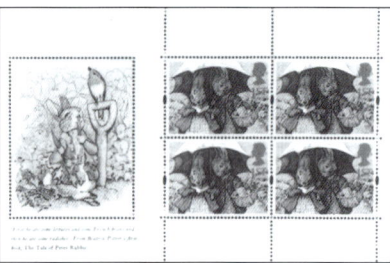

UMP62 (Actual size 162 × 96 mm.)

UMP62 (containing No. UM56 × 4) (10.8.93)	4.75

Face value 96p. (£1 from 1.11.93).

Booklet Cylinder Numbers

The cylinder numbers did not occur in the finished booklets but those used were:—1A, 1B, 1C. 1D. 1E,

The primary sheet contained two columns of four panes each.

1994 Greetings Stamps

FromGreetings Barcode Booklet KX6 (£2·60 from 8.7.96). 1994

UM63 Dan Dare and the Mekon

UM64 The Three Bears

Greetings Stamps **UM**

UM65 Rupert the Bear
UM66 Alice (*Alice in Wonderland*) 
UM67 Noggin and the Ice Dragon 
UM68 Peter Rabbit posting Letter 
UM69 Red Riding Hood and Wolf 
UM70 Orlando the Marmalade Cat 
UM71 Biggles 
UM72 Paddington Bear on Station 

Types UM63/72 were printed in a pane of ten designs together with a pane of 20 half stamp-sized labels

(Des. Newell and Sorrell)

1994 (1 February). Types UM63/72. "Messages" (1st). One elliptical perf. hole on each vertical edge. Two phosphor bands (yellow fluor). Non-fluorescent coated paper. PVAD gum. Printed in gravure by Harrison. Perf. 15 × 14, reel-fed

UM63 (= SG 1800)

UM63	(1st) gold, greenish yellow, bright purple, bistre-yellow. new blue and black ..	75	50

UM64 (= SG 1801)

UM64	(1st) gold, greenish yellow, bright purple, bistre-yellow, new blue and black ..	75	50

UM65 (= SG 1802)

UM65	(1st) gold, greenish yellow, bright purple, bistre-yellow, new blue and black ..	75	50

UM66 (= SG 1803)

UM66	(1st) gold, bistre-yellow and black	75	50

UM67 (= SG 1804)

UM67	(1st) gold, greenish yellow, bright purple, bistre-yellow, new blue and black ..	75	50

UM68 (= SG 1805)

UM68	(1st) gold, greenish yellow, bright purple, bistre-yellow, new blue and black ..	75	50

UM69 (= SG 1806)

UM69	(1st) gold, greenish yellow, bright purple, bistre-yellow, new blue and black ..	75	50

UM70 (= SG .1807)

UM70	(1st) gold, greenish yellow, bright purple, bistre-yellow, new blue and black ..	75	50

UM71 (= SG 1808)

UM71	(1st) gold. greenish yellow, bright purple, bistre-yellow, new blue and black ..	75	50

UM72 (= SG 809)

UM72	(1st) gold, greenish yellow, bright purple, bistre-yellow, new blue and black ..	75	50

First Day Cover (UM63/72)	†	12·00
Presentation Pack (UM63/72)	18·00	†
PHQ Cards *Set of* 10 (UM63/72)	16·00	30·00

Folded *se-tenant* booklet pane of ten (1st)

UMP73 *Se-tenant* pane of 10 with binding margin in centre and 20 (5 × 4) labels at right (Actual size 407 × 60 mm.)

UMP73 (containing Nos. UM63/72) (1.2.94) ..	13·00	9·00

These panes are folded five times between vertical rows 1/2, 3/4, 5/binding margin, 7/8 and 9/10.

Booklet Cylinder Numbers

Pane No.	Cyl. Nos. (No dot)	
UMP73	B1A (gold)-B1B (greenish yellow)-B1C (bright purple)-B1D (bistre-yellow)-B1E (new blue)-B1F (black)-B96 (phosphor) ..	15·00

Phosphor (with yellow fluor) was used for the first time on greetings stamps.

The phosphor cylinder number B96 occurs above B1A (gold). Between the stamps the phosphor bands are 18 mm. wide but only 12 mm. across stamps and narrow binding margin. The labels did not have phosphor bands or ellipses.

UM Greetings Stamps

Booklet Cylinder Numbers and Sheet Make-up: Harrison printed the panes on the Jumelle and the stamps were perforated by the APS machine. The panes were printed in one column of eight including the pane with cylinder numbers printed on the central binding margin. All marginal lines and crosses were trimmed off.
Sold Out: Presentation pack June 1995; booklet February 1998

Nos. UM74/UMP128 were printed by Walsall

1995 Greetings Stamps

From Greetings Barcode Booklet Nos. KX7/7a (£2·60 from 8.7.96).

UM74 "La Danse a la Campagne" (Renoir)
UM75 "Troilus and Criseyde" (Peter Brookes) 
UM76 "The Kiss" (Rodin) 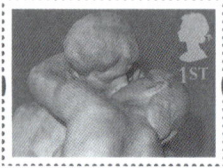
UM77 "Girls on the Town" (Beryl Cook) 
UM78 "Jazz" (Andrew Mockett) 
UM79 "Girls performing a Kathal Dance" (Aurangzeb period) 
UM80 "Alice Keppel with her Daughter" (Alice Hughes) 
UM81 "Children Playing" (L. S. Lowry) 
UM82 "Circus Clowns" (Emily Firmin and Justin Mitchell) 
UM83 Decoration from "All the Love Poems of Shakespeare" (Eric Gill) 

Types UM74/83 were printed in a pane of ten designs together with a pane of twenty half stamp-sized labels

(Des. Newell and Sorrell)

1995 (21 March). Types UM74/83. "Greetings in Art" (1st). One elliptical perf. hole on each vertical edge. Two phosphor bands (yellow fluor). Non-fluorescent coated paper. PVA gum. Printed in lithography by Walsall. Perf. 14½ × 14, sheet-fed

UM74			
UM74	(1st) greenish yellow, new blue, magenta, black and silver	75	50
UM75			
UM75	(1st) greenish yellow, new blue, magenta, black and silver	75	50
UM76			
UM76	(1st) greenish yellow, new blue, magenta, black and silver	75	50
UM77			
UM77	(1st) greenish yellow, new blue, magenta, black and silver	75	50
UM78			
UM78	(1st) greenish yellow, new blue, magenta. black and silver	75	50
UM79			
UM79	(1st) greenish yellow, new blue, magenta. black and silver	75	50
UM80			
UM80	(1st) greenish yellow, new blue, magenta, black and silver	75	50
UM81			
UM81	(1st) greenish yellow, new blue, magenta, black and silver	75	50
UM82			
UM82	(1st) greenish yellow, new blue, magenta. black and silver	75	50
UM83			
UM83	(1st) greenish yellow, new blue, magenta, black and silver	75	50
First Day Cover (UM74/83)		†	11·50
Presentation Pack (UM74/83) ..		12·00	†
PHQ Cards (UM74/83)		16·00	30·00

Folded *Se-Tenant* Booklet Pane of Ten (1st)

UMP84 (*Se-tenant* pane of 10 with binding margin in centre and 20 (5×4) labels at right (Actual size 405 × 60 mm.)

UMP84	(containing Nos. UM74/83) (21.3.95)	11·00	11·00
	a. Silver (Queen's head and "1st") and phosphor bands omitted		£15000

These panes are folded five times between vertical rows 1/2, 3/4, 5/binding margin, 7/8 and 9/10.

Booklet Plate Numbers
Colour order of plate nos. sideways reading up the margin (Yellow Fluor) Greenish yellow. new blue, magenta, black, silver

Plate Nos.

W1 (×5)	12·00
W1, W1, W1, W1, W2 (Pack £15)	18.00
W2, W1, W1, W1, W2	£475
W2, W1, W2, W1, W2 (Pack £10)	12·00
W3, W2, W3, W2, W3,	14·00
W4, W2, W3, W2, W3	12·00
W4, W2, W4, W2, W3	42·00
W4, W2, W4, W2, W4 (Pack £20)	12·00
W4, W2, W5, W2, W4	12·00
W5, W3, W6, W3, W5	12.00
W5, W3, W7, W3, W5	£200
W5, W4, W7, W3, W5	12·00
W5, W4, W7, W3, W6	12·00
W6, W5, W8, W4, W7	12·00
W6, W5, W8, W4, W8	12·00
W7, W6, W9, W5, W8	15·00
W7, W6, W9, W5, W9	12·00
W8, W7, W10, W6, W8	12·00
W9, W8, W11, W7, W10	12·00
W9, W8, W11, W7, W11	12·00

The phosphor bands are 18 mm. but only 9 mm, next to the binding margin. The labels did not have phosphor bands or elliptical perforation holes.

Booklet Plate Numbers and Sheet Make-up: The panes were printed on a Roland Favorit press in sheets containing one column of seven ordinary and one plate number pane. A Bickel sheet-fed perforator was used and the side margins were trimmed off.
Sold out: Presentation pack February 1999

As Types UM74/83 but with two phosphor bands (blue fluor)

1996 (13 February). Types UM74/83. "Greetings in Art" (1st). One elliptical perf. Hole on each vertical edge. Two phosphor bands (blue fluor). Non-fluorescent coated paper. PVA gum. Printed in lithography by Walsall. Perf. 14½ × 14, sheet fed

UM85 (= SG 1858)

UM74	(1st) greenish yellow, new blue, magenta, black and silver	75	50

UM86 (= SG 1859)

UM75	(1st) greenish yellow, new blue, magenta, black and silver	75	50

UM87 (= SG 1860)

UM76	(1st) greenish yellow, new blue, magenta, black and silver	75	50

UM88 (= SG 1861)

UM77	(1st) greenish yellow, new blue, magenta, black and silver	75	50

UM89 (= SG 1862)

UM78	(1st) greenish yellow, new blue, magenta, black and silver	75	50

UM90 (= SG 1863)

UM79	(1st) greenish yellow, new blue, magenta, black and silver	75	50

UM91 (= SG 1864)

UM80	(1st) greenish yellow, new blue, magenta, black and silver	75	50

UM92 (= SG 1865)

UM81	(1st) greenish yellow, new blue, magenta, black and silver	75	50

UM93 (= SG 1866)

UM82	(1st) greenish yellow, new blue, magenta, black and silver	75	50

UM94 (= SG 1867)

UM83	(1st) greenish yellow, new blue, magenta, black and silver	75	50

Folded *se-tenant* booklet pane of ten (1st)

As Type UMP84 but phosphor bands (blue fluor)

UMP95 (containing Nos. UM85/94) (13.2.96)	11·00	11·00

These panes are folded five times between vertical rows 1/2. 3/4, 5/binding margin, 7/8 and 9/10.

Booklet Plate Numbers
Colour order of plate nos. sideways reading up the margin Greenish yellow, new blue, magenta, black, silver

Pane No.	Plate Nos.	
UMP95	W11. W10, W13, W9, W12	12·00
	WII, W10. W13, W10, W12	14·00
	WI1, W10, W13. WII, W12	14·00
	W12, WI1, W14. WI I. W12	15·00
	W12, W12, W14. W 12, W12	90·00

Booklet Plate Numbers and Sheet Make-up: As pane No. UMP84.

1996 Greetings Stamps (first issue)

From Greetings Barcode Booklet Nos. KX8 (£2.60 from 8.7.96).

UM96 "MORE LOVE" (Mel Calman)

UM97 "Sincerely" (Charles Barsotti)

UM Greetings Stamps

UM98 "Do you have something for the Human Condition?" (Mel Calman)
UM99 "mental floss" (Leo Cullum) 
UM100 "4.55 P.M." (Charles Barsotti) 
UM101 "Dear lottery prize winner" (Larry)
UM102 "I'm writing to you because" (Mel Calman) 
UM103 "fetch this, fetch that" (Charles Barsotti) 
UM104 "My day starts before I'm ready for it" (Mel Calman) 
UM105 "The cheque in the post" (Jack Ziegler) 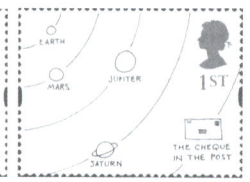

Types UM96/105 were printed in a pane of ten designs together with a pane of 20 half stamp-sized labels

(Des. Michael Wolff)

1996 (26 February). Types UM96/105 Cartoons (1st). One elliptical perf. hole on each vertical edge. "All over" phosphor (blue fluor). Non-fluorescent coated paper. PVA gum. Printed in lithography by Walsall. Perf.14½ × 14, sheet-fed

UM96 (= SG 1905)

UM96	(1st) black and bright mauve	75	40

UM97 (= SG 1906)

UM97	(1st) black and blue-green	75	40

UM98 (= SG 1907)

UM98	(1st) black and new blue ..	75	40

UM99 (= SG 1908)

UM99	(1st) black and bright violet	75	40

UM100 (= SG 1909)

UM100	(1st) black and vermilion ..	75	40

UM101 (= SG 1910)

UM101	(1st) black and new blue	75	40

UM102 (= SG 1911)

UM102	(1st) black and vermilion	75	40

UM103 (= SG 1912)

UM103	(1st) black and bright violet	75	40

UM104 (= SG 1913)

UM104	(1st) black and blue-green	75	40

UM105 (= SG 1914)

UM105	(1st) black and bright mauve ..	75	40
First Day Cover (UM96/105) ..		†	11·00
Presentation Pack (UM96/105) ..		16·00	†
PHQ Cards (UM96/105) ..		16·00	30·00

■ **Folded *se-tenant* booklet pane of ten**

UMP106 (*Se-tenant* pane of 10 with binding margin in centre and 20 (5×4) labels at right (see next page) (Actual size 405×60mm.)

20 labels with centre margin at left

■ **Pane UMP106.**

From £2·50 (£2·60 from 8.7.96)
Greetings Stamp Booklet No. KY8

UMP106 (containing Nos. UM96/105) (26.2.96) 10·00

These panes are folded five times between vertical rows 1/2, 3/4, 5/binding margin, 7/8 and 9/10.

Booklet Plate Numbers
Colour order of plate nos. sideways reading up the margin
    New blue, blue-green, bright violet, bright mauve, vermilion, black

Pane No.	Plate Nos.	
UMP106	W1, W1, W1, W1, W1, W1 (Pack £12)	12·00
	W2, W2, W2, W2, W2, W2	12·00
	W2· W2, W2, W2, W3, W2	14·00
	W2, W3, W2, W2, W2, W2 (Pack £12)	12·00
	W2, W3, W2, W2, W3, W2 (Pack £25)	12·00
	W3, W2, W2, W2, W3· W2	27·00
	W3, W3, W2, W2, W3, W2 (Pack £20)	20·00
	W4, W3, W2, W3, W4, W3	£500
	W4, W3, W3, W3, W4, W3	12·00
	W4, W4, W3. W3, W4, W3	14·00
	W5, W4, W3, W3, W4, W3	12·00
	W5, W4. W3, W3, W4, W4	14·00
	W6, W4, W4, W4, W5, W5	12·00

The "all over" phosphor printing ends on the gutter margin so that the labels are without phosphor.
Booklet Plate Numbers and Sheet Make-up: As pane Nos. UMP84 and 95.

Greetings Stamps **UM**

1996 Greetings Stamps (second issue)

From £2.60 Greetings Barcode Booklet KX8a

As Types UM96/105 but with two phosphor bands (blue fluor)

1996 (11 November). Types UM96/105 cartoons (1st). One elliptical perf. Hole on each vertical edge. Two phosphor bands (blue fluor). Non-fluorescent coated paper. PVA gum. Printed in lithography by Walsall. Perf. 14 × 14½). sheet fed

UM107 (= SG 1905p)

UM96	(1st) black and bright mauve	1·00	60

UM108 (= SG 1906p)

UM97	(1st) black and blue-green ..	1·00	60

UM109 (= SG 1907p)

UM98	(1st) black and new blue ..	1·00	60

UM110 (= SG 1908p)

UM99	(1st) black and bright violet	1·00	60

UM111 (= SG 1909p)

UM100	(1st) black and vermilion	1·00	60

UM112 (= SG 1910p)

UM101	(1st) black and new blue ..	1·00	60

UM113 (= SG 1911p)

UM102	(1st) black and vermilion	1·00	60

UM114 (= SG 1912p)

UM103	(1st) black and bright violet	1·00	60

UM115 (= SG 1913p)

UM104	(1st) black and blue-green	1·00	60

UM116 (= SG 1914p)

UM105	(1st) black and bright Mauve	1·00	60

Phosphor bands which respond to long wave u.v. light exist, see pane no. UMP117a and plate nos. W10, W8, W8, W7, W8, W8,

First Day Cover (UM107/16) ..	†	11·00

Folded *se-tenant* booklet pane of ten (1st)

As Type UMP106 but two phosphor bands (blue fluor)

UMP117	(containing Nos. UM107/16) (11.11.96)	38·00	36·00
	a. Long wave (Novaglo) phosphor bands	38·00	36·00

These panes are folded five times between vertical rows 1/2, 3/4, 5/binding, 7/8 and 9/10.

Booklet Plate Numbers

Colour order of plate nos, sideways reading up the margin
New blue, blue green, bright violet, bright mauve, vermilion, black

Pane No.	Plate Nos.	
UMP117	W7, W5, W5, W5, W6, W6	12·00
	W8, W6, W6, W6, W6, W7	25·00
	W8, W7, W6, W6, W7, W7	12·00
	W8, W7, W7, W6, W7, W7	32·00
	W9, W6, W6, W6, W7, W7	80·00
	W9, W7, W6, W6. W7, W7	32·00
	W10, W8, W8, W7, W8, W8	12·00
UMP117a	W10, W8, W8, W7, W8, W8, W11, W9. W9, W8, W9, W9	12·00

Nos. UMp117a react to long wave u.v. light.

Booklet Plate Numbers and Sheet Make-up: As pane No. UMP84.

1997 Greetings Stamps (second issue)

From £2·60 Greetings Barcode Booklets KX9/12

UM118 *Gentiana caulis* (Georg Ehret)

UM119 *Magnolia grandifaora* (Ehret)

UM120 *Camellia japonica* (Alfred Chandler)

UM121 *Tulipa* (Ehret)

UM122 *Fuchsia* "Princess of Wales" (Augusta Withers)

UM123 *Tulipa gesneriana* (Ehret)

UM124 *Gazania splendens* (Charlotte Sowerby)

UM125 *Iris latifolia* (Ehret)

UM126 *Hippeastrum rutilum* (Pierre-Joseph Redoute)

UM127 *Passiflora coerulea* (Ehret)

Types UM118/27 were printed in a pane of ten designs together with a pane of 20 half stamp-sized labels

(Des. Tutssels) (Lithography by Walsall)

1997 (6 January). Types UM118/27. 19th-century flower paintings. One elliptical perf. hole on each vertical edge. Two phosphor bands (blue fluor). Non-fluorescent coated paper. PVA gum. Printed in lithography by Walsall. Perf. 14½ × 14, sheet-fed

UM Greetings Stamps

UM118 (= SG 1955)

UM118	(1st) greenish yellow, new blue, magenta, black, blue-green and gold	50	40

UM119 (= SG 1956)

UM119	(1st) greenish yellow, new blue, magenta, black, blue-green and gold	50	40

UM120 (= SG I957)

UM120	(1st) greenish yellow, new blue, magenta, black, blue-green and gold	50	40

UM121 (= SG 1958)

UM121	(1st) greenish yellow, new blue, magenta, black, blue-green and gold	50	40

UM122 (= SG 1959)

UM122	(1st) greenish yellow, new blue, magenta. black, blue-green and gold	50	40

UM123 (= SG 1960)

UM123	(1st) greenish yellow, new blue, magenta, black, blue-green and gold	50	40

UM124 (= SG 1961)

UM124	(1st) greenish yellow, new blue, magenta. black. blue-green and gold	50	40

UM125 (= SG 1962)

UM125	(1st) greenish yellow, new blue, magenta. black, blue-green and gold	50	40

UM126 (= SG 1963)

UM126	(1st) greenish yellow, new blue, magenta, black, blue-green and gold	50	40

UM127 (SG 1964)

UM127	(1st) greenish yellow, new blue, magenta, black, blue-green and gold	50	40

Nos. UM 118/27 also exist with long wave phosphor bands. Same prices mint.

First Day Cover (UM118/27) ..	†	11·50
Presentation Pack (UM118/27) ..	16·00	†
PHQ Cards (UM118/27) ..	16·00	30·00

■ Folded *se-tenant* booklet pane of ten (1st)

UMP128 (*Se-tenant* pane of 10 with binding margin in centre and 20 (5×4) labels at right (Actual size 405×60 mm.)

UMP128	(containing Nos. UM118/27) (6.1.97) ..	11·00	11·00
	a. Long wave phosphor bands ..	11·00	11·50
	b. Gold, blue-green and phosphor omitted		28,00
	c. Wide band on stamp 7 and stamp 2 normal (KX9) ..	12·00	10·00
	d. Blue-green on labels quadrupled (KX12)		

These panes are folded five times between vertical rows 1/2, 3/4, 5/binding margin, 7/8 and 9/10.

Booklet Plate Numbers in Presentation Packs

Colour order of plate numbers placed sideways and reading up the margin
Greenish yellow, new blue, magenta, black, blue-green, gold

W1, W1, W1, W1, W1, W1	12·00
W1, W1, W2, W1, W1, W1	25·00
W1, W1, W2, W1, W1, W2	18·00
Wl, W1, W2, W1, Wl, W3	20·00
Wl, W1, W2, W1, W2, W3	15·00
Wl, Wl, W3. Wl, W2, W3	15·00
W1, W2, W3, W1, W2, W3	15·00
W1, W3, W3, W1, W2, W3	15·00
W1, W3, W4, W1, W2, W3	22·00
W2, W3, W4, W1, W2, W3	£475
W2, W3, W4, W2, W2, W3	20·00

Front Greetings Booklet Nos. KX9/12

Pane No. UMP128

Wl, W1, W1, W1, W1, W1,	22·00
Wl, W1, W2, W1, W1, W1	26·00
W1, W1, W2, W1, W1, W2	24·00
W1, W1, W2, W1, W1, W3	£110
W1, W1, W2, W1, W2, W3	40·00
W1, W1, W3, W1, W2, W3	40·00
W1, W2, W3, W1, W2, W3	28·00
W1, W3, W3, W1, W2, W3	14·00
W1, W3, W4, W1, W2, W3	£175
W2, W3, W4, W1, W2, W3	£450
W2, W3, W4, W2, W2, W3	15·00
W2, W3, W4, W2, W3, W4	12·00
W2, W3, W5, W2, W3, W4	12·00
W2, W3, W5, W2, W3, W5	£150
W2, W3, W6, W2, W3, W4	90·00
W2, W3, W6, W2, W3, W5	75·00
W3, W4, W6, W2, W3, W5	12·00
W3, W4, W6, W3, W3, W5	12·00
W3, W4, W6, W3, W3, W6	14·00
W3, W4, W7, W3, W3, W5	12·00
W3, W4, W7, W3, W3, W6	12·00
W3, W4, W7, W3, W4, W7	12·00
W4, W4, W7, W3, W4, W7	12·00
W4, W4, W8, W3, W3, W6	11·50
W4, W4, W8, W3, W3, W7	11·50
W4, W4, W8, W3, W4, W7	11·50
W5, W5, W9, W4, W3, W6	11·50

Greetings Stamps UM

Pane No. UMP128

W5, W5, W9, W4, W3, W7	11·50
W5, W5, W9, W4, W4, W7	11·50
W6, W6, W10, W5, W5, W8	11·50

Pane No. UMP128a

W6, W6, W10, W5, W5, W9	35·00
W6, W6, W10, W5, W5, WI0	£500
W6, W6, W11, W5, W5, W8	50·00
W6, W6, WII, W5, W5, W9 ,,	12·00
W6, W6, WI1, W5, W5, W10	12·00
W6, W7, WI1, W5, W5, W9	50·00
W6, W7, W12, W5, W5, W10	12·00
W6, W7, WI1, W5, W5, WI0	22·00
W7, W8, W13, W6, W5, W10	20·00
W7, W8, W13, W6, W5, W11	12·00
W7, W8, W13, W6, W6, W11	12·00
W8, W9, W14, W7, W6, W11	22·00
W9, W10, W15, W8, W7, W12	11·50
W9, W10, W16, W8, W7, W12	70·00
W9, W11, W16, W8, W7, W12	11·50
W10, W12, W16, W9, W6, W11	50·00
W11, W15, W17, WI0, W9, W15	11·50
W11, W16, W18, W10, W9, W15	14·00
W11, W16, W18, W10, W9, W16	14·00
W11, W13, W16, W10, W9, W15	22·00
W11, W13, W17, WIO, W9, W15	12·00
W11, W14, W17, W10, W9, WI5	60·00
W11, W15, W18, WI0, W9, W15	60·00
W11, W15, W18, W10, W9, W16	18·00
W12, W16, W18, WII, W9, W16	16·00
W12, W16, W19, WI I, W9, W16	14·50
W12, W17, W19, W11, W9, W16	11·50
W12, W17, W20, W11, W9, W16	22·00
W12, W18, W20, W11. W9, W16	21·50
W12, W18, W21, W11, W9, W16	11·50
W12, W18, W21, W12, W10, WI7	11·50
W13, W19, W23, W13, W11, W18	22·00
W13, W19, W23, W13, W12. W18	50·00
W14, W20. W24, W14, W12, W18	22·00
W14, W20, W25, W14, W12, W18	14·00
W15, W21, W26, W15. W13, W19	15·00
W16, W22, W27, W16, W14, W20	11·50
W17, W23, W28, W17, W15. W21	25·00
W18, W24. W29. W18, W15, W21	11·50
W18, W24, W29. W18. W15, W22	12·00
W19. W25, W29, W19, W16. W22	12·00

Booklet Sheet Make-up: The panes were printed on a Roland Favorit press in sheets containing seven ordinary and one plate number pane. The sheets were then comb perforated on a sheet-fed Bickel machine. Side margins were trimmed off before being made-up into booklets or placed in the presentation packs.

Sold at 27p. each

UM129 "Love"   UM130 "THANKS"

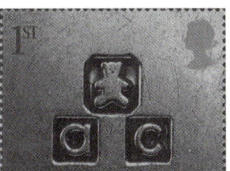

UM131 "abc" (New Baby)   UM132 "WELCOME"

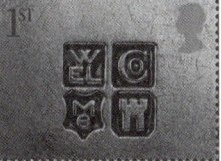

UM133 "Cheers"

2001 (6 February). Types UM129/33. "OCCASIONS".

This was a departure from previous issues in booklets. Each design was from a sheet of 100 containing two panes (10 × 5) with horizontal gutter margin.

The designs, from models created by Model Solutions, were photographed by Julian Deghy. The stamps were printed using iriodin ink which, comprising layers of pigment, reflects the light to create a shiny or metallic effect.

Perf. 14½ × 14. Two phosphor bands (blue fluor) non-fluorescent coated paper. PVA gum.

UM129 (=SG 2182)

UM129	(1st)	silver, greenish yellow, magenta, pale greenish blue, black and silver-grey	1·30	1·30

UM130 (=SG 2183)

UM130	(1st)	silver, greenish yellow, magenta, pale greenish blue, black and silver-grey	1·30	1·30

UM131 (=SG 2184)

UM131	(1st)	silver, greenish yellow, magenta, pale greenish blue, black and silver-grey	1·30	1·30

UM132 (=SG 2185)

UM132	(1st)	silver, greenish yellow, magenta, pale greenish blue, black and silver-grey	1·30	1·30

UM133 (=SG 2186)

UM133	(1st)	silver, greenish yellow, magenta, pale greenish blue, black and silver-grey	1·30	1·30

First Day Cover (UM129/33)	†	7·50
Presentation Pack (13 feb)	8·00	†
PHQ Cards (UM129/33)	8·50	13·00

Nos. UM129/33 were re-issued, as sheets of 20, including a *se-tenant* format, printed in lithography with each stamp accompanied by a half stamp-size label showing either postal symbols or a personal photograph. They were sold from 5 June 2001 at a minimum price of £5·95 (face £5·40). We do not list these.

Further packs of Nos. UM129/33 were sold from 3 July 2001. These comprised the listed stamps in gravure in blocks of ten (from sheets) with an insert describing the occasion. *(Price £15 per pack).*

UM Greetings Stamps

Cylinder Numbers (Blocks of Six)
Colour order of cylinder numbers following the Enschedé imprint reading up the margin (1A to 1F (1G phos)).
All values. Silver, greenish yellow, magenta, pale greenish blue, black, silver-grey
Perforation: Type R*
Single pane sheets

Cylinder Numbers

Two 18mm phosphor bands (blue fluor)		
No UM129 (1st)	1A-1B-1C-1D-1E-1F-1G (phosphor)	12·00
No UM130 (1st)	1A-1B-1C-1D-1E-1F-1G (phosphor)	12·00
No UM131 (1st)	1A-1B-1C-1D-1E-1F-1G (phosphor)	12·00
No UM132 (1st)	1A-1B-1C-1D-1E-1F-1G (phosphor)	12·00
No UM133 (1st)	1A-1B-1C-1D-1E-1F-1G (phosphor)	12·00

The phosphor bands do not pass over the top, gutter or bottom margins. The bands are 18mm between horizontal pairs and 9mm wide at the margins.

Secure Stock operations numbers and dates of printing
(Left margin blocks of eight)

Spec No.	SSO No.	Date	Margins at left
UM129	241	11/12/00	16·00
		12/12/00	16·00
UM130	244	11/12/00	16·00
		12/12/00	16·00
UM131	242	07/12/00	16·00
		08/12/00	16·00
UM132	242	07/12/00	16·00
		08/12/00	16·00
UM133	243	13/12/00	16·00

Sheet details
Sheet size: 100 (2 panes 10 x 5). Single pane reel-fed.

Sheet markings
Cylinder numbers: Opposite rows 8/9, left margin, boxed with Enschedé imprint opposite row 10
Margin arrows: in gutter margin opposite vertical rows 5/6
Secure Stock operations numbers and dates: left margin opposite rows 3/4
Sale date: Inscribed 6-FEB-2001 above and below vertical rows 3/4 and 9/10
Traffic lights: In right margin in order of cylinder numbers reading up opposite rows 8/9
Withdrawn: 5 February 2002

▋ 2002 Greetings Stamps

UM134 Rabbits ("a new baby")  UM135 "LOVE"

UM136 Aircraft Sky-writing "hello"  UM137 Bear pulling potted Topiary Tree (Moving Home)

UM138 Flowers ("best wishes")

2002 (5 March). Types UM134/138. "OCCASIONS". Printed in sheets of 100 containing two panes (10 x 5) with horizontal gutter margin. Perf. 15 x 14. Two 18mm phosphor bands (blue fluor) non-fluorescent coated paper. PVA gum.

UM134 (=SG 2260)

UM134	(1st)	Greenish yellow, magenta, new blue, black and lilac	1·10	1·10
	a.	As UM134 but 10mm bands	6·50	

UM135 (=SG 2261)

UM135	(1st)	Greenish yellow, magenta, new blue, black and lilac	1·10	1·10
	a.	As UM135 but 10mm bands	6·50	

UM136 (=SG 2262)

UM136	(1st)	Greenish yellow, magenta, new blue, black and lilac	1·10	1·10
	a.	As UM136 but 10mm bands	6·50	

UM137 (=SG 2263)

UM137	(1st)	Greenish yellow, magenta, new blue, black and lilac	1·10	1·10
	a.	As UM137 but 10mm bands	6·50	

UM138 (=SG 2264)

UM138	(1st)	Greenish yellow, magenta, new blue, black and lilac	1·10	1·10
	a.	As UM138 but 10mm bands	6·50	

First Day Cover (UM134/38)	†	6·75
Presentation Pack (UM134/38)	6·50	†
PHQ Cards (UM134/38)	4·50	14·00

Nos. UM134/38 were subsequently available in sheets of 20 perforated 14½ x 14, either of one design or *se-tenant*, with each stamp accompanied by a half stamp-size label showing either greetings or personal photograph.

The stamps showing 10mm wide bands came from some December printings. Vertical strips of 3 exist showing 18mm narrowing to 10mm on the third stamp.

Plate numbers (blocks of six)
Colour order of plate numbers following the Questa imprint:
New Baby: Greenish yellow, magenta, new blue, black, lilac
Love: Greenish yellow, magenta, new blue, black, silver
Hello: Greenish yellow, magenta, new blue, black,
New Home: Greenish yellow, magenta, new blue, black,
Best wishes: Greenish yellow, magenta, new blue, black, cobalt
Perforation: Type R*
Single pane sheets

		Plate Numbers
Two 18mm phosphor bands (blue fluor)		
No. UM134 (1st)	1 (x 5), 1 (phosphor)	2·75
No. UM135 (1st)	1 (x 5), 1 (phosphor)	2·75
No. UM136 (1st)	1 (x 4), 1 (phosphor)	2·75
No. UM137 (1st)	1 (x 4), 1 (phosphor)	2·75
No. UM138 (1st)	1 (x 5), 1 (phosphor)	2·75

Greetings Stamps **UM**

The phosphor bands do not pass over the top, gutter or bottom margins. The bands are 18mm between horizontal pairs and 9mm wide at the margins.
Perforation Type M on this printing shows both right and left side margins imperforate. Other margins including horizontal gutter were perforated through.

Secure Stock operations numbers and dates of printing (Left margin blocks of six)

Spec No.	SSO No.	Date	Margin at left
UM134	853	17/12/01	3·50
		09/01/02	3·50
		10/01/02	3·50
UM135	856	13/12/01	3·50
		14/01/02	3·50
		11/01/02	3·50
UM136	857	14/12/01	3·50
		08/01/02	3·50
UM137	854	15/12/01	3·50
		09/01/02	3·50
UM138	855	18/12/01	3·50
		10/01/02	3·50

Narrow bands have been reported on blocks with dates December 2001

Sheet details
Sheet size: 100 (2 panes 10 × 5). Single pane reel-fed.

Sheet markings
Plate numbers: Sideways pointing left opposite rows 8/9, left margin with imprint opposite row 10, sideways reading up.
Margin arrows: 'W' shaped in gutter margin opposite horizontal rows 5/6
Sale date: Inscribed 5-MAR-2002 above and below vertical rows 3/4 and 9/10
Secure Stock operations numbers and dates: left margin opposite horizontal rows rows 6/7 above the phosphor plate numbers
Traffic lights: In form of Questa imprint opposite rows 8/9 (New Home), right margin in same order as plate numbers reading down

Type UM136 Self adhesive

4 March 2003

(1st) printed by Questa

As No UM136 (1st) from £1·62 Barcode booklet No. PM8. Printed in gravure by Questa.
Self-adhesive and die-cut perforation 15 × 14
Two phosphor bands (blue fluor) as sheet issue but self-adhesive.

UM139 (=SG 2264a)

UM139	(1st)	greenish yellow, magenta, new blue, black	6·00	6·00

Self-adhesive Booklet pane (4 March) 2003

UMP140

From £1·62 (£1·68 from 8 May 2003) Barcode Booklet PM8 Pane comprising 2 × (1st) Printed in gravure with two phosphor bands (blue fluor) and 4 × (1st) Machin (gold). No. UM139 perf. 15 × 14 And Machin No. UJQ3 perf. 15 × 14 With one elliptical perf hole, die-cut and self-adhesive.

UMP140 (containing Nos. UM139 × 2, UJQ3 × 4) (4.3.03) 16·00
This was the first in this series of booklets to contain Greetings stamps in this case the "Hello" design from the Occasions issue. The surplus self-adhesive paper around the stamps was removed. No PM8 was initially sold at £1·62

Booklet Cylinder Numbers

Pane No.	Cyl. No.	Phos No	
UMP140	1 (× 5)	1	20·00

2003 Greetings Stamps

UM141 "Gold Star, See me, Playtime"

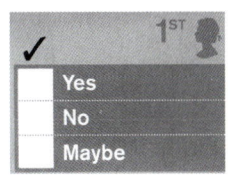

UM142 "I♥U, XXXX, S.W.A.L.K."

UM143 "Angel, Poppet, Little terror"

UM144 "Yes, No, Maybe"

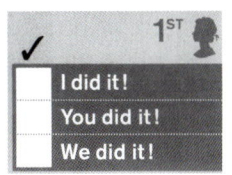

UM145 "Oops!, Sorry, Will try harder"

UM146 "I did it!, You did it!, We did it!"

(Des UNA, Sara Wiegand and Mike Exon).

(Printed in Lithography by Questa)

2003 (4 February), Types UM141/6. "OCCASIONS" Printed in sheets of 60 containing two panes (3 × 10) with vertical gutter margin. Perf 14½ × 14. Two 18mm phosphor bands (blue fluor) non-fluorescent coated paper. PVA gum

UM141 (= SG 2337)

UM141	(1st) lemon and new blue	60	50
	a. Block of six. Nos M141/6	6·50	6·00

UM142 (= SG 2338)

UM142	(1st) red and deep ultramarine	60	50

UM143 (= SG 23390)

UM143	(1st) purple and bright yellow-green	60	50

UM144 (= SG 2340)

UM144	(1st) bright yellow green and red	60	50

UM145 (= SG 2341)

UM145	(1st) deep ultramarine and lemon	60	50

UM146 (= SG 2342)

UM146	(1st) new blue and purple	60	50

Nos. UM141/6 were printed *se-tenant* blocks of six (3 × 2) Throughout the sheet.

UM Greetings Stamps

First Day Cover (UM141/6)	†	9·00
Presentation Pack (UM141/6)	8·00	†
PHQ cards (UM141/6)	5·25	18·00

Nos. UM141/6 were also issued in sheets of 20 (containing four of Nos. UM142 and UM144 and three each of the others) with *se-tenant* labels. Such sheets with the labels showing printed faces were available at £5·95 From philatelic outlets, or with personalised photographs at £14·95 from Royal Mail in Edinburgh.

Plate numbers (Blocks of 12)
Colour order of plate numbers following the Questa imprint:
Gold star: Lemon, new blue
I love you: Red, deep ultramarine
Angel: Purple, bright yellow-green
Yes: Bright yellow-green, red
Oops: Deep ultramarine, lemon
I did it: New blue, purple

Perforation Type P

Single pane sheets	Left margin		Right margin	
Nos. UM141/6	1(×6), 1 phosphor	22·00	1(×6)	22·00
	2(×6), 1 phosphor	12·00	2(×6)	12·00
	3(×6), 1 phosphor	9·00	3(×6)	9·00

There was no phosphor number on the right-hand margin. The phosphor bands do not pass over the top, gutter or bottom margins. The bands at the sides of the sheet are 9mm and 18mm between the stamps.

Dates of Printing (Right margin *se-tenant* blocks of six)

Spec Nos.	Date		Source
UM141/6	14/10/02	15·00	plate 1 (×6)
	15/10/02	10·00	plate 2 (×6)
	16/12/02	7·00	plate 3 (×6)
	17/12/02	7·00	plate 3 (×6)
	18/12/02	7·00	plate 3 (×6)

Sheet details
Sheet size: 60 (2 panes 3 × 10). Single pane reel-fed

Sheet markings
Plate numbers: Opposite rows 8/9 at each side with imprint opposite row 10. Sideways reading up
Sale date: In top margin above vertical rows 2/3 and in bottom margin below rows 5/6.
Date of printing: Right margin reading down opposite horizontal rows 1/2 in dot matrix with sheet no.
Double box with spot: Left margin opposite horizontal row 7

Withdrawn: 3 February 2004

2004 Greetings Stamps

UM147 Postman    UM148 Face

UM149 Duck    UM150 Baby

UM151 Aircraft

(Des. Satoshi Kambayashi)

Printed in Lithography by De la Rue

2004 (3 February), Types 147/51. "OCCASIONS". Printed in sheets of 50 containing two panes (5×5) with a horizontal gutter margin. Post Offices sold the sheets of 25 (5×5) and the sheets containing the two panes were sold by Royal Mail Tallents House plus the philatelic outlets. Perf. 14½×14. Two 18mm phosphor bands (blue fluor) non-fluorescent coated paper. PVA gum.

UM147 (=SG 2424)

UM147	(1st) bright mauve and black	90	90
	A. Horiz strip of 5 Nos. UM147/51	6·00	6·00

UM148 (=SG 2425)

UM148	(1st) magenta and black	90	90

UM149 (=SG 2426)

UM149	(1st) lemon and black	90	90

UM150 (=SG 2427)

UM150	(1st) pale turquoise-green and black	90	90

UM151 (=SG 2428)

UM151	(1st) bright new blue and black	90	90

Nos. UM147/51 were printed together, *se-tenant*, as horizontal strips of 5 in sheets of 25 (5×5)

Gutter Block of 10		13·00
First day Cover (UM147/51)	†	8·00
Presentation Pack UM147/51	8·00	
PHQ Cards (set of five) UM147/51	4·75	12·00

Nos. UM147/51 were also issued in sheets containing vertical strips of the five designs alternated with half stamp-size labels. These sheets with printed labels were available at £6·15 from philatelic outlets, or with personalised photographs at £14·95 From Royal Mail in Edinburgh.

Plate Numbers (Blocks of 20)
Colour and phosphor order of plate numbers reading down the margin:
(Phosphor), lemon, magenta, bright new blue, bright mauve, pale turquoise-green, black.

Perforation; Type P
Single pane sheet

Nos. UM147/51	D1(×6), D1 (phosphor)	20·00

The above includes the box with its 6 segments opposite row 2.

Sheet details
Sheet size: 50 (2 panes 5×5). Reel fed.

Greetings Stamps

Sheet markings:
Plate numbers: Opposie rows 3/4
Title: "Occasions 2004" above vertical row 1
Six box with spot: Left margin opposite horizontal row 2
Sale date: Bottom margin below vertical rows 4 and 5
Traffic lights: Right margin opposite rows 3/4 in same colour order as plate numbers.

Bicentenary of the Royal Horticultural Society (2nd issue)

Printed in Lithography

Designs as Nos. UM118, UM121 and UM125 (1997 Greeting Stamps 19th-century Flower Paintings). Each stamp with 5mm phosphor bands at left and centre (blue fluor). Non-fluorescent coated paper with PVA (bluish) gum.

Booklet stamps

Printed in lithography by Enschedé (25 May 2004)

W1666
W1667 
W1668 

Perforated 15×14 (with one elliptical hole on each vertical edge). Pane WP1669 positions in brackets
1666 (1st) As No. UM125 (R.1/1)
1667 (1st) As No. UM121 (R.1/2 and R.2./1)
1668 (1st) As No. UM118 (R.2/2)
These stamps are distinguishable by the left and centre phosphor bands. Former issues had phosphor bands at left and right sides with perforation 14½ on the horizontal edges. Since they were issued in the Prestige booklet No. DX33 they are listed under Special Issues rather than under the Greetings Stamp section.

Stitched Booklet pane (25 May 2004)

From £7·23 "The Glory of the Garden" Prestige Stamp Booklet No. DX33
Third pane comprising 4×(1st) one band at left and at centre (blue fluor) on non-fluorescent coated paper. Perforated 15×14. At left tulips with pane rouletted twice between stitched margin and to left of the four se-tenant stamps.

WP1669

WP1669 (containing Nos. W1666, W1667×2, W1668)
(25.5.04)   25·00

There were no plate numbers on the issued panes.

Smilers Booklet stamps (1st) class pane of 6

Sold at £1·80 (£1·92 From 3 April 2006).

UM152 *Guzmania splendens**
UM153 Aircraft Sky-writing "hello" 
UM154 "Love" 

UM155 Union Jack
UM156 Teddy Bear 
UM157 European Robin in Mouth of Pillar Box 

(Des. Charlotte Sowerby (UM152), Hoop Associates (UM153), A. Kitching (UM154), D. Davis (UM155), J - M. Folon (UM156), K. Lily (UM157))

Printed in gravure by Walsall

2005 (4 October). Smilers Booklet stamps inscribed (1st). Die-cut perf 15×14½. Two gradated phosphor bands (blue fluor) non-fluorescent coated paper. Self adhesive.

Issued only in booklets sold originally at £1·80, No. QA1 (see Appendix J) in which the surplus backing paper around each stamp was removed.

UM152 (=SG 2567)		
UM152 (1st) multicoloured	2·00	2·00
UM153 (=SG 2568)		
UM153 (1st) multicoloured	2·00	2·00
UM154 (=SG 2569)		
UM154 (1st) multicoloured	2·00	2·00
UM155 (=SG 2570)		
UM155 (1st) multicoloured	2·00	2·00
UM156 (=SG 2571)		
UM156 (1st) multicoloured	2·00	2·00
UM157 (=SG 2572)		
UM157 (1st) multicoloured	90	1·00
First Day Cover (UM147/51) (Tallents House)	†	12·00
First Day Cover (UM147/51) (Windsor)	†	12·00

* The flower shown appears to be of the *Compositae* family with reflex petals

(1st) £1·80 Pane 2005

Self adhesive Barcode Booklet No. QA1

Sold at £1·80 (£1·92 From 3 April 2006)
Pane of six (1st) class stamps printed in gravure on non-fluorescent coated paper with two phosphor bands (blue fluor). Die-cut perforation 15×14½.

UM Greetings Stamps

UMP158

UMP158 (containing Nos. UM152/7)(4.10.05)   12·00

Booklet Cylinder Numbers
The strip at right shows the colour bars and there was no cylinder numbers. The stamps are therefore described as multicoloured, being a combination of probably five or more cylinders.

Generic Sheet
A self-adhesive sheet of twenty inscribed "I wrote to say" containing Nos. UM153×8, UM154/55×6 Each with attached circular labels was issued on 15 January 2008 and sold at £7·35, later increased to £7·75. It was printed in lithography by Cartor.

(1st) class pane of six

Sold at £1·92 (£2·04 from 4 April 2006)

UM159 "New Baby"    UM160 "Best Wishes"    UM161 "THANK YOU"

UM162 Balloons    UM163 Firework    UM164 Champagne, Flowers and Butterflies

(Des. Alison Carmichael (UM159) Alan Kitching (UM160/1), Ivan Chermayeff (UM162), Kam Tang (UM163), Olaf Hajek (UM164) Des NB Studio.

Printed in gravure by Walsall

2006 (17 October). Smilers booklet stamps (2nd series). Occasions. Die-cut perf. 15×14½. Two gradated phosphor bands (blue fluor) non-fluorescent coated paper. Self adhesive.

Issued only in bookets sold originally at £1·92. No. QA3 in which the surplus backing paper around each stamp was removed.

UM159 (=SG 2672)

UM159 (1st) multicoloured	1·40	1·20

UM160 (=SG 2673)

UM160 (1st) multicoloured	1·40	1·20

UM161 (=SG 2674)

UM161 (1st) multicoloured	1·40	1·20

UM162 (=SG 2675)

UM162 (1st) multicoloured	1·40	1·20

UM163 (=SG 2676)

UM163 (1st) multicoloured	1·40	1·20

UM164 (=SG 2677)

UM159 (1st) multicoloured	1·40	1·20
First Day Cover (UM159/64) (Tallents House)	†	8·00
First Day Cover (UM159/64)(Grinshill Shrewsbury)†		8·00

(1st) £1·92 Pane 2006
Self-adhesive Barcode booklet No QA3

Pane of six (1st) class stamps printed in gravure on non-fluorescent coated paper with two phosphor bands (blue fluor). Die cut perforation 15 × 14½

UMP 165

UMP165 (containing Nos. UM159/64) (17.10.06)   8·00

Booklet Cylinder Numbers
The strip at right shows the colour bars and there was no cylinder numbers. The stamps are therefore described as multicoloured, being a combination of probably five or more cylinders.

UM166 "Love"

(Des. Alan Kitching)

Printed in gravure by Walsall)

2007 (16 January). Smilers Booklet Stamp (3rd series). Occasions. Die-cut perf. 15×14½ with one elliptical hole on each vertical edge. Two gradated phosphor bands (blue fluor) non-fluorescent coated paper. Self-adhesive.

UM166 (=SG 2693)

UM166 (1st) multicoloured	10·00	10·00

No. UM166 was only issued in £1·92 stamp booklets, No. SA1, in which the surplus backing paper around each stamp was removed. No. UM154 (4.10.05) did not have the elliptical perforation.

(Des. Alan Kitching)

Printed in gravure by Walsall)

2008 (15 January). Smilers Booklet Stamp (3rd series). Occasions. Die-cut perf. 15×14½ with one elliptical hole on each vertical edge. Two gradated phosphor bands (blue fluor) non-fluorescent coated paper. Self-adhesive.

UM167 (=SG 2693)

UM167 (1st) multicoloured	10·00	10·00

No. UM167 was only issued in £2·04 Stamp booklets No. SA2, in which the surplus backing paper around each stamp was removed. No. UM166 had two clear cut phosphor bands without gradated edges. This and the three uncut perforation tips on the left side of the stamp serve to distinguish Nos. UM166/7

Des. Alan Kitching.

Printed in Gravure by Walsall

2008 (28 February). Smilers Booklet Stamp (4th series). Occasions. Die-cut perf. 15 × 14½(E). Two gradated phosphor bands (blue fluor) non-fluorescent coated paper. Self-adhesive.

Issued only in booklets sold originally at £2·04, No. QA4 in which the surplus backing paper around each stamp was removed

UM168 (=SG 2819)

UM168 (1st) multicoloured	75	75

UM169 (=SG 2820)

UM169 (1st) multicoloured	75	75

UM170 (=SG 2821)

UM170 (1st) multicoloured	75	75

UM171 (=SG 2822)

UM171 (1st) multicoloured	75	75

UM172 (=SG 2823)

UM172 (1st) multicoloured	75	75

UM173 (=SG 2824)

UM173 (1st) multicoloured	75	75

(1st) £2·04 Pane 2008

Self-adhesive Barcode booklet No. QA4

Pane of six (1st) class stamps printed in gravure on non-fluorescent coated paper with two phosphor bands (blue fluor). Die cut perforation 15 × 14½(E)

UMP 174

UMP174 (containing Nos. UM168/73 (28.2.08)	9·00

Booklet Cylinder Numbers

The strip at right shows the colour bars and there were no cylinder numbers. The stamps are therefore described as multicoloured, being a combination of probably five or more cylinders.

SECTION UN
Dorothy Wilding Portrait

1998. Booklet Stamps

Printed in Gravure printed by Walsall

These stamps were issued in the Definitive Portrait Prestige Stamp Booklet issued on 10 March 1998. Printed in gravure from computer engraved cylinders they promoted the Stamp Show 2000 exhibition.

UN1

(Des. G. T. Knipe, adapted by Dew Gibbons Design Group) (Portrait by Dorothy Wilding Ltd.)

Printed in gravure by Walsall

Type UN1

Printed in Gravure by Walsall

Perforation 14 with one elliptical perf, hole on each vertical edge

20p. Light Green (1998)

1998 (10 March). Non-fluorescent coated paper. PVA gum

From £7.49 The Definitive Portrait booklet panes UNW2/3
UN1 (= SG 2031)

A. One 3 mm wide short band (blue fluor) at right			
UN1	Light green	70	75

UN2 (= SG 2031 Ea)

B. One 3 mm Wide short band (blue fluor) at left			
UN2	Light green	70	75

26p. Red-brown (1998)

1998 (10 March). Two 3 mm wide short phosphor bands (blue fluor). Non-fluorescent coated paper. PVA gum

UN3 (= SG 2032)

From £7.49 The Definitive Portrait booklet panes UNW1, UNW3/4,

UN3	Red-brown	90	95

37p. Light Purple (1998)

1998 (10 March). Two 3 mm wide short phosphor bands (blue fluor). Non-fluorescent coated paper. PVA gum

UN4 (= SG 2033)

From £7.49 The Definitive Portrait booklet panes UNW3/4			
UN4	Light purple	2·75	2·75

1998. Wilding Decimal Prestige Booklet Panes

Printed in Gravure by Walsall

From £7.49 Booklet The Definitive Portrait No. DX20
The illustrations are reduced, the actual size being 162 × 96 mm.

First pane comprising 9 × 26p. with two short phosphor bands (blue fluor) on non-fluorescent coated paper.

UNW1

UNW1 (containing No. UN3 × 9) (10.3.98)	9·50

Second pane showing Edmund Dulac, comprising 3 × 20p. short band at right and 3 × 20p. short band at left (blue fluor) on non-fluorescent coated paper.

UNW2

UNW2 (containing Nos. UN1 × 3, UN2 × 3) (10.3.98)	4·75

Third pane with stamps showing short phosphor bands comprising 2 × 20p. band at right, 2 × 20p. band at left, 2 × 26p., 2 × 37p. with two bands (blue floor) on non-fluorescent coated paper. There are no bands on the centre label.

UNW3

UNW3 (containing Nos. UN1×2, UN2×2. 9.50
UN3×2, UN4×2) (10.3.98)

Fourth pane comprising 3×26p. two short bands and 3×37p. two short bands (blue fluor) on non-fluorescent coated paper.

UNW4

UNW4 containing Nos. UN3×3. UN4×3) (10.3.98) 9·50

Pane Nos. UNW1/4 were sold separately to dealers for servicing first day covers by the Philatelic Bureau.

Cylinder Numbers

The panes were printed from computer engraved cylinders on the Chesnut press. The printer's sheets contained two columns each with five panes. The cylinder numbers do not occur in the issued booklets but it is known that the following were used. We have quoted the printers' colour descriptions.

UNW1 Brown (W1 cyl. 104). Bronze (W1 cyl. 105), Rust (W1 cyl. 133). Phos (W1 cyl. 102)
UNW2 Brown (W1 cyl. 113), Bronze (W1 cyl. 114), Light green (W1 cyl. 112), Phos (W1 cyl. 115)
UNW3 Brown (W1 cyl. 106). Bronze (W1 cyl. 108). Light green (W1 cyl. 107), Rust (W1 cyl. 109), Rhododendron (W1 cyl. 110). Phos (W1 cyl. 111)
UNW4 Black (W1 cyl. 134). Black (W1 cyl. 120), Rhododendron (W1 cyl. 118). Rust (W1 cyl. 117), Phos (W1 cyl. 116)

2001 booklet stamps inscribed 1st and 2nd

Printed in Gravure by Enschedé

UN2    UN3

(Des. Miss Enid Marx (UN2) and M.C. Farrar-Bell (UN3), adapted by GBH)

Type UN2

Printed in gravure by Enschedé

Watermark **W25** Tinted Paper

■ (2nd) Carmine-red (2002)

2002 (6 February). Perf 15 × 14 and one elliptical perf. hole on each vertical edge. One 4.5 mm centre phosphor band (blue fluor). PVA gum (bluish).

£7.29 "A Gracious Accession" booklet pane UNW5

A. Watermark W25 upright
UN5 (=SG 2258)

UN5 Carmine-red	1·20	1·00

B. Watermark W25 diagonal
UN6 (=SG 2258Ea)

UN6 Carmine-red	4·50	3·25

Type UN3

Printed in gravure by Enschede

Watermark **W25** Tinted Paper

■ (1st) Green (2002)

2002 (6 February). Perf 15 × 14 and one elliptical perf. hole on each vertical edge. Two 4.5 mm phosphor bands (blue fluor). Watermark W25. PVA gum (bluish).

£7.29 "A Gracious Accesion" booklet pane UNW5
UN7 (=SG 2259)

UN7 Green	1·25	1·25

2003 booklet stamps

Printed in Gravure by Walsall

4    5

(Des. Edmund Dulac and adapted by GBH)

Types 4/5

Printed in gravure by Walsall

Watermark **W25** Paper tinted by screen

■ (2nd) Carmine-red (2002)

2003 (2 June). Types 4/5 Watermark W25 Perf 15 × 14 and one elliptical perf. hole on each vertical edge. Two side phosphor bands (blue fluor).

£7.46 " A Perfect Coronation" booklet pane UNW6
UN8 (=SG 2378)

UN8 **4** 47p. Bistre-brown	5·00	2·50

UN9 (=SG 2379)

UN8 68p. grey-blue	5·00	2·50

UN10 (=SG 2380)

UN10 **4** £1. Deep yellow-green	50·00	45·00

Nos. UN8/10 were only available in £7.46 stamp booklets. Stamps as Nos. UN8/9, but on pale cream, were also included in the Wilding miniature sheets, Nos. UNMS1 or UNMS2. A £1 Design as No. UN10, but on phosphorised paper, was previously included in the "Stamp Show 2000" miniature sheet No. WMS1309.

2001 Wilding Decimal Prestige Booklet panes

Printed in Gravure by Enschedé

From £7.29 "A Gracious Accession" Prestige Stamp Booklet No. DX28

The other panes in the booklet are Nos. UIPP9 (Section UI) and WP1448/49 (Vol. 5).

Fourth pane printed on tinted paper comprising 5×(2nd) centre band and 4×(1st) two bands (blue fluor). No bands printed on centre label and the (2nd) class value at left is No UN6 with diagonal watermark **W25**. Perforated 15 × 14 with one elliptical perf. hole on each vertical edge. Vertical roulettes between selvedge and to left of the ??st vertical row of stamps. Printed in gravure.

UNW5

UNW5 (Containing Nos. UN5×4, UN6, UN7×4) (6.2.02)   14·00

Cylinder Numbers
No cylinder numbers occur on the issued panes.

Wilding Decimal Miniature Sheets

UNMS1 Miniature sheet

(Miniature sheet des. Rose Design. Gravure by De la Rue)

2002 (5 December). 50th Anniversary of Dorothy Wilding Portrait Definitives (1st issue).

Sheet sixe 124 × 70mm containing designs as (1952-54 issue by Enid marx (1st, 1, 2 and 5p.). Michael C. Farrar-Bell (2nd), George T. Knipe (33p.) Mary Adshead (37p.), Edmund Dulac (47, 50p.). Non-fluorescent coated paper (pale cream tinted) one 4.5mm centre band (2nd) and two bands (others) all with blue fluor. PVA (bluish gum). Watermark W25 Perf. 15 × 14 (with one elliptical perf hole on each vertical edge).

UNMS1 (=SG **MS**2326)

UNMS1	Label in green showing national emblems; 1p. orange-red; 2p. ultramarine; 5p. red-brown; (2nd) carmine-red; (1st) green; 33p. brown; 37p. magenta; 47p. bistre-brown; 50p. Green (Sold at £2.21)	10·00	10·00
First Day Cover (UNMS1)		†	10·00
Presentation Pack		£100	†

PHQ cards (set of 5)   3·00   12·00

The PHQ cards depict the (2nd), (1st), 33p., 37p., and 47p. Stamps. The (2nd) was initially sold at 19p. And (1st) at 27p.

The Presentation Pack was sold out soon after issue.

2003 Wilding Decimal Prestige Booklet panes

Printed in gravure by Walsall

From £7.46 "A Perfect Coronation" Prestige Stamp Booklet No. DX31

The other panes in the booklet are Nos. UIPP12 (Section UI) and WP1573/4 (Vol. 5)

Fouth pane printed on non-fluorescent paper with watermark **W25** comprising 2×47p., 2×68p. and £1 two bands at each side (blue fluor). Perforated 15 × 14 with one elliptical perf. hole on each vertical edge. Vertical roulettes between selvedge and the left of the first vertical row of stamps. Printed in gravure and the stamps with pale screen to resemble tinted paper.

UNW6

UNW6 (containing Nos. UN8×2, UN9×2 UN10)(2.6.03)   65·00

Cylinder Numbers
No cylinder numbers occur on the issued panes.

UNMS2 Miniature Sheet

(Miniature sheet des. Rose Design. Gravure De la Rue)

2003 (20 May). 50th Anniversary of Dorothy Wilding Portrait Definitives (2nd issue).

Sheet size 124 × 70mm containing designs as (1952-59 issued by Michael C. Farrar-Bell (4, 8p. (E)), George T. Knipe (10, 20p.) Mary Adshead (28, 34, 42p.), Edmunf Dulac (68p.). Non-fluorescent coated paper (pale cream tinted) one 4.5mm centre band (2nd) and two bands (others) all with blue fluor. PVA (bluish gum) Watermark W25 Perf 15 × 14 (with one elliptical perf. hole on each vertical edge).

UNMS2 (=SG **MS**2367)

UNMS2	Label in brown-purple showing national emblems; 4p.deep lilac; 8p. ultramarine; 10p. reddish purple; 20p. bright green; 28p. bronze-green; 34p. brown-lilac; (E) chestnut; 42p Prussian blue; 68p. rey-blue (Sold at £2.52)	10·50	11·25
	First day Cover (UNMS2)	†	13·00
	Presentation pack	18·00	†

On the previous miniature sheet, issued on 5 December 2002, the cream tint had a fine screen and was printed in gravure. The same tint on No. UNMS2 had a cream wash probably printed first in lithography. This may account for the brighter fluor response on this issue compared with UNMS1.

2005 (22 March). **50th Anniversary of First Castles Definitives.**

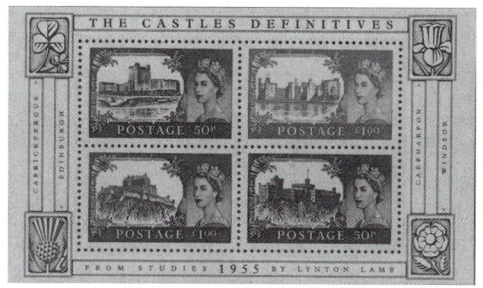

UNMS3 Miniature Sheet
(Illustration reduced to half actual size)

(Miniature sheet des. Sedley Place. Recess and Lithography Joh Enschedé)

Sheet size 127 × 73mm containing horizontal designs by Lynton Lamb as Types **T1/4** (Castle definitive of 1955-58) but with values in decimal currency, printed on pale cream. "All-over" phosphor. PVA gum. Perf. 11 × 11½.

UNMS3 (=SG **MS**2530)

UNMS3	Carrickfergus castle brownish black; £1 Caernarfon Castle dull vermilion; £1 Edinburgh Castle royal blue; 50p Windsor Castle black (Sold at £3)	10·00	10·00
	First day Cover (Tallents House)	†	12·00
	First Day Cover (Windsor)	†	12·00
	Presentation Pack	18·00	†
	PHQ Cards (set of 5)	2·20	12·00

For illustrations of the original Castle stamps see *Great Britain Specialised Catalogue Volume 3*. Individual values from the miniature sheet will not be listed separately.

XB

SECTION XB
Regional Machin Issues
1971-2000. Gravure. Isle of Man, Northern Ireland, Scotland and Wales

General Notes
Although a Post Office press notice dated 3 December 1973 designated these stamps as Country issues this term has not generally been adopted in philatelic literature and we continue to describe them as Regional issues.

Regional issues in sheets with the emblem design, were replaced by pictorial issues for Scotland and Wales in 1999 and Northern Ireland in 2001. These are listed in Section XE.

Introduction. On 7 July 1971 new stamps appeared in decimal currency showing a reduced size Machin head accompanied by emblems representing the Isle of Man, Northern Ireland, Scotland and Wales and Monmouthshire. They were all designed by Jeffery Matthews.

The ordinary postage stamps of Great Britain in the same values were not on sale at Post Offices in these regions except at the Philatelic Counters in Belfast, Cardiff, Edinburgh and Glasgow, apart from Monmouthshire where the Welsh Regionals and Great Britain stamps were on sale concurrently (see notes at the beginning of Wales). All regional stamps are valid for use throughout Great Britain with the exception of the Channel Islands and also the Isle of Man from 5 July 1973.

Printers (Harrison issue). All values issued from 1971/81 were printed in Gravure from chemically etched cylinders. As with the ordinary decimal Machin issues they were printed in double pane width, i.e. 400 stamps consisting of two panes (no dot and dot) each of 200 stamps arranged in 20 rows of ten stamps, the panes being guillotined before issue. All the 5½p. and the 8p. values were printed in single panes but from double pane cylinders. The 5p. and 7½p. were sheet-fed but all the rest were reel-fed.

Harrison printed the Prestige "BBC 75" booklet issued on 23 September 1997, in which the 26p. and 37p. regionals were printed from computer engraved cylinders.

(Walsall issue). This issue replaced the values printed in lithography. They were printed on the Chesnut press from computer engraved cylinders. The sheets are single panes of 200 (10 × 20).

Machin portrait. The original Head A with the flatter bust was used for the 3½p., 4½p., 6½p., 7p., 8½p., 10½p., 12p., 13½p. and 15p. values. Head B with the curved "shadow" was employed for the 2½p., 3p., 5p., 5½p., 7½p. and 8p. values. Head C was used for the 9p., 10p. and 11p. values.

Head A
Flatter Base

Head B
Curved Shadow

Head C
Three-dimensional effect with light background

On values of 19p. and over the Queen's head appears identical on Harrison and Walsall printings.

Multipositives. It is believed that Harrison used two multipositives for each of the Regional issues—one for the head and background and the other for the country symbol and value.

Paper and gum. The same unwatermarked papers and gums have been used as for the ordinary Machin decimal stamps and for explanation of the terms OCP, FCP, GA. PVA, PVA (bluish) and PVAD see the General Notes for Section UD in *G.B. Specialised Volume 4, Part 1*.

Perforation. All stamps are perforated 15 × 14 without ellipse unless otherwise stated. Cylinder numbers are listed according to the perforation types used and these are illustrated in Appendix I.

Phosphor bands. The remarks under this heading in the General Notes to Section UD in *G.B. Specialised Volume 4, Part 1* also apply to the regional stamps. Blue fluor was added from 1 July 1997 and this responds as dull or bright under u.v. light.

Yellow phosphor. The yellowish afterglow after exposure to long wave ultraviolet light caused by contamination in 1973 of the normal "violet" phosphor with zinc oxide, identified on Machin values, is also found on certain regional issues. This occurs only on Harrison printings, these are:

Region	Value	Cat. No.	Paper/gum	Cyl. No.	Phos. No.
Northern Ireland	3p.	XN21	FCP/PVA	1	7
Scotland	3p.	XS33	FCP GA	8	7
	5p.	XS42	FCP/PVA	7	11
Wales	3p.	XW23	FCP GA	1	7

They are recorded in footnotes below the catalogue numbers

Phosphor screens. In the regional issues the 250 screen was used for the 3p. 2 bands, 5½p. 2 bands and 8p. All the remainder to 15p. value have 150 screen.

Phosphor cylinder numbers. They normally appear synchronised in the box to the left of the cylinder number on both panes. In the case of double figure numbers in the dot pane the margins are often narrow so that the first figure is liable to be trimmed off. They also occur synchronised but displaced.

Cylinder varieties. We have only listed those that we have actually seen and know to be constant in the position given. Some of these may exist on other papers or with other gums and these will be added as they are brought to our attention. Other varieties have been reported and may be added in future editions as specimens become available for illustration. The minor flaws with Thirkell Position Finder grid reference are described and position in sheet, but without prices.

Dates of issue. Earliest known dates of issue are given for changes of paper and gum.

Regional Machin issues *Gravure Isle of Man* **XB**

Harrison & Sons Sheet Printings
1971 to 1980

Sheet Markings. Illustrations and notes apply to these regional issues as for Machin issues listed in *G.B. Specialised Volume 4, Part 1*
Cylinder Numbers. Boxed opposite R. 18/1.
Marginal Arrows. As for Machin sheets.

Perforation Guide Holes

Punched Perforation Guide Hole Box

Perforation Guide Holes. There are none on the 5p. and 7½p. On the 5½p. and 8p. a three-sided box as illustrated above appears in the left-hand margin of the no dot pane and in the right-hand margin of the dot pane it faces the other way. On the 5½p. for Northern Ireland and Scotland these occur opposite rows 13/14 and for Wales, together with all the 8p. values, they occur opposite row 14. They are punched through on the 5½p. two bands and the 8p. but were not used on the 5½p. centre band. All the remaining values have the usual "S O N" box at rows 14/15.
Marginal Rules. Wide co-extensive rule below the bottom row.
Coloured Cross. A single cross appears above and below vertical row 5 next to the marginal arrow on the no dot panes of the 5p. and 7½p.
Autotron Mark. This occurs in the colour of the stamp opposite rows 8/9 in the left-hand margin of no dot panes printed by the "Jumelle" press (Perforation Type R).
Total Sheet Values. These are preceded by "I O MAN", "N. IRELAND", "SCOTLAND" or "WALES" and occur four times on each pane opposite rows 5/7 and 15/17, reading up at left and down at right.
 Exceptionally the inscription on the 5½p. and 8p. Northern Ireland stamps is larger so that it appears opposite rows 4/7 and 15/18 and on the 6½p. and 8½p. values it reads "NORTHERN IRELAND" in full and appears in the same position as the 5½p. and 8p. On the 7p., 9p., 10p., 10½p., 11p., 12p., 13½p. and 15p. the inscription is the same except that in the upper half of the sheet it appears opposite rows 5/7 instead of 4/7.

Walsall Security Printers Ltd.
Sheet Printings July 1997 to June 1999

Sheet markings. The sheets differ from Harrison in that they are single pane, therefore no dot and dot references do not apply. The phosphor cylinder number occurs above or below the ink number but we do not list these separately.
Cylinder Numbers. Prefixed "W" and opposite row 18. left margin.

Sheet, Stock Operations Number and Date of Printing

Walsall Cylinder Number and Imprint

Date of Printing and Warrant Number. This is printed in the ink-jet style in the left margin. The position varies but we price these in blocks of 8.
Imprint. Opposite row 20 in the left margin and on the cylinder block of 6. Inscribed in capital letters "WALSALL SECURITY PRINTERS LTD".
Marginal Arrows. These are "W" shaped and are opposite vertical rows 5/6 and horizontal rows 10/11 at both sides.
Perforation. All values are perforated with an elliptical perf. hole on each vertical edge of the stamp. The gauge is 15 × 14 unless otherwise stated. Walsall used perforation 14 in the "Breaking Barriers" prestige booklet and is the only variation to the 15 × 14 standard. On sheets an on-line rotary perforator giving perf. type RE was employed. The 20p. exists with the same perf. type (RE) but a comb machine was used. We do not list single examples but give a price for a cylinder block.
Total Sheet Values. As in the Harrison issue, the country name preceeding the sheet value occurs four times on the sheet opposite horizontal rows 4/7 and 14/17 at both sides, reading up in the left and down in the right margin.

A. Isle of Man

XM3

(Des. Jeffery Matthews)

All printed by Harrison & Sons from chemically etched cylinders

2½p. Bright magenta (1971–73)

1971 (7 July). One 4 mm centre band

A. Original coated paper. PVA gum
XM12 (=SG 8)

XM12	2½p. Bright magenta		20	15
	a. Phosphor omitted .		£1500	
	b. Ankle flaw		2·50	

Cylinder Numbers (Blocks of Six)
Perforation: Type A

Cyl. No.	Phos. No.	No dot	Dot
3	5	4·00	4·00

B. Fluorescent coated paper. PVA gum

XM13	2½p. Bright magenta	90	90

Cylinder Numbers (Blocks of Six)
Perforation: Type A

Cyl. No.	Phos. No.	No dot	Dot
3	9	15·00	10·00

CYLINDER VARIETY

XM12b
White projection in ankle of bottom leg (Cyl. 3 no dot, R. 15/1)

Withdrawn: 4 July 1974

XB Regional Machin issues   Isle of Man / Northern Ireland

3p. Ultramarine (1971–73)

1971 (7 July). Two 9·5 mm bands.

A. Original coated paper. PVA gum
XM14 (=SG 9)

XM14	3p. Ultramarine	20	15
	a. Blurred emblem	2·50	

Cylinder Numbers (Blocks of Six)
Perforation: Type A

Cyl. No.	Phos. No.	No dot	Dot
4		4·00	4·00

B. Fluorescent coated paper. PVA gum (7.73)

XM 15	3p. Ultramarine	1·75	1·75
	a. Blurred emblem	4·50	

Cylinder Numbers (Blocks of Six unless otherwise stated)
Perforation: Type A

Cyl. No.	Phos. No.	No dot	Dot
1	—		25·00	25·00
1	—	7 + 35 mm (17)	32·00	† Block of eight
1	—	7 + 37 mm (17)	†	35·00 Block of eight

CYLINDER VARIETIES

XM14a, XM15a
Design at top of emblem very blurred (No dot. R. 1/9)

Minor Constant Flaw
Cyl. 1 12/2 White line below right leg of emblem (Th. B2–B3).

Withdrawn: Nos. XM14/5, 4 July 1974

5p. Reddish violet (1971)

1971 (7 July). Two 9·5 mm bands. Original coated paper. PVA gum

XM16 (=SG 10)

UM16	5p. Reddish violet	80	80
	a. Phosphor omitted	£275	

Cylinder Numbers (Blocks of Six)
Perforation: Type F

Cyl. No.	Phos. No.	No dot	Dot
4	12	7·00	7·00

Withdrawn: 4 July 1974

7½p. Chestnut (1971)

1971 (7 July). Two 9·5 mm bands. Original coated paper. PVA gum

XM17 (=SG 11)

XM17	7½p. Chestnut	90	90
	a. White flaw on 7	3·75	

Cylinder Numbers (Blocks of Six)
Perforation: Type F*

Cyl. No.	Phos. No.	No dot	Dot
4	10	10·00	9·00

CYLINDER VARIETIES

XM17a White flaw on 7 (Cyl. 4 dot. R. 12/7)

Minor Constant Flaws
Cyl. 4. 10/10 Vertical scratch from cross on crown to back of collar (Th. B5–F5)
10/11 Extension of above scratch in background to cross on crown (Th. A5/6–B5/6)

Withdrawn: 4 July 1974

Presentation Pack

XMPP2 No. 30 (7.7.71) 2½p., 3p., 5p., 7½p.   3·25
Comprises Nos. XM12, 14 and 16/17

Withdrawn: 4 July 1974

First Day Cover

XMFD1 (7.7.71) 2½p., 3p., 5p., 7½p.   3·00

B. Northern Ireland

XN4

(Des. Jeffery Matthews)

All stamps issued between 1971/80 were printed by Harrison & Sons from chemically etched cylinders.

Type XN4

2½p. Bright magenta (1971–73)

1971 (7 July). One 4 mm centre band

A. Original coated paper. PVA gum
XN18 (=SG NI12)

XN18	2½p. Bright magenta	70	60
	a. Missing pearls on crown	3·75	
	b. White patch on shoulder	3·50	

Cylinder Numbers (Blocks of Six)
Perforation: Type A

Cyl. No.	Phos. No.	No dot	Dot
4	5	9·00	7·00

B. Fluorescent coated paper. PVA gum

XN19	2½p. Bright magenta	3·00	3·00

Regional Machin issues Northern Ireland XB

Cylinder Numbers (Blocks of Six)
Perforation: Type A

Cyl. No.	Phos. No.	No dot	Dot
4	8	35·00	40·00
4	9	£120	£120
4	9–21 mm (19)	40·00	40·00

CYLINDER VARIETIES

XN18a Normal
Last two pearls at right of crown in emblem almost missing (Cyl. 4 dot, R. 3/6)

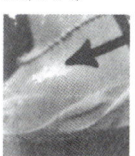

XN18b White patch on Queen's shoulder (Cyl. 4 dot, R.6/10)

Withdrawn: Nos. XN18/9. 22 January 1975

3p. Ultramarine (1971–74)

1971 (7 July). Two 9·5 mm bands.

A. Original coated paper. PVA gum
XN20 (=SG NI13)

XN20	3p. Ultramarine	30	30
	a. Phosphor omitted	50·00	

Cylinder Numbers (Blocks of Six)
Perforation: Type A

Cyl. No.	Phos. No.	No dot	Dot
1	4	3·75	3·75

B. Fluorescent coated paper. PVA gum (4.73)

XN21	3p. Ultramarine	10·00	5·00

Examples of No. XN21 exist with contaminated "yellow phosphor". Price £7 mint.

Cylinder Numbers (Blocks of Six)
Perforation: Type A

Cyl. No.	Phos. No.	No dot	Dot
1	—	£130	£140
1	7	£130	£140

Phosphor Cylinder Displacement. With ink cyl. 1, phos. cyl. 7 is known displaced up the margin 185 mm opposite row 11.

1974 (23 January). One 4 mm centre band

A. Fluorescent coated paper. PVAD gum

XN22	3p. Ultramarine		90

Cylinder Numbers (Blocks of Six)
Perforation: Type A

Cyl. No.	Phos. No.	No dot	Dot
1	8	10·00	10·00

B. Fluorescent coated paper. PVA gum (4.74)
XN23 (=SG N1 I4)

XN23	3p. Ultramarine	20	15

Cylinder Numbers (Blocks of Six)
Perforation: Type A

Cyl. No.	Phos. No.	No dot	Dot
1	8	3·00	3·00

Withdrawn: Nos. XN20/1, 22 January 1975; Nos. XN22/3, 8 April 1978

3½p. Olive-grey (1974)

1974 (23 January). Two 9·5 mm bands. Fluorescent coated paper. PVAD gum

XN24 (=SG NI15)

XN24	3½p. Olive-grey	20	25

Cylinder Numbers (Blocks of Six)
Perforation: Type R

Cyl. No.	Phos. No.	No dot	Dot
1	17	3·25	3·25

1974 (6 November). One 4 mm centre band. Fluorescent coated paper. PVAD gum

XN25 (=SG NI16)

XN25	3½p. Olive-grey	20	25
	a. White dots under chin	2·75	

Cylinder Numbers (Blocks of Six)
Perforation: Type R

Cyl. No.	Phos. No.	No dot	Dot
1	20	4·00	3.50

CYLINDER VARIETIES

XN25a
Rectangle of white dots over phosphor band below chin
(Cyl. 1 no dot, R. 4/10)

Minor Constant Flaws
Cyl. 1 2/2 One missing screening dot at edge of design over cross on crown (Th. A2)
9/3 Vertical scratch marks on Queen's cheek (Th. D4–D5)
11/2 As on 2/2

Withdrawn: Nos. XN24/ 5 September 1976

4½p. Grey–blue (1974)

1974 (6 November). Two 9·5 mm bands. Fluorescent coated paper. PVAD gum

XN26 (=SG N17)

XN26	4½p. Grey-blue	30	25

Cylinder Numbers (Blocks of Six)
Perforation: Type R

Cyl. No.	Phos. No.	No dot	Dot
1	17	4·00	4·00

XB Regional Machin issues *Northern Ireland*

CYLINDER VARIETIES

Minor Constant Flaws
Cyl. 1 3/8 White spot above necklace (Th. F4)
  9/2 White speck over pearls on right of crown in emblem (Th. A2)
  18/2 White speck in Queen's hair (Th. D5)

Withdrawn: September 1976

5p. Reddish violet (1971)

1971 (7 July). Two 9·5 mm bands. Original coated paper. PVA gum

XN27 (=SG N18)

XN27	5p. Reddish violet	1·00	1·00

Cylinder Numbers (Blocks of Six)
Perforation: Type F*

Cyl. No.	Phos. No.	No dot	Dot
4	10	12·00	12·00

Withdrawn: 22 January 1975

5½p. Violet (1974–75)

1974 (23 January). Two 9·5 mm bands. Fluorescent coated paper. PVAD gum

XN28 (=SG NI19)

XN28	5½p. Violet	20	20
	a. Phosphor omitted	£250	
	b. Right-hand band omitted		
	c. Cylinder scratch (in block of 40)	25·00	
	d. No top to cross on crown	2·40	

Cylinder Numbers (Blocks of Six)
Perforation: Type A. Single pane cylinder

Cyl. No.	Phos. No.	No dot	Dot
1	22*	3·25	†

*The phosphor 22 is shown upright but superimposed over inverted figures.

1975 (21 May). One 4 mm centre band. Fluorescent coated paper. PVAD gum

XN29 (=SG NI20)

XN29	5½p. Violet	20	25
	b. No top to cross on crown	2·40	

Cylinder Numbers (Blocks of Six)
Perforation: Type R(S).

Cyl. No.	Phos. No.	No dot	Dot
1	19	3·25	†

Normally the Swedish rotary perforator produces a single extension hole in the left-hand margin on no dot panes. Sheets from cylinder 1 have been seen with the left-hand margin fully perforated through and also with two extension holes. *Price for cylinder block* of 6 £5 mint.

CYLINDER VARIETIES

XN28c (R. 1/6) Scratch extends diagonally from R. 1/6 to R 20/7, Cyl. 1 no dot   XN28c (R. 20/7)

XN28d, XN29b
Missing top to cross on crown
(Cyl. 1 no dot, R. 11/10)

Minor Constant Flaw
Cyl. 1   1/10 Diagonal hairline scratch across Queen's shoulders (Th. G3–F6)

Withdrawn: Nos. XN28/9, 31 May 1977

6½p. Greenish Blue (1976)

1976 (14 January). One 4 mm centre band. Fluorescent coated paper. PVAD gum

XN30 (=SG NI21)

XN30	6½p. Greenish blue	20	20
	h. Blue shoulder scratch	1·75	
	c. Dark spot in hair	2·00	
	d. Collar scratch	1·75	
	e. White spot over small crown	2·00	
	f. Dark spot in band	1·75	

No. XN30 exists with the centre band misplaced to 1mm from the left of the stamp, but not over the perforations, *Price £200 mint*

Cylinder Numbers (Blocks of Six)
Perforation: Type R

Cyl. No.	Phos. No.	No dot	Dot
1	18	3·00	3·00
2	18	60·00	4·25
2	20	3·50	3·50

Perforation: Type RE

2	20	—*	2·50

*Same price as perforation type R with single extension holes in left margin.

CYLINDER VARIETIES

XN30b
Small blue scratch on back of shoulder
(Cyl. 1 dot. R. 1/4)

XN30d
Scratch from collar into background (Cyl. 1 dot, R. 13/9)

Regional Machin issues Northern Ireland XB

XN30e
White spot over small crown
Cyl. 1 dot. R. 15/3)

Multipositive Flaws: The following also occur on 6½p. Scotland cyl. 1 dot and Wales cyl. 1 dot as well as on 4½p. Wales cyl. 1 dot.

XN30c
Dark spot in hair
(Cyl. 1 dot. R. 12/8)

XN30f
Dark spot in band of crown
(Cyl. 1 dot, R. 16/6)

See also Northern Ireland 12p. cyl. 1 dot, 13½p. cyl. 2 dot, 15p. cyl. 1 dot and Wales 12p. cyl. 2 dot where these flaws are listed in positions R. 12/10 and R. 16/8. Both flaws were retouched on the Wales 15p. cyl. 1 dot.

Minor Constant Flaws:
Cyl. 1. 6/2 Small retouch at back of collar (Th. G5). Original flaw on Wales 4½p.
6/4 Blue speck on Queen's forehead (Th. C4-D4)
6/5 Blue blemish on Queen's cheek (Th. E4)
9/3 Blue spot on Queen's neck (Th. F5)
14/10 Small retouch under necklace (Th. F4)
20/2 Small speck under necklace (Th. F4-5)
Some of the above are multipositive flaws which occur to a greater or lesser extent on the 6½p. Scotland and 4½p. and 6½p. Wales from Cyl. 1 dot.

Withdrawn: March 1979

7p. Purple-brown (1978)

1978 (18 January). One 4 mm centre band. Fluorescent coated paper. PVAD gum

XN31 (=SG NI22)

XN31	7p. Purple-brown	35	25
	b. White dots left of crown	1·90	
	c. Dark spot in band of crown	1·75	
	d. Missing pearls	2·00	

Cylinder Numbers (Blocks of Six)
Perforation: Type RE

Cyl. No.	Phos. No.	No dot	Dot
1	20	35·00	45·00
1	31	3·25	3·25

CYLINDER VARIETIES

XN31b
White dots left of crown
(Cyl. 1 no dot, R. 1/8)

XN31c
Dark spot in band of crown
(Cyl. 1 no dot, R. 6/3)

XN31d Missing pearls at left of crown (Cyl. 1. no dot, R. 20/7)

Minor Constant Flaws
Cyl. 1 1/7 Two dark spots on Queen's neck (Th. F5)
3/10 Dark speck on collar (Th. G5)
4/6 White scratch touching P
14/7 Dark spot over necklace (Th. F4)

Withdrawn: March 1981

7½p. Chestnut (1971)

1971 (7 July). Two 9·5 mm bands. Original coated paper. PVA gum

XN32 (=SG NI23)

XN32	7½p. Chestnut	1·75	1·75
	a. Phosphor omitted	55·00	

Cylinder Numbers (Blocks of Six)
Perforation: Type F

Cyl. No.	Phos. No.	No dot	Dot
6	12	18·00	18·00

CYLINDER VARIETY

Minor Constant Flaw:
Cyl. 6. 20/8 Background retouch left of Queen's eye (Th. D4)

Withdrawn: 22 January 1975

8p. Rosine (1974)

1974 (23 January). Two 9·5 mm bands. Fluorescent coated paper. PVAD gum

XN33 (=SG NI24)

XN33	8p. Rosine	35	35
	a. Phosphor omitted	75·00	
	b. Lip flaw	3·25	

Cylinder Numbers (Blocks of Six)
Perforation: Type A. Single pane cylinder

Cyl. No.	Phos. No.	No dot	Dot
1	22*	3·00	†

*The phosphor 22 is shown upright but superimposed over inverted figures.

103

XB Regional Machin issues *Northern Ireland*

CYLINDER VARIETIES

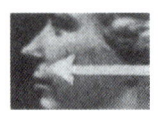

XN33b Dark spot over Queen's upper lip (Cyl. 1 no dot, R. 3/7)

Minor Constant Flaws:
Cyl. 1   15/4 Dark blemish on Queen's jaw (Th. F3)
    16/9 Coloured line below necklace (Th. F4)

Withdrawn: March 1979

8½p. Yellow–green (1976)

1976 (14 January). Two 9·5 mm bands. Fluorescent coated paper. PVAD gum

XN34 (=SG NI25)

XN34	8½p. Yellow-green	35	40
	a. Missing cross on crown	2·75	

Cylinder Numbers (Blocks of Six)
Perforation: Type R

Cyl. No.	Phos. No.	No dot	Dot
1	17	3·00	3·00

Perforation: Type RE

| 1 | 17 | 3·00* | 5·00 |
| 1 | P21 | 12·00 | 35·00 |

*Same price as perforation type R with single extension holes in left margin.

CYLINDER VARIETIES

XN34a Missing cross in crown (Cyl. 1 no dot. R. 9/I)

Minor Constant Flaw
Cyl. 1.   20/3 Blemishes on Queen's forehead (Th. C3–C4)

Withdrawn: November 1979

9p. Deep violet (1978)

1978 (18 January). Two 9·5 mm bands. Fluorescent coated paper. PVAD gum

XN35 (=SG NI26)

XN35	9p. Deep violet	40	40
	a. Phosphor omitted	25·00	
	b. Curved white flaw over jewel of crown	2·75	
	c. Missing cross on crown	3·00	
	d. Sliced 9	2·75	
	e. Left-hand band omitted	65·00	
	f. Right-hand band omitted	30·00	

Cylinder Numbers (Blocks of Six)
Perforation: Type RE

Cyl. No.	Phos. No.	No. dot	Dot
1	P21	7·00	22·00
1	30	3·00	3·00

CYLINDER VARIETIES

Listed Flaws

XN35b Curved white flaw over jewel (Cyl. 1 no dot, R. 16/10)

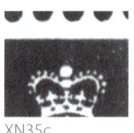

XN35c Missing cross on crown (Cyl. 1 no dot. R. 17/4) (Later retouched)

XN35d Sliced 9 (Cyl. 1 dot, R. 9/10)

Minor Constant Flaws:
Cyl. 1   10/9 Small retouch under hand (Th. D2)
    19/4 Cross on crown partly omitted (Th. A2)
Cyl. 1.   1/9 White speck under P
    6/7 Dark blemish above back of crown (Th. C6)
    6/8 Dark speck on Queen's bust (Th. G4)
    8/2 White specks under 9
    8/10 Horizontal dark scratch under Queen's bust at right (Th. G6)
    12/2 Dark speck at upper right (Th. A6)
    16/2 White cut in second finger of hand
    20/7 Dark blemish under Queen's bust (Th. G4)

Withdrawn: 30 April 1982

10p. Orange-brown (1976-80)

1976 (20 October). Two 9·5 mm bands. Fluorescent coated paper. PVAD gum

XN36 (=SG NI27)

XN36	10p. Orange-brown	40	50
	b. Right cross in crown partly missing	3·25	

Cylinder Numbers (Blocks of Six)
Perforation: Type RE

Cyl. No.	Phos. No.	No dot	Dot
1	17	3·75	3·75
1	30	21·00	£450

1980 (23 July). One 4 mm centre band. Fluorescent coated paper. PVAD gum

XN37 (=SG NI28)

XN37	10p. Orange-brown	50	50
	b. Right cross in crown partly missing	2·25	

Cylinder Numbers (Blocks of Six)
Perforation: Type RE

Cyl. No.	Phos. No.	No dot	Dot
1	20	3·75	3·75

Regional Machin issues *Northern Ireland* **XB**

CYLINDER VARIETIES

XN36/7b
Right cross in crown partly missing (Cyl. 1 dot, R. 8/3)

Minor Constant Flaws
Cyl. 1. 13/7 Small retouch at upper centre (Th. A4)
19/6 Missing screening dots in right frame (Th. G6)

Withdrawn: No. XN36, November 1982; No. XN37, sold out October 1987

10½p. Steel-blue (1978)

1978 (18 January). Two 9·5 mm bands. Fluorescent coated paper. PVAD gum

XN38 (=SG NI29)

XN38	10½p. Steel-blue	40	50
	b. Missing cross to crown	4·00	
	c. Heavy line under bust	2·75	
	d. White blob over crown	3·25	

Cylinder Numbers (Blocks of Six)
Perforation: Type RE

Cyl. No.	Phos. No.	No dot	Dot
3	30	5·00*	3·75

CYLINDER VARIETIES

Listed Flaws

XN38b Missing cross to crown (Cyl. 3 no dot, R. 4/3) (Later retouched)

XN38c Heavy line under bust (Cyl. 3 no dot, R. 18/2) (Later retouched)

XN38d White blob over crown (Cyl. 3 no dot, R. 20/8)

Minor Constant Flaws
Cyl. 3 2/3 Retouch in top right corner (Th. A6)
3/8 Cross in crown partly omitted
6/7 Dark speck left of emblem (Th. B1)
12/6 Dark speck left of 2
17/1 Dark speck under Queen's bust (Th. G4)

Withdrawn: 30 April 1982

11p. Scarlet (1976)

1976 (20 October). Two 9·5 mm bands. Fluorescent coated paper. PVAD gum

XN39 (=SG NI30)

XN39	11p. Scarlet	50	50
	a. Phosphor omitted	5·00	
	b. Left-hand band omitted	6·00	
	c. Right-hand band omitted	9·00	

Cylinder Numbers (Blocks of Six)
Perforation: Type RE

Cyl. No.	Phos. No.	No dot	Dot
1	17	4·50	3·75

CYLINDER VARIETIES

Minor Constant Flaws
Cyl. 3 1/7 White flaw in band of crown (Th. B4)
13/2 Red speck on Queen's forehead (Th. C4)
15/2 Small retouch under Queen's chin (Th. E3)
15/3 Retouch behind and below Queen's hair (Th. E5–E6)
20/8 Vertical scratch from back of Queen's hair to collar (Th. E6–F6)
The flaw on R. 20/8 also occurs on the 11p. for Scotland and for Wales.

Withdrawn: 30 April 1982

12p. Yellowish green (1980)

1980 (23 July). Phosphorised (fluorescent coated) paper. PVAD gum

XN41 (=SG NI31)

XN41	12p Yellowish green	50	50
	a. Dark spot in hair	3·00	

Cylinder Numbers (Blocks of Six)
Perforation: Type RE

Cyl. No.	No dot	Dot
1	3·75	3·75

CYLINDER VARIETIES

Multipositive Flaw
XN41a. Cyl. 1 dot, R. 12/10. See XN30c of Northern Ireland

Minor Constant Flaws
Cyl. 1. 4/5 Nick in frame bottom right (Th. G6–7)
4/10 Spot in band of crown (Th. C6)
6/6 Spot above Queen's eyebrow (Th. D4)
7/3 Dark blemish top left of 1 (Th. E1)
15/3 Retouch above Queen's eyebrow (Th. D4)
16/8 Small speck in band of crown (Th. C5)
17/3 Dark spot in hair (Th. E5)
17/5 Dark speck on bust (Th. G4)
19/3 Small dark spot on Queen's forehead (Th. C4)
20/6 Pale blemish behind Queen's neck (Th. F5)
Most of the above are multipositive flaws which occur to a greater or lesser extent on the Northern Ireland 13½p. cyl. 2 dot, 15p. cyl. 1 dot and Scotland 13p. cyl. 1 dot as well as on Wales 12p. cyl. 2 dot and 15p. cyl. 1 dot.

Withdrawn: September 1982

13½p. Purple-brown (1980)

1980 (23 July). Phosphorised (fluorescent coated) paper. PVAD gum

XN42 (=SG NI32)

XN42	13½p. Purple-brown	60	70
	a. Dark spot in hair	4·00	
	b. Dark spot in band of crown	4·00	

Cylinder Numbers (Blocks of Six)
Perforation: Type RE

Cyl. No.	No dot	Dot
2	5·50	5·50

XB Regional Machin issues Northern Ireland

CYLINDER VARIETIES
Multipositive Flaws
XN42a. Cyl. 2 dot, R. 12/10. See XN30c of Northern Ireland.
XN42b. Cyl. 2 dot, R. 16/8. See XN30f of Northern Ireland.

Minor Constant Flaws
Cyl. 2. 4/10 Spot in band of crown (Th. C5)
  6/6 Spot above Queen's eyebrow (Th. D4)
  9/5 Dark spot below necklace (Th. F5)
  15/3 Dark spot above Queen's eyebrow (Th. C4)
  17/5 Dark speck on bust (Th. G4)
  19/3 Small dark spot on Queen's forehead (Th. C4)
  20/3 Dark speck on Queen's temple (Th. D4)

Most of the above are multipositive flaws which occur to a greater or lesser extent on the Northern Ireland 12p. cyl. 1 dot, 15p. cyl. 1 dot and Scotland 13½p. cyl. 1 dot as well as on Wales 12p. cyl. 2 dot and 15p. cyl. 1 dot.

Withdrawn: August 1982

15p. Ultramarine (1980)

1980 (23 July). Phosphorised (fluorescent coated) paper. PVAD gum

XN44 (=SG NI33)

XN44	15p. Ultramarine	60	70
	a. Dark spot in hair	4·00	
	b. Dark spot in band of crown	4·00	

Cylinder Numbers (Blocks of Six)
Perforation: Type RE

Cyl. No.	No dot	Dot
1	5·50	5·50

CYLINDER VARIETIES
Multipositive Flaws:
XN44a. Cyl. 1 dot, R. 12/10. See XN30c of Northern Ireland.
XN44b. Cyl. 1 dot, R. 16/8. See XN30f of Northern Ireland.

Minor Constant Flaws
Cyl. 1. 4/10 Spot in band of crown (Th. C5)
  6/6 Spot above Queen's eyebrow (Th. D4)
  15/3 Dark spot above Queen's eyebrow (Th. C4)

The above are multipositive flaws which occur to a greater or lesser extent on the 12p. cyl. 1 dot, 13½p. cyl. 2 dot and Scotland 13½p. 1 dot as well as on Wales 12p. cyl. 2 dot and 15p. cyl. 1 dot.

Withdrawn: 14 January 1984

> All stamps issued between 1999 and 2002 were printed by Walsall, except Nos. XN49 and XN52 which were printed by Harrison and Sons.

19p. Bistre (1999)

1999 (8 June). Perf. 15 × 14(E) One 4·5 mm centre band (blue fluor). Non-fluorescent coated paper. PVA gum

XN45 (=SG NI78)

XN45	19p. Bistre	3·00	3·00

Cylinder Numbers (Blocks of Six)
Perforation: Type RE

Cyl. No.	Phos. No.	(E)
W1	W2	22·00

Warrant Number and Dates of Printing (Blocks of Eight)

Warrant No.	Date	Margin at left
545	23/3/99	30·00
	24/3/99	35·00

20p. Bright Green (1997–98)

1997 (1 July). Perf. 15×14(E). One 4·5 mm centre band (blue fluor). Non-fluorescent coated paper. PVA gum

XN46 (=SG NI79)

XN46	20p. Bright green	90	80

Cylinder Numbers (Blocks of Six)
Perforation: Type RE

Cyl. No.	Phos. No.	(E)
W1	W1	6·50

The October printing was comb instead of rotary perforated. These are the same perf. type but show no swarf residue on the gum side. *Price for comb control block of 6 £25.*

Warrant Numbers and Dates of Printing (Blocks of Eight)

Warrant No.	Date	Margin at left
398	23/4/97	9·00
	20/5/97	12·00
465	20/10/97 comb perf	20·00
	23/10/97 comb perf	—
	29/10/97 rotary perf	22·00

1998 (13 October). Perf. 14(E). One side band at right (blue fluor). Non-fluorescent coated paper. PVA gum

From £6.16 "Breaking Barriers" Prestige pane No. UEP35
XN47 (=SG NI80)

XN47	20p. Bright green	3·00	3·00

26p. Chestnut (1997–98)

1997 (1 July). Perf. 15×14(E). Two bands (blue fluor). Non-fluorescent coated paper. PVA gum

XN48 (=SG NI81)

XN48	20p. Chestnut	1·25	1·00

Cylinder Numbers (Blocks of Six)
Perforation: Type RE

Cyl. No.	Phos. No.	(E)
W1	W1	9.00
W1	—	45·00

Warrant Numbers and Dates of Printing (Blocks of Eight)

Warrant No.	Date	Margin at left
399	23/4/97	12·50
461	27/5/97	18·00
466	7/11/97	—
	10/11/97	

1997 (23 September). Perf. 15×14(E). Two bands (blue fluor). Non-fluorescent coated paper. PVA gum (bluish)

From £6·15 "BBC 75" se-tenant pane No. XBP1

XN49	26p. Chestnut	1·25	

Harrison stamps from the booklet can be distinguished from the Walsall stamps from sheets by the bluish instead of white PVA gum from Walsall. In addition the phosphor bands fluoresce bright blue under u.v. light in contrast to the dull reaction of the Walsall values. This will help in distinguishing used stamps.

1998 (13 October). Perf. 14(E). Two bands (blue fluor). Non-fluorescent coated paper. PVA gum

From £6.16 "Breaking Barriers" prestige pane No. UEP36
XN50 (=SG NI81b)

XN50	26p. Chestnut	3·00	3·00

Regional Machin issues *Northern Ireland* **XB**

37p. Bright mauve (1997)

1997 (1 July). Perf. 15×14(E). Two bands (blue fluor). Non-fluorescent coated paper. PVA gum

XN51 (=SG NI82)

XN51	37p. Bright mauve	2·25	2·25

Cylinder Numbers (Blocks of Six)
Perforation: Type RE

Cyl. No.	Phos. No.	(E)
W1	W1	16·00

Warrant Number and Date of Printing (Blocks of Eight)

Warrant No.	Date	Margin at left
400	22/4/97	22·00

1997 (23 September). Perf. 15×14(E). Two bands (blue fluor). Non-fluorescent coated paper. PVA gum (bluish)

From £6·15 "BBC 75" prestige booklet pane No. XBP1   4·25

XN52	37p. Bright mauve	2·25

38p. Ultramarine (1999)

1999 (8 June). Perf. 15×14(E). Two phosphor bands (blue fluor). Non-fluorescent coated paper. PVA gum

XN53 (=SG NI83)

XN53	38p. Ultramarine	8·00	8·00

Cylinder Numbers (Blocks of Six)
Perforation: Type RE

Cyl. No.	Phos. No.	(E)
W1	W2	60·00

Warrant Number and Date of Printing (Blocks of Eight)

Warrant No.	Date	Margin at left
546	24/2/99	80·00

Withdrawn: 29 September 2000

40p. Deep azure (2000)

2000 (25 April) perf. 15×14 (E). Two phosphor bands (blue fluor). Non-fluorescent coated paper. PVA gum

XN53A (=SG NI84)

XN53A	40p. Deep azure	60	65

Cylinder Number (Blocks of Six)
Perforation Type RE

Cyl. No.	Phos. No.	(E)
W1	W2	4·50

Warrant Number and Dates of Printing (Blocks of Eight)

SSO No.	Date	Margin at left
604	31/01/00	5·50
	01/02/00	5·50

Withdrawn: 5 March 2002

63p. Light emerald (1997)

1997 (1 July). Perf. 15×14(E). Two bands (blue fluor). Non-fluorescent coated paper. PVA gum

XN54 (=SG NI85)

XN54	63p Light emerald	5·00	5·00

Cylinder Numbers (Blocks of Six)
Perforation: Type RE

Cyl. No.	Phos. No.	(E)
W1	W1	38·00

Warrant Number and Date of Printing (Blocks of Eight)

Warrant No.	Date	Margin at left
401	22/4/97	50·00

64p. Turquoise-green (1999)

1999 (8 June). Perf. 15×14(E). Two bands (blue fluor). Non-fluorescent coated paper. PVA gum

XN55 (=SG NI86)

XN55	64p. Turquoise-green	9·00	9·00

Cylinder Numbers (Blocks of Six)
Perforation: Type RE

Cyl. No.	Phos. No.	(E)
W1	W2	65·00

Warrant Number and Date of Printing (Blocks of Eight)

Warrant No.	Date	Margin at left
547	26/02/99	90·00

Withdrawn: 29 September 2000

65p. Greenish blue (2000)

2000 (25 April). Perf 15×14 (E). Two phosphor bands (blue fluor). Non-fluorescent coated paper. PVA gum.

XN55A (=SG NI87)

XN68A	65p. Greenish blue	1·00	1·10

Cylinder Numbers (Blocks of Six)
Perforation; Type RE

Cyl. No.	Phos.	(E)
W1	W2	6·75

Warrant Number and Date of Printing (Blocks of Eight)

SSO No.	Date	Margin at left
605	01/02/00	9·75

XN56

(1st) Bright orange-red (2000)

2000 (15 February). Perf. 14(E). Two phosphor bands (blue fluor). Non-fluorescent coated paper. PVA gum

From 7·50 "Special by Design" *se-tenant* booklet pane XBP2
XN56 (=SG NI96)

XN56	(1st) Bright orange-red	3·00	3·00

2000 (25 April). Perf. 15×14(E). Two bands (blue fluor). Non-fluorescent coated paper. PVA gum

XB Regional Machin issues Northern Ireland / Scotland

XN56A (=S.C. NI88b)

XN56A	(1st) Bright orange-red	10·00	10·00

On No. XN56 the top of the emblem is below the crown but on No. XN56A this separation is very nearly non-existant. The booklet (1st) has a thinner "ST" than the above.

Cylinder Numbers (Blocks of Six)
Perforation Type RE

Cyl. No.	Phos. No.	(E)
W1	W2	55·00

Warrant Number and Dates of Printing (Blocks of Eight)

Warrant No.	Date	Margin at left
603	04/02/00	70·00
	05/02/00	70·00

Withdrawn: 5 March 2002

Presentation Packs (Northern Ireland)

XNPP2 No. 30	(7.7.71)	2½p., 3p., 5p., 7½p.	3·50
	Comprises Nos. XN18, 20, 27 and 32		
XNPP3 No. 61	(29.5.74)	3p., 3½p., 5½p., 8p.	2·25
	Comprises Nos. XN22 or 23, 24, 28 and 33		
XNPP4 No. 61	(6.11.74)	3p., 3½p., 4½p., 5½p., 8p.	4·00
	As last but with No. XN26 added		

Presumably No. XNPP4 had the 3½p. with centre band instead of two bands and no doubt it was later issued under the same stock number with the 5½p. centre band instead of two bands.

XNPP5 No. 84	(20.10.76)	6½p., 8½p., 10p., 11p.	
	Comprising Nos. XN30, 34, 36 and 39		2·00
XNPP10 No. 47	(8.6.99)	19p., 26p., 38p., 64p.	
	Comprises Nos. XN45, 58, 53 and 55		17·00
XNPP11 No. 52	(25.4.00)	1st, 40p., 65p.,	
	Comprising XN56, 53a, 55a		18·00

Withdrawn: No. XNPP2, 22 January 1975; No. XNPP3, 1974?; No. XNPP4. September 1976; XNPP5, August 1983, XNPP10, 11 March 2002.

Presentation Packs (Three Regions)

XBPP1 No. 42	(20.10.98) Twelve values	26·00

The issued pack contained one each of the 20p., 26p., 37p. and 63p. stamps from Northern Ireland, Scotland and Wales. Nos. XN46, 48, 51, 54; XS61, 63, 66, 68; and XW48, 50, 52 and 54.

Withdrawn: 29 September 2000

First Day Covers

XNFD1	(7.7.71)	2½p., 3p., (2 bands) 5p., 7½p.	3·50
XNFD2	(23.1.74)	3p. (1 band), 3½p. (2 bands), 5½p. (2 bands), 8p.	2·40
XNFD3	(6.11.74)	4½p	1·50
XNFD4	(14.1.76)	6½p., 8½p.	1·50
XNFD5	(20.10.76)	10p. (2 bands), lip.	1·75
XNFD6	(18.1.78)	7p., 9p 10½p.	1·75
XNFD7	(23.7.80)	12p., 13½p., 15p.	3·00
XNFD8	(8.6.99)	38p., 64p.	4·00
XNFD9	(25.4.00)	(1st), 40p., 65p.	7·00

No special provision was made for first day covers for the 3½p. centre band also issued on the same day as the 4½p., but of course first day covers exist with both values.

No special covers were issued for the 5½p. change to one centre band issued on 21 May 1975.

No special provision was made for first day covers for the 10p. centre band also issued on the same day as the 12p., 13½p. and 15p., but first day covers exist franked with all values.

No special provision was made for the 20p., 26p., 37p. and 63p., which replaced the same values printed in lithography issued on 23 July 1996.

No special provision was made for the 19p. bistre, which replaced the same value printed in lithography issued on 7 December 1993.

C. Scotland

XS4

(Des. Jeffery Matthews)

All stamps issued between 1971/80 were printed by Harrison & Sons from chemically etched cylinders.

Type XS4

2½p. Bright magenta (1971–73)

1971 (7 July). One 4 mm centre band

A. Original coated paper. PVA gum
XS29 (=SG S14)

XS29	2½p. Bright magenta	25	20
	a. Phosphor omitted	8·00	

Cylinder Numbers (Blocks of Six)
Perforation: Type A

Cyl. No.	Phos. No.	No dot	Dot
2	5	4·25	4·25

B. Fluorescent coated paper. Gum arabic (22.9.72)
XS30 (=SG S14Eg)

XS30	2½p. Bright magenta	30	30

Cylinder Numbers (Blocks of Six)
Perforation: Type R(S)

Cyl. No.	Phos. No.	No dot	Dot
2	9	5·00	5·00
2	9–34mm (20)	18·00	35·00

C. Fluorescent coated paper. PVA gum (6.73)

XS31	2½p. Bright magenta	7·00	
	a. Phosphor omitted	20·00	

Cylinder Numbers (Blocks of Six)
Perforation: Type A

Cyl. No.	Phos. No.	No dot	Dot
2	5	35·00	35·00
2	8	32·00	32·00

Withdrawn: Nos. XS29/31. 22 January 1975

3p. Ultramarine (1971–74)

1971 (7 July). Two 9·5 mm bands

A. Original coated paper. PVA gum
XS32 (=SG S15)

XS32	3p. Ultramarine	35	15
	a. Phosphor omitted	15·00	

Regional Machin issues *Scotland* **XB**

Cylinder Numbers (Blocks of Six)
Perforation: Type A

Cyl. No.	Phos. No.	No dot	Dot
1	4	4·00	4·00

B. Fluorescent coated paper. Gum arabic (14.12.72)
XS33 (=SG S15Eg)

XS33	3p. Ultramarine	30	30
	a. Imperforate (pair)	£425	
	b. Top margin imperforate	£350	

Examples of No. XS33 from Cyl. 8 exist with contaminated "yellow phosphor". *Price £3 mint.*

Cylinder Numbers (Blocks of Six)
Perforation: Type R(S)

Cyl. No.	Phos. No.	No dot	Dot
4	7	8·00	8·00
8	7	30·00	40·00

C. Fluorescent coated paper. PVA gum (1.73)

XS34	3p. Ultramarine	3·50	
	a. Phosphor omitted	10·00	

Cylinder Numbers (Blocks of Six)
Perforation: Type A

Cyl. No.	Phos. No.	No dot	Dot
1	7	75·00	70·00
1	—	65·00	65·00

Phosphor Cylinder Displacement. Phosphor cylinder 7 is known displaced up the margin 185 mm opposite row 10.

1974 (23 January). One 4 mm centre band
A. Fluorescent coated paper. PVA gum
XS35 (=SG S16)

XS35	3p. Ultramarine	15	15

Cylinder Numbers (Blocks of Six unless otherwise stated)
Perforation: Type A

Cyl. No.	Phos. No.	No dot	Dot
8	8	3·50	3·75
8	— 8 + 34 mm (17)	12·00	25·00 Block of eight

Dot panes from cylinder 8 have the dot at top right of 8.

B. Fluorescent coated paper. PVAD gum (9.74)

XS36	3p. Ultramarine	80	
	a. Deformed tongue	4·25	

Cylinder Numbers (Blocks of Six unless otherwise stated)
Perforation: Type A

Cyl. No.	Phos. No.	No dot	Dot
8	8	7·50	7·50
8	—8 + 32 mm (17)	55·00	55·00 Block of eight

Dot panes from cylinder 8 have the dot at top right of 8.

CYLINDER VARIETIES

XS36a
Deformed tongue
(Cyl. 8 no dot, R. 19/7)

Minor Constant Flaws
Cyl. 1. 18/1 Pale patch at lower right of value (Th. G2)
Cyl. 4. 2/9 Pale patch in background at top (Th. A5)
13/3 White speck on Queen's shoulder (Th. G4)
18/7 Dark spot in Queen's forehead (Th. C3) and small retouch on cheek (Th. D4)
19/2 White speck on top of P
Cyl. 8. 4/1 Dark spot on Queen's shoulder (Th. F4–5)
4/3 Weak letter P
10/6 White blemish on Queen's shoulder (Th. F5)

Withdrawn: Nos. XS32/4, 22 January 1975; Nos. XS35/6, 8 April 1978

3½p. Olive–grey (1974)

1974 (23 January). Two 9·5 mm bands

A. Fluorescent coated paper. PVA gum

XS37	3½p. Olive-grey	10·00	

Cylinder Numbers (Blocks of Six)
Perforation: Type A

Cyl. No.	Phos. No.	No dot	Dot
1	17	£200	£180

The dot was not inserted on the dot cylinder and the no dot cylinder box shows line breaks.

B. Fluorescent coated paper. PVAD gum. (23.1.74)
XS38 (=SG S17)

XS38	3½p. Olive-grey	20	25
	a. Phosphor omitted	50·00	

Cylinder Numbers (Blocks of Six)
Perforation: Type A

Cyl. No.	Phos. No.	No dot	Dot
1	17	3·50	3·75

1974 (6 November). One 4 mm centre band. Fluorescent coated paper. PVAD gum

XS39 (=SG S18)

XS49	3½p. Olive-grey	20	25

Cylinder Numbers (Blocks of Six)
Perforation: Type R

Cyl. No.	Phos. No.	No dot	Dot
1	20	3·00	3·50

CYLINDER VARIETY

Minor Constant Flaw
Cyl. 1 11/7 White scratch behind Queen's hair (Th. D6) (centre band only)

Withdrawn: Nos. XS37/9 September 1976

4½p. Grey–blue (1974)

1974 (6 November). Two 9·5 mm bands. Fluorescent coated paper. PVAD gum

XS40 (=SG S19)

XS40	4½p. Grey-blue	30	25
	b. White spot in 4	2·75	
	c. Blob joining hind legs	3·00	
	d. Large white spot after P	6·00	

109

XB Regional Machin issues *Scotland*

Cylinder Numbers (Blocks of Six)
Perforation: Type R

Cyl. No.	Phos. No.	No dot	Dot
1	17	10·00	18·00
	—	4·50	5·50

*The phosphor cylinder was unnumbered and inverted so that the no dot cylinder block is without phosphor number and the dot cylinder block has part of an inverted phosphor box only. The inverted cylinder box occurs in the right-hand selvedge.
Phosphor Cylinder Displacement. With ink cyl. 1, the unnumbered phos. cyl. box is known displaced up the margin 102 mm opposite row 14.

CYLINDER VARIETIES

XS40b
White spot in figure 4 (Cyl. 1 no dot, R. 2/7)

XS40c
Large white blob joining lion's hind legs (Cyl. 1 no dot, R. 3/5)

XS40d
Large white spot after P (Cyl. 1 no dot, R. 5/1) (Believed later retouched)

Withdrawn: September 1976

5p. Reddish–violet (1971–73)

1971 (7 July). Two 9·5 mm bands

A. Original coated paper. PVA gum
XS41 (=SG S20)

XS41	5p. Reddish violet	1·00	1·25

Cylinder Numbers (Blocks of Six)
Perforation: Type F*

Cyl. No.	Phos. No.	No dot	Dot
3	12	15·00	15·00

B. Fluorescent coated paper. PVA gum (6.73)

XS42	5p. Reddish violet	18·00	5·00
	a. One broad band	£200	

All examples of No. XS42 from cyl. 7 exist with contaminated "yellow phosphor". *Price £5 mint.*

Cylinder Numbers (Blocks of Six)
Perforation: Type F(L)*

Cyl. No.	Phos. No.	No dot	Dot
3	11	£120	£120
7	11	38·00	55·00

Withdrawn: Nos. XS41/2, 22 January 1975

5½p. Violet (1974–5)

1974 (23 January). Two 9·5 mm bands. Fluorescent coated paper. PVAD gum

XS43 (=SG S21)

XS43	5½p. Violet	20	20
	b. Hair flaw	2·40	
	c. Spot in 5	2·50	

Cylinder Numbers (Blocks of Six)
Perforation: Type A. Single pane cylinder

Cyl. No.	Phos. No.	No dot	Dot
1	22*	3·00	†

*The phosphor 22 is known upright but superimposed over inverted figures.

1975 (21 May). One 4 mm centre band. Fluorescent coated paper. PVAD gum

XS44 (=SG S22)

XS44	5½p. Violet	20	25
	a. Imperforate (pair)	£500	
	c. Hair flaw	2·40	
	d. Spot in 5	2·50	

Cylinder Numbers (Blocks of Six)
Perforation: Type R(S). Single pane cylinder

Cyl. No.	Phos. No.	No dot	Dot
1	19	4·25	†

Perforation: Type A

1	19	50·00	†

Normally the Swedish rotary perforator produces a single extension hole in the left-hand margin on no dot panes. The above has been seen with the left-hand margin fully perforated through and also with anything between this and a single perforation hole, sometimes with blind perforations.

CYLINDER VARIETIES

XS43b, XS44c
Dark squiggle in hair below band (Cyl. 1 no dot, R. 2/10)

XS43c, XS44d
Coloured spot in 5 (Cyl. 1 no dot. R. 11/10)

Withdrawn: 31 May 1977

6½p. Greenish Blue (1976)

1976 (14 January). One 4 mm centre band. Fluorescent coated paper. PVAD gum

XS45 (=SG S23)

XS45	6½p. Greenish blue	20	20
	a. Top margin imperforate		
	b. Dark spot in hair	1·75	
	c. Dark spot in band	1·75	
	d. Break in lion's tail	1·75	
	e. Missing claw to lower fore paw	2·00	
	f Extra claw to hind leg	2·00	

No. XS45 exists in a range of shades the most marked being dull greenish blue.

Cylinder Numbers (Blocks of Six unless otherwise stated)
Perforation: Type R

Cyl. No.	Phos. No.	No dot	Dot
1	18	2·75	2·75
1	18 +20 mm (18)	24·00	24·00
1	18 +35 mm (17)	12·00	12·00 Block of ten
1	18 +47 mm (16)	12·00	12·00 Block of ten
1	18 —44 mm (20)	7·00	7·00

Regional Machin issues Scotland XB

Perforation: Type RE

1	18	2·75*	40·00
1	20	3·00	3·00
1	20 +54 mm (76)	12·00	20·00 Block of ten

On the dot panes the dot appears before the ink cylinder 1.

*Same price as perforation type R with single extension holes in left margin.

Phosphor Cylinder Displacement. With ink cyl. 1, phos. cyl. 18 is known displaced up the margin 137 mm opposite row 13.

CYLINDER VARIETIES

XS45d Break in lion's tail (Cyl. 1 no dot, R. 1/4)

XS45e Missing claw to lower fore paw (Cyl. 1 no dot, R. 2/6)

XS45f Extra claw to upper hind leg (Cyl. 1 no dot, R. 4/3)

Multipositive Flaws
XS45b. Cyl. 1 dot, R. 12/8. See XN30c of Northern Ireland.
XS45c. Cyl. 1 dot, R. 16/6. See XN30f of Northern Ireland.

Minor Constant Flaws
Cyl. 1. 6/2 Small retouch at back of collar (Th. (G5). Original flaw on Wales 4½p.
9/3 Dark spot on Queen's neck (Th. F5)
20/2 Small speck under necklace (Th. F4–5)
The above are multipositive flaws which also occur on 6½p. Northern Ireland cyl. 1 dot and Wales cyl. 1 dot and 20/2 also on Wales 4½p. cyl. 1 dot.

Withdrawn: March 1979

7p. Purple–brown (1978)

1978 (18 January). One 4 mm centre band. Fluorescent coated paper. PVAD gum

XS46 (=SG S24)

XS46	7p. Purple-brown	30	30
	b. White spot on P.	1·75	
	c. Tail flaw	2·00	

Cylinder Numbers (Blocks of Six)
Perforation: Type RE

Cyl. No.	Phos. No.	No dot	Dot
1	20	28·00	24·00
1	31	3·00	3·00

CYLINDER VARIETIES

XS46b White spot on P (Cyl. 1 no dot, R. 8/5)

XS46c Truncated prong to tail (Cyl. 1 dot, R. 7/4)

Minor Constant Flaw
Cyl. 1 9/9 Cluster of white specks between crown and lion (Th. A–B/4–5)

Withdrawn: January 1981

7½p. Chestnut (1971–73)

1971 (7 July). Two 9·5 mm bands

XS47 (=SG S25)

A. Original coated paper. PVA gum
XS47	7½p. Chestnut	1·25	1·25
	a. Phosphor omitted	5·00	
	b. One broad band	25·00	

Cylinder Numbers (Blocks of Six)
Perforation: Type F*

Cyl. No.	Phos. No.	No. dot	Dot
6	10	18·00	18·00

B. Fluorescent coated paper. PVA gum (11.73)
| XS48 | 7½p. Chestnut | 65·00 | 18·00 |

Cylinder Numbers (Blocks of Six)
Perforation: Type F*

Cyl. No.	Phos. No.	No dot	Dot
6	11	£425	£425

CYLINDER VARIETY

Minor Constant Flaw
Cyl. 6. 4/1 Background retouch below emblem (Th. C1)

Withdrawn: Nos. XS47/8, 22 January 1975

8p. Rosine (1974)

1974 (23 January). Two 9·5 mm bands. Fluorescent coated paper. PVAD gum

XS49 (=SG S26)

| XS49 | 8p. Rosine | 45 | 40 |

Cylinder Numbers (Blocks of Six)
Perforation: Type A. Single pane cylinder

Cyl. No.	Phos. No.	No dot	Dot
1	22	3·00	†

CYLINDER VARIETY

Minor Constant Flaw
Cyl. 1 20/2 White speck on lion's tongue

Sold out: January 1979

XB Regional Machin issues *Scotland*

8½p. Yellow–green (1976)

1976 (14 January). Two 9·5 mm bands. Fluorescent coated paper. PVAD gum

XS50 (=SG S27)

XS50	8½p. Yellow-green	40	40
	b. White flaw on toes	2·50	
	c. Scratch by lion's mane	2·75	

Cylinder Numbers (Blocks of Six)
Perforation: Type R

Cyl. No.	Phos. No.	No dot	Dot
2	17	3·00	3·00

Perforation: Type RE

1	P21	5·00	3·50
2	17	3·00*	4·00
2	P21	30·00	24·00

*Same price as perforation type R with single extension holes in left margin.

CYLINDER VARIETIES

XS50b
White flaw joining toe to lion's hind paw (Cyl. 2 dot, R. 8/10)

XS50c
White scratch from mane to right fore paw (Cyl. 2 dot, R. 11/1)

Withdrawn: November 1979

9p. Deep violet (1978)

1978 (18 January). Two 9·5 mm bands. Fluorescent coated paper. PVAD gum

XS51 (=SG S28)

XS51	9p. Deep violet	40	40

Cylinder Numbers (Blocks of Six)
Perforation: Type RE

Cyl. No.	Phos. No.	No dot	Dot
1	P21	3·50	3·50
1	30	3·50	3·50

CYLINDER VARIETIES

Minor Constant Flaws:
Cyl. 1. 6/7 Blemish in background behind Queen's neck (Th. F6)
7/7 Damaged claw on lion's right hind paw (Th. C1)
10/3 Pale blemish at lower right edge (Th. G6)
11/7 Dark scratch over crown (Th. B5–A6)
12/7 Diagonal dark scratch over crown (Th. A5–B6)
17/2 Dark speck on Queen's shoulder (Th. F4–F5)
20/2 Dark spot over crown (Th. B5)

Withdrawn: 30 April 1982

10p. Orange–brown (1976-80)

1976 (20 October). Two 9·5 mm bands. Fluorescent coated paper. PVAD gum

XS52 (=SG S29)

XS52	10p. Orange-brown	45	50
	b. Dark spot on lion's thigh	2·75	

Cylinder Numbers (Blocks of Six)
Perforation: Type RE

Cyl. No.	Phos. No.	No dot	Dot
4	17	3·50	3·50
4	30	4·50	4·50

1980 (23 July). One 4 mm centre band. Fluorescent coated paper. PVAD gum

XS53 (=SG S30)

XS53	10p. Orange-brown	40	50

Cylinder Numbers (Blocks of Six)
Perforation: Type RE

Cyl. No.	Phos. No.	No dot	Dot
4	20	3·50	3·50

CYLINDER VARIETIES

XS52b Dark spot on lion's thigh (Cyl. 4 dot. R. 18/3) Retouched on No. XS53

Minor Constant Flaws
Cyl. 4. 3/5 Pale blemish on jaw line (Th. E4)
3/9 Pale spot on bust (Th. G4)
13/7 Pale blemish in upper background (Th. A4)
19/6 Brown mark touching front of Queen's neck (Th. E4-F4)

Withdrawn: No. XS52, January 1981; XS53 sold out, February 1987

10½p. Steel–blue (1978)

1978 (18 January). Two 9·5 mm bands. Fluorescent coated paper. PVAD gum

XS54 (=SG S31)

XS54	10½p. Steel-blue	45	50

Cylinder Numbers (Blocks of Six)
Perforation: Type RE

Cyl. No.	Phos. No.	No dot	Dot
1	30	3·25	3·25

CYLINDER VARIETIES

Minor Constant Flaws
Cyl. 1 5/3 White speck under lion (Th. D2)
5/9 Dark speck on Queen's cheek (Th. D3)
8/5 White speck to right of small figure 1
15/7 Dark speck in Queen's hair (Th. D4)
18/1 Dark dot in front of necklace (Th. F4)
Cyl. 1. 2/1 White dot over P

Withdrawn: February 1982

11p. Scarlet (1976)

1976 (20 October). Two 9·5 mm bands. Fluorescent coated paper. PVAD gum

XS55 (=SG S32)

XS55	11p. Scarlet	50	50
	a. Phosphor omitted	2·00	
	b. Left-hand band omitted	40·00	

c. Right-hand band omitted 35·00

Cylinder Numbers (Blocks of Six)
Perforation: Type RE

Cyl. No.	Phos. No.	No dot	Dot
1	17	3·25	3·25
1	17-30mm (20)	20·00	†
1	30	5·00	5·00

CYLINDER VARIETIES

Minor Constant Flaws
Cyl. 1 10/2 Red spot in background (Th. A5)
11/17 White speck on collar (Th. G4)
20/8 Vertical scratch from back of Queen's hair to collar (Th. E6—F6) (less pronounced than on 11p. Northern Ireland)

Withdrawn: February 1982

12p. Yellowish green (1980)

1980 (23 July). Phosphorised (fluorescent coated) paper. PVAD gum

XS57 (=SG S33)

| XS57 | 12p. Yellowish green | 50 | 50 |

Cylinder Numbers (Blocks of Six)
Perforation: Type RE

Cyl. No.	No dot	Dot
2	3·50	3·50

CYLINDER VARIETIES

Minor Constant Flaws
Cyl. 2. 2/3 Pale blemish in background touching Queen's lips (Th. E3)
4/3 Retouch to necklace (Th. F4)
10/6 Pale patch in background upper right (Th. A5)

Withdrawn: September 1982

13½p. Purple-brown (1980)

1980 (23 July). Phosphorised (fluorescent coated) paper. PVAD gum

XS58 (=SG S34)

| XS58 | 13½p. Purple-brown | 70 | 80 |
| | a. Pale spot on dress | 3·00 | |

Cylinder Numbers (Blocks of Six)
Perforation: Type RE

Cyl. No.	No dot	Dot
1	4·75	4·75

CYLINDER VARIETIES

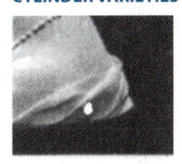

XS58a
Pale spot on dress
(Cyl. 1 dot, R. 6/4)

Minor Constant Flaws
Cyl. 1. 4/10 Spot in band of crown (Th. C6)
6/6 Spot above Queen's eyebrow (Th. D4)
9/5 Dark spot below necklace (Th. F5)
15/3 Retouch above Queen's eyebrow (Th. D4)
17/1 Pale blemishes touching lion's head
17/5 Dark speck on bust (Th. G4) and retouch in front of Queen's lips (Th. D3)
18/1 Pale blemish on shoulder (Th. G4)
20/3 Dark speck on Queen's temple (Th. D4)

Most of the above multipositive flaws which occur to a greater or lesser extent on the Northern Ireland 12p. cyl 1 dot, 13½p. cyl. 2 dot and 15p. cyl. 1 dot as well as on Wales 12p. cyl. 2 dot and 15p. cyl. 1 dot.

Withdrawn: August 1982

15p. Ultramarine (1980)

1980 (23 July). Phosphorised (fluorescent coated) paper. PVAD gum

XS60 (=SG S35)

| XS60 | 15p. Ultramarine | 60 | 70 |

Cylinder Numbers (Blocks of Six)
Perforation: Type RE

Cyl. No.	No dot	Dot
1	4·50	4·50

CYLINDER VARIETIES

Minor Constant Flaws
Cyl. 1 3/2 White specks in front of eye (Th. D3)
10/3 Retouch in background opposite Queen's lips (Th. D2–E2)
10/4 Diagonal white scratch touches lower lip (Th. D3)
20/5 Diagonal line of dots across lion's left hind leg (Th. B2–C2)
20/8 Small retouch above lip (Th. D3)

Withdrawn: 14 January 1984

> All stamps printed between 1997 and 2000 were printed by Walsall except Nos. XS64 and XS67, which were printed by Harrison & Sons

20p. Bright green (1997–98)

1997 (1 July). Perf. 15×14(E). One 4.5 mm centre phosphor band (blue fluor). Non-fluorescent coated paper. PVA gum

XS61 (=SG S90)

| XS61 | 20p. Bright green | 1·00 | 90 |

Cylinder Numbers (Blocks of Six)
Perforation: Type RE

Cyl. No.	Phos. No.	(E)
W1	W1	7·50
W1	W2	£150

Warrant Numbers and Dates of Printing (Blocks of Eight)

Warrant Nos.	Date	Margin at left
394	17/4/97	10·00
	18/4/97	10·00
	21/5/97	10·00
	22/5/97	10.00
	23/5/97	14·00
513	26/8/98	14·00 (source WIW2)
	27/8/98	£150

Regional Machin issues — Scotland

1998 (13 October). Perf. 14(E). One side band at right (blue fluor). Non-fluorescent coated paper. PVA gum

From £6.16 Land Speed Prestige pane No. UEP35
XS62 (=SG S90a)

| XS62 | 20p. Bright green | 3·50 | 3·50 |

26p. Chestnut (1997)

1997 (1 July). Perf. 15×14(E). Two bands (blue fluor). Non-fluorescent coated paper. PVA gum

XS63 (=SG S91)

| XS63 | 26p. Chestnut | 1·20 | 1·20 |

Cylinder Numbers (Blocks of Six)
Perforation: Type RE

Cyl. No.	Phos. No.	(E)
W1	W1	3·00

Warrant Numbers and Dates of Printing (Blocks of Eight)

Warrant No.	Date	Margin at left
395	21/4/97	12·00
	15/5/97	15·00
	17/5/97	17·00
	27/5/97	13·00
	28/5/97	35·00
	29/5/97	30·00

1997 (23 September). Perf. 15×14(E). Two bands (blue fluor). Non-fluorescent coated paper. PVA gum (bluish)

From £6.15 "BBC 75" se-tenant pane No. XBP1
| XS64 | 26p. Chestnut | 1·20 |

1998 (13 October). Perf. 14(E). Two phosphor bands (blue fluor). Non-fluorescent coated paper. PVA gum

From £6.16 "Breaking Barriers" Prestige pane No. UEP36
XS65 (=SG S91a)

| XS65 | 26p. Chestnut | 3·50 | 3·50 |

37p. Bright mauve (1997)

1997 (1 July). Perf. 15×14(E). Two bands (blue fluor). Non-fluorescent coated paper. PVA gum

XS66 (=SG S92)

| XS66 | 37p. Bright mauve | 1·50 | 1·50 |

Cylinder Numbers (Blocks of Six)
Perforation: Type RE

Cyl. No.	Phos. No	(E)
W1	W1	11·00

Warrant Numbers and Dates of Printing (Blocks of Eight)

Warrant No.	Date	Margin at left
396	24/4/97	14·00
461	30/10/97	28·00

1997 (23 September). Perf 15×14(E). Two bands (blue fluor). Non-fluorescent coated paper. PVA gum (bluish)

From £6.15 "BBC 75" se-tenant pane No. XBP1
| XS67 | 37p. Bright mauve | 1·50 |

63p. Light emerald (1997)

1997 (1 July). Perf 15×14(E). Two phosphor bands (blue fluor). Non-fluorescent coated paper. PVA gum

XS68 (=SG S93)

| XS68 | 63p. Light emerald | 4·00 | 4·00 |

Cylinder Numbers (Blocks of Six)
Perforation: Type RE

Cyl. No.	Phos. No.	(E)
W1	W1	30·00

Warrant Numbers and Dates of Printing (Blocks of Eight)

Warrant No.	Date	Margin at left
397	22/4/97	35·00
462	14/11/97	50·00

XS69

(1st) Bright orange-red (2000)

2000 (15 February). Perf. 14(E). Two phosphor bands (blue fluor). Non-fluorescent coated paper. PVA gum

From £7·50 Special by Design se-tenant booklet pane XBP2
XS69 (=SG S108)

| XS69 | (1st) Bright orange-red | 3·00 | 3·25 |

Presentation Packs

XSPP2 No. 27	(7.7.71) 2½p., 3p., 5p., 7½p. Comprises Nos. XS29, 32, 41 and 47	3·50
XSPP3 No. 62	(29.5.74) 3p., 3½p., 5½p., 8p. Comprises Nos. XS35, 38, 43 and 49	2·50
XSPP4 No. 62	(6.11.74) 3p., 3½p.,4½p., 5½p., 8p. As last but with No. XS40 added	4·00

Presumably No. XSPP4 had the 3½p. with centre band instead of two bands and no doubt it was later issued under the same stock number with the 5½p. centre band instead of two bands.
| XSPP5 No. 85 | (20.10.76) 6½p., 8½p 10p., 11p. Comprises Nos. XS45, 50, 52 and 55 | 2·00 |

Withdrawn: No. XSPP2, 22 January 1975; No. XSPP3, 1974?; No. XSPP4, September 1976; No. XSPP5, August 1983

First Day Covers

XSFD1	(7.7.71)	2½p 3p. (2 bands). 5p., 7½p.	†	3·00
XSFD2	(23.1.74)	3p. (1 band), 3½p. (2 bands)	†	
		5½p. (2 bands), 8p.	†	2·50
XSFD3	(6.11.74)	4½p.	†	1·50
XSFD4	(14.1.76)	61p., 8 p.,	†	1·50
XSFD5	(20.10.76)	10p. (2 bands), 11p.	†	1·50
XSFD6	(18.1.78)	7p., 9p., 10½p.	†	1·75
XSFD7	(23.7.80)	12p., 13½p., 15p.	†	2·75
XSFD8	(7.12.93)	19p., 25p., 30p., 41p.,	†	6·00
XSFD9	(23.7.96)	20p., 26p., 37p., 63p.,	†	8·75

No special provision was made for first day covers for the 3½p. centre band also issued on the same day as the 4½p., but of course first day covers exist with both values.

No special covers were issued for the 5½p., change to one centre band issued on 21 May 1975.

No special provision was made for first day covers for the 10p. centre band also issued on the same day as the 12p., 13½p., and 15p., but first day covers exist franked with all values.

No special provision was made for the 20p., 26p., 37p. and 63p., which replaced the same values printed in lithography issued on 23 July 1996.

1977–78 Experimental Machine Packets

These are small cartons containing loose stamps for sale in vending machines and it is not practical to list them in detail.

The experiment was confined to the Scottish Postal Board area, where six vending machines were installed, the first becoming operational in Dundee about February 1977. The cartons contain labels inscribed "ROYAL MAIL STAMPS", their total face value (30p. or 60p.) and their contents. There are several versions of the labels and styles of packets.

At first the 30p. packet contained two 6½p. and two 8½p. Scottish Regional stamps and the 60p. packet had four of each. The stamps could be in pairs or blocks but also in strips or singles.

With the change in postal rates on 13 June 1977 these packets were withdrawn on 11 June and on the 13th the contents were changed, giving three 7p. and one 9p. for the 30p. packet and double this for the 60p. packet. However, this time ordinary British Machin stamps were used. Moreover the Edinburgh machine, situated in an automatic sorting area, was supplied with 7p. stamps with two phosphor bands instead of the new centre band 7p. stamps, despite instructions having been given to withdraw the two band stamps. However, the demand for these packets was too great to be filled and by 27 June the machine was closed down. It was brought back into use on 16 August 1977, supplying 7p. stamps with the centre band.

The 6½p. and 8½p. Scottish Regional packets were put on sale at the Edinburgh Philatelic Bureau in June 1977 and withdrawn in April 1978. The packets with the 7p. and 9p. Machin stamps were put on sale at the Bureau in June 1977 and withdrawn in December 1978. This suggests that these machines were withdrawn once the 50p. coin machines dispensing 50p. folded booklets were operational in Scotland.

D. Wales

From the inception of the Regional stamps, the Welsh versions were tendered to members of the public at all Post Offices within the former County of Monmouthshire but the English alternatives were available on request. Offices with a Monmouthshire address but situated outside the County, namely Beachley, Brockweir, Redbrook, Sedbury, Tutshill, Welsh Newton and Woocroft, were not supplied with the Welsh Regional stamps.

With the re-formation of Counties, Monmouthshire became known as Gwent and was also declared to be part of Wales. From 1 July 1974, therefore, except for the offices mentioned above, only Welsh Regional stamps were available at the offices under the jurisdiction of Newport, Gwent.

XW4

(Des. Jeffery Matthews)

All stamps issued between 1971 and 1980 were printed by Harrison & Sons from chemically etched cylinders.

Type XW4

2½p. Bright magenta (1971–73)

1971 (7 July). One 4 mm centre band

XW18 (=SG W13)

A. Original coated paper. PVA gum

XW18	2½p. Bright magenta	20	20
	a. Imperf. top margin	£450	
	b. Phosphor omitted	7·50	
	c. Extra line in dragon	3·00	
	d. Extra hind leg claw	2·00	
	e. Severed snout	4·00	
	f. Spur to hindmost foot	2·00	
	g. Weak tips to wings	2·00	
	h. Extra line in wing	2·25	
	i. White flaw by tip of dragon's tongue	2·00	

Cylinder Numbers (Blocks of Six)
Perforation: Type A

Cyl. No.	Phos. No.	No dot.	Dot
3	5	4·00	5·25*

B. Fluorescent coated paper. Gum Arabic (22.9.72)

XW19 (=SG W13Eg)

XW19	2½p. Bright magenta	20	
	a. Imperforate (pair)	£600	
	d. Weak tips to wing	2·25	
	c. Extra line in wing	2·50	

Cylinder Numbers (Blocks of Six)
Perforation: Type R(S)

Cyl. No.	Phos. No.	No dot	Dot
3	9	5·50	9·00

A block with displaced phosphor no. to row 20 has been reported.

C. Fluorescent coated paper. PVA gum (1973)

XW20	2½p. Bright magenta	90	20
	a. Spur to hindmost foot	4·00	
	b. Weak tips to wings	4·50	
	c. Extra line in wing	4·75	
	d. White flaw by arrow from dragon's mouth	4·50	

Cylinder Numbers (Blocks of Six)
Perforation: Type A

Cyl. No.	Phos. No.	No dot	Dot
3	9	30·00	20·00

CYLINDER VARIETIES

XW18c
Extra curved line from top of dragon's head to bottom of central leg
(No dot, R. 4/6)

XW 18d
Extra claw to hind leg
(No dot, R 18/6)

XW18e
Snout completely severed
(Dot, R. 3/1) (Later retouched)

XW 18f, 20a
Spur to hindmost foot (Dot, R. 3/5)

XW18g, 19d, 20b
Weak tips to wings
(Dot, R. 15/2)

XW18h, 19c, 20c
Extra line in wing
(Dot. R. 18/8)

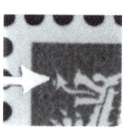

XW18i, 20d
White flaw by dragon's mouth
(Dot, R. 19/l)

Minor Constant Flaws:
Cyl. 3.   2/9 Retouch on Queen's shoulder (Th. F4–5)
   14/5 Pink marks in dragon's foreleg (Th. B1)

Withdrawn: Nos. XW18/20. 22 January 1975

3p. Ultramarine (1971–74)

1971 (7 July) Two 9·5 mm bands

XW21 (=SG W14)

A. Original coated paper. PVA gum

XW21	3p. Ultramarine	25	20
	a. Phosphor omitted	30·00	
	b. Break in line in dragon by head	2·50	
	c. Similar break and forelegs joined by white flaw	2·50	
	d. Break in line in dragon by foot	2·75	
	e. "v" flaw by claw on hindmost leg	2·50	

Cylinder Numbers (Blocks of Six)
Perforation: Type A

Cyl. No.	Phos. No.	No dot	Dot
1	4	5·00*	3·75

B. Fluorescent coated paper. PVA gum (2.73)

XW22	3p. Ultramarine	6·50	1·50
	a. One broad band	85·00	
	b. Break in line in dragon by head	10·00	
	c. Similar break and forelegs joined by white flaw	10·00	
	d. Break in line in dragon by foot	10·00	
	e. "v" flaw by claw on hindmost leg	10·00	

Cylinder Numbers (Blocks of Six)
Perforation: Type A

Cyl. No.	Phos. No.	No dot	Dot
1	7	55·00*	50·00

C. Fluorescent coated paper. Gum Arabic (6.6.73)

XW23 (=SG W14Eg)

XW23	3p. Ultramarine	25
	a. Phosphor omitted	12·00
	b. Break in line in dragon by head	3·50
	c. Similar break and forelegs joined by white flaw	3·50
	d. Break in line in dragon by foot	3·75
	e. "v" flaw by claw on hindmost leg	3·50
	f. Phosphor band at left omitted	£150
	g. Phosphor band at right omitted	£150

Examples of No. XW23 only exist with contaminated "yellow phosphor".

Cylinder Numbers (Blocks of Six)
Perforation: Type R(S)

Cyl. No.	Phos. No.	No dot	Dot
1	7	15·00	18·00

1974 (23 January). One 4mm centre band. Fluorescent coated paper. PVA gum

XW24 (=SG W15)

XW24	3p. Ultramarine	25	25
	b. Break in line in dragon by head	2·25	
	c. Broken body line and forelegs joined by white flaw	1·75	
	d. Break in line in dragon by foot	1·75	
	e. "v" flaw by claw of hindmost leg	1·75	

Cylinder Numbers (Blocks of Six)
Perforation: Type A

Cyl. No.	Phos. No.	No dot	Dot
1	8*	3·50*	3·50

*Exists without phosphor number showing due to a dry print.

CYLINDER VARIETIES

XW21/4b
Broken body line near head
(No dot, R. 2/1)

XW21/4c
Broken body line and forelegs joined (No dot, R. 6/10)

XW21/4d
Broken body line near foot
(Dot, R. 10/10)

XW21/4e
"v" flaw appearing as extra claw to hind leg
(No dot, R. 18/1)

Minor Constant Flaws:
Cyl. 1   8/1 Missing tips to dragon's nose and arrow from mouth (Th. A1)
8/9 Small coloured spot in fork of dragon's tongue (Th. A1) and three white dots at back of Queen's hair (Th. E6)

Withdrawn: Nos. XW21/3, 22 January 1975; No. XW24, 8 April 1978

3½p. Olive-grey (1974)

1974 (23 January). Two 9·5 mm bands. Fluorescent coated paper. PVAD gum

XW26 (=SG W16)

XW26	3½p. Olive-grey	20	30
	b. Break in line in dragon	2·25	
	c. White spot in value	3·00	

Cylinder Numbers (Blocks of Six)
Perforation: Type R

Cyl. No.	Phos. No.	No dot	Dot
2	17	3·50	3·50

CYLINDER VARIETIES

XW26/7b
Broken body line
(Cyl. 2 dot, R. 3/7)

XW26/7c
Large white spot before P of value (Cyl. 2 dot, R. 17/5)

Minor Constant Flaws
Cyl. 2.   6/5 Dark scratch across Queen's jaw (Th. E4)
11/2 Disturbance between figure 1 and P in value

1974 (6 November). One 4 mm centre band. Fluorescent coated paper. PVAD gum

XW27 (=SG W17)

XW27	3½p. Olive-grey	20	30
	b. Break in line in dragon	2·25	
	c. White spot in value	3·00	

Cylinder Numbers (Blocks of Six)
Perforation: Type R

Cyl. No.	Phos. No.	No dot	Dot
2	20	3·50	3·50

A no dot cylinder block of 6 has been seen without a phosphor cylinder number.

CYLINDER VARIETIES

Minor Constant Flaws
Cyl. 2.   6/5 Dark scratch across Queen's jaw (Th. E4)
11/2 Disturbance between figure 1 and P in value

Withdrawn: Nos. XW26/7, September 1976

4½p. Grey-blue (1974)

1974 (6 November). Two 9·5 mm bands. Fluorescent coated paper. PVAD gum

XW28 (S.G.W18)

XW28	4½p. Grey-blue	30	30
	b. Scratch below eye	2·00	
	c. Dark spot in hair	2·00	
	d. Spot in crown	2·00	

Cylinder Numbers (Blocks of Six)
Perforation: Type R

Cyl. No.	Phos. No.	No dot	Dot
1	17	3·50	3·50

CYLINDER VARIETIES

XW28b
Vertical scratch below Queen's eye
(Cyl. 1 dot, R. 5/4)

Multipositive Flaws
XW28c. Cyl. 1 dot, R. 12/8. See XN30c of Northern Ireland.
XW28d. Cyl. 1 dot, R. 16/6. See XN30f of Northern Ireland.

Minor Constant Flaws
Cyl. 1.   3/7 Scratch through dragon's wing extending through head into left margin on stamp (Th. A2-B1)
6/2 White patch at back of collar (Th. G5)
6/4 Small retouch on Queen's forehead (Th. C4–D4)
6/5 Dotted line on Queen's cheek (Th. E4)
7/7 Dark speck in front of Queen's hair (Th. B3)
14/10 Small retouch under necklace (Th. F4)
16/8 Dark speck on Queen's cheek (Th. D4)
17/1 White speck in hair below band of diadem (Th. D5)
20/2 Small speck under necklace (Th. F4–5)
Some of the above are multipositive flaws which occur to a greater or lesser extent on the 6½p. Northern Ireland, Scotland and Wales from Cyl. 1 dot.

Withdrawn: September 1976

5p. Reddish violet (1971–73)

1971 (7 July). Two 9·5 mm bands

A. Original coated paper. PVA gum
XW29 (=SG W19)

XW29	5p. Reddish violet	1·25	1·25
	a. Phosphor omitted	20·00	
	b. One broad band	60·00	
	c. Extra claw	3·50	

Cylinder Numbers (Blocks of Six)
Perforation: Type F`

Cyl. No.	Phos. No.	No dot	Dot
3	12	15·00	15·00

B. Fluorescent coated paper. PVA gum (6.73)

XW30	5p. Reddish violet	15·00	4·00
	a. Phosphor omitted	35·00	
	c. Extra claw	16·00	

XB Regional Machin issues *Wales*

Cylinder Numbers (Blocks of Six)
Perforation: Type F*

Cyl. No.	Phos. No.	No dot	Dot
3	11	£120	£120

CYLINDER VARIETIES

Normal

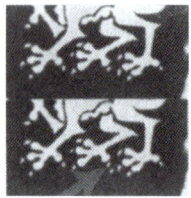

XW29c, 30c Extra claw on dragon's hind foot (Cyl. 3 dot, R. 17/2)

Minor Constant Flaw:
Cyl. 3   18/1 Extensive retouching above Queen's head (Th. A3–5)

Withdrawn: Nos. XW29/30, 22 January 1975.

5½p. Violet (1974–75)

1974 (23 January). Two 9·5mm bands. Fluorescent coated paper. PVAD gum

XW31 (=SG W20)

XW31	5½p. Violet	25	30
	a. Phosphor omitted	£180	
	b. Spot on forehead.	2·00	

Cylinder Numbers (Blocks of Six)
Perforation: Type A. Single pane cylinder

Cyl. No.	Phos. No.	No dot	Dot
1	22*	2·75	†

*The phosphor 22 is shown upright but superimposed over inverted figures.

Cyl. 1 (XW32)

Cyl. 2 (XW32d)

1975 (21 May). 4mm centre band. Fluorescent coated paper. PVAD gum

XW32 (=SG W21)

XW32	5½p. Violet	25	30
	a. Imperforate (pair)	£600	
	b. Top margin imperforate		
	c. Spot on forehead	2·00	
	d. Low emblem and value (1977, ex. Cyl 2)	£350	

Cylinder Numbers (Blocks of Six)
Perforation: Type R(S). Single pane only

Cyl. No.	Phos. No.	No dot	Dot
1	19	3·25	†

Perforation: Type A. Single pane only

2	19	£2250	†

Normally the Swedish rotary perforator produces a single extension hole in the left-hand margin on no dot panes. Sheets from cylinder 1 have been seen with the left-hand margin fully perforated through or else with four to six extension holes, the rest being blind perforations.

CYLINDER VARIETIES

XW31b, 32c
Dark spot on forehead
(Cyl. 1 no dot, R. 15/9)

Minor Constant Flaws:
Cyl. 1   2/1 Vertical scratch on Queen's cheek (Th. D4)
         10/4 Vertical scratch on Queen's neck (Th. E4–D4)

Withdrawn: Nos. XW31/2, 31 May 1977

6½p. Greenish Blue (1976)

1976 (14 January). One 4mm centre band. Fluorescent coated paper. PVAD gum

XW33 (=SG W22)

XW33	6½p. Greenish blue	20	20
	a. Dark blob in diadem	2·50	
	b. Blue mark on wing	2·25	
	c. White spot by arrow	1·75	
	d. Blue spot in hair	1·75	
	e. Blue spot in band	1·75	
	f. Missing tip to dragon's wing	1·75	
	g. Blunted arrow	2·25	

Cylinder Numbers (Blocks of Six unless otherwise stated)
Perforation: Type R

Cyl. No.	Phos. No.	No dot	Dot
1	18	2·75	2·75

Perforation: Type RE

1	20	55·00	55·00
1	—	12·00	12·00
2	20	18·00	7·00
2	20+65 mm (16)	50·00	45·00 Block of ten

On the dot panes the dot appears before the ink cylinder 1.
Phosphor Cylinder Displacement: With ink cyl. 1, phos. cyl. 20 is known displaced up the margin 433 mm opposite row 1.

Regional Machin issues *Wales* **XB**

CYLINDER VARIETIES

XW33a Dark blob on central cross (Cyl. 1 no dot, R. 14/9)

XW33b Blue mark on dragon's wing (Cyl. 1 dot, R. 4/8)

XW33c White spot by arrow (Cyl. 1 dot, R. 11/9)

XW33f Missing tip to dragon's wing (Cyl. 1 dot, R. 20/7)

XW33g Blunted arrow behind wing (Cyl. 1 dot, R. 4/6)

Multipositive Flaws
XW33d. Cyl. 1 dot, R. 12/8. See XN30c of Northern Ireland.
XW33e. Cyl. 1 dot, R. 16/6. See XN30f of Northern Ireland.

Minor Constant Flaws:
Cyl. 1. 6/2 Small retouch on back of collar (Th. G5). Original flaw on Wales 4½p.
6/4 Blue speck on Queen's forehead (Th. C4–D4)
6/5 Blue blemish on Queen's cheek (Th. E4)
9/3 Blue spot on Queen's neck (Th. F5)
14/6 White flaw under band of crown (Th. D5) and missing cylinder dots in bottom frame (Th. H6)
14/10 Small retouch under necklace (Th. F4)
16/8 Dark spot on Queen's cheek (Th. D4)
17/2 White speck in fold of collar (Th. G5)
19/3 Dark speck in Queen's shoulder (Th. G4)
19/5 Small retouch on Queen's shoulder adjoining back of collar (Th. F5)
20/2 Small speck under necklace (Th. F4-5)
20/8 Two white spots in Queen's hair (Th. D5)
Some of the above are multipositive flaws which occur to a greater or less extent on the 6½p. Northern Ireland and Scotland and 4½p. Wales from Cyl. 1 dot.

Withdrawn: April 1979

■ 7p. Purple–brown (1978)

1978 (18 January). One 4 mm centre band. Fluorescent coated paper. PVAD gum

XW34 (=SG W23)			
XW34	7p. Purple-brown	25	25

Cylinder Numbers (Blocks of Six)
Perforation: Type RE

Cyl. No.	Phos. No.	No dot	Dot
1	18	9·00	5·00
1	31	5·00	5·00

Perforation: Type A

1	20	12·00	30·00

CYLINDER VARIETIES

Minor Constant Flaws
Cyl. 1. 4/6 Dark spot below back of Queen's hair (Th. E6)
5/5 White scratch from top of design through crown and hair to dress (Th. A5–G5)
15/6 Dark spot on Queen's bust (Th. G6)
16/4 Curved scratch from Queen's neck to ear (Th. F4–E4)
20/8 Three white spots on Queen's neck (Th. E4)

Withdrawn: May 1980

■ 7½p. Chestnut (1971)

1971 (7 July). Two 9·5 mm bands. Original coated paper. PVA gum

XW35 (=SG W24)			
XW35	7½p. Chestnut	1·75	1·75
	a. Phosphor omitted	95·00	

Cylinder Numbers (Blocks of Six)
Perforation: Type F*

Cyl. No.	Phos. No.	No dot	Dot
7	10	18·00	18·00

Withdrawn: 22 January 1975

■ 8p. Rosine (1974)

1974 (23 January). Two 9·5 mm bands. Fluorescent coated paper. PVAD gum

XW36 (=SG W25)			
XW36	8p. Rosine	30	35
	a. Two wing-tips missing	3·75	
	b. Phosphor omitted	£800	

Cylinder Numbers (Blocks of Six)
Perforation: Type A. Single pane cylinder

Cyl. No.	Phos. No.	No dot	Dot
1	22	3·50	†

CYLINDER VARIETIES

XW36a Two wing-tips missing (Cyl. 1, R. 12/3)

Minor Constant Flaw
Cyl. 1 2/8 White spot on Queen's temple (Th. D4)

Withdrawn: March 1979

■ 8½p. Yellow- green (1976)

1976 (14 January). Two 9·5 mm bands. Fluorescent coated paper. PVAD gum

XW37 (=SG W26)			
XW37	8½p. Yellow-green	30	35
	b. White spot over crown	2·50	

119

Regional Machin issues — Wales

Cylinder Numbers (Blocks of Six)
Perforation: Type R

Cyl. No.	Phos. No.	No dot	Dot
1	17	3·25	3·25

Perforation: Type RE

Cyl. No.	Phos. No.		No dot	Dot
1	17		3·25*	9·00
1	17	−30mm (20)	90·00	
1	P21		18·00	4·00
1	P21	−29mm (20)	£100	£100

*Same price as perforation type R with single extension holes in left margin.

CYLINDER VARIETIES

XW37b
White spot over crown (Cyl. 1 no dot, R. 8/1)

Minor Constant Flaw
Cyl. 1   17/2 Small white line between claws of dragon's hind foot (Th. C2)

Withdrawn: April 1979 but put on sale again at the Philatelic Bureau in June and finally withdrawn in October 1979.

9p. Deep violet (1978)

1978 (18 January). Two 9·5mm bands. Fluorescent coated paper. PVAD gum

XW38 (=SG W27)

XW38	9p. Deep violet		40	40

Cylinder Numbers (Blocks of Six)
Perforation: Type RE

Cyl. No.	Phos. No.	No dot	Dot
2	P21	4·50	4·50
2	30	3·50	3·50

CYLINDER VARIETIES

Minor Constant Flaws:
Cyl. 2   2/4 Dark blemish touching back of collar (Th. F6–G6)
7/1 Dark speck in background near back of crown (Th. D6)
7/4 Dark blemish touching back of Queen's neck (Th. F5)
9/5 Dark specks above crown (Th. B5–B6)
9/8 Dark specks on Queen's neck (Th. E4)
15/8 Dark speck above crown (Th. A5)
20/8 Vertical scratch at upper right extending into margin (Th. A5)

Withdrawn: 30 April 1982

10p. Orange–Brown (1976)

1976 (20 October). Two 9·5mm bands. Fluorescent coated paper. PVAD gum

XW39 (=SG W28)

XW39	10p. Orange-brown		40	40

Cylinder Numbers (Blocks of Six)
Perforation: Type RE

Cyl. No.	Phos. No.	No dot	Dot
2	P21	3·50	3·50
2	30	£200	£275

1980 (23 July). One 4mm centre band. Fluorescent coated paper. PVAD gum

XW40 (=SG W29)

XW40	10p. Orange-brown		40	40
	a. Two white dots on tongue		2·50	
	b. Extra claw		2·50	

Cylinder Numbers (Blocks of Six)
Perforation: Type RE

Cyl. No.	Phos. No.	No dot	Dot
2	20	3·50	3·50

CYLINDER VARIETIES

Normal

XW40a
Two white dots above dragon's tongue
(Cyl. 2 no dot, R. 3/10)

XW40b
Extra claw on dragon's hind foot
(Cyl. 2 no dot, R. 20/10)

Minor Constant Flaws:
Cyl. 2   8/4 White spot below dragon's wing tip (Th. A3)
13/5 Dark speck on Queen's neck (Th. F5)
15/4 Dark speck behind Queen's neck under hair (Th. E5)
18/9 Disturbance on Queen's cheek (Th. D4)
19/2 White speck on Queen's forehead (Th. C4)
19/4 Dark spot on Queen's forehead (Th. C3)

Withdrawn: No. XW39, January 1981; No. XW40, sold out February 1987

10½p. Steel–blue (1978)

1978 (18 January). Two 9·5mm bands. Fluorescent coated paper. PVAD gum

XW41 (=SG W30)

XW41	10½p. Steel-blue		45	45

Cylinder Numbers (Blocks of Six)
Perforation: Type RE

Cyl. No.	Phos. No.	No dot	Dot
3	30	3·50	3·50

CYLINDER VARIETIES

Minor Constant Flaws
Cyl. 3   3/10 Background blemish behind Queen's hair (Th. E6)
9/5 Blemish on Queen's cheek (Th. D–E/3-4)

Withdrawn: 30 April 1982

Regional Machin issues *Wales* **XB**

11p. Scarlet (1976)

1976 (20 October). Two 9·5 mm bands. Fluorescent coated paper. PVAD gum

XW42 (=SG W31)

XW42	11p. Scarlet	45	45
	b. Front wing-tip missing	2·75	
	c. Two wing tips missing	3·25	

Cylinder Numbers (Blocks of Six)
Perforation: Type RE

Cyl. No.	Phos. No.	No dot	Dot
1	17	5·50*	3·50
1	30	—	£1000

CYLINDER VARIETIES

XW42b
Front wing tip missing
(Cyl. 1 no dot, R. 15/7)

XW42c
Two wing tips missing
(Cyl. 1 no dot, R. 16/9 and 20/1)

Minor Constant Flaws
Cyl. 1.   13/2 Two dark specks on Queen's cheek (Th. D4)
19/6 Pale blemish on Queen's neck above necklace (Th. F4)
20/8 Vertical scratch from back of Queen's hair to collar (Th. E6–F6) (as on 11p. Northern Ireland)

Withdrawn: 30 April 1982

12p. Yellowish green (1980)

1980 (23 July). Phosphorised (fluorescent coated) paper. PVAD gum

XW44 (=SG W32)

XW44	12p. Yellowish green	50	50
	a. Dark spot in hair	2·75	

Cylinder Numbers (Blocks of Six)
Perforation: Type RE

Cyl. No.	No dot	Dot
2	3·75	3·75

CYLINDER VARIETIES

Multipositive Flaw
XW44a. Cyl. 2 dot, R. 12/10. See XN30c of Northern Ireland.

Minor Constant Flaws
Cyl. 2.   6/6 Spot above Queen's eyebrow (Th. D4)
10/6 Dark spot in background above crown (Th. A5)
15/3 Retouch above Queen's eyebrow (Th. C4)
16/8 Retouch in band of crown (Th. C5)
17/5 Dark speck on bust (Th. G4)
20/6 Pale blemish behind Queen's neck (Th. F5)
Most of the above are multipositive flaws which occur to a greater or lesser extent on the 15p. cyl. 1 dot and Northern Ireland 12p. cyl. 1 dot, 13½p. cyl. 2 dot and 15p. cyl. 1 dot as well as on Scotland 13½p. cyl. 1 dot.

Withdrawn: September 1982

13½p. Purple–brown (1980)

1980 (23 July). Phosphorised (fluorescent coated) paper. PVAD gum

XW45 (=SG W33)

XW45	13½p. Purple-brown	60	70

Cylinder Numbers (Blocks of Six)
Perforation: Type RE

Cyl. No.	No dot	Dot
2	4·75	4·75

CYLINDER VARIETIES

Minor Constant Flaws
Cyl. 2 10/2 Short scratch on Queen's dress (Th. G6)
12/1 Distorted lower curve to figure 3
18/1 Retouch left of Queen's ear-ring (Th. D/E4)

Withdrawn: August 1982

15p. Ultramarine (1980)

1980 (23 July). Phosphorised (fluorescent coated) paper. PVAD gum

XW47 (=SG W34)

XW47	15p. Ultramarine	60	70

Cylinder Numbers (Blocks of Six)
Perforation: Type RE

Cyl. No.	No dot	Dot
1	4·75	4·75

CYLINDER VARIETIES

Minor Constant Flaws
Cyl. 1.   4/10 Spot in band of crown (Th. C5) and spot on LQueen's neck (Th. E4)
6/6 White spot above Queen's eyebrow (Th. D4)
9/5 Dark spot below necklace (Th. F5)
12/10 Retouch in hair (Th. D5)
15/2 Blemishes in background behind portrait (Th. F6–G6)
15/3 Retouch on Queen's hairline above eyebrow (Th. C4)
16/8 Retouch in band of crown (Th. C5)
17/7 Retouch to Queen's upper lip (Th. D3)
Most of the above are multipositive flaws which occur to a greater or lesser extent on the 12p. cyl. 2 dot and Northern Ireland 12p. cyl. 1 dot, 13½p. cyl. 2 dot and 15p. cyl. 1 dot as well as on Scotland 13½p. cyl. 1 dot.

Withdrawn: 14 January 1984

> All stamps printed between 1997 and 2000 were printed by Walsall except Nos. XW51 and XW53 which were printed by Harrison & Son

XW5

Without "p". The removal of the "p" on the value of the stamps was to bring the stamps in line with the Welsh Language Act.

XB Regional Machin issues *Wales*

Type XW5

20p. Bright green (1997-98)

1997 (1 July). Perf 15×14(E). One 4.5 mm centre band (blue fluor). Non-fluorescent coated paper. PVA gum

XW48 (=SG W79)

| XW48 | 20p. Bright green | 80 | 80 |

This value was pre-released and the earliest reported use is 16 May 1997.

Examples of No. XW48 exist 1 mm wider overall due to an extra horizontal perforation hole from printing Warrant No. 402. (*With left margin attached price £14 mint*). This error was from column 1 and examples exist in cyl. and Warrant blocks.

Cylinder Numbers (Blocks of Six)
Perforation: Type RE

Cyl. No.	Phos. No.	(E)
W1	W1	6·00
W1	W2	6·00

Warrant Numbers and Dates of Printing (Blocks of Eight)

Warrant Nos.	Date	Margin at left
402	9/4/97	9·00
	14/4/97	8·00
	12/5/97	20·00
463	5/11/97	18·00
	6/11/97	12·00
	7/11/97	18·00
514	11/8/98	9·00 (source W1(W2))
	12/8/98	12·00
	14/8/98	12·00
	20/8/98	12·00
	21/8/98	12·00
	24/8/98	12·00
	25/8/98	18·00
515	28/7/98	20·00
	29/7/98	20·00

1998 (13 October). Perf. 14(E). One side band at right (blue fluor). Non-fluorescent coated paper. PVA gum

From £6·16 "Breaking Barriers" Prestige pane No. UEP35
XW49 (=SG W79a)

| XW49 | 20p. Bright green | 3·00 | 3·00 |

26p. Chestnut (1997–98)

1997 (1 July). Perf. 15×14(E). Two bands (blue fluor). Non-fluorescent coated paper. PVA Gum

XW50 (=SG W80)

| XW50 | 26p. Chestnut | 1·00 | 1·00 |

Cylinder Numbers (Blocks of Six)
Perforation: Type RE

Cyl. No.	Phos. No.	(E)
W1	W1	7·50
W1	W2	20·00

Warrant Numbers and Dates of Printing (Blocks of Eight)

Warrant No.	Date	Margin at left
403	12/4/97	10·00
	15/4/97	10·00
WT403	9/5/97	10·00
403	15/5/97	40·00
464	11/11/97	18·00 (source W1(W2))
	12/11/97	18·00
	13/11/97	14·00
	14/11/97	25·00

1997 (23 September). P. 15×14(E). Two bands (blue fluor). Non-fluorescent coated paper. PVA gum (bluish)

From £6·15 "BBC 75" *se-tenant* pane No. XBP1 XW51
| XW51 | 26p. Chestnut | | 1.00 |

1998 (13 October). Perf. 15×14(E). Two phosphor bands (blue fluor). Non-fluorescent coated paper. PVA gum

£6.16 "Breaking Barriers" pane No. UEP36
XW53 (=SG W80a)

| XW52 | 26p. Chestnut | 3·00 | 3·00 |

37p. Bright mauve (1997)

1997 (1 July). Perf. 15×14(E). Two bands (blue fluor). Non-fluorescent coated paper. PVA gum

XW53 (=SG W81)

| XW53 | 37p. Bright mauve | 2·75 | 2·75 |

Cylinder Numbers (Blocks of Six)
Perforation: Type RE

Cyl. No.	Phos. No.	(E)
W1	W1	20·00

Warrant Number and Dates of Printing (Blocks of Eight)

Warrant No.	Date	Margin at left
404	12/4/97	30·00
	14/4/97	28·00

1997 (23 September). Perf 14×15 (E). Two bands (blue fluor). Non-fluorescent coated paper. PVA gum (bluish)

From £6.15 "BBC 75" *se-tenant* pane No. XBP1
| XW54 | 37p. Bright mauve | | 75 |

63p. Light Emerald (1997)

1997 (1 July). Perf 14×15 (E). Two bands (blue fluor). Non-fluorescent coated paper. PVA gum

XW55 (=SG W82)

| XW55 | 63p. Light emerald | 5·00 | 5.00 |

Cylinder Numbers (Blocks of Six)
Perforation: Type RE

Cyl. No.	Phos. No.	(E)
W1	W1	35·00

Warrant Number and Date of Printing (Blocks of Eight)

Warrant No.	Date	Margin at left
405	13/4/97	45·00

XW56

(1st) Bright Orange-red (2000)

2000 (15 February). Perf. 14.(E). Two phosphor bands (blue fluor). Non-fluorescent coated paper. PVA gum

From £7·50 "Special by Design" *se-tenant* booklet pane XBP2
XW56 (=SG W97)

XW56	(1st) Bright orange-red	3·00	2·75

Presentation Packs

XWPP2 No. 28	(7.7.71) 2½p., 3p., 5p., 7½p. Comprises Nos. XW I8, 21, 29 and 35	3·50
XWPP3 No. 63	(29.5.74) 3p., 3½p., 5½p., 8p. Comprises Nos. XW24, 26, 31 and 36	2·50
XWPP4 No. 63	(6.11.74) 3p., 3½p., 4½p., 5½p., 8p. As last but with No. XW28 added	4·00

Presumably No. XWPP4 had the 3½p. with centre band instead of two bands and no doubt it was later issued under the same stock number with the 5½p. centre band instead of two bands.

XWPP5 No. 86	(20.10.76) 6½p., 8½p 10p., 11p. Comprises Nos. XW33. 37, 39 and 42	2·00
XWPP6 No. 39	(1.7.97) 20p., 26p 37p., 63p. Comprises Nos. XW48, 50, 52 and 54	17·00

Withdrawn: No. XWPP2, 22 January 1975 No. XWPP3, 1974?; No. XWPP4, September 1976; No. XWPP5, August 1983

First Day Covers

XWFD1	(7.7.71)	2½p., 3p. (2 bands), 5p., 7½p.	† 3·00
XWFD2	(23.1.74)	3p. (1 band), 3½p. (2 bands), 5½p. (2 bands), 8p.	† 2·50
XWFD3	(6.11.74)	4½p.	† 1·50
XWFD4	(14.1.76)	6½p. 8½p.	† 1·50
XWFD5	(20.10.76)	10p. (2 bands), 11p.	† 1·50
XWFD6	(18.1.78)	7p., 9p., 10 p.	† 1·75
XWFD7	(23.7.80)	12p., 13½p., 15p.	† 3·00
XWFD8	(1.7.97)	20p., 26p., 37p., 63p.	6·00

No special provision was made for first day covers for the 3½p. centre band also issued on the same day as the 4½p., but of course first day covers exist with both values.

No special covers were issued for the 5½p. change to one centre band issued on 21 May 1975.

No special provision was made for first day covers for the 10p. centre band also issued on the same day as the 12p., 13½p. and 15p., but first day covers exist franked with all values.

No special provision was made for the same values issued on 1 July 1997 for Northern Ireland and Scotland. They are identical to the lithographed stamps which they replaced with "p" after the value.

SECTION XC
Regional Machin Issues
1981-96. Printed by Lithography.

General Notes

Introduction. Following the decision to employ the lithographic process to print five denominations of the Machin issues in 1980 the Post Office placed further contracts with John Waddington Ltd for Scottish issues and The House of Questa for the Northern Ireland and Welsh Regional stamps issued on 8 April 1981. In April 1986 Questa took over from Waddington the work of printing Scottish regional issues.

Printing process. Details are given under this heading in the General Notes to Section UG in Part 1 of this catalogue.

Machin portrait. Reduced size Machin head portraits have been used but none of the basic listings occur with more than one type and it is not necessary to include head types in the descriptions of each stamp.

Plates. Most printings are recorded with two plates, one in a deeper shade than the other. As an exception the 13p. printed by Questa in 1984 for Northern Ireland and Wales had grey as the second plate.

Minor constant flaws. Numerous minor flaws caused by specks of dust settling on the printing plate and preventing the ink from reaching the area appear as white inkless rings and are known as litho "ring" flaws. Minor flecks of colour are similarly caused. As such flaws only affect part of a printing and cannot be regarded as constant we do not record them.

Regional issues for Northern Ireland, Scotland and Wales printed by The House of Questa

Sheet arrangement and markings. The sheet make-up and markings are as described and illustrated in Section UG in Part 1 of this catalogue. The "Total Sheet Value" inscription on the Questa sheets varied in position as follows: 1981 (11½p., 14p., 18p. and 22p., rows 15/16), 1982 (12½p.), 15½p., 19½p., and 26p., rows 14/17), 1983 (12½p. (p1. 18/1), 16p., 20p. and 28p., rows 15/16). From 1984 all values had the country name added, repeated on the sheets reading up at left and down at right opposite rows 4/7 and 14/17. The value of the sheet is shown with a decimal point placed at the centre between the figures for all values except the 22p. where it is placed between the figures in the full stop position.

The 1996 issue (20p., 26p., 37p. and 63p.), were printed by Questa on a Mitsubishi press. The solid ink bar used for quality control between odd and even numbered panes did not appear.

Perforation. All values are comb perforated 14 or, from January 1984 15×14 with perforation Type L and later, Type L(P) as described in Appendix I. On plate blocks (I) indicates an imperf. left margin and (P) is perforated. Plate blocks from the *right feed* have margins perforated through.

Re-introduction of Perforation 14. During the second half of 1992 some printings of current values were perforated with the previous 14 gauge. The stamps affected were the Northern Ireland 18p. (bright green), Scotland 18p. (bright green), 24p. (chestnut), 28p. (deep bluish grey), 39p., and Wales 18p. (bright green) and 24p. (chestnut). Dates of issue for these varieties are uncertain and we give the earliest confirmed dates of use known to us. Only the Scotland 18p. perforated 14 was available from the Philatelic Bureau.

Introduction of the elliptical perforation hole. The 19p., 25p., 30p. and 41p. values were the first regional stamps to be issued with an elliptical perforation hole designated (E) in each vertical edge. They appeared on 7 December 1993 with perforation 15×14 from the right leaving plate blocks Perf. Type P.

Paper and gum. Original coated paper was used for the 11½p. value and one printing of the Northern Ireland 12½p. Thereafter fluorescent coated paper with PVAD gum was used for the 12½p. and 13p. values. Other values were printed on phosphorised paper with the fluorescent additive in the coating. On the 22p. value, printed in yellow-green phosphorised (advanced coated) paper was employed and this was later used for other values PVA gum was replaced by PVAD gum for issues from 1982 except for the Northern Ireland 12½p. No. XNL5. From April 1987 values for second class mail were issued with PVA gum and a 4 mm phosphor band printed at the left-hand side or right of centre.

In 1988 paper supplied by Henry Leigh & Slater to Questa for the 19p., 23p. and 32p. issued on 8 November had PVAD gum without the greenish dye additive, described as (PVAD (clear)) in the listings. The 14p. issued at the same time was printed on paper with PVA gum from Coated Papers Limited (CPL). In 1989 the Scotland and Wales 19p. values were printed on phosphorised paper with PVA gum as an experiment using CPL paper. All regions used CPL paper for the 15p., 20p., 24p., and 34p. with PVAD (clear) except 15p. with PVA gum issued on 28 November 1989. Of the 1990 issues only the 17p. was on CPL paper with Harrison supplying phosphorised paper for 22p., 26p. and 37p. values. The Scotland and Wales 22p., 26p. and 37p. issued on 14 May 1991 and the regional issues of 3 December 1991 were all printed on paper supplied by CPL.

Phosphor bands. Values for second class mail have been issued with a phosphor band which gives a violet after-glow following irradiation by short-wave ultraviolet light. The bands, which are continuous, were probably applied using a litho process as opposed to gravure.

In 1986 the 12p. second class mail value was printed with a short phosphor band on each stamp in the sheet. This reduced wear on the perforator pins and the measure was continued with the 13p., 14p., 15p., 17p. and 19p. values.

Phosphor Bands (Yellow Fluor). The first regional stamps to appear with phosphor bands (yellow fluor) occurred in the Beatrix Potter Prestige booklet issued on 10 August 1993. The bands are 4 mm wide at the edges of the pane and 7·5 mm between the stamps. At the same time non-fluorescent paper replaced both the fluorescent coated paper with phosphor bands and phosphorised (advanced coated) paper. After the postage rate increase of 1 November 1993 the 19p., 25p., 30p. and 41p. all appeared on the non-fluorescent coated paper on which the phosphor (yellow fluor) was overprinted by typography.

Blue Fluor. From July 1995 blue fluor replaced yellow fluor in the phosphor on the 19p. and 25p. values for each region. Following the rate increase of 8 July 1996 the 20p. one band, 26p., 37p. and 63p. two bands were issued with blue fluor.

For General Notes describing the issues printed by John Waddington Ltd., see Section XC under Scotland.

In 1997 Walsall Security Printers Ltd. gained the contract to print regional stamps in sheet format from Questa. These issues, printed in gravure, are listed in Section XB.

A. Northern Ireland

Type XN4 as illustrated in Section XB printed by Questa

Two Types of Crown

I

II

Type I. Crown with pearls individually drawn
Screened background: 13p., 17p. (grey-blue), 28p. (deep violet-blue).
Solid background: 26p. (rosine), 31p.
Type II. Crown with first three pearls at left are joined
Screened background: 28p. (deep violet-blue), 31p.
Solid background: 13p., 17p., (grey-blue), 26p. (rosine)
No other values exist with both types in the same colour.

11½p. Drab (1981)

1981 (8 April). Perf. 14. One 4mm band at left. Original coated paper. PVA gum

XNL1 (=SG NI34)

XNL1	11½p. Drab		85	85

Plate Numbers (Blocks of Six)
Double Pane Plates
Plate Nos. in right margin

Pl. Nos.	Row 1	Row 20
1, 1	6·00	6·00
2, 2	7·50	7·50

Withdrawn: 26.2.83

12p. Bright emerald (1986)

1986 (7 January). Perf. 15×14. One 4mm band at left. Fluorescent coated paper. PVAD gum

XNL2 (=SG NI35)

XNL2	12p. Bright emerald	90	90

Plate Numbers (Blocks of Six)
Double Pane Plates
Plate Nos. in left margin

Pl. Nos.	(P)
1, 1	6·50
2, 2	7·50

1986 (July). Perf. 15×14. One short band at left. Fluorescent coated paper. PVAD gum

XNL3	Bright emerald	90	90

Plate Numbers (Blocks of Six)
Double Pane Plates
Plate Nos. in left margin

Pl. Nos.	(P)
3, 3	7·50
4, 4	7·50

No. XNL3 was printed with the 4mm wide phosphor band at left cut short opposite the perforations at the top and bottom.

Sold out: Nos. XNL 2/3, 10.87

12½p. Light emerald (1982–84)

1982 (24 February). Perf. 14. One 4mm band at left. Fluorescent coated paper. PVAD gum

XNL4 (=SG NI36)

XNL4	12½p. Light emerald	60	60

Plate Numbers (Blocks of Six)
Double Pane Plates
Plate Nos. in right margin

Pl. Nos.	Row 1	Row 20
1, 1	18·00	30·00
2, 2	8·00	8·00
1, 3	—	—
2, 4	8·00	8·00
3, 3	5·00	5·00
4, 4	6·00	6·00

Plate Nos. in left margin

Pl. Nos.	(I)	Pl. Nos.	(P)
1, 1	30·00	2, 2	30·00

1984 (28 February). Perf. 15×14. One 4mm band at left

A. Original coated paper. PVA gum

XNL5	12½p. Light emerald	5·25	5·25

Plate Numbers (Blocks of Six)
Double Pane Plates
Plate Nos. in left margin

Pl. Nos.	(I)	Pl. Nos.	(P)
1, 1	38·00	2, 2	£175

B. Fluorescent coated paper. PVAD gum (6.84)
XNL6 (=SG NI36a)

XNL6	12½ Light emerald	5·25	5·25

Plate Numbers (Blocks of Six)
Double Pane Plates
Plate Nos. in left margin

Pl. Nos.	(I)	Pl. Nos.	(P)
1, 3	38·00	2, 4	35·00

Withdrawn: No. XNL4, 28 February 1985, Nos. XNL5/6, 28 June 1985

13p. Pale chestnut (1984–87)

1984 (23 October). Perf. 15×14. One 4mm band at left. Fluorescent coated paper. Type I. PVAD gum

XNL7 (=SG NI37)

XNL7	13p. Pale chestnut	80	50
	a. Phosphor omitted		

XC Regional Machin Issues Lithography Northern Ireland

Plate Numbers (Blocks of Six)
Double Pane Plates (Second plate number is grey)
Plate Nos. in left margin

Pl. Nos.	(l)	Pl. Nos.	(P)
1, 1	7·50	2, 2	7·50
3, 3	10·00	4, 4	8·00
5, 5	7·50	6, 6	7·50

Plate No. 1, 1 exists with a short imperforate section at base below the 8th perforation.

1986 (28 November). Perf. 15×14. One short band at left. Fluorescent coated paper. Type II

A. PVAD gum

| XNL8 | 13p. Pale chestnut | 2·50 | |

Plate Numbers (Blocks of Six)
Double Pane Plates (Second plate number is chestnut)
Plate Nos. in left margin

Pl. Nos.	(l)	Pl. Nos.	(P)
1, 1	16·00	2, 2	20·00

B. PVA gum (14.4.87)
XNL9 (=SG NI37Ea)

| XNL9 | 13p. Pale chestnut | 1·50 | 1·00 |

Plate Numbers (Blocks of Six)
Double Pane Plates (Second plate number is chestnut)
Plate Nos. in left margin

Pl. Nos.	(l)	Pl. Nos.	(P)
1, 1	10·00	1, 1	10·00
		2, 2	9·00
		3, 3	—
		4, 4	10·00

Plate No. 2, 2 exists with a short imperforate section at base below the 8th perforation. *Price for plate 2, 2 £25.*
Withdrawn: No. XNL7, 14 April 1988; Nos. XNL 8/9, 4 September 1989

14p. Grey-blue (1981)

1981 (8 April). Perf. 14. Phosphorised (fluorescent coated) paper. PVA gum

XNL10 (=SG NI38)

| XNL10 | 14p. Grey-blue | 75 | 75 |

Plate Numbers (Blocks of Six)
Double Pane Plates
Plate Nos. in right margin

Pl. Nos	Row 1	Row 20
1, 1	5·50	5·50
2, 2	5·50	5·50

Withdrawn: 14 January 1984

14p. Deep blue (1988)

1988 (8 November). Perf. 15×14. One 4mm short band (right of centre). Fluorescent coated paper. PVA gum

XNL11 (=SG NI39)

| XNL11 | 14p. Deep blue | 75 | 60 |

Plate Numbers (Blocks of Six)
Double Pane Plates
Plate Nos. in left margin

Pl. Nos.	(P)
1, 1	6·00
2, 2	6·00
3, 3	32·00
4, 4	27·00

Withdrawn: 27 November 1990

15p. Bright blue (1989)

1989 (28 November). Perf. 15×14. One 4mm short band (right of centre). Fluorescent coated paper. PVA gum

XNL12 (=SG NI40)

| XNL12 | 15p. Bright blue | 90 | 60 |

Plate Numbers (Blocks of Six)
Double Pane Plates
Plate Nos. in left margin

Pl. Nos.	(P)
1, 1	6·25
2, 2	6·25
3, 3	7·00
4, 4	7·00

Plate No. 4, 4 exists with a short imperforate section at base below the 8th perforation. *Price for plate 4, 4 £18.*
Withdrawn: 14 September 1991

15½p. Pale violet (1982)

1982 (24 February). Perf. 14. Phosphorised (fluorescent coated) paper. PVAD gum

XNL13 (=SG NI41)

| XNL13 | 15½p. Pale violet | 80 | 80 |

Plate Numbers (Blocks of Six)
Double Pane Plates
Plate Nos. in right margin

Pl. Nos.	Row 1	Row 20
1	5·50	5·50
2	5·50	5·50

Withdrawn: 29 April 1984

16p. Drab (1983–84)

1983 (27 April). Perf. 14. Phosphorised (fluorescent coated) paper. PVAD gum

XNL15 (=SG NI42)

| XNL15 | 16p. Drab | 1·00 | 1·00 |

Plate Numbers (Blocks of Six)
Double Pane Plates
Plate Nos. in left margin

Pl. No.	(l)	Pl. No.	(P)
1	18·00	2	7·00

1984 (28 February). Perf. 15×14. Phosphorised (fluorescent coated) paper. PVAD gum

XNL16 (=SG NI42a)

| XNL16 | 16p. Drab | 8·25 | 8·50 |

Plate Numbers (Blocks of Six)
Double Pane Plates
Plate Nos. in left margin

Pl. No.	(I)	Pl. No.	(P)
3	55·00	4	55·00

Withdrawn: No. XNL15, 28 February 1985; No. XNL16, 7 February 1987

17p. Grey-blue (1984-86)

1984 (23 October). Perf. 15 × 14. Phosphorised paper. Type I. PVAD gum

A. Fluorescent coated paper

XNL17	17p. Grey-blue	1·50	1·25

Plate Numbers (Blocks of Six)
Double Pane Plates
Plate Nos. in left margin

Pl. No.	(I)	Pl. No.	(P)
1	10·00	2	10·00

B. Advanced coated paper (25.2.86)
XNL18 (=SG NI43)

XNL18	17p. Grey-blue	90	95

Plate Numbers (Blocks of Six)
Double Pane Plates
Plate Nos. in left margin

Pl. No.	(I)	Pl. No.	(P)
3	6·00	4	6·00

1986 (9 September). Perf. 15 × 14. Phosphorised (advanced coated) paper. Type II. PVAD gum

XNL19 (=SG NI43Ea)

XNL19	17p. Grey-blue	£150	£120

Plate Numbers (Blocks of Six)
Double Pane Plates
Plate Nos. in left margin

Pl. Nos.	(I)	Pl. Nos.	(P)
1, 1	£800	2, 2	£800

Withdrawn: No. XNL17, 24 February 1987; No. XNL18/19, sold out October 1987

17p. Deep blue (1990)

1990 (4 December). Perf. 15 × 14. One 4 mm short band (right of centre). Fluorescent coated paper. PVA gum

XNL20 (=SG NI44)

XNL20	17p. Deep blue	1·00	80

Plate Numbers (Blocks of Six)
Double Pane Plates
Plate Nos. in left margin

Pl. Nos.	(P)	Pl. Nos.	(P)
1, 1	6·50	3, 3	25·00
2, 2	6·50	4, 4	17·00

Withdrawn: 13 September 1992

18p. Deep violet (1981)

1981 (8 April). Perf. 14. Phosphorised (fluorescent coated) paper. PVA gum

XNL21 (=SG NI45)

XNL21	18p. Deep violet	1·00	1·00

Plate Numbers (Blocks of Six)
Double Pane Plates
Plate Nos. in right margin

Pl. Nos.	Row 1	Row 20
1, 1	5·50	5·50
2, 2	5·50	5·50

Withdrawn: 14 January 1984

18p. Deep olive-grey (1987)

1987 (6 January). Perf. 15 × 14. Phosphorised (advanced coated) paper. PVAD gum

XNL22 (S.G.NI46)

XNL22	18p. Deep olive-grey	1·00	90

Plate Numbers (Blocks of Six)
Double Pane Plates
Plate Nos. in left margin

Pl. Nos.	(I)	Pl. Nos.	(P)
1, 1	6·50	2, 2	6·50
3, 3	£950	3, 3	£140
		4, 4	£200

Withdrawn: 4 September 1989

18p. Bright green (1991–93)

1991 (3 December). One 4 mm short band (right of centre). Fluorescent coated paper. PVA gum

A. PERF. 15 × 14
XNL23 (=SG NI47)

XNL23	18p. Bright green	1·00	95

Plate Numbers (Blocks of Six)
Double Pane Plates
Plate Nos. in left margin

Pl. Nos.	(P)
1, 1	6·50
2, 2	6·50
3, 3	90·00
4, 4	90·00

B. PERF. 14 (31.12.92)
XNL24 (=SG NI47a)

XNL24	18p. Bright green	5·00	5·00

Plate Numbers (Blocks of Six)
Double Pane Plates
Plate Nos. in left margin

Pl. Nos.	(P)
1, 1	30·00
2, 2	30·00

1993 (10 August). Perf. 15 × 14. One side band (yellow fluor) at left. Non-fluorescent coated paper. PVA gum

From £6 (£5·64) "The Story of Beatrix Potter" booklet pane XD1
XNL25 (=SG NI48)

XNL25	18p. Bright green	2·25	2·25

Withdrawn: No. XNL23, 6 December 1994. No. XNL24 was not available from the Bureau.

19p. Bright orange-red (1988)

1988 (8 November). Perf. 15 × 14. Phosphorised (advanced coated) paper. PVAD (clear) gum

XNL26 (S.G.NI49)

XNL26	19p. Bright orange-red	1·00	1·00

Plate Numbers (Blocks of Six)
Double Pane Plates
Plate Nos. in left margin

Pl. Nos.	(P)	Pl. Nos.	(P)
1, 1	6·00	3, 3	6·50
2, 2	6·00	4, 4	9·00

Withdrawn: 27 November 1990

19p. Bistre (1993–96)

1993 (7 December). Perf. 15 × 14(E). One 4 mm short phosphor band (yellow fluor) right of centre. Non-fluorescent coated paper. PVA gum

XNL27 (=SG NI69)

XNL27	19p. Bistre	90	80

Plate Numbers (Blocks of Six)
Double Pane Plates
Plate Nos. in left margin

Pl. No.	(P)
1, 1	6·00
2, 2	6·00
3, 3	40·00
4, 4	40·00

1994 (26 July). Perf. 15 × 14(E). One side phosphor band (yellow fluor) at left. Non-fluorescent coated paper. PVA gum

From £6.04 Northern Ireland booklet *se-tenant* panes XDNI1/2
XNL28 (=SG NI70)

XNL28	19p. Bistre	1·25	1·75
	a. Phosphor omitted	£950	

1995 (25 April). Perf. 15 × 14 and one elliptical perf. hole on each vertical edge. One side phosphor band (yellow fluor) at right. Non-fluorescent coated paper. PVA gum

From £6 National Trust booklet *se-tenant* pane XD2
XNL29 (=SG NI70Ec)

XNL29	19p. Bistre	2·50	2·50

1996 (1 February). Perf. 15 × 14(E). One 4 mm short band (blue fluor) right of centre. Non-fluorescent coated paper. PVA gum

XNL30	19p. Bistre	1·25	1·25

Plate Numbers (Blocks of Six)
Double Pane Plates
Plate Nos. in left margin

Pl. Nos.	(P)
3, 3	9·00
4, 4	9·00

Withdrawn: No. XNL27, 29 March 1996; No. XNL30, 22 July 1997

19½p. Olive-grey (1982)

1982 (24 February). Perf. 14. Phosphorised (fluorescent coated) paper. PVAD gum

XNL31 (=SG NI50)

XNL31	19½p. Olive-grey	1·50	1·75

Plate Numbers (Blocks of Six)
Double Pane Plates
Plate Nos. in right margin

Pl. Nos.	Row 1	Row 20
1	14·00	12·00
2	14·00	18·00

Withdrawn: 29 April 1984

20p. Brownish black (1989)

1989 (28 November). Perf 15 × 14. Phosphorised (advanced coated) paper. PVAD (clear) gum

XNL32 (=SG NI51)

XNL32	20p. Brownish black	1·00	80

Plate Numbers (Blocks of Six)
Double Pane Plates
Plate Nos. in left margin

Pl. Nos.	(P)	Pl. Nos.	(P)
1, 1	6·50	3, 3	6·50
2, 2	12·00	4, 4	6·50

Withdrawn: 14 September 1991

20p. Bright green (1996)

1996 (23 July). Perf. 15 × 14(E). One 4·5 mm centre band (blue fluor). Non-fluorescent coated paper. PVA gum

XNL33 (= SG.NI71)

XNL33	20p. Bright green	1·50	1·50

Plate Numbers (Blocks of Six)
Double Pane Plates
Plate Nos. in left margin

Pl. Nos.	(P)
1, 1	12·00
2, 2	12·00

Withdrawn: 1 December 1997

20½p. Ultramarine (1983)

1983 (27 April). Perf. 14. Phosphorised (fluorescent coated) paper. PVAD gum

XNL36 (=SG NI52)

XNL36	20½p. Ultramarine	4·50	4·25

Plate Numbers (Blocks of Six)
Double Pane Plates
Plate Nos. in left margin

Pl. No.	(I)	Pl. No.	(P)
1	27·00	2	27·00

Withdrawn: 28 June 1985

22p. Blue (1981)

1981 (8 April). Perf. 14. Phosphorised (fluorescent coated) paper. PVA gum

XNL37 (=SG NI53)

XNL37	22p. Blue	1·10	1·10

Plate Numbers (Blocks of Six)
Double Pane Plates
Plate Nos. in right margin

Pl. Nos.	Row 1	Row 20
1, 1	9·00	8·00
2, 2	8·00	8·00

Withdrawn: 29 April 1984

22p. Yellow-green (1984)

1984 (23 October). Perf. 15 × 14. Phosphorised (advanced coated) paper. PVAD gum

XNL38 (=SG NI54)

XNL38	22p. Yellow-green	1·10	1·10

Plate Numbers (Blocks of Six)
Double Pane Plates
Plate Nos. in left margin

Pl. Nos.	(I)	Pl. Nos.	(P)
1, 1	7·50	2, 2	7·50

Withdrawn: 27 November 1990

22p. Bright orange-red (1990)

1990 (4 December). Perf. 15 × 14. Phosphorised (advanced coated) paper. PVAD gum

XNL39 (=SG NI55)

XNL39	22p. Bright orange-red	1·25	90

Plate Numbers (Blocks of Six)
Double Pane Plates
Plate Nos. in left margin

Pl. Nos.	(P)
1, 1	7·50
2, 2	7·50

Withdrawn: 13 September 1992

23p. Bright green (1988)

1988 (8 November). Perf. 15 × 14. Phosphorised (advanced coated) paper. PVAD (clear) gum

XNL40 (=SG NI56)

XNL40	23p. Bright green	1·25	1·10

Plate Numbers (Blocks of Six)
Double Pane Plates
Plate Nos. in left margin

Pl. Nos.	(P)
1, 1	7·50
2, 2	7·50

Withdrawn: 27 November 1990

24p. Indian red (1989)

1989 (28 November). Perf. 15 × 14. Phosphorised (advanced coated) paper. PVAD (clear) gum

XNL41 (=SG NI57)

XNL41	24p. Indian red		

Plate Numbers (Blocks of Six)
Double Pane Plates
Plate Nos. in left margin

Pl. Nos.	
1, 1	
2, 2	7·50

Withdrawn: 14 September 1991

24p. Chestnut (1991–93)

1991 (3 December). Perf. 15 × 14. Phosphorised (advanced coated) paper. PVA gum

XNL42 (=SG NI58)

XNL42	24p. Chestnut	1·10	90

Plate Numbers (Block of Six)
Double Pane Plates
Plate Nos. in left margin

Pl. Nos.	(P)	Pl. Nos.	(P)
1, 1	6·50	3, 3	7·00
2, 2	6·50	4, 4	7·00

1993 (10 August). Perf. 15 × 14. Two bands (yellow fluor). Non-fluorescent coated paper. PVA gum

From £6 (£5·64) "The Story of Beatrix Potter" booklet pane XD1
XNL43 (=SG NI59)

XNL43	24p. Chestnut	2·25	2·50

Withdrawn: No. XNL42, 6 December 1994

25p. Red (1993–96)

1993 (7 December). Perf. 15 × 14(E). Two 8 mm bands (yellow fluor). Non-fluorescent coated paper. PVA gum

XNL44 (=SG NI72)

XNL44	25p. Red		75	75
	a. 11.5 mm between bands (25.4.95, ex. XD2)		1·00	1·00
	b. Phosphor omitted		£950	

The distance between the phosphor bands on No. XNL44 is 12·5 mm

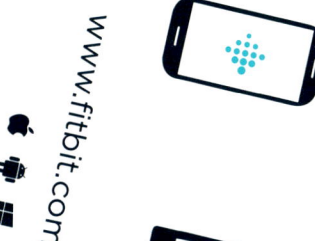

XC Regional Machin Issues Lithography *Northern Ireland*

Plate Numbers (Blocks of Six)
Double Pane Plates
Plate Nos in left margin

Pl. Nos.	(P)
1, 1	5·00
2, 2	5·00
3, 3	50·00
4, 4	90·00
5, 5	45·00
6, 6	45·00

1996 (5 March). Perf. 15 × 14(E). Two bands (blue fluor). Non-fluorescent coated paper. PVA gum

A. Two 8 mm bands

XNL45	25p. Red	1·25	1·25

Plate Numbers (Blocks of Six)
Double Pane Plates
Plate Nos. in left margin

Pl. Nos.	(P)
5, 5	9·00
6, 6	9·00

B. Two 9 mm phosphor bands.

From £6·48 European Football Championship booklet pane UHP18 (14.5.96)

XNL46	25p. Red	2·00	2·00

Withdrawn: No. XNL44, 30 August 1996; No. XNL45, 22 July 1997

26p. Rosine (1982–87)

1982 (24 February). Perf. 14 Phosphorised (fluorescent coated) paper. Type I. PVAD gum

XNL48 =SG NI60

XNL48	26p. Rosine	1·25	1·25

Plate Numbers (Blocks of Six)
Double Pane Plates
Plate Nos. in right margin

Pl. Nos.	Row 1	Row 20
1	9·00	9·00
2	27·00	27·00
3	8·50	8·50
4	8·50	8·50

1987 (27 January). Perf. 15 × 14. Phosphorised (advanced coated) paper. Type II. PVAD gum

XNL49 (=SG NI60a)

XNL49	26p. Rosine	3·00	3·25

Plate Numbers (Blocks of Six)
Double Pane Plates
Plate Nos. in left margin

Pl. No.	(I)	Pl. No.	(P)
1	20·00	2	20·00

Withdrawn: No. XNL48, 26 January 1988; No. XNL49, 4 September 1989

26p. Drab (1990)

1990 (4 December). Perf. 15 × 14. Phosphorised (advanced coated) paper. PVAD gum

XNL50 (=SG NI61)

XNL50	26p. Drab	1·75	1·75

Plate Numbers (Blocks of Six)
Double Pane Plates
Plate Nos. in left margin

Pl. Nos.	(P)
1, 1	11·00
2, 2	11·00

Withdrawn: 13 September 1992

26p. Red-brown (1996)

1996 (23 July). Perf. 15 × 14 (E). Two bands (blue fluor). Non-fluorescent coated paper. PVA gum

XNL51 (=SG NI73)

XNL51	26p. Red-brown	1·75	1·75
	a. Two long wave phosphor bands (1997)		
	ab. Double printed phosphor bands	75·00	

No. XNL51a came from a late printing of plates 2, 2.

No. XNL51ab affected the whole sheet but our price is for an example from horizontal row 1 which clearly shows the double printing. Stamps from the rest of the sheet can be identified only by a slight difference in registration and these are outside the scope of the listing. The variety with the top margin will show the horizontal phosphor band which occurs above the "W" sheet marking.

Plate Numbers (Blocks of Six)
Double Pane Plates
Plate Nos. in left margin

Pl. Nos.	(P)	
1, 1	12·00	
2, 2	12·00	
2, 2	£150	Long wave phosphor

Withdrawn: 1 December 1997

28p. Deep violet-blue (1983–87)

1983 (27 April). Perf. 14. Phosphorised (fluorescent coated) paper. Type I. PVAD gum

XNL52 (=SG NI62)

XNL52	28p. Deep violet-blue	1·50	1·50

Plate Numbers (Blocks of Six)
Double Pane Plates
Plate Nos. in left margin

Pl. No.	(I)	Pl. No.	(P)
1	9·00	2	9·00

1987 (27 January). Perf. 15 × 14. Phosphorised (advanced coated) paper. Type II. PVAD gum

XNL53 (=SG NI62a)

XNL53	28p. Deep violet-blue	1·25	1·25

Plate Numbers (Blocks of Six)
Double Pane Plates
Plate Nos. in left margin

Pl. No.	(l)	Pl. No.	(P)
1	8·00	2	8·00

Withdrawn: No. XNL52, 26 January 1988; No. XNL53, 27 November 1990

28p. Deep bluish grey (1991)

1991 (3 December). Perf. 15 × 14. Phosphorised (advanced coated) paper. PVA gum

XNL54 (=SG NI63)

XNL54	28p. Deep bluish grey	1·50	1·50

Plate Numbers (Blocks of Six)
Double Pane Plates
Plate Nos. in left margin

Pl. Nos.	(P)
1, 1	9·00
2, 2	9·00

Withdrawn: 6 December 1994

30p. Deep olive-grey (1993)

1993 (7 December). Perf. 15 × 14(E). Two bands (yellow fluor). Non-fluorescent coated paper. PVA gum

XNL55 (=SG NI74)

XNL55	30p. Deep olive-grey	1·25	1·25
	a. Phosphor omitted	£950	

Plate Numbers (Blocks of Six)
Double Pane Plates
Plate Nos. in left margin

Pl. Nos.	(P)
1, 1	8·00
2, 2	8·00

Withdrawn: 22 July 1997

31p. Bright purple (1984–87)

1984 (23 October). Perf. 15 × 14. Phosphorised (fluorescent coated) paper. Type I. PVAD gum

XNL57 (=SG NI64)

XNL57	31p. Bright purple	1·75	2·00

Plate Numbers (Blocks of Six)
Double Pane Plates
Plate Nos. in left margin

Pl. No.	(l)	Pl. No.	(P)
3	12·00	4	12·00

1987 (14 April). Perf. 15 × 14. Phosphorised (advanced coated) paper. Type II. PVAD gum

XNL58 (=SG NI64Ea)

XNL58	31p. Bright purple	1·90	1·75

Plate Numbers (Block of Six)
Double Pane Plates
Plate Nos. in left margin

Pl. No.	(l)	Pl. No.	(P)
5	13·00	6	13·00

Withdrawn: No. XNL57, 14 April 1988; No. XNL58, 4 September 1989

32p. Greenish blue (1988)

1988 (8 November). Perf. 15 × 14. Phosphorised (advanced coated) paper. PVAD (clear) gum

XNL59 (=SG NI65)

XNL59	32p. Greenish blue	1·75	1·75

Plate Numbers (Blocks of Six)
Double Pane Plates
Plate Nos. in left margin

Pl. Nos.	(P)
1, 1	11·00
2, 2	11·00

Withdrawn: 27 November 1990

34p. Deep Bluish Grey (1989)

1989 (28 November). Perf. 15 × 14. Phosphorised (advanced coated) paper. PVAD (clear) gum

XNL60 (=SG NI66)

XNL60	34p. Deep bluish grey	1·75	1·75

Plate Numbers (Blocks of Six)
Double Pane Plates
Plate Nos. in left margin

Pl. Nos.	(P)
1, 1	11·00
2, 2	11·00

Withdrawn: 14 September 1991

37p. Rosine (1990)

1990 (4 December). Perf. 15 × 14. Phosphorised (advanced coated) paper. PVAD gum

XNL61 (=SG NI67)

XNL61	37p. Rosine	2·00	2·50

Plate Numbers (Blocks of Six)
Double Pane Plates
Plate Nos. in left margin

Pl. Nos.	(P)
1, 1	12·00
2, 2	12·00

Withdrawn: 13 September 1992

37p. Bright mauve (1996)

1996 (23 July). Perf. 15 × 14 (E). Two bands (blue fluor). Non-fluorescent coated paper. PVA gum

XNL62 (=SG NI75)

XNL62	37p. Bright mauve	2·75	3·00

XC Regional Machin Issues Lithography — Northern Ireland

Plate Numbers (Blocks of Six)
Double Pane Plates
Plate Nos. in left margin

Pl. Nos.	(P)
1, 1	18·00
2, 2	18·00

Withdrawn: 1 December 1997

39p. Bright mauve (1991)

1991 (3 December). Perf. 15 × 14. Phosphorised (advanced coated) paper. PVA gum

XNL63 =SG NI68)

XNL63	39p. Bright mauve	2·00	2·25
	a. Error. Fluorescent coated paper*	25·00	

*Under ultraviolet light the paper appears very bright and is without any phosphor reaction.

Plate Numbers (Blocks of Six)
Double Pane Plates
Plate Nos. in left margin

Pl. Nos.	(P)
1, 1	12·00
1, 1 Fluorescent coated paper	£180
2, 2	12·00
3, 3	15·00
4, 4	14·00

Withdrawn: 6 December 1994

41p. Grey-brown (1993)

1993 (7 December). Perf. 15 × 14(E). Two bands (yellow fluor). Non-fluorescent coated paper. PVA gum

XNL64 (=SG NI76)

XNL64	41p. Grey-brown	1·50	1·75
	a. Phosphor omitted	£950	

Plate Numbers (Blocks of Six)
Double Pane Plates
Plate Nos. in left margin

Pl. Nos.	(P)
1, 1	10·00
2, 2	10·00

Withdrawn: 22 July 1997

63p. Light emerald (1996)

1996 (23 July). Perf. 15 × 14(E). Two bands (blue fluor). Non-fluorescent coated paper. PVA gum

XNL65 (=SG NI77)

XNL65	63p. Light emerald	5·00	5·00

Plate Numbers (Blocks of Six)
Double Pane Plates
Plate Nos. in left margin

Pl. Nos.	(P)
1, 1	30·00
2, 2	30·00

Withdrawn: 1 December 1997

Further issues of 1999 in this design are listed in Section XB (Gravure).

Presentation Packs (Northern Ireland)

XNPP6 No. 129d (28.10.81)	7p., 9p., 10½p., 11½p., 12p., 13½p., 14p., 15p., 18p., 22p.	9·00

Comprises Nos. XN31, 35, 38, 41/2, 44, XNL1, 10, 21 and 37.

XNPP7 No. 4 (3.8.83)	10p., 12½p., 16p., 20½p., 26p., 28p.	18·00

Comprises Nos. XN37, XNL4, 15, 36, 48 and 52.

XNPP8 No. 8 (23.10.84)	10p., 13p., 16p., 17p., 22p., 26p., 28p., 31p.	18·00

Comprises Nos. XN37, XNL7, 16, 17, 38, 48, 52 and 57.

XNPP9 No. 12 (3.3.87)	12p., 13p., 17p., 18p., 22p., 26p., 28p., 31p.	20·00

Comprises Nos. XNL3, 8, 18, 22, 38, 49, 53 and 57
Withdrawn: No. XNPP6, August 1983; No. XNPP7, October 1984; No. XNPP8, 2 March 1987; No. XNPP9, 31 December 1991

Presentation Packs (Three Regions)

XPP2 No. 17 (8.11.88)	Twelve values	17·00

The issued pack contained one each of the 14p., 19p., 23p. and 32p. stamps from Northern Ireland. Scotland and Wales. Nos. XNL11, 26, 40, 59; XSL10, 27, 44, 68; XWL10, 27, 41 and 60.
For No. XPP1 see the Wilding Section XA in Volume 3 of this catalogue.

XPP3 No. 20 (28.11.89)	Twelve values	16·00

The issued pack contained one each of the 15p., 20p., 24p. and 34p. stamps from Northern Ireland, Scotland and Wales. Nos. XNL12, 32, 41, 60; XSL13, 34, 47, 69; XWL11, 33, 42 and 61.

XPP4 No. 23 (4.12.90)	Twelve values	16·00

The issued pack contained one each of the 17p., 22p., 26p. and 37p. stamps from Northern Ireland, Scotland and Wales. Nos. XNL20, 39, 50, 61; XSL20, 43, 56, 70; XWL18, 39, 52 and 62.

XPP5 No. 26 (3.12.91)	Twelve values	16·00

The issued pack contained one each of the 18p., 24p., 28p. and 39p. stamps from Northern Ireland, Scotland and Wales. Nos. XNL23, 42, 54, 63; XSL24, 48, 62, 73; XWL22, 43, 56 and 64.

Values with elliptical perforation holes from 1993.

XPP6 No. 31 (7.12.93)	Twelve values	16·00

The issued pack contained one each of the 19p., 25p., 30p. and 41p. stamps from Northern Ireland, Scotland and Wales. Nos. XNL27, 44, 55, 64; XSL30, 51, 64, 75; XWL29, 47, 57 and 65.

XPP7 No. 36 (23.7.96)	Twelve values	26·00

The issued pack contained one each of the 20p., 26p., 37p. and 63p. stamps from Northern Ireland, Scotland and Wales. Nos. XNL33, 51, 62, 65; XSL35, 59, 72, 76; XWL34, 53, 63 and 67.
Withdrawn: No. XPP2, 27 November 1990; No. XPP3, 14 September 1991; No. XPP4, 13 September 1991; No. XPP5, 6 December 1994; No. XPP6, 22 July 1997; No. XPP7, 31 December 1998

First Day Covers

XNLFD1 (8.4.81)	11½p., 14p., 18p., 22p.	2·50
XNLFD2 (24.2.82)	12½p., 15½p., 19½p., 26p.	4·00
XNLFD3 (27.4.83)	16p., 20½p., 28p.	4·00
XNLFD4 (23.10.84)	13p., 17p., 22p., 31p.	4·75
XNLFD5 (7.1.86)	12p.	2·00
XNLFD6 (6.1.87)	18p.	2·00
XNLFD7 (8.11.88)	14p., 19p., 23p., 32p.	4·25

XNLFD8 (28.11.89)	15p., 20p., 24p., 34p.	5·00
XNLFD9 (4.12.90)	17p., 22p., 26p., 37p.	5·00
XNLFD10 (3.12.91)	18p., 24p., 28p., 39p.	5·50
XNLFD11 (7.12.93)	19p., 25p., 30p., 41p.	6·00
XNLFD12 (26.7.94)	N.I. *se-tenant* pane	8·00
XNLFD13 (23.7.96)	20p., 26p., 37p., 63p.	8·75

For further issues of 1999 see Section XB.
Pictorial designs are listed in Section XE.

B. Scotland

John Waddington Printings
(April 1981 to March 1986)

Sheet arrangement and markings. The sheet make-up and markings are as described in Section UG of Part 1 of this catalogue except that the sheets were serially numbered in black after printing for checking purposes. The country name appeared before "Total Sheet Value".
Perforation. All Waddington printings were comb perforated 14 with perforation Type L which is described in Appendix I. Questa printings were perforated 15 × 14.
Paper and gum. Fluorescent coated paper was used for the 11½p., 12½p. and 13p. values and phosphorised paper with fluorescent additive was employed for other values. The phosphorised (advanced) coated paper gives a stronger reaction to ultraviolet on the 22p. printed in yellow green and this paper was employed for other values. The gum was PVAD except for the 11½p., 12½p. and 13p. which have PVA.
Phosphor bands. The 11½p., 12½p. and 13p. have a 4 mm phosphor band printed at the left-hand side. This reacts violet after irradiation by short-wave ultraviolet light. The phosphor band was applied by typography and a phosphor cylinder number appears synchronised in the printed box. The bands stop short in the top and bottom sheet margins.

For details of Questa printings see the introduction to this section.

Type XS4 as illustrated in Section XB
Printed by Waddington (1981-86)
or Questa (1986-96)

Two Types of Lion

| I | II |

Type I. No line across bridge of nose
Screened background: 13p., 17p. (grey-blue) 31p., Waddington ptgs. Solid background: 22p. (yellow-green), 26p. (rosine) Waddington ptgs.
Type II. Line joins nose to the eye
Screened background: 13p., 17p. (grey-blue) 31p. Waddington ptgs.
Solid background: 13p., 17p. (grey-blue), 22p. (yellow-green), 26p. (rosine) 31p., Questa ptgs. 22p. (yellow-green) Waddington ptg.

The Questa 22p. shows a pale portrait compared to the same stamp from Waddington.
No other values exist with both types in the same colour.

■ 11½p. Drab (1981)

Printed by Waddington

1981 (8 April). Perf. 14. One 4 mm phosphor band at left. Fluorescent coated paper. PVA gum

XSL1 (=SG S36)

XSL1	11½p. Drab		80	80
	a. Imperforate between stamp and right margin		95·00	
	b. Phosphor omitted		£700	

Plate Numbers (Blocks of Eight)
Double Pane Plates
Plate Nos. in top margin

Pl. Nos.	Phos. No.	Dot	No dot
1A, 1B	1A	20·00	£160
1A, 2B	1A	£275	£275
2A, 2B	1A	5·00	5·00
3A, 3B	1A	90·00	90·00
4A, 4B	1A	35·00	8·00
5A, 4B	1A	10·00	20·00
6A, 4B	1A	80·00	80·00
6A, 5B	1A	£130	£130
7A, 6B	1A	£1100	£1000

Withdrawn: 26 February 1983

■ 12p. Bright emerald (1986)

Printed by Waddington

1986 (7 January). Perf. 14. One 4 mm phosphor band at left. Fluorescent coated paper. PVA gum

XSL2 (=SG S37)

XSL2	12p. Bright emerald	2·00	2·00

Plate Numbers (Blocks of Six)
Double Pane Plates
Plate Nos. in left margin

Pl. Nos.	Phos. No.	Dot (I)	No dot (P)
1A, 1B	1A	12·00	12·00

Printed by Questa

1986 (29 April). Perf. 15 × 14. One short phosphor band at left. Fluorescent coated paper. PVAD gum

XSL3 (=SG S52)

XSL3	12p. Bright emerald	2·00	2·25

Plate Numbers (Blocks of Six)
Double Pane Plates
Plate Nos. in left margin

Pl. Nos.	(I)	Pl. Nos.	(P)
1, 1	12·00	2, 2	12·00

No. XSL3 was printed with the 4 mm wide phosphor band at left cut short opposite the perforations at the top and bottom of each stamp in the sheet.
Withdrawn: No. XSL2, 28 April 1987; No. XSL3, sold out October 1987

XC Regional Machin Issues Lithography *Scotland*

12½p. Light emerald (1982)

Printed by Waddington

1982 (24 February). Perf. 14. One 4mm phosphor band at left. Fluorescent coated paper. PVA gum

XSL4 (=SG S38)

XSL4	12½p.	Light emerald	60	70
		b. With varnish coating (12.83)	20·00	

Plate Numbers (Blocks of Eight)
Double Pane Plates
Plate Nos. in top margin

Pl. Nos.	Phos. Nos.	Dot	No dot
1A, 1B	1B/1A	5·00	5·00
2A, 2B	1B/1A	5·00	5·00
3A, 3B	1B/1A	40·00	7·00
4A, 4B	1B/1A	10·00	15·00
4A, 4B	2B/2A	£400	4500
5A, 4B	2B/2A	70·00	80·00
5A, 5B	2B/2A	32·00	70·00

Plate Numbers (Blocks of Six)
Double Pane Plates
Plate Nos. in left margin

Pl. Nos.	Phos. Nos.	Dot (I)	No dot (P)
6A, 6B	2B/2A	12·00	9·00
7A, 7B	2B/2A With varnish coating	£150	£730
8A, 8B	2B/2A	7·00	5·00

The phosphor number is "A" on dot or "B" on no dot plate blocks.
   On No. XSL4b the varnish coating completely covers the stamp but the phosphor band is visible under u.v. light.
Withdrawn: 28 June 1985

13p. Pale chestnut (1984–87)

Printed by Waddington

1984 (23 October). Perf. 14. One 4mm phosphor band at left. Fluorescent coated paper. PVA gum

A. Type I
XSL5 (=SG S39)

XSL5	13p. Pale chestnut.	85	75
	a. Phosphor omitted	£700	

Plate Numbers (Blocks of Six)
Double Pane Plates
Plate Nos. in left margin

Pl. Nos.	Phos. Nos.	Dot (I)	No dot (P)
1A, 1B	1A	5·50	5·50

B. Type II (1.85)
XSL6 (S.G.S39Ea)

XSL6	13p. Pale chestnut	8·00	8·00
	a. Phosphor omitted	£750	

Plate Numbers (Blocks of Six)
Double Pane Plates
Plate Nos. in left margin

Pl. Nos.	Phos. Nos.	Dot (I)	No dot (P)
2A, 2B	1A	48·00	48·00
3A, 3B	1A	48·00	48·00
3A, 4B	1A	48·00	48·00

Printed by Questa

1986 (4 November). Perf. 15 × 14. One 4mm short phosphor band at left. Fluorescent coated paper. Type II

A. PVAD gum

XSL7	13p. Pale chestnut		1·00

Plate Numbers (Blocks of Six)
Double Pane Plates
Plate Nos. in left margin

Pl. Nos.	(I)	Pl. Nos.	(P)
1, 1	6·00	2, 2	6·00

B. PVA gum (14.4.87)
XSL8 (=SG S53)

XSL8	13p. Pale chestnut	70	75

Plate Numbers (Blocks of Six)
Double Pane Plates
Plate Nos. in left margin

Pl. Nos.	(I)	(P)
3, 3	6·00	25·00
4, 4	†	4·75
5, 5	†	4·75
6, 6	†	4·75
7, 7	†	42·00
8, 8	†	45·00
9, 9	†	42·00
10,10	†	4·75

Plate Nos. 5, 5 and 6, 6 exist with a short imperforate section at base below the 8th perforation. *Price for plates* 5, 5 £65 *and* 6, 6 £75.
Withdrawn: Nos. XSL5/6, 3 November 1987; No. XSL7, 14 April 1988; No. XSL8, 4 September 1989

14p. Grey-blue (1981)

Printed by Waddington

1981 (8 April). Perf. 14. Phosphorised (fluorescent coated) paper. PVAD gum

XSL9 (=SG S40)

XSL9	14p. Grey-blue	75	75

Plate Numbers (Blocks of Eight)
Double Pane Plates
Plate Nos. in top margin

Pl. Nos.	Dot	No dot
2A, 1B	6·00	6·00
2A, 2B	35·00	14·00
3A, 3B	70·00	8·00
4A, 3B	£120	£110
4A, 4B	6·50	20·00

Withdrawn: 14 January 1984

Regional Machin Issues Lithography *Scotland* **XC**

14p. Deep blue (1988–89)

Printed by Questa

1988 (8 November). Perf. 15 × 14. One 4 mm short phosphor band (right of centre). Fluorescent coated paper. PVA gum

XSL10 (=SG S54)

XSL10	14p. Deep blue	60	70

Plate Numbers (Blocks of Six)
Double Pane Plates
Plate Nos. in left margin

Pl. Nos.	(P)
1, 1	4·00
2, 2	4·00
3, 3	4·00
4, 4	4·50
5, 5	4·00
6, 6	4·50
7, 7	4·00
8, 8	4·00
9, 9	50·00
10, 10	10·00

1989 (21 March). Perf. 15 × 14. One 4 mm phosphor band (right of centre). Fluorescent coated paper. PVA gum

From £5 "The Scots Connection" booklet pane No. XDS2

XSL11	14p. Deep blue	1·00	1·00

No. XSL10 shows the phosphor band short at top or bottom of the stamp whereas on No. XSL11 the band is continuous.

1989 (21 March). Perf. 15 × 14. One 4 mm phosphor band at left. Fluorescent coated paper. PVA gum

From £5 "The Scots Connection" booklet se-tenant pane No. XDS3

XSL12 (=SG S55)

XSL12	14p. Deep blue	80	90

Withdrawn: No. XSL10, 27 November 1990

15p. Bright blue (1989)

Printed by Questa

1989 (28 November). Perf. 15 × 14. One 4 mm short phosphor band (right of centre). Fluorescent coated paper. PVA gum

XSL13 (=SG S56)

XSL13	15p. Bright blue	70	70
	a. Imperforate (3 sides) (block of four)	£275	

No. XSL13a occurred in the second vertical row of two sheets. The price is for a block of four including the left-hand vertical pair imperforate on three sides.

Plate Numbers (Blocks of Six)
Double Pane Plates
Plate Nos. in left margin

Pl. Nos.	(P)
1, 1	5·00
2, 2	5·00
3, 3	20·00
4, 4	5·50
5, 5	7·00
6, 6	10·00
7, 7	5·50
8, 8	5·00

Plate Nos. 3, 3; 4, 4 and 5, 5 exist with a short imperforate section at base below the 8th perforation. *Price for plates* 3, 3 £40: 5, 5 £28. (Plates 4, 4 are scarce in this state.)

Withdrawn: 14 September 1991

15½p. Pale violet (1982)

Printed by Waddington

1982 (24 February). Perf. 14. Phosphorised (fluorescent coated) paper. PVAD gum

XSL14 (=SG S41)

XSL14	15½p. Pale violet	80	80

Plate Numbers (Blocks of Eight)
Double Pane Plates
Plate Nos. in top margin

Pl. Nos.	Dot	No dot
1A, 1B	8·00	24·00
2A, 1B	28·00	25·00
3A, 1B	£550	£550
3A, 2B	7·50	9·00
4A, 3B	15·00	£120
5A, 3B	45·00	£110
6A, 4B	7·00	15·00

Withdrawn: 29 April 1984

16p. Drab (1983)

Printed by Waddington

1983 (27 April). Perf. 14. Phosphorised (fluorescent coated) paper. PVAD gum

XSL15 (=SG S42)

XSL15	16p. Drab	80	85

Plate Numbers (Blocks of Six)
Double Pane Plates
Plate Nos. in left margin

Pl. Nos.	Dot (I)	No dot (P)
1A, 1B	5·50	5·50
2A, 2B*	5·50	5·50
3A, 3B	42·00	60·00
4A, 4B	27·00	65·00
5A, 4B	5·50	40·00

*This printing was on paper produced by Harrisons for print quality trials by Waddingtons. Under both ordinary and ultraviolet light this paper appeared similar to the paper it replaced.

Withdrawn: 31 October 1986

17p. Grey-blue (1984–86)

Printed by Waddington

1984 (23 October). Perf. 14. Phosphorised (fluorescent coated) paper. Type I. PVAD gum

XSL16 (S.G.S43)

XSL16	17p. Grey-blue	1·50	1·50

Plate Numbers (Blocks of Six)
Double Pane Plates Plate Nos. in left margin

Pl. Nos.	Dot (I)	No dot (P)
1A, 1B	10·00	10·00
1A, 2B	12·00	10·00

XC Regional Machin Issues Lithography — Scotland

1985 (January). Perf. 14. Phosphorised (fluorescent coated) paper. Type II

A. PVAD gum

| XSL 17 | 17p. Grey-blue | 1·75 | 1·50 |

Plate Numbers (Blocks of Six)
Double Pane Plates
Plate Nos. in left margin

Pl. Nos.	Dot (I)	No dot (P)
2A, 3B	11·00	11·00
2A, 4B	12·00	12·00
2A, 5B	11·00	11·00
3A, 5B	25·00	25·00

B. PVA gum (25.6.85)
XSL18 (=SG S43Ea)

| XSL18 | 17p. Grey-blue | 1·75 | 1·50 |

Plate Numbers (Blocks of Six)
Double Pane Plates
Plate Nos. in left margin

Pl. Nos.	Dot (I)	No dot (P)
2A, 4B	11·00	†

No. XSL18 was an experimental issue printed on paper made by Henry & Leigh Slater Ltd.

Printed by Questa

1986 (29 April). Perf. 15×14. Phosphorised (advanced coated) paper. Type II. PVAD gum

XSL19 (=SG S57)

| XSL19 | 17p. Grey-blue | 4·00 | 4·00 |

Plate Numbers (Blocks of Six)
Double Pane Plates
Plate Nos. in left margin

Pl. Nos.	(I)	Pl. Nos.	(P)
1, 1	25·00	2, 2	25·00

Sold out: Nos. XSL16/18, May 1986; No. XSL19, October 1987.

17p. Deep blue (1990)

Printed by Questa

1990 (4 December). Perf. 15×14. One 4mm Short phosphor band (right of centre). Fluorescent coated paper. PVA gum

XSL20 (=SG S58)

| XSL20 | 17p. Deep blue | 1·00 | 1·10 |

Plate Numbers (Blocks of Six)
Double Pane Plates
Plate Nos. in left margin

Pl. Nos.	(P)
1, 1	7·00
2, 2	7·00
3, 3	7·50
4, 4	7·50
5, 5	9·00
6, 6	95·00

Withdrawn: 13 September 1992

18p. Deep violet (1981)

Printed by Waddington

1981 (8 April). Perf. 14. Phosphorised (fluorescent coated) paper. PVAD gum

XSL21 (=SG S44)

| XSL21 | 18p. Deep violet | 80 | 80 |

Plate Numbers (Blocks of Eight)
Double Pane Plates
Plate Nos. in top margin

Pl. Nos.	Dot	No dot
1A, 1B	5·00	5·00

Withdrawn: 14 January 1984

18p. Deep olive-grey (1987–88)

Printed by Questa

1987 (6 January). Perf. 15×14. Phosphorised (advanced coated) paper

A. PVAD gum
XSL22 (=SG S59)

| XSL22 | 18p. Deep olive-grey | 1·10 | 85 |

Plate Numbers (Blocks of Six)
Double Pane Plates
Plate Nos. in left margin

Pl. Nos.	(I)	(P)
1, 1	7·00	†
2, 2	†	7·50
3, 3	15·00	8·00
4, 4	†	7·00
5, 5	†	10·00
6, 6	†	10·00
7, 7	†	50·00
8, 8	†	50·00

Plate Nos. 3, 3; 4, 4 and 6, 6 exist with a short imperforate section at base below the 8th perforation. *Price for plates 3, 3 £55; 4, 4 £18 and 6, 6 £90.*

B. PVAD (clear) gum (29.3.88)

| XSL23 | 18p. Deep olive-grey | 1·40 |

This printing was on phosphorised (advanced coated) paper supplied to Questa by Henry & Leigh Slater Ltd. The PVAD gum did not have the green dye additive.

Plate Numbers (Blocks of Six)
Double Pane Plates
Plate Nos. in left margin

Pl. Nos.	(P)
5, 5	8·50
6, 6	8·50

Withdrawn: 4 September 1989

18p. Bright green (1991–93)

1991 (3 December). One 4mm short phosphor band (right of centre). Fluorescent coated paper. PVA gum

A. Perf. 15×14
XSL24 (=SG S60)

| XSL24 | 18p. Bright green | 1·25 | 90 |

Regional Machin Issues Lithography Scotland XC

Plate Numbers (Blocks of Six)
Double Pane Plates
Plate Nos. in left margin

Pl. Nos.	(P)
1, 1	8·00
2, 2	8·00
3, 3	9·00
4, 4	9·00
11, 11	9·00
12, 12	9·00

B. Perf. 14 (26.9.92. Philatelic Bureau. 23.2.93)
XSL25 (=SG S60a)

XSL25	18p. Bright green	1·00	1·00
	a. Phosphor omitted	£1250	

Plate Numbers (Blocks of Six)
Double Pane Plates
Plate Nos. in left margin

Pl. Nos.	(P)
5, 5	8·00
6, 6	8·00
7, 7	6·50
8, 8	6·50
9, 9	6·50
10, 10	6·50

1993 (10 August). Perf. 15×14. One side phosphor band (yellow fluor) at left. Non-fluorescent coated paper. PVA gum

From £6 (£5.64) "The Story of Beatrix Potter" booklet pane XD1
XSL26 (=SG S61)

XSL26	18p. Bright green	2·75	3·00

Withdrawn: No. XSL24/5, 6 December 1994

19p. Bright orange-red (1988–89)

Printed by Questa

1988 (8 November). Perf. 15×14. Phosphorised (advanced coated) paper

A. PVAD (clear) gum (cream back)
XSL27 (=SG S62)

XSL27	19p. Bright orange-red	70	70

No. XSL27 is known pre-released on 4 November at Edinburgh. The same note below No. XSL23 applies here.

Plate Numbers (Blocks of Six)
Double Pane Plates
Plate Nos. in left margin

Pl. Nos.	(P)
1, 1	4·75
2, 2	4·75

B. PVA gum (white back) (25.4.89)

XSL28	19p. Bright orange-red	70	

This paper was supplied as an experiment by Coated Papers Limited of Leek, Staffordshire. It can be distinguished by the whiter gummed side from No. XSL27 which is cream. Both are similar under ultraviolet.

Plate Numbers (Blocks of Six)
Double Pane Plates
Plate Nos. in left margin

Pl. Nos.	(P)
3, 3	4·75
4, 4	4·75

1989 (21 March). Perf. 15×14. Two phosphor bands. Fluorescent coated paper. PVA gum

From £5 "The Scots Connection" booklet se-tenant pane No. XDS3
XSL29 (=SG S63)

XSL29	19p. Bright orange-red	2·25	2·00

Withdrawn: No. XSL27, 24 April 1990; No. XSL28, 27 November 1990

19p. Bistre (1993–95)

Printed by Questa

1993 (7 December). Perf. 15×14(E). One 4mm short phosphor band (yellow fluor) right of centre. Non-fluorescent coated paper. PVA gum

XSL30 (=SG S81)

XSL30	19p. Bistre	80	70

Plate Numbers (Blocks of Six)
Double Pane Plates
Plate Nos. in left margin

Pl. Nos.	(P)
1, 1	5·00
2, 2	5·00
3, 3	5·50
4, 4	6·00
5, 5	6·00
6, 6	6·00
7, 7	14·00
8, 8	8·00
9, 9	55·00
10, 10	40·00

Plate Nos. 5, 5 and 6, 6 exist with a short imperforate section at base below the 9th perforation. *Price for plate* 5, 5 £50 *and* 6, 6 £22.

1995 (25 April). Perf. 15×14(E). One side phosphor band (yellow fluor) at right. Non-fluorescent coated paper. PVA gum

From £6 National Trust booklet se-tenant pane XD2
XSL31 (=SG S82)

XSL31	19p. Bistre	3·00	3·25

1995 (12 October). Perf. 15×14(E). One 4mm short phosphor band (blue fluor) right of centre. Non-fluorescent coated paper. PVA gum

XSL32	19p. Bistre	80	80

XC Regional Machin Issues Lithography Scotland

Plate Numbers (Blocks of Six)
Double Pane Plates
Plate Nos. in left margin

Pl. Nos.	(P)
11, 11	5·00
12, 12	5·00
13, 13	50·00
14, 14	65·00

Withdrawn: No. XSL30, 29 March 1996; No. XSL32, 22 July 1997

19½p. Olive-grey (1982)

Printed by Waddington

1982 (24 February). Perf. 14. Phosphorised (fluorescent coated) paper. PVAD gum

XSL33 (=SG S45)

XSL33	19½p. Olive-grey	1·75	1·75

Plate Numbers (Blocks of Eight)
Double Pane Plates
Plate Nos. in top margin

Pl. Nos.	Dot	No dot
1A, 1B	14·00	14·00

Withdrawn: 29 April 1984

20p. Brownish black (1989)

Printed by Questa

1989 (28 November). Perf. 15 × 14. Phosphorised (advanced coated) paper. PVAD (clear) gum

XSL34 (=SG S64)

XSL34	20p. Brownish black	95	95

Plate Numbers (Blocks of Six)
Double Pane Plates
Plate Nos. in left margin

Pl. Nos.	(P)
1, 1	6·50
2, 2	6·50
3, 3	6·50
4, 4	7·00
5, 5	7·00
6, 6	7·00

Withdrawn: 14 September 1991

20p. Bright green (1996)

Printed by Questa

1996 (23 July). Perf. 15 × 14(E). One 4.5 mm centre phosphor band (blue fluor). Non-fluorescent coated paper. PVA gum

XSL35 (=SG S83)

XSL35	20p. Bright green	1·50	1·50
	a. One long wave phosphor band (1997)	2·00	2·00

No. XSL35a came from plates 3, 3 and 4, 4.

Plate Numbers (Blocks of Six)
Double Pane Plates
Plate Nos. in left margin

Pl. Nos.	(P)
1, 1	9·00
2, 2	9·00
3, 3	12·00
4, 4	12·00

Withdrawn: 1 December 1997

20½p. Ultramarine (1983)

Printed by Waddington

1983 (27 April). Perf. 14. Phosphorised (fluorescent coated) paper. PVAD gum

XSL38 (=SG S46)

XSL38	20½p. Ultramarine	3·50	3·50

Plate Numbers (Blocks of Six)
Double Pane Plates
Plate Nos. in left margin

Pl. Nos.	No dot	Dot (I) (P)
1A, 1B	21·00	21·00

Withdrawn: 28 June 1985

22p. Blue (1981)

Printed by Waddington

1981 (8 April). Perf. 14. Phosphorised (fluorescent coated) paper. PVAD gum

XSL39 (=SG S47)

XSL39	22p. Blue	1·00	1·00

Plate Numbers (Blocks of Eight)
Double Pane Plates
Plate Nos. in top margin

Pl. Nos.	Dot	No dot
4A, 1B	9·00	9·00

Withdrawn: 29 April 1984

22p. Yellow-green (1984–87)

Printed by Waddington

1984 (23 October). Perf. 14. Phosphorised (advanced coated) paper. PVAD gum

A. Type I
XSL40 (=SG S48)

XSL40	22p. Yellow-green	4·25	4·25

Plate Numbers (Blocks of Six)
Double Pane Plates
Plate Nos. in left margin

Pl. Nos.	Dot (I)	No dot (P)
1A, 1B	26·00	26·00

B. Type II (1.86)
XSL41 (=SG S48Ea)

XSL41	22p. Yellow-green	50·00	30·00

Regional Machin Issues Lithography *Scotland* **XC**

Plate Numbers (Blocks of Six)
Double Pane Plates
Plate No. in left margin

Pl. Nos.	Dot (I)	No dot (P)
2A, 2B	£275	£275
3A, 2B	£300	£275

Printed by Questa

1987 (27 January). Perf. 15 × 14. Phosphorised (advanced coated) paper. Type II. PVAD gum

XSL42 (=SG S65)

XSL42	22p. Yellow-green	1·25	1·50

Plate Numbers (Blocks of Six)
Double Pane Plates
Plate Nos. in left margin

Pl. Nos.	(I)	Pl. Nos.	(P)
1, 1	7·50	2, 2	7·50

Withdrawn: Nos. XSL40/41, 26 January 1988; No. XSL42, 27 November 1990

22p. Bright orange-red (1990)

Printed by Questa

1990 (4 December). Perf. 15 × 14. Phosphorised (advanced coated) paper

A. PVAD gum
XSL43 (S.G.S66)

XSL43	22p. Bright orange-red	1·25	90

Plate Numbers (Blocks of Six)
Double Pane Plates
Plate Nos. in left margin

Pl. Nos.	(P)
1, 1	7·00
2, 2	7·00
3, 3	26·00
4, 4	7·00
5, 5	£300
6, 6	14·00

B. PVA gum (white back) (14.5.91)

XSL44	22p. Bright orange-red	1·40

Plate Numbers (Blocks of Six)
Double Pane Plates
Plate Nos. in left margin

Pl. Nos.	(P)
7, 7	9·00
8, 8	9·00
9, 9	22·00
10, 10	10·00

Withdrawn: 13 September 1992

23p. Bright green (1988–89)

Printed by Questa

1988 (8 November). Perf. 15 × 14. Phosphorised (advanced coated) paper. PVAD (clear) gum

XSL45 (S.G.S67)

XSL45	23p. Bright green	1·25	1·10

Plate Numbers (Blocks of Six)
Double Pane Plates
Plate Nos. in left margin

Pl. Nos.	(P)
1, 1	7·50
2, 2	7·50

1989 (21 March). Perf. 15 × 14. Two phosphor bands. Fluorescent coated paper. PVA gum

From £5 "The Scots Connection" booklet *se-tenant* pane No. XDS3
XSL46 (=SG S68)

XSL46	23p. Bright green	14·00	14·00

Withdrawn: No. XSL45, 27 November 1990

24p. Indian red (1989)

Printed by Questa

1989 (28 November). Perf. 15 × 14. Phosphorised (advanced coated) paper. PVAD (clear) gum

XSL47 (=SG S69)

XSL47	24p. Indian red	1·25	1·25

Plate Numbers (Blocks of Six)
Double Pane Plates
Plate Nos. in left margin

Pl. Nos.	(P)
1, 1	7·50
2, 2	7·50

Withdrawn: 14 September 1991

24p. Chestnut (1991–93)

Printed by Questa

1991 (3 December). Phosphorised (advanced coated) paper. PVA gum

A. Perf. 15 × 14
XSL48 (=SG S70)

XSL48	24p. Chestnut	1·40	1·25

Plate Numbers (Blocks of Six)
Double Pane Plates
Plate Nos. in left margin

Pl. Nos.	(P)
1, 1	8·50
2, 2	8·50
3, 3	9·00
4, 4	9·00
7, 7	10·00
8, 8	10·00
9, 9	10·00
10, 10	8·50
11, 11	8·50
12, 12	10·00

B. Perf. 14 (10.92)
XSL49 (=SG S70a)

XSL49	24p. Chestnut	6·00	6·00

XC Regional Machin Issues Lithography Scotland

Plate Numbers (Blocks of Six)
Double Pane Plates
Plate Nos. in left margin

Pl. Nos.	(P)
5, 5	55·00
6, 6	35·00
7, 7	55·00
8, 8	38·00

1993 (10 August). Perf. 15 × 14. Two bands (yellow fluor). Non-fluorescent coated paper. PVA gum

From £6 (£5.64) "The Story of Beatrix Potter" booklet pane XDI
XSL50 (=SG S71)

XSL50	24p. Chestnut	2·75	3·00

Withdrawn: No. XSL48, 6 December 1994. No. XSL49 was not available from the Bureau.

25p. Red (1993–96)

Printed by Questa

1993 (7 December). Perf. 15 × 14(E). Two 8 mm phosphor bands (yellow fluor). Non-fluorescent coated paper. PVA gum

XSL51 (=SG S84)

XSL51	25p. Red	1·10	1·00
	a. 11·5 mm between bands (25.4.95, ex. XD2)	1·25	1·25

The distance between the phosphor bands on No. XSL51 is 12·5 mm.

Plate Numbers (Blocks of Six)
Double Pane Plates
Plate Nos. in left margin

Pl. Nos.	(P)
1, 1	6·00
2, 2	6·00
3, 3	7·00
4, 4	7·00
5, 5	8·00
6, 6	9·00
7, 7	12·00
8, 8	12·00

1995 (3 August). Perf. 15 × 14 and one elliptical perf. hole on each vertical edge. Two phosphor bands (blue fluor). Non-fluorescent coated paper. PVA gum

A. Two 8 mm Phosphor bands

XSL52	25p. Red	1·25	1·25

This was sold by the Philatelic Bureau from 20 October 1995.

Plate Numbers (Blocks of Six)
Double Pane Plates Plate Nos. in left margin

Pl. Nos.	(P)
9, 9	7·50
10, 10	7·50
11, 11	12·00
12, 12	12·00

B. Two 9 mm phosphor bands.
From £6.48 European Football Championship booklet pane UHP18 (14.5.96)

XSL53	25p. Red	2·00	2·00

Withdrawn: No. XSL51, 29 March 1996; No. XSL52, 22 July 1997.

26p. Rosine (1982–87)

Printed by Waddington

1982 (24 February). Perf. 14. Phosphorised (fluorescent coated) paper. Type I. PVAD gum

XSL55 (S.G.S49)

XSL55	26p. Rosine	1·25	1·25

Plate Numbers (Blocks of Eight)
Double Pane Plates
Plate Nos. in top margin

Pl. Nos.	Dot	No dot
1A, 1B	10·00	10·00

Printed by Questa

1987 (27 January). Perf. 15 × 14. Phosphorised (advanced coated) paper. Type II. PVAD gum

XSL56 (=SG S72)

XSL56	26p. Rosine	3·75	4·00

Plate Numbers (Blocks of Six)
Double Pane Plates
Plate Nos. in left margin

Pl. No.	(I)	Pl. No.	(P)
1	23·00	2	23·00

Withdrawn: 4 September 1989

26p. Drab (1990)

Printed by Questa

1990 (4 December). Perf. 15 × 14. Phosphorised (advanced coated) paper.

A. PVAD gum
XSL57 (=SG S73)

XSL57	26p. Drab	1·25	1·25

Plate Numbers (Blocks of Six)
Double Pane Plates
Plate Nos. in left margin

Pl. Nos.	(P)
1, 1	7·50
2, 2	7·50

B. PVA gum (white back) (14.5.91)

XSL58	26p. Drab	1·40

Plate Numbers (Blocks of Six)
Double Pane Plates
Plate Nos. in left margin

Pl. Nos.	(P)
1, 1	9·00
2, 2	9·00

Withdrawn: 13 September 1992

26p. Red-brown (1996)

Printed by Questa

1996 (23 July). Perf. 15×14(E). Two phosphor bands (blue fluor). Non-fluorescent coated paper. PVA gum

XSL59 (=SG S85)

XSL59	26p. Red-brown	1·75	2·00
	b. Horizontal band at top and two misplaced short bands at foot		

No. XSL59b came from a phosphor shift on a sheet with a top row showing the horizontal phosphor band, normally above the "W" sheet marking, placed across ten stamps. The vertical side bands were short and the rest of the sheet was normal.

Plate Numbers (Blocks of Six)
Double Pane Plates
Plate Nos. in left margin

Pl. Nos.	(P)
1, 1	10·00
2, 2	10·00
3, 3	11·00
4, 4	11·00

Withdrawn: 1 December 1997

28p. Deep violet-blue (1983–87)

Printed by Waddington

1983 (27 April). Perf. 14. Phosphorised (fluorescent coated) paper. PVAD gum

XSL60 (=SG S50)

XSL60	28p. Deep violet-blue	1·25	1·25

Plate Numbers (Blocks of Six)
Double Pane Plates
Plate Nos. in left margin

Pl. Nos.	Dot (I)	No dot (P)
1A, 1B	7·50	7·50

Printed by Questa

1987 (27 January). Perf. 15×14. Phosphorised (advanced coated) paper. PVAD gum

XSL61 (=SG S74)

XSL61	28p. Deep violet-blue	1·25	1·25

Plate Numbers (Blocks of Six)
Double Pane Plates
Plate Nos. in left margin

Pl. No.	(I)	Pl. No.	(P)
1	7·50	2	7·50

Withdrawn: No. XSL60. 26 January 1988; No. XSL61. 27 November 1990

28p. Deep bluish grey (1991)

Printed by Questa

1991 (3 December). Phosphorised (advanced coated) paper. PVA gum

A. Perf 15×14
XSL62 (=SG S75)

XSL62	28p. Deep bluish grey	1·25	1·50

Plate Numbers (Blocks of Six)
Double Pane Plates
Plate Nos. in left margin

Pl. Nos.	(P)
1, 1	7·50
2, 2	7·50

B. Perf. 14 (18.2.93)
XSL63 (=SG S75a)

XSL63	Deep bluish grey	8·00	8·00

Plate Numbers (Blocks of Six)
Double Pane Plates
Plate Nos. in left margin

Pl. Nos.	(P)
1, 1	48·00
2, 2	48·00

Withdrawn: No. XSL62, 6 December 1994. No. XSL63 was not available from the Bureau.

30p. Deep olive-grey (1993)

Printed by Questa

1993 (7 December). Perf. 15×14(E). Two 8mm phosphor bands (yellow fluor). Non-fluorescent coated paper. PVA gum

XSL64 (=SG S86)

XSL64	30p. Deep olive-grey	1·25	1·25

Plate Numbers (Blocks of Six)
Double Pane Plates
Plate Nos. in left margin

Pl. Nos.	(P)
1, 1	7·50
2, 2	7·50
3, 3	11·00
4, 4	11·00

Plate No. 2, 2 exists with two perforation holes in bottom margin. *Price for plate 2, 2 £55.*
Withdrawn: 22 July 1997

31p. Bright purple (1984–86)

Printed by Waddington

1984 (23 October). Perf 14. Phosphorised (fluorescent coated) paper. PVAD gum

A. Type I
XSL65 (=SG S51)

XSL65	31p. Bright purple	2·50	2·50

Plate Numbers (Blocks of Six)
Double Pane Plates
Plate Nos. in left margin

Pl. Nos.	Dot (I)	No dot (P)
1A, 1B	15·00	15·00

B. Type II (4.11.85)
XSL66 (=SG S51Ea)

XSL66	31p. Bright purple	£130	£100

Plate Numbers (Blocks of Six)
Double Pane Plates
Plate Nos. in left margin

Pl. Nos.	Dot (I)	No dot (P)
2A, 2B	£750	£800

Printed by Questa

1986 (29 April). Perf. 15 × 14. Phosphorised (advanced coated) paper. Type II. PVAD gum

XSL67 (=SG S76)

XSL67	31p. Bright purple	2·25	2·25

Plate Numbers (Blocks of Six)
Double Pane Plates
Plate Nos. in left margin

Pl. No.	(I)	Pl. Nos.	(P)
1	14·00	2, 2	14·00

Sold out: Nos. XSL65/66, December 1986
Withdrawn: No. XSL67, 4 September 1989

32p. Greenish blue (1988)

Printed by Questa

1988 (8 November). Perf. 15 × 14. Phosphorised (advanced coated) paper. PVAD (clear) gum

XSL68 (=SG S77)

XSL68	32p. Greenish blue	1·75	2·00

Plate Numbers (Blocks of Six)
Double Pane Plates
Plate Nos. in left margin

Pl. Nos.	(P)
1, 1	11·00
2, 2	11·00

Withdrawn: 27 November 1990

34p. Deep bluish grey (1989)

Printed by Questa

1989 (28 November). Perf. 15 × 14. Phosphorised (advanced coated) paper. PVAD (clear) gum

XSL69 (=SG S78)

XSL69	34p. Deep bluish grey	1·75	1·75

Plate Numbers (Blocks of Six)
Double Pane Plates
Plate Nos. in left margin

Pl. Nos.	(P)
1, 1	11·00
2, 2	11·00

Withdrawn: 14 September 1991

37p. Rosine (1990)

Printed by Questa

1990 (4 December). Perf. 15 × 14. Phosphorised (advanced coated) paper

A. PVAD gum
XSL70 (=SG S79)

XSL70	37p. Rosine	2·00	2·25

Plate Numbers (Blocks of Six)
Double Pane Plates
Plate Nos. in left margin

Pl. Nos.	(P)
1, 1	12·00
2, 2	12·00

B. PVA gum (white back) (14.5.91)

XSL71	37p. Rosine		2·25

Plate Numbers (Blocks of Six)
Double Pane Plates
Plate Nos. in left margin

Pl. Nos.	(P)
1, 1	14·00
2, 2	14·00

Withdrawn: 13 September 1992

37p. Bright mauve (1996)

Printed by Questa

1996 (23 July). Perf. 15 × 14(E). Two phosphor bands (blue fluor). Non-fluorescent coated paper. PVA gum

XSL72 (=SG S87)

XSL72	37p. Bright mauve	2·75	3·00

Plate Numbers (Blocks of Six)
Double Pane Plates
Plate Nos. in left margin

Pl. Nos.	(P)
1, 1	17·00
2, 2	17·00

Withdrawn: 1 December 1997

39p. Bright mauve (1991–92)

Printed by Questa

1991 (3 December). Phosphorised (advanced coated) paper. PVA gum

A. Perf 15 × 14
XSL73 (=SG S80)

XSL73	39p. Bright mauve	2·00	2·25

Plate Numbers (Blocks of Six)
Double Pane Plates
Plate Nos. in left margin

Pl. Nos.	(P)
1, 1	12·00
2, 2	12·00
3, 3	12·00
4, 4	14·00

B. Perf. 14 (11.92)
XSL74 (=SG S80a)

XSL74	39p. Bright mauve	7·00	7·00

Plate Numbers (Blocks of Six)
Double Pane Plates
Plate Nos. in left margin

Pl. Nos.	(P)
1, 1	42·00
2, 2	42·00

Withdrawn: No. XSL73, 6 December 1993. No. XSL74 was not available from the Bureau.

41p. Grey-brown (1993)

Printed by Questa

1993 (7 December). Perf. 15×14(E). Two 8mm phosphor bands (yellow fluor). Non-fluorescent coated paper. PVA gum

XSL75 (=SG S88)

XSL75	41p. Grey-brown	1·75	2·00
	a. Phosphor omitted	£300	

Plate Numbers (Blocks of Six)
Double Pane Plates
Plate Nos. in left margin

Pl. Nos.	(P)
1, 1	11·00
2, 2	11·00

Withdrawn: 22 July 1997

63p. Light emerald (1996)

Printed by Questa

1996 (23 July). Perf. 15×14(E). Two phosphor bands (blue fluor). Non-fluorescent coated paper. PVA gum

XSL76 (=SG S89)

XSL76	63p. Light emerald	4·00	4·25

Plate Numbers (Blocks of Six)
Double Pane Plates
Plate Nos. in left margin

Pl. Nos.	(P)
1, 1	24·00
2, 2	24·00

Withdrawn: 1 December 1997

Presentation Packs

Presentation Packs containing stamps of Northern Ireland, Scotland and Wales are listed after those of Northern Ireland.

XSPP6 No. 129b (28.10.81)	7p., 9p., 10½p., 11½p., 12p., 13½p., 14p., 15p., 18p., 22p.	9·00

Comprises Nos. XS46, 51, 54, 57/8, 60, XSL1, 9, 21 and 39.

XSPP7 No. 2 (3.8.83)	10p., 12½p., 16p., 20½p., 26p., 28p.	18·00

Comprises Nos. XS52, XSL4, 15, 38, 55 and 60.

XSPP8 No. 6 (23.10.84)	10p., 13p., 16p., 17p., 22p., 26p., 28p., 31p.	17·00

Comprises Nos. XS53, XSL5, 15, 16, 40, 55, 60 and 64.

XSPP9 No. 10 (3.8.71)	12p., 13p., 17p., 18p 22p., 26p., 28p., 31p.	20·00

Comprises Nos. XSL3, 7, 19, 22, 42, 56, 61 and 67.
Withdrawn: No. XSPP6, August 1983; No. XSPP7, October 1984; No. XSPP8. 2 March 1987; No. XSPP9, 31 December 1991

First Day Covers

XSLFD1 (8.4.81)	11½p., 14½p 18p., 22p.	2·50
XSLFD2 (24.2.82)	12½p., 15½p., 19½p., 26p.	3·50
XSLFD3 (27.4.83)	16p., 20½p., 28p.	4·00
XSLFD4 (23.10.84)	13p., 17p., 22p., 31p.	4·00
XSLFD5 (7.1.86)	12p.	2·00
XSLFD6 (6.1.87)*	18p.	1·80
XSLFD7 (8.11.88)	14p., 19p., 23p., 32p,	4·25
XSLFD8 (21.3.89)	Scots Connection *se-tenant* pane	14·00
XSLFD9 (28.11.89)	15p., 20p., 24p., 34p.	5·00
XSLFD10 (4.12.90)	17p., 22p., 26p., 37p.	5·00
XSLFD11 (3.12.91)	18p., 24p., 28p., 39p.	5·50
XSLFD12 (7.12.93)	19p., 25p., 30p., 41p.	6·00
XSLFD13 (23.7.96)	20p., 26p., 37p., 63p.	8·75

*The Questa printings issued on 27 January 1987 for 22p., 26p. and 28p, were affixed to No. XSLFD6 in error by the Edinburgh Philatelic Bureau; three weeks earlier than the official date of release.

C. Wales

Type XW4 as illustrated in Section XB printed by Questa

Two Types of Dragon

I	II

Type I. Thin wing tips and tail. Eye not joined to nose
Screened background: 13p., 17p. (grey-blue). 28p., (deep violet blue)
Solid background: 26p. (rosine)

Type II. Thick wing tips and tail. Eye joined to the nose
Screened background: 28p. (deep violet blue)
Solid background: 13p., 17p. (grey-blue), 26p. (rosine)
No other values exist with both types in the same colour.

11½p. Drab (1981)

1981 (8 April). Perf. 14. One 4mm phosphor band at left. Original coated paper. PVA gum

XWL1 (=SG W35)

XWL1	11½p. Drab	90	80

Plate Numbers (Blocks of Six)
Double Pane Plates
Plate Nos. in right margin

Pl. Nos.	Row 1	Row 20
1, 1	5·75	5·75
2, 2	5·75	5·75

Withdrawn: 26 February 1983

12p. Bright emerald (1986)

1986 (7 January). Perf. 15×14. One 4mm band at left. Fluorescent coated paper. PVAD gum

XWL2 (=SG W36)

XWL2	12p. Bright emerald	2·00	2·00

Plate Numbers (Blocks of Six)
Double Pane Plates
Plate Nos. in left margin

Pl. Nos.	(l)	Pl. Nos.	(P)
1, 1	12·00	2, 2	12·00

1986 (July). Perf. 15×14. One short phosphor band at left. Fluorescent coated paper. PVAD gum

XWL3	12p. Bright emerald	4·50	3·00

No. XWL3 was printed with the 4mm wide phosphor band at left cut short opposite the perforations at the top and bottom of each stamp in the sheet.

Plate Numbers (Blocks of Six)
Double Pane Plates
Plate Nos. in left margin

Pl. No.	(l)	Pl. Nos.	(P)
3, 3	26·00	4, 4	26·00

Sold out: Nos. XWL2/3, September 1987

12½p. Light emerald (1982–84)

1982 (24 February). Perf. 14. One 4mm band at left. Fluorescent coated paper. PVAD gum

XWL4 (=SG W37)

XWL4	12½p. Light emerald	70	70

Plate Numbers (Blocks of Six)
Double Pane Plates
Plate Nos. in right margin

Pl. Nos.	Row 1	Row 20
1, 1	6·00	6·00
2, 2	4·50	4·50
3, 1	8·00	8·00
4, 2	30·00	30·00

Plate Nos. in left margin

Pl. Nos.	(l)	Pl. Nos.	(P)
1, 1	15·00	2, 2	45·00

1984 (10 January). Perf. 15×14. One 4mm band at left. Fluorescent coated paper. PVAD gum

XWL5 (=SG W37a)

XWL5	12½p. Light emerald	4·75	4·25

Plate Numbers (Blocks of Six)
Double Pane Plates
Plate Nos. in left margin

Pl. Nos.	(l)	Pl. Nos.	(P)
1, 1	30·00	2, 2	30·00
1, 3	35·00	2, 4	£650

Withdrawn: No. XWL4, 28 February 1985; No. XWL5, 28 June 1985

13p. Pale chestnut (1984–87)

1984 (23 October). Perf. 15×14. One 4mm band at left. Fluorescent coated paper. Type I. PVAD gum

XWL6 (=SG W38)

XWL6	13p. Pale chestnut	60	60

Plate Numbers (Blocks of Six)
Double Pane Plates (Second plate number is grey)
Plate Nos. in left margin

P1. Nos.	(l)	Pl. Nos.	(P)
1, 1	4·50	2, 2	4·50
1, 3	8·00	2, 4	£225
3, 3	22·00	4, 4	22·00
5, 3	3·50	6, 4	3·50
7, 5	4·50	8, 6	5·00

1987 (January). Perf. 15×14. One short phosphor band at left. Fluorescent coated paper. Type II

A. PVAD gum

XWL7	13p. Pale chestnut	3·75

Examples of No. XWL7 showing a "continuous" phosphor band similar to No. XWL6, but Type II, were from an overinked printing.

Plate Numbers (Blocks of Six)
Double Pane Plates (Second plate number is chestnut)
Plate Nos. in left margin

Pl. Nos.	(l)	Pl. Nos.	(P)
1, 1	24·00	2, 2	24·00

B. PVA gum (14.4.87)
XWL8 (=SG W38Ea)

XWL8	13p. Pale chestnut	1·90	1·75

Plate Numbers (Blocks of Six)
Double Pane Plates (Second plate number is chestnut)
Plate Nos. in left margin

Pl. Nos.	(P)
1, 1	12·00
2, 2	12·00
3, 3	15·00
4, 4	12·00

Withdrawn: No. XWL6, 1 April 1988; Nos. XWL7/8, 4 September 1989

14p. Grey-blue (1981)

1981 (8 April). Perf. 14. Phosphorised (fluorescent coated) paper. PVA gum

XWL9 (=SG W39)

XWL9	14p. Grey-blue	70	70

Regional Machin Issues Lithography Wales XC

Plate Numbers (Blocks of Six)
Double Pane Plates
Plate Nos. in right margin

Pl. Nos.	Row 1	Row 20
1, 1	4·50	4·50
2, 2	7·50	7·50
1, 3	5·50	6·00
2, 4	18·00	18·00

Withdrawn: 14 January 1984

14p. Deep blue (1988)

1988 (8 November). Perf. 15×14. One 4mm short band (right of centre). Fluorescent coated paper. PVA gum

XWL10 (=SG W40)

XWL10	14p. Deep blue	75	75

Plate Numbers (Blocks of Six)
Double Pane Plates
Plate Nos. in left margin

Pl. Nos.	(P)
1, 1	4·75
2, 2	4·75
3, 3	5·50
4, 4	5·00
5, 5	5·00
6, 6	5·00

Withdrawn: 27 November 1990

15p. Bright blue (1989)

1989 (28 November). Perf. 15×14. One 4mm short band (right of centre). Fluorescent coated paper. PVA gum

XWL11(=SG W41)

XWL11	15p.	Bright blue	80	75
		a. Phosphor omitted		

Plate Numbers (Blocks of Six)
Double Pane Plates
Plate Nos. in left margin

Pl. Nos.	(P)
1, 1	5·00
2, 2	5·00
3, 3	50·00
4, 4	60·00
5, 5	5·00
6, 6	5·50

Plate No. 6, 6 exists with a short imperforate section at base below the 8th perforation. *Price for plate* 6, 6 £12.
Withdrawn: 14 September 1991

15½p. Pale violet (1982)

1982 (24 February). Perf. 14. Phosphorised (fluorescent coated) paper. PVAD gum

XWL12 (=SG W42)

XWL12	15½p. Pale violet	75	75

Plate Numbers (Blocks of Six)
Double Pane Plates
Plate Nos. in right margin

Pl. Nos.	Row 1	Row 20
1	5·00	5·00
2	5·50	5·50
3	45·00	45·00
4	25·00	25·00
5	£550	£550
6	£550	£650

Withdrawn: 29 April 1984

16p. Drab (1983–84)

1983 (27 April). Perf. 14. Phosphorised (fluorescent coated) paper. PVAD gum

XWL13 (=SG W43)

XWL13	16p. Drab	1·75	1·75

Plate Numbers (Blocks of Six)
Double Pane Plates
Plate Nos. in left margin

Pl. Nos.	(I)	Pl. Nos.	(P)
1	11·00	2	18·00
3	£160	4	48·00

1984 (10 January). Perf. 15×14. Phosphorised (fluorescent coated) paper. PVAD gum

XWL14 (=SG W43a)

XWL14	16p. Drab	1·75	1·75

Plate Numbers (Blocks of Six)
Double Pane Plates
Plate Nos. in left margin

Pl. Nos.	(I)	Pl. Nos.	(P)
3	18·00	4	11·00
5	11·00	6	11·00

Withdrawn: No. XWL13, 10 January 1985; No. XWL14, 7 February 1987

17p. Grey-blue (1984–86)

1984 (23 October). Perf. 15×14. Phosphorised paper. Type I. PVAD gum

A. Fluorescent Coated Paper
XWL15 (=SG W44)

XWL15	17p. Grey-blue	70	80

Plate Numbers (Blocks of Six)
Double Pane Plates
Plate Nos. in left margin

Pl. Nos.	(I)	Pl. Nos.	(P)
1	8·00	2	18·00
3	4·50	4	4·50

The following plate number blocks are on paper of intermediate brightness and were issued with those listed above. The paper used was a forerunner to the brighter advanced coated paper of February 1986.

Pl. Nos.	(I)	Pl. Nos.	(P)
3	£180	4	45·00
5	5·00	6	5·00
7	15·00	8	5·00

B. Advanced Coated Paper (25.2.86)

XWL16	17p. Grey-blue	1·00

Plate Numbers (Blocks of Six)
Double Pane Plates
Plate Nos. in left margin

Pl. Nos.	(I)	Pl. Nos.	(P)
7	6·50	8	6·50

1986 (18 August). Perf. 15×14. Phosphorised (fluorescent coated) paper. Type II. PVAD gum

XWL17 (=SG W44Ea)

XWL17	17p. Grey-blue	55·00	45·00

Plate Numbers (Blocks of Six)
Double Pane Plates
Plate Nos in left margin

Pl. Nos.	(I)	Pl. Nos.	(P)
1, 1	£325	2, 2	£325

Withdrawn: No. XWL15, 24 February 1987; No. XWL16/17, sold out October 1987

17p. Deep blue (1990)

1990 (4 December). Perf. 15×14. One 4 mm short band (right of centre). Fluorescent coated paper. PVA gum

XWL18 (=SG W45)

XWL18	17p.	Deep blue	90	80
		a. Phosphor omitted	18·00	

Plate Numbers (Blocks of Six)
Double Pane Plates
Plate Nos. in left margin

Pl. Nos.	(I)	P1. Nos.	(P)
1, 1	5·50	3, 3	6·50
2, 2	5·50	4, 4	6·50

Withdrawn: 13 September 1992

18p. Deep violet (1981)

1981 (8 April). Perf. 14. Phosphorised (fluorescent coated) paper. PVA gum

XWL19 (=SG W46)

XWL19	18p. Deep violet	1·00	95

Plate Numbers (Blocks of Six)
Double Pane Plates
Plate Nos. in right margin

Pl. Nos.	Row 1	Row 20
1,1	6·00	6·00
2,2	6·00	6·00

Withdrawn: 14 January 1984

18p. Deep olive-grey (1987)

1987 (6 January). Perf. 15×14. Phosphorised (advanced coated) paper.

A. PVAD gum
XWL20 (S.G.W47)

XWL20	18p. Deep olive-grey	95	90

Plate Numbers (Blocks of Six)
Double Pane Plates
Plate Nos. in left margin

Pl. Nos.	(I)	Pl. Nos.	(P)
1, 1	5·75	2, 2	5·75
3, 3	5·75	3, 3	9·00
		4, 4	5·75
		5, 5	9·50
		6, 6	15·00

Plate No. 4, 4 exists with a short imperforate section at base below the 8th perforation. *Price for plate 4, 4 £30.*

B. PVAD (clear) gum (29.3.88)

XWL21	18p. Deep olive-grey	1·00

This printing was on paper supplied to Questa by Henry & Leigh Slater Ltd. The PVAD gum did not have the green dye additive.

Plate Numbers (Blocks of Six)
Double Pane Plates
Plate Nos. in left margin

Pl. Nos.	(P)
5, 5	6·00
6, 6	6·00

Withdrawn: 4 September 1989

18p. Bright green (1991–93)

1991 (3 December). One 4 mm short phosphor band (right of centre). Fluorescent coated paper. PVA gum

A. Perf. 15×14
XWL22 (=SG W48)

XWL22	18p. Bright green	75	75
	a. Phosphor omitted	£200	

Plate Numbers (Blocks of Six)
Double Pane Plates
Plate Nos. in left margin

Pl. Nos.	(P)
1, 1	4·50
2, 2	4·50
3, 3	7·00
4, 4	7·50
5, 5	6·00
6, 6	6·00
7, 7	90·00
8, 8	£250

B. Perf. 14 (12.1.93)
XWL23 (=SG W48b)

XWL23	18p. Bright green	7·50	7·50

Plate Numbers (Blocks of Six)
Double Pane Plates Plate Not, in left margin

Pl. Nos.	(P)
5, 5	45·00
6, 6	45·00

Regional Machin Issues Lithography Wales XC

1992 (25 February). Perf. 15 × 14. One 4 mm band (right of centre). Fluorescent coated paper. PVA gum

From £6 Wales booklet pane No. XDW1

| XWL24 | 18p. Bright green | 2·00 | 2·00 |

No. XWL22 shows the phosphor band short at top or bottom of the stamp whereas on No. XWL24 the band was continuous.

1992 (25 February). Perf. 15 × 14. One narrow band at right. Fluorescent coated paper. PVA gum

From £6 Wales booklet se-tenant pane No. UHP9
XWL25 (=SG W49)

| XWL25 | 18p. Bright green | 2·00 | 2·00 |

1993 (10 August). Perf. 15 × 14. One side band (yellow fluor) at left. Non-fluorescent coated paper. PVA gum

From £6 (£5.64) "The Story of Beatrix Potter" booklet pane XD1
XWL26 (=SG W49Eb)

| XWL26 | 18p. Bright green | 2·00 | 2·00 |

Withdrawn: No. XWL22, 6 December 1994. No. XWL23 was not available from the Bureau.

19p. Bright orange-red (1988)

1988 (8 November). Perf. 15 × 14. Phosphorised (advanced coated) paper

A. PVAD (clear) Gum
XWL27 (=SG W50)

| XWL27 | 19p. Bright orange-red | 1·00 | 80 |

Plate Numbers (Blocks of Six)
Double Pane Plates
Plate Nos. in left margin

Pl. Nos.	(P)
1, 1	6·00
2, 2	6·00
3, 3	20·00
4, 4	20·00

B. PVA gum (white back) (20.6.89)

| XWL28 | 19p. Bright orange-red | 1·00 |

The note below Scotland No. XSL.28 also applies here.

Plate Numbers (Blocks of Six)
Double Pane Plates
Plate Nos. in left margin

Pl. Nos.	(P)
3, 3	6·00
4, 4	6·00

Withdrawn: No. XWL27, 19 June 1990; No. XWL28, 27 November 1990.

19p. Bistre (1993)

1993 (7 December). Perf 15 × 14(E). One 4 mm short band (yellow fluor) (right of centre). Non-fluorescent coated paper. PVA gum

XWL29 (=SG W70)

| XWL29 | 19p. Bistre | 80 | 70 |

Plate Numbers (Blocks of Six)
Double Pane Plates Plate Nos. in left margin

Pl. Nos.	(P)
1, 1	4·75
2, 2	4·75
3, 3	5·50
4, 4	5·50
5, 5	45·00
6, 6	55·00

1995 (25 April). Perf. 15 × 14(E). One side band (yellow fluor) at right. Non-fluorescent coated paper. PVA gum

From £6 "National Trust" booklet se-tenant pane XD2
XWL30 (=SG W71)

| XWL30 | 19p. Bistre | 3·75 | 4·00 |

1995 (2 November). Perf 15 × 14(E). One 4 mm short band (blue fluor) right of centre. Non-fluorescent coated paper. PVA gum

| XWL31 | 19p. Bistre | 1·50 | 1·25 |

This was sold by the Philatelic Bureau from 9 November 1995.

Plate Numbers (Blocks of Six)
Double Pane Plates
Plate Nos. in left margin

Pl. Nos.	(P)
7, 7	9·00
8, 8	9·00

Withdrawn: No. XWL29, 29 March 1996; No. XWL31, 22 July 1997

19½p. Olive-grey (1982)

1982 (24 February). Perf. 14. Phosphorised (fluorescent coated) paper. PVAD gum

XWL32 (=SG W51)

| XWL32 | 19½p. Olive-grey | 1·75 | 2·00 |

Plate Numbers (Blocks of Six)
Double Pane Plates
Plate Nos. in right margin

Pl. Nos.	Row 1	Row 20
1	11·00	11·00
2	17·00	17·00

Withdrawn: 29 April 1984

20p. Brownish black (1989)

1989 (28 November). Perf. 15 × 14. Phosphorised (advanced coated) paper. PVAD (clear) gum

XWL33 (=SG W52)

| XWL33 | 20p. Brownish black | 90 | 90 |

Plate Numbers (Blocks of Six)
Double Pane Plate
Plate Nos. in left margin

Pl. Nos	(P)
1, 1	5·50
2, 2	5·50
3, 3	6·50
4, 4	24.00
5, 5	8·00
6, 6	8·00

Withdrawn: 14 September 1991

20p. Bright green (1996)

1996 (23 July). Perf. 15 × 14(E). One 4.5mm centre band (blue fluor). Non-fluorescent coated paper. PVA gum

XWL34 (=SG W72)

| XWL34 | 20p. Bright green | 1·75 | 2·00 |

No. XWL34 was pre-released and used on 9 July 1996 in Pembrokeshire.

Plate Numbers (Blocks of Six)
Double Pane Plates
Plate Nos. in left margin

Pl. Nos.	(P)
1, 1	11·00
2, 2	11·00
3, 3	35·00
4, 4	40·00

Withdrawn: 1 December 1997

20½p. Ultramarine (1983)

1983 (27 April). Perf. 14. Phosphorised (fluorescent coated) paper. PVAD gum

XWL36 (=SG W53)

| XWL36 | 20½p. Ultramarine | 3·75 | 3·75 |

Plate Numbers (Blocks of Six)
Double Pane Plates
Plate Nos. in left margin

Pl. No	(I)	Pl. No.	(P)
1	23·00	2	23·00

Withdrawn: 28 June 1985

22p. Blue (1981)

1981 (8 April). Perf. 14. Phosphorised (fluorescent coated) paper. PVA gum

XWL37 (=SG W54)

| XWL37 | 22p. Blue | 1·10 | 1·10 |

Plate Numbers (Blocks of Six)
Double Pane Plates
Plate Nos. in right margin

Pl. Nos.	Row 1	Row 20
1, 1	6·50	6·50
2, 2	6·50	6·50

Withdrawn: 29 April 1984

22p. Yellow-green (1984)

1984 (23 October). Perf. 15 × 14. Phosphorised (advanced coated) paper. PVAD gum

XWL38 (=SG W55)

| XWL38 | 22p. Yellow-green | 95 | 1·10 |

Plate Numbers (Blocks of Six)
Double Pane Plates
Plate Nos. in left margin

Pl. Nos.	(I)	Pl. Nos.	(P)
1, 1	5·75	2, 2	5·75
1, 3	5·75	2, 4	5·75

Withdrawn: 27 November 1990

22p. Bright orange-red (1990)

1990 (4 December). Perf. 15 × 14. Phosphorised (advanced coated) paper

A. PVAD gum
XWL39 (=SG W56)

| XWL39 | 22p. Bright orange-red | 1·00 | 1·10 |

Plate Numbers (Blocks of Six)
Double Pane Plates
Plate Nos. in left margin

Pl. Nos.	(P)
1, 1	6·00
2, 2	6·00
3, 3	6·50
4, 4	10·00

B. PVA gum (white back) (14.5.91)

| XWL40 | 22p. Bright orange-red | 1·00 |

Plate Numbers (Blocks of Six)
Double Pane Plates
Plate Nos. in left margin

Pl. Nos.	(P)
5, 5	6·00
6, 6	6·00

Withdrawn: 13 September 1992

23p. Bright green (1988)

1988 (8 November). Perf. 15 × 14. Phosphorised (advanced coated) paper. PVAD (clear) gum

XWL41 (=SG W57)

| XWL41 | 23p. Bright green | 1·00 | 1·10 |

Plate Numbers (Blocks of Six)
Double Pane Plates Plate Nos. in left margin

Pl. Nos.	(P)
1, 1	6·00
2, 2	6·00

Withdrawn: 27 November 1990

24p. Indian red (1989)

1989 (28 November). Perf. 15 × 14. Phosphorised (advanced coated) paper. PVAD (clear) gum

XWL42 (=SG W58)

| XWL42 | 24p. Indian red | 1·25 | 1·25 |

Plate Numbers (Blocks of Six)
Double Pane Plates
Plate Nos in left margin

Pl. Nos.	(P)
1, 1	8·00
2, 2	8·00

Withdrawn: 14 September 1991

Regional Machin Issues Lithography *Wales* XC

24p. Chestnut (1991-93)

1991 (3 December). Phosphorised (advanced coated) paper. PVA gum

A. Perf 15 × 14
XWL43 (=SG W59)

XWL43	24p. Chestnut	75	75

Plate Numbers (Blocks of Six)
Double Pane Plates
Plate Nos. in left margin

Pl. Nos.	(P)
1, 1	4·50
2, 2	4·50
3, 3	8·00
4, 4	£275
5, 5	5·00
6, 6	5·00
7, 7	5·00
8, 8	5·00

Plate Nos. 3, 3 and 4, 4 exist with a short imperforate section at base below the 10th perforation *Price for plate* 3, 3 £10 *and* 4, 4 £275.

B. Perf. 14 (14.9.92)
XWL44 (=SG W59b)

XWL44	24p. Chestnut	7·50	7·50

Plate Numbers (Blocks of Six)
Double Pane Plates
Plate Nos. in left margin

Pl. Nos.	(P)
3, 3	45·00
4, 4	45·00

1992 (25 February). Perf. 15 × 14. Two 9.5 mm bands. Fluorescent coated paper. PVA gum

From £6 Wales booklet *se-tenant* pane No. UHP9
XWL45 (=SG W60)

XWL45	24p. Chestnut	1·25	1·50
	a. Phosphor omitted	£375	

1993 (10 August). Perf. 15 × 14. Two bands (yellow fluor). Non-fluorescent coated paper. PVA gum

From £6 (£5.64) "The Story of Beatrix Potter" booklet pane XD1
XWL46

XWL46	24p. Chestnut	2·50	2·50

Withdrawn: No. XWL43, 6 December 1994. No. XWL44 was not available from the Bureau.

25p. Red (1993-96)

1993 (7 December). Perf. 15 × 14(E). Two 8 mm bands (yellow fluor). Non-fluorescent coated paper. PVA gum

XWL47 (=SG W73)

XWL47	25p. Red	1·25	1·00
	a. 11·5 mm, between bands (25.4.95, ex. XD2)	1·50	1·50

The distance between the phosphor bands on No. XWL47 is 12·5 mm.

Plate Numbers (Blocks of Six)
Double Pane Plates
Plate Nos. in left margin

Pl. Nos.	(P)
1, 1	7·50
2, 2	7·50
3, 3	£250
4, 4	£175
5, 5	8·00
6, 6	8·00
7, 7	9·00
8, 8	8·50

1995 (31 July). Perf. 15 × 14(E). Two bands (blue fluor). Non-fluorescent coated paper. PVA gum

A. Two 8 mm Phosphor bands

XWL48	25p. Red	1·50	1·50

Plate Numbers (Blocks of Six)
Doable Pane Plates
Plate Nos. in left margin

Pl. Nos.	(P)
9, 9	9·00
10, 10	9·00
11, 11	70·00
12, 12	70·00

B. Two 9 mm Phosphor bands.
From £6.48 European Football Championship booklet pane UHP18 (14.5.96)

XWL49	25p. Red	1·50	1·50

Withdrawn: No. XWL47, 29 March 1996; No. XWL48, 22 July 1997

26p. Rosine (1982–87)

1982 (24 February). Perf. 14. Phosphorised (fluorescent coated) paper. Type I. PVAD gum

XWL50 (=SG W61)

XWL50	26p. Rosine	1·10	1·10

Plate Numbers (Blocks of Six)
Double Pane Plates
Plate Nos. in right margin

Pl. No.	Row 1	Row 20
1	7·00	7·00
2	9·00	9·00

1987 (27 January). Perf. 15 × 14. Phosphorised (advanced coated) paper. Type II. PVAD gum

XWL51 (=SG W61a)

XWL51	26p. Rosine	5·75	6·00

Plate Numbers (Blocks of Six)
Double Pane Plates
Plate Nos. in left margin

Pl. No.	(I)	Pl. No.	(P)
1	35·00	2	35·00

Withdrawn: No. XWL50, 26 January 1988; No. XWL51, 4 September 1989

XC Regional Machin Issues Lithography *Wales*

26p. Drab (1990)

1990 (4 December). Perf. 15 × 14. Phosphorised (advanced coated) paper. PVAD gum

XWL52 (=SG W62)

XWL52	26p. Drab	1·75	1·75

Plate Numbers (Blocks of Six)
Double Pane Plates
Plate Nos. in left margin

Pl. Nos.	(P)
1, 1	10·50
2, 2	10·50

Withdrawn: 13 September 1992

26p. Red-brown (1996)

1996 (23 July). Perf. I5 × 14(E). Two bands (blue fluor). Non-fluorescent coated paper. PVA gum

XWL53 (=SG W74)

XWL53	26p. Red-brown	2·00	2·25

No. XWL53 was pre-released and used on 9 July 1996 in Pembrokeshire.

Plate Numbers (Blocks of Six)
Double Pane Plates
Plate Nos. in left margin

Pl. Nos.	(P)
1, 1	12·00
2, 2	12·00
3, 3	38·00
4, 4	50·00

Withdrawn: 1 December 1997

28p. Deep violet-blue (1983–87)

1983 (27 April). Perf. 14. Phosphorised (fluorescent coated) paper. Type I. PVAD gum

XWL54 (=SG W63)

XWL54	28p. Deep violet-blue	1·50	1·50

Plate Numbers (Blocks of Six)
Double Pane Plates
Plate Nos. in left margin

Pl. No.	(I)	Pl. No.	(P)
1	9·00	2	9·00

1987 (27 January). Perf. 15 × 14. Phosphorised (advanced coated) paper. Type II. PVAD gum

XWL55 (=SG W63a)

XWL55	28p. Deep violet-blue	1·50	1·50

Plate Numbers (Blocks of Six)
Double Pane Plates
Plate Nos. in left margin

Pl. No.	(I)	P1. No.	(P)
1	9·00	2	9·00

Withdrawn: No. XWL54, 26 January 1988

28p. Deep bluish grey (1991)

1991 (3 December). Perf. 15 × 14. Phosphorised (advanced coated) paper. PVA gum

XWL56 (=SG W64)

XWL56	28p. Deep bluish grey	1·50	1·50

Plate Numbers (Blocks of Six)
Double Pane Plates
Plate Nos. in left margin

Pl. Nos.	(P)
1, 1	9·00
2, 2	9·00

Withdrawn: 6 December 1994

30p. Deep olive-grey (1993)

1993 (7 December). Perf. 15 × 14(E). Two bands (yellow fluor). Non-fluorescent coated paper. PVA gum

XWL57 (=SG W75)

XWL57	30p. Deep olive-grey	1.25	1.25

Plate Numbers (Blocks of Six)
Double Pane Plates
Plate Nos. in left margin

Pl. Nos.	(P)
1, 1	7·50
2, 2	7·50
3, 3	8·00
4, 4	8·00

Withdrawn: 22 July 1997

31p. Bright purple (1984-87)

1984 (23 October). Perf. 15 × 14. Phosphorised paper. PVAD gum

A. Fluorescent Coated Paper
XWL58 (=SG W65)

XWL58	31p. Bright purple	1·75	1·75

Plate Numbers (Blocks of Six)
Double Pane Plates
Plate Nos. in left margin

Pl. No.	(I)	Pl. No.	(P)
3	10·00	4	13·00
5	10·00	6	10·00

B. Advanced Coated Paper (27.1.87)

XWL59	31p. Bright purple	2·00	2·00

Plate Numbers (Blocks of Six)
Double Pane Plates
Plate Nos. in left margin

Pl. No.	(1)	Pl. No.	(P)
5	12·00	6	12·00

Withdrawn: No. XWL58, 26 January 1988; No. XWL59, 4 September 1989

Regional Machin Issues Lithography Wales XC

32p. Greenish blue (1988)

1988 (8 November). Perf. 15×14. Phosphorised (advanced coated) paper. PVAD (clear) gum

XWL60 (=SG W66)

| XWL60 | 32p. Greenish blue | 1·75 | 1·75 |

Plate Numbers (Blocks of Six)
Double Pane Plates
Plate Nos. in left margin

Pl. Nos.	(P)
1, 1	10·00
2, 2	10·00

Withdrawn: 27 November 1990

34p. Deep bluish grey (1989)

1989 (28 November). Perf. 15×14. Phosphorised (advanced coated) paper. PVAD (clear) gum

XWL61 (=SG W67)

| XWL61 | 34p. Deep bluish grey | 1·75 | 1·75 |

Plate Numbers (Blocks of Six)
Double Pane Plates
Plate Nos. in left margin

Pl. Nos.	(P)
1, 1	10·00
2, 2	10·00

Withdrawn: 14 September 1991

37p. Rosine (1990)

1990 (4 December). Perf. 15×14. Phosphorised (advanced coated) paper. PVAD gum

XWL62 (=SG W68)

| XWL62 | 37p. Rosine | 2·25 | 2·25 |

Plate Numbers (Blocks of Six)
Double Pane Plates
Plate Nos. in left margin

Pl. Nos.	(P)
1, 1	14·00
2, 2	14·00

Withdrawn: 13 September 1992

37p. Bright mauve (1996)

1996 (23 July). Perf. 15×14(E). Two bands (blue fluor). Non-fluorescent coated paper. PVA gum

XWL63 (=SG W76)

| XWL63 | 37p. Bright mauve | 2·75 | 3·00 |

Plate Numbers (Blocks of Six)
Double Pane Plates
Plate Nos. in left margin

Pl. Nos.	(P)
1, 1	17·00
2, 2	17·00

Withdrawn: 1 December 1997

39p. Bright mauve (1991)

1991 (3 December). Perf. 15×14. Phosphorised (advanced coated) paper. PVA gum

XWL64 (=SG W69)

| XWL64 | 39p. Bright mauve | 2·25 | 2·25 |

Plate Numbers (Blocks of Six)
Double Pane Plates
Plate Nos. in left margin

Pl. Nos.	(P)
1, 1	14·00
2, 2	14·00

Withdrawn: 6 December 1994

41p. Grey-brown (1993-96)

1993 (7 December). Perf. 15×14(E). Two bands (yellow fluor). Non-fluorescent coated paper. PVA gum

XWL65 (=SG W77)

| XWL65 | 41p. Grey-brown | 2·00 | 2·00 |

Plate Numbers (Blocks of Six)
Double Pane Plates
Plate Nos. in left margin

Pl. Nos.	(P)
1, 1	12·00
2, 2	12·00

1996 (30 April). Perf. 15×14(E). Two 8 mm bands (blue fluor). Non-fluorescent coated paper. PVA gum

| XWL66 | 41p. Grey-brown | 2·50 | 2·50 |

Plate Numbers (Blocks of Six)
Double Pane Plates
Plate Nos. in left margin

Pl. Nos.	(P)
1, 1	15·00
2, 2	15·00

Withdrawn: No. XWL65. 30 August 1996; No. XWL66, 22 July 1997

63p. Light emerald (1996)

1996 (23 July). Perf. 15×14(E). Two bands (blue fluor). Non-fluorescent coated paper. PVA gum

XWL67 (=SG W78)

| XWL67 | 63p. Light emerald | 4·50 | 4·75 |

Plate Numbers (Blocks of Six)
Double Pane Plates
Plate Nos. in left margin

Pl. Nos	(P)
1, 1	27·00
2, 2	27·00

Withdrawn: 1 December 1997

Presentation Packs

Presentation Packs containing stamps of Northern Ireland, Scotland and Wales are listed after those of Northern Ireland.

XWPP6 No. 129c (28.10.81)	7p., 9p., 10½p., 11½p., 12p., 13½p., 14p., 15p., 18p., 22p.	9·00

Comprises Nos. XW34, 38, 41, 44/5, 47, XWL1, 9, 19 and 37.

XWPP7 No. 3 (3.8.83)	10p., 12 p., 16p., 20½p., 26p., 28p.	20·00

Comprises Nos. XW40, XWL4, 13, 36, 50 and 54.

XWPP8 No. 7 (23.10.84)	10p., 13p., 16p., 17p., 22p., 26p., 28p., 31p.	17·00

Comprises Nos. XW40, XWL6, 14, 15, 38, 50, 54 and 58.

XWPP9 No. 11 (3.3.87)	12p., 13p., 17p., 18p., 22p., 26p., 28p., 31p.	20·00

Comprises Nos. XWL2, 6, 16, 20, 38, 51, 55 and 59.

Withdrawn: No. XWPP6, August 1983; No. XWPP7, October 1984; No. XWPP8, sold out October 1986: No. XWPP9, 31 December 1991

First Day Covers

XWLFD1 (8.4.81)	11½p., 14p., 18p., 22p.	2·50
XWL,FD2 (24.2.82)	12½p., 15½p., 19½p., 26p.	3·50
XWLFD3 (27.4.83)	16p., 20½p., 28p.	3·50
XWLFD4 (23.10.84)	13p., 17p., 22p., 31p.	4·25
XWLFD5 (7.1.86)	12p.	2·00
XWLFD6 (6.1.87)	18p.	2·00
XWLFD7 (8.11.88)	14p., 19p., 23p., 32p.	4·50
XWLFD8 (28.11.89)	15p., 20p., 24p., 34p.	5·00
XWLFD9 (4.12.90)	17p., 22p., 26p., 37p.	5·00
XWLFD10 (3.12.91)	18p., 24p., 28p., 39p.	5·50
XWLFD11 (25.2.92)	Cymru-Wales se-tenant pane	10·00
XWLFD12 (7.12.93)	19p., 25p., 30p., 41p.	6·00
XWLFD13 (23.7.96)	20p., 26p., 37p., 63p.	7·00

SECTION XD
Regional Machin Prestige Booklet Panes
1989-95. Printed in Lithography by Questa 1997. Printed in Gravure by Harrison

For regional pictorial panes from Prestige Booklets, see Section XE.

The illustrations are reduced, the actual size being 162×95 mm.

A. NORTHERN IRELAND

From £6.04 "Northern Ireland" booklet No. DX16

Third pane comprising 2×19p. band at left, 4×25p., 30p. and 41p. with two phosphor bands (yellow fluor) on non-fluorescent coated paper. There are no bands on the centre label. Printed in lithography.

XDNI1

XDNI1	(containing Nos. XNL28×2, XNL44×4, XNL55, XNL64) (26.7.94)	8·00
	b. One broad band	

No. XDNI1b comprised all stamps with a 10·5mm band misplaced to right. One example reported which may have ben split into single stamps.

Fourth pane comprising 19p. band at left, 25p., 30p. and 41p. with two phosphor bands (yellow fluor) on non-fluorescent coated paper. Printed in lithography.

XDNI2

XDNI2	(containing Nos. XNL28, XNL44, XNL55, XNL64) (26 7.94)	6·00
	a. Phosphor omitted	

Plate Numbers: The printer's sheet contained 3 columns each with four panes without plate numbers.

B. SCOTLAND

From £5 "The Scots Connection" booklet No. DX10

First pane comprising 9×19p, phosphorised (advanced coated) paper. Printed in lithography.

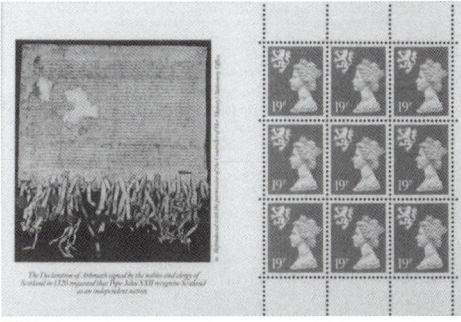

XDS1

XDS1 (containing No. XSL27×9) (21.3.89)		5·50

Pane Nos. XDS1 and XDS4 were printed on HLS paper, see Section XC under General Notes.

Second pane comprising 6×14p. with 4 mm band to right of centre. Printed in lithography.

XDS2

XDS2 (containing No. XSL11×6) (21.3.89)		3·50

Pane No., XDS2/3 were printed on CPL paper with PVA gum. The phosphor bands were continuous on this pane.

Third pane comprising 5×14p. band at left: 2×19p. and 23p. two bands. Printed in lithography.

153

XD Regional Machin prestige Booklet Panes

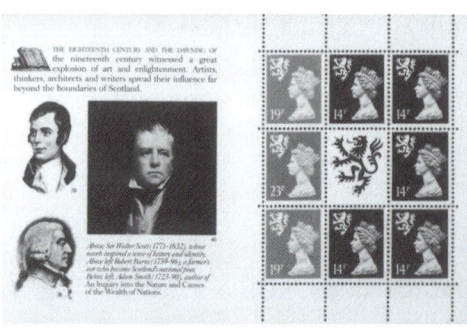

XDS3

XDS3 (containing Nos. XSL12×5, XSL29×2, XSL46) (21.3.89)   18·00
  a. Error. Imperforate pane   £1750
  b. First vertical row imperf. on 3 sides (top, left and bottom)
  c. Partly imperf. (top row imperf, centre row perf. at left, right and bottom, bottom row perf.)
  d. Partly imperf. (top two rows imperf., bottom row perf. at left, right and bottom sides)

The error No. XDS3b was perforated as a normal pane of six. The phosphor bands stopped short in the horizontal margins.

Fourth pane comprising 6×19p. phosphorised (advanced coated) paper. Printed in lithography.

XDS4

XDS4 (containing No. XSL27×6) (21.3.89)   4·50

Plate Numbers: The printer's sheet contained 3 columns each with four panes but none of the plate numbers appeared on the sheets.

C. WALES

From £6 "Wales" booklet No. DX13

Second pane comprising 6×18p. with 4 mm band to right of centre. Printed in lithography.

XDW1

XDW1 (containing No. XWL24×6) (25.2.92)   3·25
  a. Phosphor omitted

Three examples of No. XDW1a were reported.

Fourth pane comprising 6×24p. phosphorised (advanced coated) paper. Printed in lithography.

XDW2

XDW2 (containing No. XWL43×6) (25.2.92)   5·00

Plate Numbers: The printer's sheet contained 3 columns each with four panes. Plate numbers were not used.

D. Panes containing stamps from three regions

(a) Printed in Lithography by Questa

From £6 (£5.64) "The Story of Beatrix Potter" booklet, No. DX15

Second pane comprising 3×18p. band at left and 3×24p. two phosphor bands (yellow fluor) on non-fluorescent coated paper. Printed in lithography.

XD1

XD1 (containing Nos. XNL25, XNL43, XSL26, XSL50, XWL26, XWL46) (10.8.93) 14·00

Plate Numbers: The printer's sheet contained 3 columns each with four panes.

From £6 "National Trust" booklet, No. DX17

Third pane comprising 3 × 19p. band at right and 3 × 25p. two bands (yellow fluor). Printed in lithography.

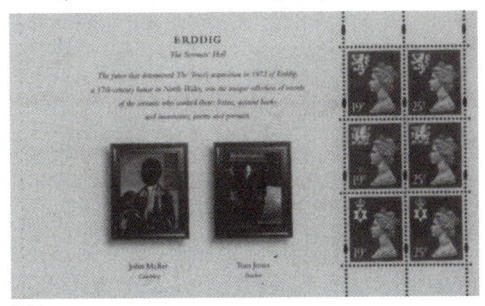

XD2

XD2 (containing Nos. XNL29, XNL44a, XSL31, XSL51a, XWL30, XWL47a) (25.4.95) 10·00
    b. Partly imperf. (top row imperf., second row part perf. at sides, perf. at bottom, bottom row perf.)

Plate Numbers: The printer's sheet contained 3 columns each with four panes. There were no plate numbers on the sheets and markings were trimmed off.

(b) Printed in Gravure by Harrison/De La Rue

From £6.15 "BBC 75" Booklet, No DX19

First pane comprising 3 × 26p. (chestnut) and 3 × 37p. (bright mauve) with two phosphor bands (blue fluor) on non-fluorescent coated paper. Printed in gravure from computer engraved cylinders.

XBP1

XBP1 (containing Nos. XN49, XN52, XS64, XS67, XW51, XW53) (23.9.97) 6·00

Cylinder Numbers: The cylinder numbers were trimmed off the finished sheets. The stamps were printed from computer engraved cylinders on the Jumelle press. The sheets were made up of three columns of four panes.

(b) Printed in Gravure by Walsall

From £7·50 "Special by Design" booklet, No. DX24

The first and fourth panes are Nos. UIPP6/7 (Section UI), the third pane is No. UEP39 (Section UD).

Second pane comprising 9x(1st) (bright orange-red) with two phosphor bands (blue fluor) on non-fluorscent coated paper. Printed in gravure from computer engraved cylinders.

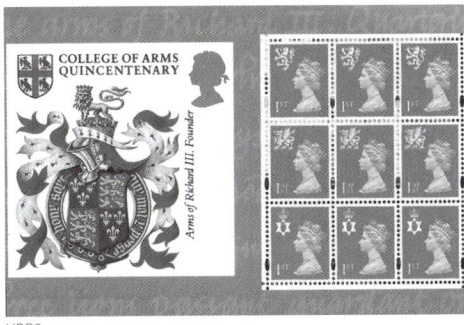

XBP2

XBP2 (containing Nos. XN56×3, XS69×3, XW56×3) (15.2.00) 13·00

Cylinder Numbers
The cylinder numbers were trimmed off the finished sheets. The stamps were printed on the Chesnut press but sheet make-up is not known.

SECTION XE
Regional Pictorial Issues
Printed in Gravure.

General Notes
On 12 May 1999 the new Welsh Assembly held its first session; on the same day the Scottish Parliament reconvened as a separate entity after having been in abeyance for nearly 300 years after it merged with the English Parliament under the Act of Union in 1707. These historic events were marked on 8 June 1999, by the release of pictorial stamps showing the Queen's head in silver as used on special stamps.

Northern Ireland pictorial regionals were issued on 6 March 2001, wholly printed in litho (see section XF) and subsequently in gravure (from 27 March 2001).

Pictorial regionals for England appeared on 23 April 2001.

A. ENGLAND
Printer. The sheet stamps were printed by De La Rue in gravure. The sheets contained 200 stamps arranged in 20 horizontal rows of ten stamps each. There was no gutter margin.

Paper and gum. The stamps were printed on non-fluorescent coated paper with PVA (bluish) gum.

Perforation. The sheets were perforated 15 × 14 with one elliptical perf. hole opposite each vertical edge as in the case of Machins. Also the machine was the rotary APS perforator attached to the Jumelle press.

Phosphor bands. Values above (2nd) class had two gradated edge phosphor bands with blue fluor. The (2nd) class had one centre band again with blue fluor.

The English regional stamps are printed by other firms when issued in booklets. These stamps usually exhibit differences from their sheet counterparts

XEN1 Three Lions

XEN2 Crowned Lion with Shield of St. George

XEN3 Oak Tree

XEN4 Tudor Rose

(Des. Sedley Place, from sculptures by David Dathan and photographed by Chris Ridley.)

Printed in Gravure by De La Rue

■ (2nd) slate-green and silver without borders

2001 (23 April). Perf. 15 × 14(E). One 4.5 mm centre band blue fluor) Non-fluorescent coated paper. PVA gum (bluish)

XEN1 (=SG EN1)

XEN1	(2nd) slate-green and silver	1·00	1·00

No. XEN1 was in initially sold at 19p.

Cylinder Numbers (Blocks of Six)
Perforation Type RE
Double pane cylinders. Jumelle Press

	No dot	Dot
(2nd) 1 (silver)–2 (slate-green)–50 (phosphor)	7·00	7·00

Warrant Numbers and Dates of Printing (Blocks of Eight)

Spec. No.	Value	SSO No.	Date	Margin at left or right
XEN1	(2nd)	851	09/02/01	9·00
			12/02/01	9·00
			15/02/01	10·00
			16/02/01	10·00
			22/02/01	10·00
			23/02/01	10·00
			08/03/01	10·00
		852	07/03/01	10·00
			21/03/01	10·00
			22/03/01	10·00
			23/03/01	10·00

Printed by Questa in Gravure

2002 (24 September). Perf. 15 × 14(E). One centre phosphor band (blue fluor). Non-fluorescent coated paper. PVA gum

From £6.83 "Across the Universe" booklet *se-tenant* pane No. XEP1

XEN1A	(2nd) slate-green and silver	1·50	1·50

■ (1st) without borders

2001 (23 April). Perf. 15 × 14(E). Two bands (blue fluor) Non-fluorescent coated paper. PVA gum (bluish)

XEN2 (=SG EN2)

XEN2	(1st) lake-brown and silver	1·00	1·00

No. XEN2 was initially sold at 27p.

Cylinder Numbers (Blocks of Six)
Perforation Type RE
Double pane cylinders. Jumelle Press

	No dot	Dot
(1st) 1 (silver)–1 (lake brown)– 49 (phosphor)	7·00	7·00
1–3–49 (phosphor)	7·00	7·00
1–4–49 (phosphor)	7·00	7·00

Warrant Numbers and Dates of Printing (Blocks of Eight)

XEN2	(1st)	849	05/02/01	5·00	1-1

	06/12/01	5·00	
	07/02/01	7·00	
	08/02/01	7·00	
	01/03/01	7·00	
	05/03/01	7·00	
	06/03/01	7·00	
850	27/03/01	7·00	1-3
	28/03/01	7·00	1-3, 1-4
	29/03/01	7·00	1-4
	30/03101	7·00	
	25/04/01	7·00	

Printed by Questa in Gravure

2002 (24 September). Perf. 15×14(E). Non-fluorescent coated paper. PVA gum Two phosphor bands

From £6·83 "Across the Universe" booklet *se-tenant* pane No. XEP1

XEN2A (1st) lake-brown and silver	1·75	1·75

Nos. XEN1A and XEN2A have PVA gum without the bluish dye used by De La Rue. Used examples can be distinguished by checking the screen with 10 times lens. The Questa printing has a coarse screen on both values compared to De La Rue.

(E) without borders

2001 (23 April). Perf. 15×14(E). Two bands (blue fluor) Non-fluorescent coated paper. PVA gum (bluish)

XEN3 (=SG EN3)

XEN3 (E) olive-green and silver	1·75	1·75

No. XEN3, was initially sold at 36p., representing the basic European airmail rate which was increased to 37p. from 2 July, 2001.

Cylinder Numbers (Blocks of Six)
Perforation Type RE
Double pane cylinders. Jumelle Press

		No dot	Dot
(E)	1 (silver)–1 (olive-green -49 (phosphor)	12·00	12·00

Warrant Numbers and Dates of Printing (Blocks of Eight)

XEN3	(E)	853	01/02/01	9·00
			02/02/01	6·00

65p. without borders

2001 (23 April). Perf. 15×14(E). Two bands (blue fluor)Non-fluorescent coated paper. PVA gum (bluish)

XEN4 (=SG EN4)

XEN4 65p. deep reddish lilac and silver	1·00	1·10

Cylinder Numbers (Blocks of Six)
Perforation Type RE
Double pane cylinders. Jumelle Press

		No dot	Dot
65p.	1(silver) I (deep reddish lilac)–49 (phosphor)		20·00
		20·00	

Warrant Numbers and Dates of Printing (Blocks of Eight)

XEN4	65p.	854	30/01/01	9·75
			12/03/01	12·50

68p without borders

2002 (4 July). Perf 15 × 14(E). Two bands (blue fluor). Non-fluorescent coated paper. PVA gum (bluish)

XEN5 (=SG EN5)

XEN5	68p. deep reddish lilac and silver (4.7.02)	3.00
		3.00

Cylinder Numbers (Blocks of Six)
Perforation Type RE
Double pane cylinders. Jumelle Press

		No dot	Dot
68p.	1(silver) I (deep reddish lilac)–49 (phosphor)		20·00
		20·00	

Warrant Number and Dates of Printing (Blocks of Eight)

Spec. No.	Value	SSO No.	Date	Margin at left or right
XEN5	68p.	943	01/05/02	25·00
			02/05/02	25·00

(2nd) with borders

Printed by De La Rue at West Byfleet in Gravure

2003 (14 October). Perf. 15×14(E). One 4.5 mm centre band (blue fluor) Non-fluorescent coated paper. PVA gum

XEN6 (=SG EN6)

XEN6	(2nd) slate-green and silver	75	60

XEN6 was initially sold at 20p.

Cylinder Numbers (Blocks of Eight)
Peforation Type RE
Double pane cylinders

		No dot	Dot
(2nd)	D1 (slate-green)-D1 (silver)-D1 (phosphor)		4·50
		4·50	

Dates of Printing
XEN6 23/6/03

(1st) with borders

2003 (14 October). Perf. 15×14(E). Two bands (blue fluor) Non-fluorescent coated paper. PVA gum

XEN7 (=SG EN7)

XEN7	(1st) lake-brown and silver	80	75

XEN7 was initially sold at 28p.

Cylinder Numbers (Blocks of six)
Peforation Type RE
Double pane cylinders

		No dot	Dot
(1st)	D1(lake-brown)-D1(silver)-D1(phosphor)		5·00
		5·00	

Dates of Printing
XEN7 28/06/03

XE Regional Pictorial Issues Gravure *England*

(E) with borders

2003 (14 October). Perf. 15 × 14(E). Two bands (blue fluor) Non-fluorescent coated paper. PVA gum

XEN8 (=SG EN8)

XEN8	(E) olive-green and silver	2·00	2·00

XEN8 was initially sold at 38p., representing the basic European airmail rate which was increased to 40p. From 1 April 2004.

Cylinder Numbers (Blocks of six)
Peforation Type RE
Double pane cylinders

		No dot	Dot
(E)	D1(olive-green)-D1(silver)-		14·00
	D1(phosphor)	14·00	

Dates of Printing
XEN8 28/06/03

40p with borders

Printed by De La Rue in Gravure

2004 (11 May). Perf. 15 × 14(E). Two phosphor bands (blue fluor) Non-fluorescent coated paper. PVA gum (bluish)

XEN9 = (SG EN9)

XEN9	40p. olive green and silver	1·50	1·50

Cylinder Numbers (Blocks of Six)
Perforation type RE
Double pane cylinders
Two phosphor bands

	No dot	Dot
40p. D1(olive-green)-D1(silver)D1(phosphor) 12·50		12·50

The bands are 13 mm wide between stamps but only 6.5 mm at the vertical sheet margin. They react In both short and long wave ultraviolet light.

Dates of Printing

Spec. No.	Dates
XEN9	08/03/04, 22/03/04

Printed by Walsall in Gravure

2005 (24 February). Perf. 15 × 14 and one (E). Non-fluorescent coated paper. Two phosphor bands (bright blue fluor). PVA gum

From £7.43 "The Bronte Sisters" Prestige pane No. XEP2

XEN9A	**XEN3** 40p. olive-green and silver	60

No. XEN9 (11.5.04) from sheets printed by De La Rue has bluish PVA gum. There is a 4 to 5 screening dot shading border between the "0" of value and the frame of the booklet stamps but this shading is only 3 screening dots on De La Rue stamp No. XEN9.

42p with borders

Printed by Walsall in Gravure

2005 (5 April). Perf. 15 × 14(E). Two phosphor bands (bright blue fluor). Non-fluorescent coated paper. PVA gum

XEN10	42p. olive-green and silver	1·25	1·25

Cylinder Numbers (Blocks of Six)
Perforation Type RE
Single pane cylinders

	No dot
42p. W1 (olive-green)- W1 (silver)-W1 (phosphor)	9·00

The bands are bright especially on the white borders. They react to both short and long wave ultraviolet light.

Dates of Printing
Spec. No.   Date
XEN10   20/12/04, 21/12/04

Withdrawn: 25 July 2006

Printed by De La Rue in Gravure

2005 (10 May). Perf. 15 × 14(E). Two phosphor bands (dull blue fluor). Non-fluorescent coated paper. PVA gum

XEN10A (=SG EN10)

XEN10A	42p. olive-green and silver	1·25	1·25

Cylinder Numbers (Blocks of Six)
Perforation Type RE
Double pane cylinders

		No dot	Dot
42p.	D1 (olive-green)-D1(silver)-		
	D1(phosphor)	5·25	5·25

The bands are 13 mm wide between stamps but only 6.5 mm at the vertical sheet margin. They react dull to both short and long wave ultraviolet light.

Dates of Printing
Spec. No.   Date
XEN10A   19/04/05, 20/04/05

44p with borders

Printed by De La Rue in Gravure

2006 (28 March). Perf. 15 × 14(E). Two phosphor bands (blue fluor). Non-fluorescent coated paper. PVA gum

XEN11 (=SG EN11)

XEN11	44p. olive-green and silver	1·50	1·50

Cylinder Numbers (Blocks of Six)
Perforation Type RE
Double pane cylinders

		No dot	Dot
44p.	D1 (olive-green)-D1(silver)-		5·75
	D1(phosphor)	5·75	

The bands are 13 mm wide between stamps but only 6.5 mm at the vertical sheet margin. They react to both short and long wave ultraviolet light.

Dates of Printing
Spec. No.   Dates
XEN11   07/02/06, 08/02/06

48p with borders

Printed by De La Rue in Gravure

2007 (27 March). Perf. 15 × 14(E). Two bands (blue fluor). Non-fluorescent coated paper. PVA gum

XEN12 (=SG EN12)

XEN12	48p. olive-green and silver	1·25	1·25

Cylinder Numbers (Blocks of Six)
Perforation Type RE
Double pane cylinders

Two phosphor bands		No dot	Dot
48p.	D1(olive-green)-D2(silver)-		8·00
	(D1phosphor)	8·00	

The bands are 13 mm wide between stamps but only 6.5 mm at the vertical sheet margin.

Dates of Printing
Spec. No.   Date
XEN12   11/01/07, 14/01/07

Regional Pictorial Issues Gravure *England* **XE**

■ 50p. with borders

Printed by De La Rue in Gravure

2008 (1 April). Perf. 15 × 14(E). Two bands (blue fluor). Non-fluorescent coated paper. PVA gum

XEN13 (=SG EN13)

XEN13	50p. olive-green and silver	90	85

Cylinder Numbers (Blocks of Six)
Perforation Type RE
Double pane cylinders comprising No dot and Dot panes.

Two phosphor bands		No dot	Dot
50p.	D1(olive-green)-D2(silver)-D1(phosphor)	5·75	5·75

The bands are 13 mm wide between stamps but only 6·5 mm at the vertical sheet margin.

Dates of Printing

Spec. No.	Date
XEN13	14/01/08

■ 56p. With borders

2009 (31 March). Perf 15×14(E). Two bands (blue fluor). Non-fluorescent coated paper. PVA gum

XEN14 (=SG EN13a)

XEN14	56p. Olive-green and silver	1·25	1·25

Cylinder Numbers (Blocks of Six)
Perforation Type RE
Double pane cylinders comprising No dot and Dot panes.

Two phosphor bands		Dot left	Dot right
56p.	D1(olive-green)-D1(silver)-D1(phosphor)	6·50	6·50

The bands are 13 mm wide between stamps but only 6·5 mm at the vertical sheet margin.

Dates of Printing

Spec. No.	Date	Left pane	Right pane
XEN14	28/01/09	8·50	8·50

2004 (16 March). As last but horizontal screen

From £7.44 "letters by night" booklet *se-tenant* pane No. XSP3
XEN15A

XEN15A	68p. deep reddish lilac and silver	1·10

The screen on No. XEN10A is one of diamond dots in a vertical pattern the opposite of No. XEN4.

■ 68p with borders

2003 (14 October). Perf. 15 × 14(E). Two bands (blue fluor) Non-fluorescent coated paper. PVA gum

XEN15 (=SG EN14)

XEN15	68p. deep reddish lilac and silver	2·50	2·50

Cylinder Numbers (Blocks of Six)
Perforation Type RE
Double pane cylinders. Jumelle Press

		No dot	Dot
68p.	1(silver) I (deep reddish lilac)–49 (phosphor)	7·25	7·25

Cylinder Numbers (Blocks of Six)
Peforation Type RE
Double pane cylinders

		No dot	Dot
68p.	D1(deep reddish lilac)-D1(silver)	16·00	16·00

Warrant Number and Dates of Printing (Blocks of Eight)

Spec. No.	Value	SSO No.	Date	Margin at left or right
XEN15	68p.	943	01/05/02	10·00
			02/05/02	10·00

■ 72p. with borders

Printed by De La Rue in Gravure

2006 (28 March). Perf 15 × 14(E). Two bands (blue fluor). Non-fluorescent coated paper. PVA gum

XEN16 (=SG EN15)

XEN16	72p. deep reddish lilac and silver	2·50	2·50

Cylinder Numbers (Blocks of Six)
Perforation Type RE
Double pane cylinders

		No dot	Dot
72p.	D1 (deep reddish lilac)-D1 (silver)-D1 (phosphor)	9·00	9·00

The bands are 13 mm ,wide between stamps but only 6·5 mm at the vertical sheet margin. They react to both short and long wave ultraviolet light.

Dates of Printing

Spec. No.	Dates			
XEN16	03/02/06,	09/02/06,	10/02/06,	07/07/06,
	10/07/06			

Printing dates confirmed by Jim Bond of Exeter.

■ 78p. with borders

2007 (27 March). Perf. 15 × 14(E). Two bands (blue fluor). Non-fluorescent coated paper. PVA gum.

XEN17 (=SG EN16)

XEN17	78p. deep reddish lilac and silver	2·50	2·50

Cylinder Numbers (Blocks of Six)
Perforation Type RE
Double pane cylinders

		No dot	Dot
78p.	D1(deep reddish lilac)-D1(silver)-D1(phosphor)	16·00	16·00

The bands are 13 mm wide between stamps but only 6·5 mm at the vertical sheet margin.

Dates of Printing

Spec. No.	Dates
XEN17	12/01/07, 13/01/07,

81p. Deep reddish lilac and silver

Printed by De La Rue in gravure

2008 (1 April). Perf. 15 × 14(E). Two bands (blue fluor). Non-fluorescent coated paper. PVA gum

XEN18 (=SG EN17)

XEN18	81p. deep reddish lilac and silver	2·00	2·00

Cylinder Numbers (Blocks of Six)
Perforation Type RE
Double pane cylinders comprising No dot and Dot panes.

Two phosphor bands	No dot	Dot
81p. D1 (deep reddish lilac)-D1(silver)-D1(phosphor)	9·00	9·00

The bands are 13 mm wide between stamps but only 6·5 mm at the vertical sheet margin.

Dates of Printing

Spec. No.	Date
XEN18	11/01/08, 14/01/08, 17/01/08,

90p. with borders

Printed by De La Rue in gravure

2009 (31 March). Perf. 15 × 14(E). Two bands (blue fluor). Non-fluorescent coated paper. PVA gum

XEN19 (=SG EN17a)

XEN19	90p. deep reddish lilac and silver	2·00	2·00

Cylinder Numbers (Blocks of Six)
Double pane. Perforation Type RE

Two phosphor bands	No dot	Dot
90p. D1 (deep reddish lilac)-D1(silver)-D1(phosphor)	11·00	11·00

The bands are 13 mm wide between stamps but only 6·5 mm at the vertical sheet margin.

Dates of Printing

Spec. No.	Date	Left pane	Right pane
XEN19	28/01/09	14·00	14·00

Miniature sheets containing England stamps

2007 (23 April). Celebrating England

(sold at £2·24, £2·28 from 7.4.07)

XEMS1

(Miniature sheet des. Peter Crowther, Clare Melinsky and Silk Pearce. Gravure De La Rue)
Issued on St. George's Day, the miniature sheet was the second of a series of four with the title "The Four Countries" and similar in format to the Scottish miniature sheet (30.11.2006). The St. George's flag stamp bottom right was by Peter Crowther and the sheet background is a photograph of Blackmore Vale, Dorset by David Noton. Sheet size 123 × 70 mm and printed on non-fluorescent coated paper with two gradated phosphor (blue fluor) bands all with PVA gum. Perf 15 × 14 (E) or 15½ × 14 (78p.).

XEMS1 (=SG MSEN19)

XEMS1, (1st) St. George's flag, 78p. St. George, 78p. Houses of Parliament, London, (Sold at £2·24)	9·00	9·00
First Day Cover (XEMS1)	†	9·00
Presentation Pack (XEMS1)	10·00	
PHQ Cards (Set of 5)	4·00	15·00

Cylinder Numbers: No cylinder numbers appeared on the printer's sheet margins. The following colours were used; magenta, greenish yellow, new blue, black, grey, brown and silver. Before separation the printer's sheet contained 15 miniature sheets arranged (3 × 5).

Generic Sheet: A sheet inscribed ""GLORIOUS ENGLAND" containing 20 (4 × 5) (1st) class self-adhesive Crowned Lion seated stamps was issued on 23 April 2007 and sold at £7·35. It was printed in Lithography by Cartor. The four vertical rows were separated by labels showing ten English scenes repeated twice with the England flag. This sheet was also available with personal photographs on labels at £14·95.

2007 (17 May). New Wembley Stadium

(sold at £2·38, £2·46 from 7.4.08)

XEMS2

Des. Roundel. Gravure De La Rue

The large Crowned Lion design is as Type **W1477** but with "WORLD CUP 2002" inscription omitted. The Wembley Arch designed by Lord Foster forms the background. Sheet size 113 × 103 mm and printed on non-fluorescent coated paper with one centre phosphor band (2nd) or two gradated bands (others) (blue fluor) with PVA gum. Perf. 14½ × 14 (1st) or 15 × 14 (E) (2nd, 78p.).

XEMS2 (=SG **MS**2740)

XEMS2 (1st) as Type W1477; (2nd) No. XEN2×2; 78p. No. XEN17×2 And one central stamp size label.	7·00	
	7·00	
First Day Cover	†	7·50

Withdrawn: 16 May 2008

Generic Sheet. A sheet inscribed "Memories of Wembley Stadium" containing 20 (4 × 5) (1st) class Crowned Lion seated stamps was issued on 17 May 2007 and sold at £7·35. It was printed in Lithography by Cartor. The four vertical rows were separated by labels showing scenes dated from 1923–2007.

Miniature sheets containing stamps of all four regions

2006 (9 November) Lest We Forget (1st issue)

(sold at £3·20, £3·22 from 2.4.07)

WMS 1886 Miniature Sheet (illustration reduced to half size)

(Des. Hat-trick Design. Gravure by De La Rue)

Perf. 14½ (1st) or 15 × 14(E) PVA gum
Sheet size 124 × 71 mm containing (1st) Poppies on barbed wire and stamp designs as Nos. XEN11, XW70, XS71 and XN70.

Two gradated phosphor bands

WMS1886 (=SG MS2685)

WMS1886	9·00	9·00
First Day Cover		9·50
Presentation Pack	12·00	

The Northern Ireland 72p. was printed in Gravure for the first time.
Generic Sheet: A sheet inscribed "WE WILL REMEMBER THEM" containing 20 (4 × 5) (1st) class poppy stamps from the miniature sheet No. WMS1886 was issued on 9 November 2006 and sold at £6·95, later increased to £7·35. It was printed in Lithography by Cartor. The four vertical rows were separated by labels showing sculptures on the Cenotaph and other memorials detailed on the other labels.

First Day Covers

XEFD1	(23.4.01) (2nd), (1st), (E), 65p.	3·25
XEFD2	(4.7.02) 68p	3·50
XEFD3	(14.10.03) (2nd), (1st), (E), 68p	3·50
XEFD4	(11.5.04) 40p.	2·75
XEFD5	(5.4.05) 42p.	1·40
XEFD6	(27.3.07) 48p., 78p	4·00
XEFD7	(1.4.08) 50p., 81p.	4·00
XEFD8	(31.3.09) 56p., 90p.	4·75

Presentation Packs (England)

XEPP1	No. 54 (23.4.01) (2nd), (1st), (E), 65p	7·50
XEPP2	No. 63 (14.10.03) (2nd), (1st), (E), 68p	6·00

Presentation Packs (Four Regions) (stamps with borders)

XECP1 No. 59 (4.7.02) Four values 45

The issued pack contained one each 68p. from England, Northern Ireland and Wales. Nos. XEN5. XN61, XS75 and XW62.

XECP2 No. 68 (11.5.04) Four values .... 6·25

The issued pack contained one each 40p. from England, Northern Ireland, Scotland and Wales. Nos. XEN9. XN68, XS79 and XW66.

XECP6 No. 79 (1.4.08) Eight values .... 11·50

The issued pack contained one each 50p. and 81p. from England, Northern Ireland, Scotland and Wales.

XECP7 No. 81 (29.9.08) Sixteen values .... 16·00

The issued pack contained one each (2nd), (1st), 50p. and 81p. from England, Northern Ireland, Scotland and Wales.

XECP3 No.69 (5.4.05) Four values .... 8·00

The issued pack contained one each 42p. from England, Northern Ireland, Scotland and Wales.

XECP4 No. 73 (28.3.06) Eight values .... 10·00

The issued pack contained one each 44p. and 72p. from England, Northern Ireland, Scotland and Wales.

XECP5 No.76 (27.3.07) Eight values .... 12·50

The issued pack contained one each 48p. and 78p. from England, Northern Ireland, Scotland and Wales.

XECP8 No. 85 (31.3.09) Eight values .... 13·50

The issued pack containe one each 56p. And 90p. From England, Northern Ireland, Scotland and Wales.

PHQ Cards (stamps with borders)

XEC2	(Nos. XEN6/8, 10) (Set of 4)	1·70	4·00

PHQ Cards (stamps without borders)

XEC 1	(Nos. XEN1/4) (Set of 4)	8·00	14·00

B NORTHERN IRELAND

Printer. Sheet stamps were printed in Gravure from computer engraved cylinders. The sheets were single pane of 200 in 20 horizontal rows of ten.
Paper and gum. Non-fluorescent coated paper with PVA gum was used.
Perforation. The sheets were perforated 15 × 14 with an ellipse as in Section XB.
Phosphor bands. The 2nd class no value indicated stamps have a single centre band. Other values have two bands with gradated edges so band widths are indistinct. Blue fluor was used and the bands stop short on the sheet margins.

SHEET MARKINGS

Cylinder Numbers. Opposite R. 18/1 and 19/1 (64p.) and R. 18/1 (others).
Warrant Numbers and Dates of Printing. In the left margin opposite rows 8/10 between the inscribed country name and "W" shaped sheet mark. As usual the sheet number follows the date in dot matrix style. For similar inscription see Section XB.
Imprint. Opposite R. 20/1 in two lines reading up.
Marginal Arrows. Opposite horizontal rows 10/11 and vertical rows 5/6 at both sides. "W" shaped.
Total Sheet Values. This applies to the 64p. value where the inscription is opposite horizontal rows 4/6 and 14/16 at both sides of the sheet, reading up at left and down at right, The country name is opposite rows 7 and 17, both sides and reading up at left and down at right.
Postage rates. See Section UI for postage rates charged for 2nd, 1st and European airmail with dates of validity.

■ (2nd) with borders

Printed by De La Rue in Gravure

2007 (20 September). Perf. 15 × 14(E). One 4 mm centre band (blue fluor) Non-fluorescent coated paper. PVA gum.

XN73 (=SG NI102)

XN73	(2nd) bright magenta, greenish yellow, new blue and black	60 70

The Gravure printing shows the "2nd" very close to the base compared to the litho printing.

Cylinder Numbers (Blocks of Six)
Perforation Type RE
Double pane cylinders

One 4 mm centre band		No dot	Dot
(2nd)	D1(bright magenta)-D1(greenish yellow)-D1(new blue)- D1(phosphor)		4·25 4·25

Dates	of	Printing

Spec. No.	Dates	
XN73	26/07/07	

■ (1st) with borders

Two phosphor bands (blue fluor)
XN74 (=SG NI103)

XN74	(1st) greenish yellow, new blue and black	80	75

The phosphor bands are gradated to the vertical sides and differ from the sharp straight edge of the litho printing.

Cylinder Numbers (Blocks of Six)
Perforation Type RE
Double pane cylinders

Two phosphor bands			
(1st)	D1(greenish yellow)-D1(new blue)- D1(black)-D1(phosphor)		4·75 4·75

Dates of Printing

Spec. No.	Dates
XN74	21/06/07

■ 48p with borders

Printed by De La Rue in Gravure

2007 (27 March). Perf. 15 × 14(E). Two bands (blue fluor). Non-fluorescent coated paper. PVA gum

XN75 (=SG NI106)

XN75	48p. olive-grey and black	1·20	1·20

Cylinder Numbers Blocks of Six)
Perforation Type RE
Double pane cylinders

Two phosphor bands		No dot	Dot
48p.	D1(olive-grey)-D(black)-D(phosphor)	8·00	8·00

The bands are 13 mm wide between stamps but only 6.5 mm at the vertical sheet margin.

Printing dates

Spec. No.	Dates
XN75	17/01/07

■ 50p with borders

Printed by De La Rue in Gravure

2008 (1 April). Perf. 15 × 14(E). Two bands (blue fluor). Non-fluorescent coated paper. PVA gum

XN76 (=SG NI105)

XN76	50p. olive-grey and black	1·20	1·20

Cylinder Numbers (Blocks of Six)
Perforation Type RE
Double pane cylinders comprising 50p. Wales at left and 50p. Northern Ireland at right. The 81p similar comprising Northern Ireland at right and 81p. Scotland at left. All No Dot.

Two phosphor bands		No dot
50p.	D1(olive-orey)-D1(black)-D1(phosphor)	8·00

The bands are 13 mm wide between stamps but only 6.5 mm at the vertical sheet margin.

Dates of Printing

Spec. No.	Dates
XN76	21/01/08

■ 56p with borders

Printed by De La Rue in Gravure

2009 (31March). Perf. 15 × 14(E). Two bands (blue fluor). Non-fluorescent coated paper. PVA gum

XN77 (=SG NI105a)

XN77	56p. olive-grey and black	1·25	1·25

Cylinder Numbers (Blocks of Six)
Perforation Type RE
Double pane cylinders comprising 56p. Wales at left and 56p. Northern Ireland at right.

Two phosphor bands		Dot Right
56p.	D1(olive-orey)-D1(black)-D1(phosphor)	6·50

The bands are 13 mm wide between stamps but only 6.5 mm at the vertical sheet margin.

Dates of Printing

Spec. No.	Dates
XN77	03/02/09

78p. with borders

2007 (27 March). Perf 15 × 14(E). Two bands (blue fluor). Non-fluorescent coated paper. PVA gum

XN70A (=SG NI10h)

XN78	78p. bright magenta, greenish yellow and black	2·00 2·00

Cylinder Numbers Blocks of Six)
Perforation Type RE
Double pane cylinders

Two phosphor bands		No dot	Dot
78p.	D (bright magenta)-D (greenish yellow)-D (black)- D (phosphor)	13·00	13·00

The bands are 13 mm wide between stamps but only 6.5 mm at the vertical sheet margin.

Printing dates

Spec. No.	Dates
XN78	18/01/07

81p. with borders

XN79 (=SG NI107)

XN79	81p. bright magenta, greenish yellow and black	2·00 2·00

Cylinder Numbers (Blocks of Six)
Perforation Type RE
Double pane cylinders comprising 81p Scotland at left and 81p. Northern Ireland at right.

Two phosphor bands		No Dot
81p.	D1 (bright magenta)-D1(greenish yellow)-D1(black)-D1 (phosphor)	13·00

The bands are 13 mm wide between stamps but only 6.5 mm at the vertical sheet margin.

Dates of Printing

Spec. No.	Dates
XN79	21/01/08

90p. with borders

2009 (31 March). Perf. 15 × 14(E). Two bands (blue fluor), Non-fluorescent coated paper. PVA gum.

XN80 (=SG NI107a)

XN80	90p. bright magenta, greenish yellow and black	2·00 2·00

Cylinder Numbers (Blocks of Six)
Perforation Type RE
Double pane cylinders comprising 90p Scotland at left and 90p. Northern Ireland at right.

Two phosphor bands		Dot Right
90p.	D1 (bright magenta)-D1(greenish yellow)-D1(black)-D1 (phosphor)	11·00

The bands are 13 mm wide between stamps but only 6.5 mm at the vertical sheet margin.

Dates of Printing

Spec. No.	Dates
XN80	04/02/09

First Day Covers

XNFD15 (28.3.06) 44p., 72p	†	2·75
XNFDI6 (27.3.07) 48p., 78p	†	4·00
XNFDI7 (1.4.08) 50p., 81p.	†	4·00
XNFD18 (31.3.09) 56p., 90p.	†	4·75

C. SCOTLAND

Printer. Sheet stamps were printed in Gravure from computer engraved cylinders. The sheets were single pane of 200 in 20 horizontal rows of ten.
Paper and gum. Non-fluorescent coated paper with PVA gum was used.
Perforation. The sheets were perforated 15 × 14 with an ellipse as in Section XB.
Phosphor bands. The 2nd class no value indicated stamps have a single centre band. Other values have two bands with gradated edges so band widths are indistinct. Blue fluor was used and the bands stop short on the sheet margins.

SHEET MARKINGS

Cylinder Numbers. Opposite R. 18/1 and 19/1 (64p.) and R. 18/1 (others).
Warrant Numbers and Dates of Printing. In the left margin opposite rows 8/10 between the inscribed country name and "W" shaped sheet mark. As usual the sheet number follows the date in dot matrix style. For similar inscription see Section XB.
Imprint. Opposite R. 20/1 in two lines reading up.
Marginal Arrows. Opposite horizontal rows 10/11 and vertical rows 5/6 at both sides. "W" shaped.
Total Sheet Values. This applies to the 64p. value where the inscription is opposite horizontal rows 4/6 and 14/16 at both sides of the sheet, reading up at left and down at right, The country name is opposite rows 7 and 17, both sides and reading up at left and down at right.
Postage rates. See Section UI for postage rates charged for 2nd, 1st and European airmail with dates of validity.

XS70 Scottish Flag    XS71 Scottish Lion

XS72 Thistle    XS73 Tartan

(Des. Anton Morris (2nd). Frank Pottinger (1st). Tim Chalk (E), Tartan (64p.) supplied by Kinloch Anderson. Adapted by Tayburn of Edinburgh)

XE Regional Pictorial Issues Gravure *Scotland*

(2nd) without borders

Printed in Gravure by Walsall

1999 (8 June). Perf. 15 × 14(E). One 4·5 mm Centre band (blue fluor). Non-fluorescent coated paper. PVA gum

XS70 (= SG S94)

XS70	(2nd) new blue, blue and silver		75	75

Cylinder Numbers (Blocks of Six)
Perforation Type RE
Single pane cylinders. Chesnut press
One 4·5 mm centre phosphor band

(2nd)	W1 (new blue)-W1 (blue)-W1 (silver)-W1 (phosphor)		5·00

Warrant Numbers and Dates of Printing (Blocks of Eight)

Spec. No.	Value	SSO No.	Date	Margin at left
XS70	(2nd)	549	26/04/99	—
			27/04/99	7·00
			28/04/99	7·00
			07/05/99	—
			08/05/99	—
		560	03/06/99	8·50
			18/06/99	8·50

Printed by De La Rue in Gravure

2002 (5 June). As Walsall but with PVA (bluish) gum. One 4.5 mm centre band (blue fluor)

XS70B	**XS70** (2nd) new blue, blue and silver		75	75

Cylinder Numbers (Blocks of Six)
Perforation Type RE
Double pane cylinders

		No dot	Dot
One 4.5 mm centre phosphor band			
(2nd)	1 (new blue)-1 (blue)-1 (silver)-50 (phosphor)	5·00	5·00

Warrant Number and Date of Printing (Blocks of Eight)

Spec. No.	Value	SSO No.	Date	Margin at left or right
XS70B	(2nd)	935	13/05/02	7·00

(1st) without borders

1999 (8 June) Perf 15 × 14(E). Two bands (blue fluor). Non-fluorescent coated paper. PVA gum

Two phosphor bands (blue fluor)
XS71 (= SG S95)

XS71	(1st) greenish yellow, deep rose-red, rose-red and silver	1·00	1·00

Cylinder Numbers (Blocks of Six)
Perforation Type RE
Double pane cylinders

		No dot	Dot
Two phosphor bands			
(1st)	1 (deep rose-red)-1 (rose-red)-1 (greenish yellow) (silver)-49 (phosphor)	7·00	7·00

Warrant Numbers and Dates of Printing (Blocks of Eight)

Spec. No.	Value	SSO No.	Date	Margin at left
XS71	(1st)		09/04/99	9·00
			10/04/99	—
			11/04/99	10·00
			12/04/99	9·00
			13/04/99	9·00
			30/04/99	—
			01/05/99	9·00
		561	27/05/99	—
			28/05/99	—

2002 (5 June). As Walsall but with PVA (bluish) gum. Two phosphor bands (blue fluor)

XS71B	**XS71** (1st) greenish yellow, deep rose-red, rose-red and silver		1·00	1·00

Warrant Number and Date of Printing (Blocks of Eight)

Spec. No.	Value	SSO No.	Date	Margin at left or right
XS71B	(1st)	936	10/05/02	9·00

Printed by Questa in Gravure

2002 (24 September). Perf 15 × 14(E) Two phosphor bands (blue fluor). Non-fluorescent coated paper. PVA gum

£6.83 "Across the Universe" booklet *se-tenant* pane No. XEP11

XS71C	**XS71** (1st) greenish yellow, deep rose-red, rose-red and silver		1·00

No. XS71C can be distinguished by a gap in the red screening around the lion's tongue and tail. In addition the screening is diamond shaped and horizontal as opposed to the Walsall screen which is vertical on No. XS71.

(E) without borders

2001 (6 March). Perf. 15 × 14(E). Two bands (blue fluor). Non-fluorescent coated paper. PVA gum

XS72 (= SG S96)

XS72	(E) bright lilac, deep lilac and silver		2·00	2·00

No. XS72 was initially sold at 30p., representing the basic European airmail rate.

Cylinder Numbers (Blocks of Six)
Perforation Type RE
Single pane cylinders. Chesnut press
Two phosphor bands

(E)	W1 (bright lilac)-W1 (deep lilac)-W1 (silver)-W1 (phosphor)		14·00

Warrant Numbers and Dates of Printing (Blocks of Eight)

XS72	(E)	551	16/04/99	10·00
			17/04/99	10·00
			30/04/99	—
		558	12/10/99	10·00

64p. without borders

2000 (25 April). Perf. 15 × 14(E). Two bands (blue fluor). Non-fluorescent coated paper. PVA gum

XS73 (= SG S97)

XS73	64p. greenish yellow, bright magenta, new blue, grey-black and silver		9·00	9·00

Cylinder Numbers (Blocks of Six)
Perforation Type RE
Single pane cylinders. Chesnut press
Two phosphor bands

64p.	W1 (greenish yellow)-W1 (bright magenta)-W1 (new blue)-W1 (grey- black)-W1 (phosphor)-W1 (silver)		50·00

Regional Pictorial Issues Gravure   *Scotland*   **XE**

Warrant Numbers and Dates of Printing (Blocks of Eight)

XS73	64p.	552	15/04/99	70·00
			16/04/99	70·00

65p. without borders

2000 (25 April). Perf 15 × 14(E). Two bands (blue fluor). Non-fluorescent coated paper. PVA gum

XS75 (=SG S99)

XS74	65p. greenish yellow, bright magenta. new blue, grey-black and silver	3·00	3·25

Cylinder Numbers (Blocks of Six)
Perforation Type RE
Single pane cylinder. Chesnut oress

		Dot
Two phosphor bands		
65p.	W1 (greenish yellow)-W1 (bright magenta)-W1 (new blue)-W1 (grey-black)-W1 (phosphor)–W1 (silver)	20·00

Warrant Number and Date of Printing (Blocks of Eight)

Spec. No.	Value	SSO No.	Date	Margin at left or right
XS74	65p.	606	11/02/00	26·00

68p. without borders

2002 (4 July). Perf 15 × 14(E). Two bands (blue fluor). Non-fluorescent coated paper. PVA gum

XS75 (=SG S99)

XS75	68p. greenish yellow, bright magenta. new blue, grey-black and silver (4.7.02)	3·25	3·25

Cylinder Numbers (Blocks of Six)
Perforation Type RE
Double pane cylinders

		No dot	Dot
Two phosphor bands			
68p.	1 (black)-1 (new blue)-1 (bright magenta)-1 (greenish yellow)-1 (silver)-49 (phosphor)	21·00	21·00

Warrant Number and Date of Printing (Blocks of Eight)

Spec. No.	Value	SSO No.	Date	Margin at left or right
XS75	68p.	944	07/05/02	28·00

(2nd) with borders

Printed by De La Rue at West Byfleet in Gravure

2003 (14 October). Perf. 15 × 14(E). One 4.5 mm centre band (blue fluor). Non-fluorescent coated paper. PVA gum.

XS76 =(SG S 109)

XS76	(2nd) new blue, blue and silver	60	60

Cylinder Numbers (Blocks of Eight)
Perforation Type RE
Double pane cylinders

		No dot	Dot
One 4.5 mm centre phosphor band			
(2nd)	D1 (new blue)-D1 (blue)-D1(silver)-D 1(phosphor)	5·50	5·50

Dates. of Printing

Spec. No.	Dates
XS76	26/06/03

2004 (16 March). As last but honeycomb screen

From £7.44 "Letters by Night" booklet *se-tenant* pane No. XSP3

XS76A	(2nd) new blue, blue and silver	60

The screen on No. XS76 consists of vertical rows of dashes and dots when seen with a 10x lens.

(1st) with borders

2003 (14 October). Perf. 15 × 14(E). One 4.5 mm centre band (blue fluor). Non-fluorescent coated paper. PVA gum.

Two phosphor bands (blue fluor)

XS77 (=SG S110)

XS77	(1st) rose-red, greenish yellow, deep rose-red and silver	85	85

Dates. of Printing

Spec. No.	Dates
XS77	26/06/03

(E) with borders

2003 (14 October). Perf. 15 × 14(E). One 4.5 mm centre band (blue fluor). Non-fluorescent coated paper. PVA gum.

XS78 (=SG S111)

XS78	(E) bright lilac, deep lilac and silver	2·50	2·50

Cylinder Numbers (Blocks of Eight)
Perforation Type RE
Double pane cylinders

Two phosphor bands			
(E)	D1(brightl lilac)-D1(deep lilac)-D1(silver)-D1 (Phosphor)	21·00	21·00

On the two band values the bands are 13 mm wide between stamps but only 6.5 mm at the vertical sheet margin. They react to both short and long wave ultraviolet light.

Dates. of Printing

Spec. No.	Dates
XS78	27/06/03

40p with borders

Printed by De La Rue in Gravure

2004 (11 May). Type XS72 with white borders. Perf. 15 × 14 (E). Two phosphor bands (blue fluor). Non-florescent coated paper. PVA gum

XS79 (=SG S112)

XS79	40p. bright lilac deep lilac and silver	1·75	1·75

Cylinder Numbers (Blocks of Eight)
Perforation Type RE
Double pane cylinders

		No dot	Dot
Two phosphor bands			
40p.	D1, (bright lilac)-D1(deep lilac)-D1(silver)-D1. phosphor)		16·00
		16·00	

The bands are 13 mm wide between stamps but only 6.5 mm at the vertical sheet margin. They react to both short and long wave ultraviolet light

XE Regional Pictorial Issues Gravure *Scotland*

Dates of Printing

Spec. No	Dates
XS79	05/03/04

42p with borders

Printed by Walsall in Gravure

2005 (5 April). Perf. 15 × 14(E). Non-fluorescent coated paper. Two phosphor bands (blue fluor). PVA gum

XS80	42p. bright lilac, deep lilac and silver	1·75	1.75

Cylinder Numbers (Blocks of Six)
Perforation Type RE
Single pane cylinders

Two phosphor bands		No dot
42p.	W1 (bright lilac)-W1 (deep lilac)-W1 (silver)-W 1 (phosphor)	12·00

The bands are bright especially on the white borders. They react to both short and long wave ultraviolet light.

Dates of Printing

Spec. No.	Dates
XS80	16/12/14, 18/12/04, 19/12/04

Withdrawn: 25 July 2006

Printed by De La Rue in Gravure

2005 (10 May). Perf. 15 × 14(E). Non-fluorescent coated paper. Two phosphor bands (dull blue fluor). PVA gum

XS80A (=SG S113)

XS80A	42p. bright lilac, deep lilac and silver	1·75	1·75

Cylinder Numbers (Blocks of Six)
Perforation Type RE
Double pane cylinders

Two phosphor bands		No dot	Dot
42p.	D1 (bright lilac)-D1 (deep lilac)-D1 (silver)-Dl (phosphor)	12·00	12·00

The bands are 13 mm wide between stamps but only 6.5 mm at the vertical sheet margin. They react dull to both short and long wave ultraviolet light.

Dates of Printing

Spec. No	Date
XS80A	19/04/05

44p with borders

Printed by De La Rue in Gravure

2006 (28 March). Perf, 15 × 14 (E). Non-fluorescent coated paper. Two phosphor bands (blue fluor). PVA gum

XS81 (=SG S114)

XS81	44p. bright lilac, deep lilac and silver	1·50	1·50

Cylinder Numbers (Blocks of Six)
Perforation Type RE
Double pane cylinders

Two phosphor bands		No dot	Dot
44p.	D1 (bright lilac)-D1 (deep lilac)-D1 (silver)-D1(phosphor)	10·50	10·50

The bands are 13 mm wide between stamps but only 6.5 mm at the vertical sheet margin. They react. to both short and long wave ultraviolet light.

Dates of Printing

Spec. No.	Dates
XS81	06/02/06

48p with borders

Printed by De La Rue in Gravure

2007 (27 March). Perf. 15 × 14(E). Two bands (blue fluor). Non-fluorescent coated paper. PVA gum

XS82 (=SG S115)

XS82	48p. bright lilac, deep lilac and silver	90	90

Cylinder Numbers (Blocks of Six)
Perforation Type RE
Double pane cylinders

Two phosphor bands		No dot	Dot
48p.	D1(bright lilac)-D2(deep lilac)-D1(silver)-D1(phosphor)	6·25	6·25

The bands are 13mm wide between stamps but only 6·5 mm at the vertical sheet margin.

Dates of Printing

Spec. No.	Dates
XS82	14/01/07

50p with borders

Printed by De La Rue, in Gravure

2008 (1 April). Perf. 15 × 14(E). Two bands (blue fluor). Non-fluorescent coated paper. PVA gum

XS83 (=SG S116)

XS83	50p. bright lilac, deep lilac and silver	80	75

Cylinder Numbers (blocks of Six)
Perforation Type RE
Double pane cylinders comprising 50p. Scotland at left and 81p. Wales at right. The 81p. similar comprising Scotland at left and Northern Ireland at right. All No Dot.

Two phosphor bands		No dot
50p.	D1(bright lilac)D1(deep lilac)D1(silver(-D1(phosphor)	5·75

The bands are 13mm wide between stamps but only 6.5 mm at the vertical sheet margin.

Dates of Printing

Spec. No.	Dates
XS83	15/01 /08

56p. with borders

Printed by De La Rue, in Gravure

2009 (31 March). Perf. 15 × 14(E). Two bands (blue fluor). Non-fluorescent coated paper. PVA gum

XS84 (=SG S116a)

XS84	56p. bright lilac, deep lilac and silver	1·25	1·25

Cylinder Numbers (blocks of Six)
Perforation Type RE
Double pane cylinders comprising 56p. Scotland at left and 90p. Wales at right. .

Two phosphor bands		Dot Right
56p.	D1(bright lilac)D1(deep lilac)D1(silver)-D1(phosphor)	6·50

The bands are 13mm wide between stamps but only 6.5 mm at the vertical sheet margin.

Dates of Printing

Regional Pictorial Issues Gravure *Scotland* **XE**

Spec. No.	Dates
XS84	04/02/09

68p. with borders

2003 (14 October). Perf. 15 × 14(E). One 4.5 mm centre band (blue fluor). Non-fluorescent coated paper. PVA gum.

XS85 (=SG S113)

XS85	68p. bright magenta, greenish yellow, new blue, grey-black and silver	2·00	2·00

No. XS78 was initially sold at 38p., representing the basic European airmail rate which was increased to 38p. from 8 May 2003.

Cylinder Numbers (Blocks of Eight)
Perforation Type RE
Double pane cylinders

Two phosphor bands		
68p.	D1(bright magenta)-D1(greenish yellow)-D1(new blue)-D1(grey-black)-D1(silver)-D1(phosphor)	17·00 17·00

On the two band values the bands are 13mm wide between stamps but only 6.5 mm at the vertical sheet margin. They react to both short and long wave ultraviolet light.

Dates. of Printing

Spec. No.	Dates
XS85	28/06/03, 30/06/03

Printed by De La Rue in Gravure

72p. with borders

XS86 (=SG S116)

XS86	72p. bright magenta, greenish yellow, new blue, grey-black and silver	1·75 1·75

Cylinder Numbers (Blocks of Six)
Perforation Type RE
Double pane cylinders

Two phosphor bands		No dot	Dot
72p.	D1(bright magenta)-D1 (greenish yellow)-D1 (new blue)- D1 (grey-Flack)-D1 (silver)-D1 (phosphor)	12·00	12·00

The bands are 13mm wide between stamps but only 6.5 mm at the vertical sheet margin. They react. to both short and long wave ultraviolet light.

Dates of Printing

Spec. No.	Dates
XS86	08/02/06, 09/02/06

78p with borders

XS87 (=SG S119)

XS87	78p. bright magenta, greenish yellow, new blue, grey-black and silver	1·50 1·50

Cylinder Numbers (Blocks of Six)
Perforation Type RE
Double pane cylinders

Two phosphor bands		No dot	Dot
78p.	D1 (bright magenta)-D1 (greenish yellow)-D2(new blue. D1 (grey-black) D1 (silver)-D1 (phosphor)	10·50	10·50

The bands are 13 mm wide between stamps but only 6·5 mm at the vertical sheet margin.

Dates of Printing

Spec. No.	Dates
XS87	16/01/07

81p with borders

XS88 (=SG S120)

XS88	81p. bright magenta, greenish yellow, new blue, grey-black and silver	1·40 1·30

Cylinder Numbers (blocks of Six)
Perforation Type RE
Double pane cylinders comprising 81p. Scotland at left and 81p. Northern Ireland at right. .

Two phosphor bands		No dot
81p.	D1 (bright magenta)-D1(greenish yellow)-D1(new blue)-D1(grey-black)-D1(silver)-D1(phosphor)	9·00

The bands are 13 mm wide between stamps but only 6.5 mm at the vertical sheet margin.

Dates of Printing

Spec. No.	Dates
XS88	18/01/08

90p with borders

2009 (31 March). Perf. 15 × 14(E). Two bands (blue fluor). Non-fluorescent coated paper. PVA gum

XS89 (=SG S120a)

XS89	90p. bright magenta, greenish yellow, new blue, grey-black and silver	2·00 2·00

Cylinder Numbers (blocks of Six)
Perforation Type RE
Double pane cylinders comprising 90p. Scotland at left and 56p. Northern Ireland at right

Two phosphor bands		No dot
90p.	D1 (bright magenta)-D1(greenish yellow)-D1(new blue)-D1(grey-black)-D1(silver)-D1(phosphor)	11·00

The bands are 13mm wide between stamps but only 6.5 mm at the vertical sheet margin.

Dates of Printing

Spec. No.	Dates
XS89	04/02/09

XE Regional Pictorial Issues Gravure *Scotland*

Miniature sheets containing Scotland Stamps

2004 (5 October) Scottish Parliament

(sold at £1·57)

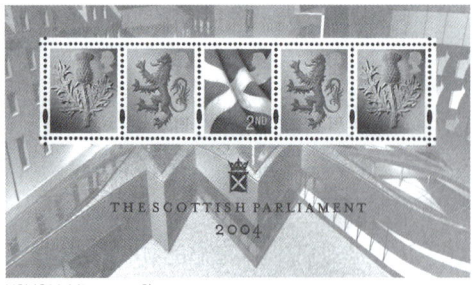

XSMS90 Miniature Sheet
(Illustration reduced to half actual size)

(Minature sheet des. Howard Brown. Gravure De La Rue)

2004 (5 October). Opening of new Scottish Parliament building, Edinburgh

Issued to mark the opening of the Scottish Parliament on 9 October by Her Majesty The Queen. The official crest of the Parliament is shown on a background of an architects' computer simulation of part of the Parliament building.

Sheet size 123 × 70 mm containing designs as Type Nos. **XS70** (2nd), **XS71** (1st) and **XS72** 40p. (original 1999 issue but with white borders) by Anton Morris (2nd), Frank Pottinger (1st) and Tim Chalk (E). Non-fluorescent coated paper one centre band (2nd) and two bands others all with blue fluor. PVA gum. Perf 15 × 14 (with one elliptical perf hole on each vertical edge.

XSMS90 (=SG **MS**S120)

Scottish Flag and National Emblems:		
(2nd) new blue, blue, silver; (1st) greenish yellow, deep rose-red. rose-red silver; 40p. bright lilac, deep lilac, silver	6·00	6·00
First Day cover (XSMS90)	†	8·00

Withdrawn: 4 October 2005

2006 (30 November) "Celebrating Scotland"

(sold at £2·08, £2·12 from 2.4.07)

XSMS91 Miniature sheet
(Illustration reduced to half actual size)

(Miniature sheet des. Silk Pearce. Gravure De La Rue)
2006 (30 November). Celebrating Scotland

Issued on St. Andrew's Day this was the first of a series of four with the title "The Four Countries". The Scottish Lion Rampant design is at top left and a new design bottom right showing the Saltire flag (Peter Crowther) above this (72p.) St. Andrew (Claire Melinsky). Edinburgh Castle at night is depicted on the other 72p. Sheet size 124 × 71mm and printed on non-fluorescent coated paper with two gradated phosphor (blue fluor) bands all with PVA gum. Perf 15 × 14(E) or 14½ × 14 (72p.).

XSMS91 (=SG **S**SI2I)

As Type XS71, (1st) Scottish Flag, 72p. St. Andrew, 72p. Edinburgh Castle	6·00	6·00
Presentation Pack (XSMS91)	8·00	
First Day Cover (XSMS91)	6·50	

250th Birth Anniversary of Robert Burns

(sold at £2·66, £2·78 from 6.4.09)

XSMS96 Miniature Sheet

(Illustration reduced to half actual size)
(Minature sheet des. Tayburn.Gravure Enschedé)

2009 (22 January). 250th Birth Anniversary of Robert Burns

The miniature sheet contains two new designs celebrating Robert Burns with a se-tenant block of Scottish regional stamps. The stamp at left shows Burns ploughing and the famous line from one of his most celebrated poems. The plough has disturbed a mouse from its nest from a copper plate engraving by James Sargent Storer. The stamp on the right depicts a famous portrait of the poet by Alexander Nasmyth. The sheet background shows the poets birthplace at Alloway, near Ayr. Sheet size 145 × 74 mm. and printed on nonfluorescent coated paper with two gradated phosphor (blue fluor) bands all with PVA gum. Perf. 14½ (1st). or se-tenant block 15 × 14 (E)

XSMS96 (=S.G. MSS137)

(2nd) as No. XS76, (1st) "A Man's, For a' that" (34 × 34 mm.); (1st) No. XS77; (1st) Portrait of Burns (34 × 34 mm.); 50p. No.XS79E; 81p.

XS81B (Sold at £2.66)	6·00	6·00
First Day Cover (XSMS96)	6·50	
Presentation Pack (XSMS96)	7·25	

Individual values from the miniature sheet will not be listed separately.

First Day Covers

XSFD8	(8.6.99) (2nd), (1st), (E), 64p.	†	6·00
XSFD9	(25.4.00) (65p.), (1st), (E), 64p.	†	3·50
XSFD10	(4.7.02) 68p.		3·50
XSFD11	(14.10.03) (2nd), (1st), (E), 68p.		3·25
XSFD12	(11.5.04) 40p.	†	2·75
XSFD13	(5.4.05) 42p.	†	1·40
XSFD14	(28.3.06) 44p., 72p.	†	2·75
XSFD15	(27.3.07) 48p., 78p	†	4·00
XSFD16	(1.4.08) 50p., 81p.	†	4·75
XSFD19	(31.3.09) 56p., 90p.		4·75

Presentation Packs

XSPP6	No. 45 (8.6.99) (2nd), (1st), (E), 64p.	2·50

XSPP12	No. 55 (12.3.02) (2nd), (1st), (E), 65p.		15·00
XSPP13	No. 64 (14.10.03) (2nd), (1st), (E), 68p.		15·00

PHQ Cards

XSC1	(Nos. XS70/73) (Set of 4)	8·00	14·00
XSC2	(Nos. XS76/8,80) (Set of 4)	1·70	4·00

D. WALES

Printer. The stamps were printed by in Gravure from computer engraved cylinders. The sheets were single pane of 200 in twenty horizontal rows of ten.
Paper and gum. Non-fluorescent coated paper with PVA gum was used.
Perforation. The sheets were perforated 15 × 14 with an ellipse as in Section XB.
Phosphor bands. The 2nd class no value indicated stamps have a single centre band. Other values have two bands with gradated edges so band widths are indistinct. Blue fluor was used and the bands stop short on the sheet margins.

SHEET MARKINGS

Cylinder Numbers. Opposite R. 18/1 and 19/1 (64p.) and R. 18/1 (others).
Warrant Numbers and Dates of Printing. In the left margin opposite rows 8/10 between the inscribed country name and "W" shaped sheet mark. As usual the sheet number follows the date in dot matrix style. For similar inscription see Section XB.
Imprint. Opposite R. 20/1 in two lines reading up.
Marginal Arrows. Opposite horizontal rows 10/11 and vertical rows 5/6 at both sides. "W" shaped.
Total Sheet Values. This applies to the 64p. value where the inscription is opposite horizontal rows 4/6 and 14/16 at both sides of the sheet, reading up at left and down at right, The country name is opposite rows 7 and 17, both sides and reading up at left and down at right.
Postage rates. See Section UI for postage rates charged for 2nd, 1st and European airmail with dates of validity.

XW56
Leek

XW57
Welsh Dragon

XW58
Daffodil

XW59
Prince of Wales Feathers

(Des. David Petersen (2nd), Tony and Gideon Petersen (1st), Ieuan Rees (E), Rhiannon Evans (64p.). Adapted by Tutssels).

(2nd) without borders

(Printed in Gravure by Walsall)

1999 (8 June). Perf. 15 × 14(E). One 4·5 mm Centre band (blue fluor) Non-fluorescent coated Paper. PVA gum.

XW56 (= SG W83)

XW56	(2nd) orange-brown, yellow-orange and black	50	60

Cylinder Numbers (Blocks of Six)
Perforation Type RE
Single pane cylinders. Chesnut press
One 4·5 mm centre phosphor band

(2nd)	W1 (orange-brown)-W1 (yellow-orange)-W1 (black)-W1 (phosphor)	4·25

Warrant Numbers and Dates of Printing (Blocks of Eight)

Spec. No.	Value	SSO No.	Date	Margin at left
XW56	(2nd)	553	29/04/99	5·00
			13/05/99	9·00
		558	14/05/99	8·00
			01/06/99	7·00

Printed by Walsall

2000 (18 September). Perf. 14. One phosphor side band at right (blue fluor) Non-fluorescent coated paper. PVA gum

From £7 "A Treasury of Trees" se-tenant booklet pane XWP1
XW56A (=SG W83a)

XW56A	(2nd) orange-brown, yellow-orange and black	4·00	4·00

Printed by De la Rue in Gravure

2003 (28 May). Perf. 15 × 14(E). One 4.5mm centre band (blue fluor) Non-fluorescent coated paper. PVA gum

XW56B (=SG W83a)

XW56B	(2nd) yellow brown- orange and black	80	75

Cylinder Numbers (Block of Six)
Perforation Type RE
Double pane cylinders

One 4.5 mm. centre phosphor band	No dot	Dot
(2nd) D1(yellow brown) D1(orange-brown)-D1(black)-D1(phosphor)	5·25	5·25

Date of Printing (Blocks of Eight)

Spec. No.	Value	Date	Margin at left or rigid
XW56B	(2nd)	08/4/03	7·00

Withdrawn: 13 October 2004

XE Regional Pictorial Issues Gravure *Wales*

(1st) without borders

1999 (8 June). Perf 15 × 14(E). Two bands (blue fluor). Non-fluorescent coated paper. PVA gum

XW57 (=SG W84)

XW57	(1st) blue-green, greenish yellow, silver and black	1·00	1·00

Cylinder Numbers (Blocks of Six)
Perforation Type RE
Single pane cylinders. Chesnut press
Two phosphor bands

(1st)	W1 (blue-green)-W1 (greenish yellow)-W1 (silver)-W1 (black)-W1 (phosphor)	3·00

Warrant Numbers and Dates of Printing (Blocks of Eight)

Spec. No.	Value	SSO No.	Date	Margin at left
XW57	(1st)	554	18/04/99	9·00
			19/04/99	9·00
			20/04/99	—
		559	12/05/99	10·00

Printed by De la Rue in Gravure

2003 (4 March). Perf 15 × 14(E). Two bands (blue fluor). Non-fluorescent coated paper. PVA gum

XW57A

XW57A	(1st) blue-green, greenish yellow, silver and black	1·00	1·00

No. XW57A is distinguishable by the diamond dot screen on the Queen's head. The black screen appears solid on Walsall not on No. XW57A. This was printed at Byfleet on the ATN press formally owned by The House of Questa. The stamp was initially sold at 20p. which was increased to 21p. from 1.4.04.
This was the first Welsh value to be printed by De La Rue and was initially sold at 27p. which was increased to 28p. from 8.5.03.

Cylinder Numbers (Block of Six)
Perforation Type RE
Double pane cylinders

Two phosphor bands

(1st)	1(blue-green)-1(greenish yellow)-1(silver)-1(black)- 51(phosphor)	7·00	7·00

Date of Printing (Blocks of Eight)

Spec. No.	Value	Date	Margin at left or right
XW57A	(1st)	08/11/02,	9·00
		11/11/02	9·00

Withdrawn: 13 October 2004(

(E) without borders

1999 (8 June). Perf 15 × 14(E). Two bands (blue fluor). Non-fluorescent coated paper. PVA gum

XW58 (= SG W85)

XW58	(E) greenish blue, deep greenish blue and grey- black	1·75	1·75

No. XW58 was initially sold at 30p., the latter representing the basic European airmail rate.

Cylinder Numbers (Blocks of Six)
Perforation Type RE
Single pane cylinders. Chesnut press
Two phosphor bands

(E)	W1 (greenish blue)-W1 (deep greenish blue)-W1 (grey-black)-W1 (phosphor)	12·00

Warrant Numbers and Dates of Printing (Blocks of Eight)

Spec. No.	Value	SSO No.	Date	Margin at left
XW58	(E)	555	21/04/99	15·00

64p without borders

1999 (8 June). Perf 15 × 14(E). Two bands (blue fluor). Non-fluorescent coated paper. PVA gum

XW59 (= SG W86)

XW59	64p. violet, gold, silver and black	9·00	9·00

Cylinder Numbers (Blocks of Six)
Perforation Type RE

Two phosphor bands

64p.	W1 (violet)-W1 (gold)-W1 (silver)-W1 (black)-W1 (phosphor)	55·00

Warrant Numbers and Dates of Printing (Blocks of Eight)

Spec. No.	Value	SSO No.	Date	Margin at left
XW59	64p.	556	22/04/99	65·00

65p without borders

Printed by Walsall in Gravure

2000 (25 April). Perf 15 × 14(E). Two bands 9bluer fluor). Non-fluorescent coate dpaper PVA gum

XW60 (=SG W87)

XW60	65p. violet. gold, silver and black	3·25	3·25

Cylinder Numbers (Blocks of Six)
Perforation Type RE
Single pane cylinder. Chesnut press
Colours reading down the margin

Two phosphor bands

65p.	W1 (violet)—W1 (gold)—W1 (silver) W1 (black) W1(phosphor)	21·00

Warrant Number and Date of Printing (Block of Eight)

SSO No.	Date	Margin at left
607	10/02/00	28·00

68p without borders

Printed by De La Rue in Gravure

2002 (4 July). Perf. 15 × 14(E). Two bands (blue fluor). Non-fluorescent coated paper. PVA gum

XW61 (=SG W88)

XW61	68p. violet, gold, silver and black	3·25	3·25

Cylinder Numbers (Blocks of Six)
Perforation Type RE
Double pane cylinders

Two phosphor bands		No dot	Dot
68p.	1 (violet)-1 (gold)-1 (silver)-1 (black)-49 (phosphor)	21·00	21·00

Regional Pictorial Issues Gravure Wales XE

Warrant Number and Date of Printing (Blocks of Eight)

Spec. No.	Value	SSO No.	Date	Margin at left or right
XW62	68p.	945	08/05/02	28·00

(2nd) with borders

Printed by De La Rue at West Byfleet in Gravure

2003 (14 October). Perf. 15 × 14(E). One 4·5 mm. centre band (blue fluor). Non-fluorescent coated paper. PVA gum

XW62 (=SG W98)

XW62	(2nd) yellow-orange, orange- brown and black	80	75

Cylinder Numbers (Blocks of Eight)
Perforation Type RE
Double pane cylinders

One 4.5 mm. centre phosphor band		No dot	Dot
(2nd)	D1(yellow-orange)-D1(orange-brown)-D1(black)-D1(phosphor)	5·25	5·25

On the two band values the bands are 13 mm. wide between stamps but only 6.5 mm. at the vertical sheet margin. They react to both short and long wave ultraviolet light.

Dates of Printing (Blocks of Eight)

Spec. No.	Date
XW62	25/06/03

(1st) with borders

Two phosphor bands (blue fluor)

2003 (14 October). Perf 15 × 14(E). Two bands (blue fluor). Non-fluorescent coated paper. PVA gum

XW63 (=SG W99)

XW63	(1st) blue-green, greenish yellow, silver and black	80	75

Cylinder Numbers (Blocks of Eight)
Perforation Type RE
Double pane cylinders

Two phosphor bands		No dot	Dot
(1st)	D1(blue-green)-D1(greenish yellow)-D1(silver)- D1(black)-D1(phosphor)	6·00	6·00

On the two band values the bands are 13 mm. wide between stamps but only 6.5 mm. at the vertical sheet margin. They react to both short and long wave ultraviolet light.

Dates of Printing

Spec. No.	Date
XW63	25/06/03

Generic Sheet: A sheet inscribed "GLORIOUS WALES" containing 20 (4x5) (1st) class self-adhesive Welsh Dragon stamps was issued on 1 March 2007 and sold at £6·95, later increased to £7·35. It was printed in Lithography by Cartor. The four vertical rows were separated by labels showing ten Welsh scenes repeated with Welsh and English inscriptions on a background of the flag photographed by Andy Seymour.

This sheet was also available with personal photographs on labels at £14·95.

(E) with borders

Printed by De La Rue in Gravure

2003 (14 October). Perf. 15 × 14(E). Two bands (blue fluor). Non-fluorescent coated paper. PVA gum

XW64 (=SG W100)

XW64	(E) greenish blue, deep greenish blue and grey-black	2·50	2·50

Cylinder Numbers (Blocks of Eight)
Perforation Type RE
Double pane cylinders

		No dot	Dot
Two phosphor bands			
(E)	D1(greenish blue)-D1(deep greenish blue)- D1(grey-black)-D1(phosphor)	16·00	16·00

On the two band values the bands are 13 mm. wide between stamps but only 6.5 mm. at the vertical sheet margin. They react to both short and long wave ultraviolet light.

Dates of Printing

Spec. No.	Date
XW64	25/06/03

40p with borders

Printed by De La Rue in Gravure

2004 (11 May). Perf. 15 × 14(E). Two phosphor bands (blue fluor). Non-fluorescent coated paper. PVA gum

XW65 (SG W101)

XW65	40p. greenish blue, deep greenish blue and grey-black	1·50	1·50

Cylinder Numbers (Blocks of Eight)
Perforation Type RE
Double pane cylinders

Two phosphor bands	No dot	Dot
D1 40p. (greenish blue)-D1(deep greenish blue)- D1(grey-black, (-D1 (phosphor).	10·00	10·00

The bands are 13mm wide between stamps but only 6.5 mm. at the vertical sheet margin. They react to both short and long wave ultraviolet light.

Date of Printing

Spec No.	Date
XW65	08/03/04

42p with borders

Printed by Walsall in Gravure

2005 (5 April). Perf. 15 × 14(E). Non-fluorescent coated paper. Two phosphor bands (blue fluor). PVA gum

XW66	42p. greenish blue, deep greenish blue and grey-black	1·50	1·50

Cylinder Numbers (Blocks of Six)
Perforation Type RE
Single pane cylinders

Two phosphor bands	No dot
42p. W1 (greenish blue l-W 1 (deep greenish blue)-W1 (grey-black)-W1 (phosphor)	10·00

The bands are bright especially on the white borders. They react to both short and long wave ultraviolet light.

Dates of Printing

Spec. No.	Dates
XW66	16/12/04, .7/12/04

Withdrawn: 25 July 2006

XE Regional Pictorial Issues Gravure *Wales*

Printed by De La Rue in Gravure

2005 (10 May). Perf. 15 × 14(E). Non-fluorescent coated paper. Two phosphor bands (dull blue fluor). PVA gum

XW66A (=SG W102)

XW66A	42p. greenish blue, deep greenish blue and grey-black	1·50	1·50

Cylinder Numbers (Blocks of Six)
Perforation Type RE
Double pane cylinders

Two phosphor bands	No dot	Dot
42p. Dl (greenish blue)-Dl (deep greenish blue)-D1 (grey- black)-Dl (phosphor)	10·00	10·00

The bands are 13mm. wide between stamps but only 6.5 mm. at the vertical sheet margin. They react dull to both short and long wave ultraviolet light.

Date of Printing

Spec. No.	Date
XW66A	18/04/05

44p with borders

Printed by De La Rue in Gravure

2006 (28 March). Perf. 15 × 14(E). Non-fluorescent coated paper. Two phosphor bands (blue fluor). PVA gum

XW67 (=SG W103)

XW67	44p. greenish blue, deep greenish blue and grey-black	1·50	1·50

Cylinder Numbers (Blocks of Six)
Perforation Type RE
Double pane cylinders

Two phosphor bands	No dot	Dot
44p. D1 (greenish blue)-D1 (deep greenish blue)-D1 (grey-black)-D1 (phosphor)	10·00	10·00

The bands are 13mm wide between stamps but only 6·5 mm. at the vertical sheet margin. They react to both short and long wave ultraviolet light.

Dates of Printing

Spec. No.	Date
XW67	10/02/06, 13,/02/06

48p with borders

Printed by De La Rue in Gravure

2007 (27 March). Perf. 15 × 14(E). Two bands (blue fluor). Non-fluorescent coated paper.PVA gum

XW68 (=SG W104)

XW68	48p. greenish blue, deep greenish blue and grey-black	90	90

Cylinder Numbers (Blocks of Six)
Perforation Type RE
Double pane cylinders

Two phosphor bands	No dot	Dot
48p. D1(greenish blue)-D1(deep greenish blue)-D1(grey- black)-D1(phosphor)	6·25	6·25

The bands are 13 mm. wide between stamps but only 6 5 mm. at the vertical sheet margin.

Dates of Printing

Spec. No.	Date
XW68	18/01/07

50p with borders

Printed by De La Rue in Gravure

2008 (1 April). Perf. 15 × 14(E). Two bands (blue fluor). Non-fluorescent coated paper. PVA gum

XW69 (=SG W105)

XW69	50p. greenish blue, deep greenish blue and grey-black	1·00	1·00

Cylinder Numbers (Blocks of Six)
Perforation Type RE:
Double pane cylinders comprising 50p. Wales at left and 50p. Northern Ireland at right. The Wales 81p. was paired at right with the Scotland 50p. at left. All No Dot.

Two phosphor bands	No dot
50p. D1(greenish blue)-D1(deep greenish blue)-D1(grey-black)- D1(phosphor)	7·00

The bands are 13mm wide between stamps but only 6.5 mm. at the vertical sheet margin.

Dates of Printing

Spec. No.	Date
XW69	21/01/08

56p with borders

Printed by De La Rue in Gravure

2009 (31 March). Perf. 15 × 14(E). Two bands (blue fluor). Non-fluorescent coated paper. PVA gum

XW70 (=SG W105a)

XW70	56p. greenish blue, deep greenish blue and grey-black	1·25	1·25

Cylinder Numbers (Blocks of Six)
Perforation Type RE:
Double pane cylinders comprising 56p. Wales at left and 56p. Northern Ireland at right.

Two phosphor bands	Dot left
56p. D1(greenish blue)-D1(deep greenish blue)-D1(grey-black)- D1(phosphor)	7·00

The bands are 13mm wide between stamps but only 6.5 mm. at the vertical sheet margin.

Dates of Printing

Spec. No.	Date
XW77	03/02/09

68p with borders

2003 (14 October). Perf. 15 × 14(E). Two bands (blue fluor). Non-fluorescent coated paper. PVA gum

XW71 (=SG W102)

XW71	68p. violet, gold, silver and black	2·00	2·00

Cylinder Numbers (Blocks of Eight)
Perforation Type RE
Double pane cylinders

Two phosphor bands	No dot	Dot
68p. D1(violet)-D1(gold)-D1(silver)- D1(black)	13·00	13·00

On the two band values the bands are 13 mm. wide between stamps but only 6.5 mm. at the vertical sheet margin. They react to both short and long wave ultraviolet light.

Dates of Printing (Block of Eight)

Spec. No.	Date
XW71	27/6/03

72p with borders

XW70 (=SG W105)

XW72	72p. violet, gold, silver and black	2·00	2·00

Cylinder Numbers (Blocks of Six)
Perforation Type RE
Double pane cylinders

Two phosphor bands		No dot	Dot
72p.	D1 (violet)-D1 (gold)-D1 (silver)-D1 (black)-D1 (phosphor)	13·00	13·00

The bands are 13 mm wide between stamps but only 6.5 mm. at the vertical sheet margin. They react to both short and long wave ultraviolet light.

Dates of Printing

Spec. No.	Date
XW72	14/02/06

78p. with borders

2007 (27 March). Perf. 15×14(E). Two bands (blue fluor). Non-fluorescent coated paper. PVA gum.

XW73 (=SG W108)

XW73	78p. violet, gold, silver and black	1·40	1·30

Cylinder Numbers (Blocks of Six)
Perforation Type RE
Double pane cylinders

Two phosphor bands		No dot	Dot
78p.	D1(violet)-D1(gold)-D1(silver)-D1(black)-D1(phosphor)	9·00	9·00

The bands are 13 mm. wide between stamps but only 6 5 mm. at the vertical sheet margin.

Dates of Printing

Spec. No.	Date
XW73	18/01/07, 19/01/07

81p with borders

2008 (1 April). Perf. 15×14(E). Two bands (blue fluor). Non-fluorescent coated paper. PVA gum.

XW74 (=SG W109)

XW74	81p. violet, gold, silver and black	1·75	1·75

Cylinder Numbers (Blocks of Six)
Perforation Type RE:
Double pane cylinders comprising 50p. Wales at left and 50p. Northern Ireland at right. The Wales 81p. was paired at right with the Scotland 50p. at left. All No Dot.

Two phosphor bands	No dot
81p. D1 (violet)-D1(gold)D1(silver)-D1(black)-D1(phosphor)	11·50

The bands are 13 mm wide between stamps but only 6.5 mm. at the vertical sheet margin.

Dates of Printing

Spec. No.	Date
XW74	15/01/08

90p with borders

XW75 (=SG W109a)

XW75	90p. violet, gold, silver and black	1·75	1·75

Cylinder Numbers (Blocks of Six)
Perforation Type RE:
Double pane cylinders comprising 56p. Scotland at left and 90p. Wales at right.

Two phosphor bands	No dot
81p. D1 (violet)-D1(gold)-D1(silver)-D1(black)-D1(phosphor)	11·50

The bands are 13 mm wide between stamps but only 6.5 mm. at the vertical sheet margin.

Dates of Printing

Spec. No.	Date
XW75	29/01/09

Minature Sheets containing Welsh stamps

2006 (1 March) Welsh Assembly Miniature Sheet

(sold at £2·23)

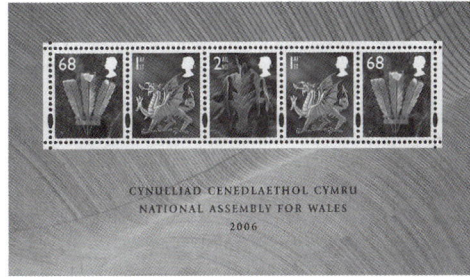

XWMS75 Miniature Sheet

(Illustration reduced to half actual size)
(Miniature sheet des. Silk Pearce. Gravure De La Rue)

2006 (1 March). Opening of new Welsh Assembly Building, Cardiff

Issued to mark the opening of the Welsh Assembly building located on the waterfront area of Cardiff Bay. The pale brown background of the miniature sheet features detail of the wooden roof of the building photographed by Gordon Brown and Taylor Woodrow Construction Ltd. Sheet size 123x70mm. containing designs as Type Nos. **XW56** (2nd), **XW57** (1st) and **XW59** 68p. (original 1999 issue but with white borders) by David Petersen (2nd), Tony and Gideon Petersen (1st) and Rhiannon Evans 68p. Non-fluorescent coated paper one centre band (2nd) and two bands (others) all with blue fluor. PVA gum. Perf 15 × 14 (with one elliptical perf hole on each vertical edge).

XWMS75 (=SG MSW109)

XWMS75	Welsh National Emblems; (2nd) orange-brown, yellow-orange and black; (1st) blue-green, greenish yellow, silver and black; 68p. violet, gold, silver and black	5·00	5·00
First Day Cover (XWMS75)		†	6·00

Withdrawn: 28 February 2007

First Day Covers

XWFD9	(8.6.99) (2nd). (1st), (E), 64p.	6·00
XWFD10	(25.4.00) 65p.	3·00
XWFD11	(4.7.02) 68p.	1·75
XWFD12	(14.10.03) (2nd), (1st), (E), 68p.	3·25
XWFD13	(11.5.04) 40p.	2·75
XWFD14	(5.5-4.05) 42p.	1·40
XWFD15	(28.3.06) 44p., 72p	2·75
XWFD16	(27.3.07) 48p., 78p.	3·50
XWFD17	(1.4.08) 50p., 81p.	4·00
XWFD18	(31.3.09) 56p., 90p.	4·75

Presentation Packs

XWPP7	No. 46 (8.6.99) (2nd), (1st). (E), 64p.	14·00
XWPP11	No. 51 (25.4.00) 65p.	2·50
XWPP13	No. 56 (12.3..02) (2nd), (1st), (E), 65p.	18·00
XWPP14	No. 65 (14.10.03) (2nd), (1st), (E), 68p.	7·00

PHQ Cards

XWC1	(XW57/9)	8·00	14·00
XWC2	(Nos. XW62/4,71)	2·00	6·00

SECTION XF
Regional Pictorial Issues
1999. Printed in Lithography

A. ENGLAND

(1st) with white borders

Printed by Enschedé in Lithography

2007 (20 September). Perf. 15 × 14(E). Two bands (blue fluor). Non-fluorescent coated paper. PVA gum

From £7.66 British Army Uniforms pane XEP3

XEN13 (=SG EN18)

XEN2 (1st) lake-brown and silver	4·25	4·25

A design as No. XEN13 but self-adhesive was issued on 23 April 2007 in sheets of 20, each stamp accompanied led by a *se-tenant* label showing an English scene. These sheets were printed in lithography, perforated 15 × 14 without the elliptical holes, and sold at £7·35 each. They were also available with personalised photographs on labels at £14·95 from the Royal Mail in Edinburgh.

Miniature sheets including stamps of all four regions printed by Lithography

2007 (8 November) Lest We Forget (2nd issue)

(sold at £3·46, £3·48 from 7.4.08)

WMS1997 Miniature Sheet (illustration reduced to half, size)

(Des. Hat-trick Design. Lithography by De La Rue)

Perf. 14½ (1st) or 15 × 14(E) (others). PVA gum

Sheet size 124 × 70 mm containing (1st) Soldiers in poppy flower and designs as Nos. XEN11A, XW70A, XS81A and XN75 (78p.). Two phosphor bands

WMS1997 (=SG **MS**2796)

WMS1997	10·00	10·00
First Day Cover		11·00
Presentation Pack (P.O. pack No. 405)	10·00	

2008 6 November Lest We Forget (3rd issue)

(sold at £3·60, £3·63 from 6.4.09)

WMS2088 Miniature Sheet Illustration reduced to half size)

(Des. Hat-trick Design. Lithography by De La Rue)

Perf. 14½ (1st) or 15 × 14)(E) (others). PVA gum

Sheet size 24x70mm containing (1st) Soldier's face in poppy flower and designs as Nos. XEN11B, XW70B, XS81B and XN70B (81p.). Two phosphor bands (Sold at £3·60)

WMS2088 (=SG **MS**2886)

WMS2008	10·00	10·00
First Day Cover		11·00
Presentation Pack (P.O. Pack No. 419)	10·00	

XF Regional Pictorial Issues *Lithography Northern Ireland*

B. NORTHERN IRELAND

2001. Printed in Lithography.

Printer. Initially, the stamps were printed by Walsall Security Printers in Lithography. The sheets of 200 were in 20 rows of ten stamps in each.

Perforation. The sheets were perforated 15×14 with one elliptical perforation hole on each vertical edge.

Phosphor bands. All values had two bands with gradated edges and blue fluor with the exception of the second class value which had one centre band.

XN60 Basalt Columns, Giant's Causeway

XN61A Aerial view of Patchwork Fields

XN60B Linen Pattern

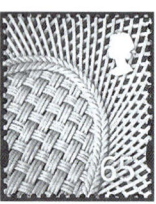

XN60C Vase Pattern from Belleck:

(Des. Rodney Miller Associates from photographs by Christopher Hill (2nd), Richard Cooke (1st). David Pauley (E), Tiff Hunter 65p.)

■ (2nd) without borders

Printed by Walsall in Lithography

2001 (6 March). Perf. 15×14(E). Non-fluorescent coated paper. PVA gum. One 4·5 mm centre band blue fluor)

XN60 (=SG NI89)

XN60	(2nd) black, new blue, bright magenta and greenish yellow	75	75

Plate Numbers (Blocks of Six)
Colour order of plate numbers reading down the margin to the Walsall imprint : Black, new blue, bright magenta and greenish yellow

Perforation Type RE
Single pane plates

Value	Pl. No.	Phos. No.	
(2nd)	W1 (x4)	WI	5·00

Secure Stock Operations Numbers and Dates of Printing
(Blocks of Eight)

Spec. No.	Value	SGNo.	Date	Margin at left
XN60	(2nd)	659	3/1/01, 4/1/01	7·50

2003 (25 February). Perf. 15×14(E). Non-fluorescent coated paper. One 5mm centre phosphor band (blue fluor). PVA gum (bluish)

From £6·99 " Microcosmos" Prestige stamp booklet No. DX30 printed by Enschedé in Lithography.

XN60A

XN60A	(2nd) black, new blue, bright magenta and greenish yellow	75

■ (1st) without borders

2001 (6 March). Perf. 15×4(E). Two bands (blue flour). Non-florescent coated paper. PVA gum.

XN61 (=SG NI90)

XN61	(1st) black, new blue, and greenish yellow	1·20 1·20

Plate Numbers (Blocks of Six)
Colour order of plate numbers reading down the margin to the Walsall imprint :Black, new blue and greenish yellow

Perforation Type RE
Single pane plates

Value	Pl. No.	Phos. No.	
(1st)	W1 (x3)	W1	8·00

Secure Stock Operations Numbers and Dates of Printing
(Blocks of Eight)

Spec. No.	Value	SGNo.	Date	Margin at left
XN61	(1st)	658	21/12/01	11·00

2003 (25 February). Perf 15×14(E). Two bands (blue fluor). Non-fluorescent coated paper. PVA gum.

From £6·99 "Microcosmos" Prestige stamp booklet No. DX30. Printed by Enschedé in Lithography

XN61A

XN61A	XN61A	(1st) black, new blue and greenish yellow	1·20

On No. XN61A the bands have a straight edge with points whereas Walsall printings were gradated.

■ (E) without borders

2001 (6 March) Perf 15×14(E). Two bands (blue fluor). Non-fluorescent coated paper. PVA gum

XN62 (=SG NI91)

XN62	(E) black. new blue and pale orange	1·50 1·50

No X62 was initially sold at 36p., the basic European airmail rate. This was increased to 37p. from 2 July 2001.

Plate Numbers (Blocks of Six)
Colour order of plate numbers reading down the margin to the Walsall imprint : Black, new blue and pale orange

Perforation Type RE
Single pane plates

Value	Pl. No.	Phos. No.	
(E)	W1 (x3)	W1	10·00

Regional Pictorial Issues *Lithography Northern Ireland* **XF**

Secure Stock Operations Numbers and Dates of Printing
(Blocks of Eight)

Spec. No.	Value	SGNo.	Date	Margin at left
XN62	(E)	660	5/1/01	14·00

2002 (15 October) Perf 15×14(E). Two bands (blue fluor). Non-fluorescent coated paper. PVA gum (bluish).

Printed by De La Rue in Lithography

XN62A

XN62A	(E) greenish yellow, new blue, black (15.10.02)		1·50

No. XN62A was initially sold at 37p.
  No X62A has sharp edge bands and Walsall gradated bands on No. XN60B. The De La Rue has blue tinted PVA.

Plate Numbers (Blocks of Six)
Colour order of plate numbers reading down the margin to the De La Rue imprint (E) greenish yellow, new blue, black (greenish yellow does not show on the stamp)

Perforation Type RE
Double Pane Plates
Two phosphor bands

Value	Pl. Nos.	Phos. No.	
(E)	1A (x3)	P19	10·00
	1B (x3)	P19	10·00

Date of Printing
No SSO number. Date of printing 17/06/02

65p without borders

2001 (6 March) Perf 15×14(E). Two bands (blue flour). Non-fluorescent coated paper. PVA gum

XN63 (=SG NI92)

XN63	65p. black, bright magenta and greenish yellow	3·00	3·00

Plate Numbers (Blocks of Six)
Colour order of plate numbers reading down the margin to the Walsall imprint : Black, bright magenta and greenish yellow

Perforation Type RE
Single pane plates

65p.	W1 (x3)	W1	20·00

Secure Stock Operations Numbers and Dates of Printing
(Blocks of Eight)

Spec. No.	Value	SGNo.	Date	Margin at left
XN63	65p.	661	20/12/01	20·00

68p without borders

Printed by De La Rue in Lithography

XN64 (=SG NI93)

XN64	68p. black, bright magenta and greenish yellow (4.7.02)	3·25	3·25

Plate Numbers (Blocks of Six)
Colour order of plate numbers reading down the margin to the De La Rue imprint 68p. Greenish yellow, bright magenta and black (2)

Perforation Type RE
Double pane plates

Two phosphor bands

Value	Pl. Nos.	Phos. No.	
68p.	1A (×4)	P19	21·00
	1B (×4)	P19	21·00

Date of Printing (Blocks of Eight)

Spec. No.	Value	Date	Margin at left or right
XN64	68p.	26/04/02	28·00

(2nd) with borders

Printed by De La Rue at West Byfleet

2003 (14 October). Perf 15×14(E). Non-fluorescent coated paper. PVA gum One 4.5 mm centre band (blue fluor)

XN65 (=SG NI94)

XN65	(2nd) black, new blue, bright magenta and greenish yellow	1·00	1·00

Plate Numbers (Blocks of Eight)
Colour order of plate numbers reading down the margin to the De La Rue imprint :Black, new blue, bright magenta and greenish yellow

Perforation Type RE
Double pane plates

One 4.5 mm centre phosphor band

Value	Pl. Nos.	Phos. No.	
(2nd)	D1a(×4)	D1a	9·00
	D1b (×4)	D1b	9·00

Dates of Printing

Spec. No.	Dates
XN65	24/06/03, 25/06/03,

(1st) with borders

Printed by De La Rue at West Byfleet

2003 (14 October). Perf 15×14(E). Two bands (blue fluor). Non-fluorescent coated paper. PVA gum

Two phosphor bands (blue fluor)
XN66 (=SG NI95)

XN66	(1st) black, new blue and greenish yellow	1·00	1·00

Plate Numbers (Blocks of Eight)
Colour order of plate numbers reading down the margin to the De La Rue imprint: Black, new blue and greenish yellow

Perforation Type RE
Double pane plates

Two phosphor bands

Value	Pl. Nos.	Phos. No.	
(1st)	D1a(x-)	D1a	9·00
	D1b (×)	D1b	9·00

Dates of Printing

Spec. No.	Dates
XN66	27/06/03

XF Regional Pictorial Issues Lithography Northern Ireland

Printed by Enschedé in Lithography

2007 (20 September). Perf. 15 × 14(E). Two bands (blue fluor). Non-fluorescent coated paper. PVA gum

From £7·66 British Army Uniforms pane XEP3 (20.9.07)

XN66A

XN66A	(1st) . black, new blue, and greenish yellow	4·25	4·25

On the DLR printing the bands are 7 mm apart but on No. XN66A the gap is 11 mm

A design as No. XN66A but self-adhesive was issued on 11 March 2008 in sheets of 20, each stamp accompanied by a *se-tenant* label showing a Northern Ireland scene. These sheets were printed in Lithography, perforated 15 × 14 without the elliptical holes, and sold at £7·35 each. They were also available with personalised photographs on the labels at £14.95 from the Royal Mail in Edinburgh.

2008 (29 September). Perf15 × 14(E). Two bands (dull blue fluor). Non-fluorescent coated paper. PVA gum

From £9·72 Country 50th Anniversary booklet pane XNP86

XN66B

XN66B	(1st) black, new blue, and greenish yellow	1·00	1·00
	a. black omitted		

No. XN66Ba comes from an example of booklet pane XNP86 with a progressive dry print of black.

(E) with borders

Printed by De La Rue at West Byfleet

2003 (14 October). Perf 15 × 14(E). Two bands (blue fluor). Non-fluorescent coated paper. PVA gum

XN67 (=SG NI96)

XN67	(E) black and new blue	2·50	2·50

No XN67 was initially sold at 38p., the latter representing the basic European airmail rate which was increased to 38p. from 8 May 2003.

Plate Numbers (Blocks of Eight)
Colour order of plate numbers reading down the margin to the De La Rue imprint : Black and new blue

Perforation Type RE
Double pane plates

Value	Pl. Nos.	Phos. No.	
(E)	D1a (x-)	D1a	22·00
	D1b (x1)	D1b	22·00

Dates of Printing
Spec. No.	Dates
XN67	24/06/03

40p with white borders

Printed by De La Rue in Lithography

2004 (11 May). Perf. 15 × 14(E). Two bands (blue fluor) Non-fluorescent coated paper. PVA gum

XN68 (=SG NI97)

XN68	40p. black and new blue	1·75	1·75

Plate Numbers (Blocks of Eight)
Colour order of plate number reading down the margin to the De La Rue imprint 40p Black and new blue

Perforation Type RE
Double pane plates

Two phosphor bands.
Value	Pl. Nos.	Phos. No.	
40p.	D1a(x2)	D1a	16·00
	D1b(x2)	D1b	16·00

Dates of Printings
Spec. No.	Date
XN68	18/02/04

42p with borders

Printed by Walsall in Lithography

2005 (5 April). Perf. 15 × 14(E). Non-fluorescent coated paper. Two phosphor bands (blue fluor). PVA gum

XN69 (=SG NI98)

XN69	42p. black, new blue and orange-yellow	1·75	1·75

Plate Numbers (Blocks of Six)
Colour order of plate numbers reading down the margin to the Walsall imprint 42p. Black, new blue and orange-yellow

Perforation Type P
Single pane plates

Two phosphor bands *No dot*
42p.	W1 (black)-W1 (new blue)-W1 (orange-yellow)-	
	W1 (phosphor)	12·00

The bands are bright especially on the white borders. They react to both short and long wave ultraviolet light.

Dates of Printing
Spec. No.	Date
XN69	15/12/04, 16/12/04

Withdrawn: 25 July 2006

Printed by De La Rue in Lithography

2005 (26 July). Perf. 15 × 14(E). Non-fluorescent coated paper. Two phosphor bands (dull blue fluor). PVA gum

XN69B (=SG NI98a)

XN69B	42p. black, new blue and greenish yellow	1·75	1·75

Cylinder Numbers (Blocks of Six)
Perforation Type RE

Two phosphor bands (double pane 1a (left) and 1b (right))
42p.	D1a (black)-D 1 a (new blue) D1a (greenish yellow)-D1a (phosphor)	12·00
	D1b (x3), D1b (phosphor)	12·00

The bands are 13 mm wide between stamps but only 6.5 mm at the vertical sheet margin. They react dull to both short and long wave ultraviolet light.

Dates of Printing
Spec. No.	Date
XN69B	03/06/05

44p with borders

Printed by De La Rue in Lithography

2006 (28 March). Perf. 15 × 14(E). Non-fluorescent coated paper. Two phosphor bands (blue fluor). PVA gum

XN70 (=SG NI99)

XN70	44p. black, new blue and greenish yellow	1·00	1·00

Plate Numbers (Blocks of Six)
Perforation Type RE

Regional Pictorial Issues Lithography Northern Ireland **XF**

Two phosphor bands (single pane 1a (left))

44p.	D1a (black)-D1a (new blue)-D1a (greenish yellow)-D1a (phosphor)	7·00

The bands are 13mm wide between stamps but only 6.5mm at the vertical sheet margin. They react dull to both short and long wave ultraviolet light.

68p with borders

Printed by De La Rue at West Byfleet

2003 (14 October). Perf 15 × 14(E). Two bands (blue fluor). Non-fluorescent coated paper. PVA gum

XN71 (=SG NI98)

XN71	68p. black, bright magenta, and greenish yellow	2·75	2·75

Plate Numbers (Blocks of Eight)
Perforation Type RE

Two phosphor bands

68p.	D1a (x.1)	D1a	24·00
	D1b (xt)	D1b	24·00

Dates of Printing

Spec. No.	Dates
XN69	26/06/03

72p with borders

Printed by De La Rue in Lithography

2006 (28 March). Perf. 15 × 14(E). Non-fluorescent coated paper. Two phosphor bands (blue fluor). PVA gum

XN72 (=SG NI101)

XN72	72p. black, greyish black, bright magenta and greenish yellow	2·50	2·50

Plate Numbers (Blocks of Six)
Perforation Type RE

Two phosphor bands (single pane 1a (left))

72p.	D1a (black)-D1a (greyish black)-D1a (bright magenta)- D2a (greenish yellow)-D1a (phosphor)	17·00

The bands are 13mm wide between stamps but only 6.5mm at the vertical sheet margin. They react dull to both short and long wave ultraviolet light.

Dates of Printing

Spec. No.	Dates
XN72	30/01/06

Presentation Packs

XNPP12 No. (6.3.01) (2nd), (1st), (E). 65p.	7·00
XNPP13 No. 66 (14.10.03)(2nd), (1st), (E), 68p	7·00

First Day Covers

XNFD10 (6.3.01) (22nd). (1st). (E), 65p.		5·00
XNFD11 (4.7.02) 68p		2·50
XNFD12 (4.10.03) (2nd), (1st), (E), 68p		3·25
XNFD13 (1.5.04) 40p	†	2·75
XNFD14 (5.4.05) 42p.	†	1·40
XNFD15 (28.3.06) 44p., 72p.		2·75

PHQ Cards

XNIC1 Nos. XN60/3 (Set of 4)	8·00	14·00
XNIC2 (Nos. XN65/7, 80) (Set of 4)	2·00	10·00

Decimal Wilding stamps

Booklet stamps printed in Lithography by De La Rue

From £9.72 50th Anniversary of the Country Definitives booklet No. DX43

XN82

XN83   XN84

2008 (29 September). 50th Anniversary of the Country definitives (2nd issue). Perf. 15 × 14 (E). Two bands (blue fluor). Non-fluorescent coatred paper. PVA gum

From £9·72 50th Anniv. fo the Country Definitives Prestige Stamp book. DX43

XN82 (= SG NI112)

XN82 (1st) deep lilac	1·25	1·25

XN83 (= SG NI113)

XN83 (1st) green	1·25	1·25

XN84 (= SG NI114)

XN84 (1st) deep claret	1·25	1·25

Miniature Sheet containing Northern Ireland stamps

2008 (11 March) "Celebrating Northern Ireland" Miniature sheet

(sold at £2·24, £2·28 from 7.4.08)

XNMS80 Miniature Sheet
(Ilustration reduced to half actual size)

(Minature sheet des. David Lyons, Clare Melinsky, Ric Ergenhright and Silk Pearce. Lithography De La Rue)

2008 (11 March). **Celebrating Northern Ireland**

This was, the third in the series of miniature sheets celebrating the four countries. The background features the Antrim countryside. Sheet size 123 × 70mm and printed on non-fluorescent coated paper with two phosphor (blue fluor) bands with PVA gum. Perf. 15 × 14 (E) or 15½ × 14 (78p.).

XNMS80 (=SG MSNI110)

As Type XNMS80, (1st) (Carrickfergus Castle, (1st) Giant's Causeway, 78p. Saint Patrick, by Clare Melinsky, 78p. Queen's Bridge and Friendship Beacon, Belfast (Sold at £2·24)	6·00	6·00
First Day Cover (XNMS80)		6·00
Presentation Pack (P.O. Pack No. 410)	8·00	
PHQ Cards (Set of 5)	14·00	17·00

Individual values from the miniature sheet are not listed separately.

The five PHQ cards depict the complete miniature sheet and the four stamps within it.

Cylinder Numbers
No cylinder numbers appeared on the printer's sheet margins. Before separation the printers sheet contained 15 miniature sheets arranged (3 × 5).

Miniature sheet containing Wilding stamps from three regions

50th Anniversary of the Country Definitives.

Miniature Sheet (sold at £3·24, £3·51 from 6.4.09)

XNMS81 Miniature Sheet

(Illustration reduced to half actual size)
(Miniature sheet des. Sedley Place. Gravure De La Rue)

2008 (29 September). 50th Anniversary of the Country definitives

This miniature sheet and the prestige booklet were issued on the same day to mark the issue, on 18 August 1958, of the first regional stamps. These were for the 3d. letter rate at the time. The 6d. and 1s.3d. followed for Northern Ireland, Scotland and Wales. The miniature sheet shows the 1958 designs as 1st Class, values on a pale cream tinted background. Sheet size 124 × 70 mm and printed on non-fluorescent coated paper with two 6.5 mm gradated phosphor bands (blue fluor) with PVA gum. Perf. 15 × 14 (E).

XNMS81 (=SG MSN111)

As Type XNMS81, (lst)x9 top row as Nos. XW1, XS1, XW14, wq XS22; bottom row as Nos. XN1, XW11,XS16,XN11,XN14 (Sold at £324)	8·25	8·25
First Day Cover (XNMS81)	†	10·00
Presentation Pack (P.O. Pack No. 410)	8·25	
PHQ Cards (set of 10)	6·00	14·00

Individual values from the miniature sheet are not listed separately.

The ten PHQ cards depict the nine individual values and the miniature sheet.

Cylinder Numbers:
No cylinder numbers appeared on the printer's sheet margins.
Generic Sheet: A sheet inscribed "GLORIOUS NORTHERN IRELAND" containing 20 (4 × 5) (1st) class self-adhesive Aerial View of Patchwork Fields stamps was issued on 11 March 2008 and sold at £7·35. It was printed in Lithography by Cartor. The four vertical rows were separated by labels showing ten Northern Ireland scenes repeated twice with a Giant's Causeway background.

Regional Pictorial Issues Lithography Scotland/Wales **XF**

C. SCOTLAND

▇ (1st) with borders

Printed by Enschedé in Lithography

2007 (20 September). Perf. 15 × 14(E). Two bands (dull blue fluor). Non-fluorescent coated paper. PVA gum

From £7·66 British Army Uniforms pane XEP3

XS83 (=SG S131)

XS83	(1st) rose-red, greenish yellow, deep rose-red and silver	4·25	4·25

No. XS83 shows an 11mm gap between the two phosphor bands, which is wide compared to the De La Rue printing

Printed by De La Rue in Lithography

2008 (29 September). Perf. 15 × 14 (E). Two bands (dull blue fluor). Non-fluorescent coated paper. PVA gum

From £9·72 Country 50th Anniversary booklet pane XSP95 (29.9.08)

XS84

XS84	(1st) rose-red, greenish yellow, deep rose-red and silver	1·00	1·00

No. XS84 shows a 7 mm gap between the two phosphor bands which is narrow compared to the Enschedé litho printing.

▇ Decimal Wilding stamps

Booklet stamps printed in lithography by De La Rue

From £9·72 50th Anniversary of the County Definitives Prestige Stamp Booklet No. DX43

XS92   XS93   XS94

2008 (29 September). 50th anniversary of the country definitives (2nd issue). Perf. 15 × 14 (E). Two bands (blue fluor). Non-fluorescent coated paper. PVA gum

XS92 (= SG S134)

XS92	(1st) deep lilac	1·25	1·25

XS93 (=SG S135)

XS93	(1st) green	1·25	1·25

X894 (= SG S136)

XS94	(1st) deep claret	1·25	1·25

D. WALES

▇ (1st) with white borders

Printed by Enschedé in Lithography.

2007 (20 September). Perf. 15 × 14(E). Two bands (blue fluor). Non-fluorescent coated paper. PVA gum

From £7·66 British Army Uniforms pane XEP3 (20.9.07)
XW76 (=SG W120)

XW76	(1st) blue green, greenish yellow, silver and black	4·25	4·25

A design as No. XW76 but self-adhesive was issued on 1 March 2007 in sheets of 20, each stamp accompanied by a *se-tenant* label showing a Welsh scene. These sheets were printed in Lithography, perforated 15 × 14 without the elliptical holes, and sold at £6·55 each. They were also available with personalised photographs on the labels at £14·95 from the Royal Mail in Edinburgh.

Printed by De La Rue in Lithography

2008 (29 September). Perf. 15 × 14 (E). Two bands (dull blue fluor). Non-fluorescent coated paper. PVA gum

From £9·72 Country 50th Anniversary booklet pane XWP79

XW77

XW77	(1st) blue-green, greenish yellow, silver and black	1·00	1·00

No. XW73 shows a 7 mm. gap between the two phosphor bands which is narrow compared to the Enschedé litho printing.

▇ Decimal Wilding Stamps

Booklet stamps printed in lithography by De La Rue

From £9·72 50th Anniversary of the Country Definitives Prestige Stamp Booklet No. DX43

XW76   XW77   XW78

2008 (29 September). 50th Anniversary of the Country Definitives (2nd Issue). Perf. 15 × 14 (E). Two bands (blue flour) Non-fluorescent coated paper. PVA gum

XW76 (SGW122)

XW76	(1st) deep blue	1·25	1·25

XW77 (SGW123)

XW77	(1st) green	1·25	1·25

XW78 (SGW124)

XW78	(1st) deep claret	1·25	1·25

XG

SECTION XG
Regional Pictorial Booklet Panes

A. Panes containing stamps of more than one region

From £7·44 "Letters by Night" A Tribute to the Travelling Post Office Booklet No. DX32

XSP3

The other panes in the booklet are No. WP1593, WP1627 (Section W) and UIPP13 (Section UI) in Vol .4

First pane comprising (2nd) 4·5 mm centre band Scotland and English 68p. two bands (blue fluor) ×3 each *se-tenant* on non-fluorescent coated paper. Perforated 15 × 14 with one elliptical perf. hole on each vertical edge and printed in Gravure. Vertical roulettes each side of Night Mail train at left

XSP3 (containing Nos. XS76A × 3, XEN4A × 3) (16.3.04)   8·50

Marginal Inscription: This pane is inscribed "Q5736RMatl Page13, StampPane (CyanMagYellowBlk877" at left.

From £7·49 "World of Invention" Prestige Stamp Booklet No. DX38

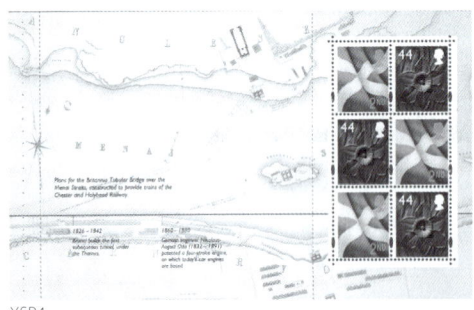

XSP4

The other panes in the booklet are Nos. WP19234 (Section W) and UEP47

First pane comprising Scotland 38(2nd) 4.5 mm centre band and Wales 3 × 44p. two bands (blue fluor) each pair *se-tenant* on non-fluorescent coated paper. The margin shows map of Menai Straits. The pane is rouletted twice between stitched margin and to left of the six *se-tenant* stamps. Perforated 15 × 14 with one elliptical perf, hole on each vertical edge and printed in Gravure.

XSP4 (containing Nos. XS76 × 3, XW66C × 3) (1.3.07)   3·00

From £7·66 British Army Uniforms Prestige Stamp Booklet No. DX40

XEP3

Printed by Enschedé in Lithography

Fourth pane comprising one each of the (1st) from Wales, England, Northern Ireland and Scotland two bands (blue fluor), on non-fluorescent coated paper and all labels without bands. The labels showing cap badges of the Coldstream Welsh, Grenadier (centre label), Scots and Irish Guards.

XEP3 (containing Nos. XW72, XEN13, XN71, XS83)   17·00
    (20.9.07)

There were no cylinder numbers or other marks on the issued panes.

From £9.72 50th Anniversary of the Country Definitives Prestige Stamp Booklet No. DX43

XNP85

The booklet contains panes XNP85/6, XSP95 and XWP79

First pane printed in Lithography comprising 9x(1st) 2 bands (blue fluor) on non-fluorescent coated paper and perforated 15814 (E) arranged in vertical *se-tenant* strips for each country, Northern Ireland (col. 1) Wales (col. 2) and Scotland (col. 3). The pane margin shows a coat of arms. The pane is rouletted twice between stitched margin and to left of the nine *se-tenant* stamps.

XNP85 (containing Nos. XN82/4, XW76/8, XS92/4)
    (29.9.08)   7·00

B. ENGLAND

From £6.83 "Across the Universe" Prestige Stamp Booklet No. DX29

XEP1

Printed by Questa in Gravure

First pane comprising 4×(2nd) and 5×(1st) including one (1st) Scotland in the centre. One centre band (2nd) and two gradated bands (others) (blue fluor) on non-fluorescent coated paper. Perforated 15×14 with one elliptical perf. hole on each vertical edge. Showing the Constellation Leo at left with a vertical roulette each side

XEP1	(containing Nos. XEN1 A×4, XEN2A×4. XS71C) (24.9.02)	8·50

Cylinder Numbers
No cylinder numbers occur on the issued panes.

From £7·43 "The Brontë Sisters" Prestige Stamp Booklet No. DX34

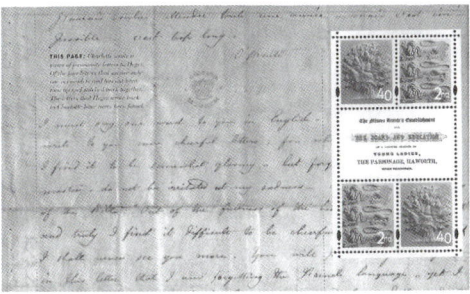

XEP2

The other panes in the booklet are Nos. WP1732/33 (Section W) and UIPP15 (Section UI).

Second pane comprising 2 booklet (2nd) 4·5mm centre band and 2x40p. two bands (blue fluor) *se-tenant* on non-fluorescent coated paper. Perforated 15×14 with one elliptical perf. hole on each vertical edge and printed in Gravure. Vertical roulettes each side of Charlotte's letter to Heger at left

XEP2 (containing Nos. XEN6A×2,XEN9A×2 (24.2.05)	3·75

There were no cylinder numbers or other marks on the issued panes.

C. NORTHERN IRELAND

From £6.99 (£7.24 from 8.5.03) "Microcosmos" Prestige Stamp Booklet No. DX30

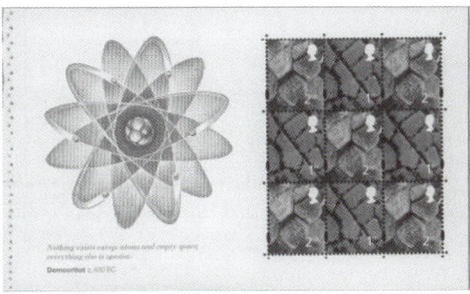

XNP1

The other panes in the Booklet are Nos. UIP11 (Section UE) and WP1534/5 (Vol. 5).

First pane comprising 5×(2nd) and 4×(1st), one centre band (2nd) and two straight edge bands (1st) (blue fluor) on non-fluorescent coated paper. Perforated 15×14 with one elliptical perf. hole on each vertical edge. Showing atoms in empty space with vertical roulette each side

XNP1 (=SG NI89)

XNP1(containing Nos. XN60Ax5, XN61Ax4) (25.2.03)	5·50

Plate Numbers
No plate numbers occur on the issued panes.

From £9.72 50th Anniversary of the Country Definitives Prestige Stamp Booklet No. DX43

Third pane printed in Lithography comprising 6 Northern Ireland (1st) 2 bands (blue fluor) on non-fluorescent coated paper and perforated 15×14 (E) arranged in three horizontal *se-tenant* pairs. The pane margin shows the Flax plant. The pane is rouletted twice between stitched margin and to left of the six *se-tenant* stamps.

XNP86

XNP86	(containing Nos. XN82/4, XN66ax3) (29.9.08)	4·75

One pane of XNP86 is known with black partially omitted, leaving two examples of XN66a with the colour missing completely.

"D. SCOTLAND

From £7.03 "The Life of the Century, The Queen Mother" (Booklet No. DX25
2000. Printed in Gravure by Questa

XSP1

The other panes in the booklet are Nos. UIPP7 (Section UI), WP1336 and WP1335 (Vol.5)
First pane comprising 6×(2nd) centre band with 2×65p. two 4·5 mm phosphor bands (blue fluor) on non-fluorescent coated paper. There are no bands on the centre label. Perforated 15×14 with one elliptical perf. hole on each vertical edge and printed in Gravure. Portrait rouletted at both sides.

| XSP1 (containing No. XS70A×6. XS74A×2) (4.8.00) | 7·00 |

Cylinder Numbers
Printed on the ATN, Applications Technologies Nouvelle press. Cylinder numbers were trimmed off but "Page 3" printed in red appears at the bottom right on the margin.

From £6.76 "Unseen & unheard". Centenary of the Royal Navy Submarine Service Booklet No. DX27

XSP2

Printed in Gravure by Questa
The other panes in the book et are Nos. WP1389/91 (Vol. 5)
Fourth pane comprising 4×(1st) and 4×(E) two bands (blue fluor) on non-fluorescent coated paper. There are no bands on the centre label. Perforated 15×14 with one elliptical perf. hole on each vertical edge and printed in Gravure. Vertical roulettes each side of the pane text.

| XSP2 (containing Nos. XS71A×4, XS72A×4) (22.10.01) | 7·75 |

Nos. XS7 I A and XS72A acre initially sold at 27p. and 37p. the latter representing the basic European airmail rate.

Cylinder Numbers
Cylinder numbers did not appear on the issued panes.

Stitched booklet pane (29 September) 2008

From £9.72 50th Anniversary of the Country Definitives Booklet No. DX43

The booklet contains panes XNP85/6, XSP95 and XWP79.
    Second pane printed in Lithography comprising 6 Scotland (1st) 2 bands (blue fluor) on non-fluorescent coated paper and perforated 15×14 (E) arranged in three horizontal *se-tenant* pairs. The pane margin shows the Scottish Lion depicted on the 1st class stamp designed by Tayburn. The pane is rouletted twice between stitched margin and to left of the ‚six *se-tenant* stamps.

XSP95

| XSP95 (containing Nos.)XS84×3, AS91.4) (29.9.08) | 4·75 |

Presentation Pack
| XWPP11 No. 46 (8.6.99) (2nd), (1st), (E), 64p. | 2·50 |

First Day Cover
| XWFD10 (4.7.02) (2nd), (1st), (E), 64p | † | 3·00 |

PHQ Cards
| XWC1 (XW57/60) (Set of 4) | 1·50 | 3·75 |

E. WALES

From £9·72 50th Anniversary of the Country Definitives booklet No. DX43

The booklet comprises panes XNP85/6, XSP95 and XWP79.
    Fourth pane printed in Lithography comprising 6 Wales (1st) 2 bands (blue fluor) on non-fluorescent coated paper and perforated 15×14 (E) Arranged in three horizontal *se-tenant* pairs. The pane margin shows the outline of the Welsh Dragon. The pane is rouletted twice between stitched margin and to left of the six *se-tenant* stamps.

XWP79

| XWP79 containing Nos. XW73×3, XW76/8) (29.9.08) | 4·75 |

SECTION Y
Royal Mail Postage Labels 1984
Royal Mail Fast Stamps 2008

Royal Mail Postage Labels

General Note

These imperforate labels were issued as an experiment by the Post Office. Special microprocessor controlled machines were installed at four Post Offices in Cambridge, London, Southampton and Windsor to provide an after-hours sales service to the public. The machines printed and dispensed the labels according to the coins inserted and the buttons operated by the customer. Values were initially available in ½p. steps to 16p. and in addition, the labels were sold at philatelic counters in two packs containing either 3 values (3½p., 12½p., 16p.) or 32 values (1p. to 16p.). From 28 August 1984 the machines were adjusted to provide values up to 17p. After 31 December 1984 labels including ½p. values were withdrawn. The machines were taken out of service on 30 April 1985, but the labels remained on sale at the Philatelic Bureau for a further 12 months.

The test was not successful and the experiment was not repeated.

The set of seventeen values were available in *black* with specimen imprint from the National Postal Museum to commemorate the Penny Black's 150th anniversary. Black ink was added to red on 23 May 1990 which produced blackish red labels.

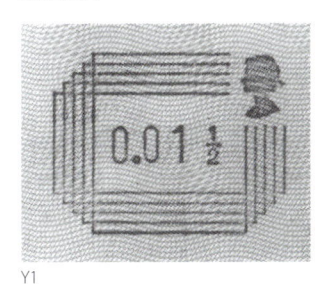

Y1

(Des. Martin Newton)

Machine postage-paid impression in red on unwatermarked phosphorised paper with grey-green background design.

Two Value Types (All values)

Type I   Type II

Type I. The 0 appears broad and the serif to 1 is solid.
Type II. The 0 is less broad and the serif to 1 appears to be curved at the top.

Types I and II came from the packs sold by the Philatelic Bureau and Type II came from the vending machines. Prices are the same for either type.

The following combinations were sold in "packs" (inscribed transparent envelopes) by the Philatelic Bureau and at philatelic counters.

YPP1	Set of 3 values (1.5.84) 3½p., 12½p., 16p.		2·50	3·00
YPP2	Set of 32 values (1.5.84) ½p. to 16p.		15·00	22·00
YPP3	Set of 2 values (28.8.84) 16½p., 17p.		4·00	3·00

1984. Imperforate. PVAD gum

Y1	**Y1**	1.5.84	½p.		25	40
			a. Value shown as 0·00 in error		45·00	
+			b. White paper		£100	
			ba. Value shown as 0·00 in error		£120	
Y2		1.5.84	1p.		30	45
			a. White paper		£100	
Y3		1.5.84	1p.		35	50
Y4		1.5.84	2p.		35	50
			a. White paper		£100	
Y5		1.5.84	2p.		40	55
Y6		1.5.84	3p.		45	60
			b. Printed on the gum		£300	
Y7		1.5.84	3½p.		50	65
Y8		1.5.84	4p.		55	70
Y9		1.5.84	4½p.		60	70
Y10		1.5.84	5p.		65	80
Y11		1.5.84	5½p.		70	85
Y12		1.5.84	6p.		75	90
Y13		1.5.84	6½p.		80	95
Y14		1.5.84	7p.		85	1·00
Y15		1.5.84	7½p.		90	1·00
Y16		1.5.84	8p.		95	1·00
Y17		1.5.84	8½p.		1·00	1·10
Y18		1.5.84	9p.		1·00	1·10
Y19		1.5.84	9½p.		1·10	1·25
Y20		1.5.84	10p.		1·10	1·25
Y21		1.5.84	10½p.		1·10	1·25
Y22		1.5.84	11p.		1·25	1·40
Y23		1.5.84	11½p.		1·25	1·40
Y24		1.5.84	12p.		1·25	1·40
Y25		1.5.84	12½p.		1·40	1·50
			a. White paper		£100	
			b. Printed on the gum		£225	
Y26		1.5.84	13p.		1·40	1·50
			b. Printed on the gum		£300	
Y27		1.5.84	13½p.		1·40	1·50
Y28		1.5.84	14p.		1·40	1·50
Y29		1.5.84	14½p.		1·50	1·60
Y30		1.5.84	15p.		1·50	1·60
Y31		1.5.84	15½p.		1·50	1·60
Y32		1.5.84	16p.		1·50	1·60
			a. White paper			
			b. Printed on the gum		£225	
Y33		28.8.84	16½p.		2·25	1·75
			b. Printed on the gum		£300	
Y34		28.8.84	17p.		2·25	1·75
			b. Printed on the gum		£300	

The labels printed on plain white paper came from a machine in which an engineer had left this paper in the machine by mistake. The error was quickly discovered but not before a quantity of labels were sold.

The labels printed on the gum side only came from a roll of paper which was placed in a machine incorrectly.

Withdrawn: No. YPP1. 28 June 1985, Nos. YPP2/3, April 1986

Labels inscribed "Post Paid" are outside the scope of this catalogue. They were not dispensed by vending machine or sold by the Philatelic Bureau.

First Day Cover

YFD1 (1.5.84)	3½p., 12½p., 16p.	6·50

The Philatelic Bureau only serviced first day covers bearing the 3½p., 12½p. and 16p. labels on 1 May 1984 although first day boxes were provided for collectors to post covers with all values. No first day cover facilities were available for the 16½p. and 17p. values on 28 August 1984.

Royal Mail Fast Stamps 2008

General Note

Following trials of a number of self-service machines capable of dispensing postage labels, Royal Mail began installing "Post and Go" machines in larger post offices in October 2008. In addition to postage labels, the machines, manufactured by Wincor- Nixdorf, dispense stamps with a pre-printed background and an inkjet printed indicator of the service required together with a four-part code.

The first machines were sited at the Galleries post office in Bristol and came into use on 8 October 2008. They dispensed five different labels, dependent on the service; the code at the foot of the stamp referring to the branch in which the machine is sited, the machine number within the branch, and the session and transaction numbers.

FT 1

(Printed in gravure by Walsall Security Printers, inkjet printed service indicator)

2008 (8 October). Type FT1. Black inscription on olive-brown background. Two 4mm. bands (blue fluor) each side of the Queen's head. Non-flourescent coated paper. Self-adhesive Die cut perforation 14½

YFS1 (=S.G.FS1)

YFS1	"1st Class Up to 100g"	1.25	1.40

YFS2 (=S.G.FS2)

YFS2	"1st Large Up to 100g"	1.50	1.75

YFS3 (=S.G.FS3)

YFS3	"Europe Up to 20g"	1.50	1.75

YFS4 (=S.G.FS4)

YFS4	"Worldwide Up to10g"	1.75	2.00

YFS5 (=S.G.FS5)

YFS5	"Worldwide Up to20g"	2.50	2.75
	Set of 5	7.50	7.75

The backing paper is yellowish and it is understood that the faststamps come in rolls of 1,500 and that 99 labels or stamps is the limit printed in one session.

Examples exist with the band at right placed left to show a small strip clear of the right perforations. The number of bands on the stamp remains at two and we do not list them. The machine issuing the stamps can jam causing misprints and these are outside the scope of the catalogue. Faulty software has been known to cause small variations in the size of the printed impression.

Stamps issued from a Belfast machine were incorrectly dated along with the corresponding receipt.

Post & Go Pack

YPP1	Post & Go Stamp Pack containing Nos. YFS1/5	8·00

The pack contains separate stamps. These are reproductions of the first "Post and Go" stamps printed at the Galleries post office, Bristol. They differ from machine printed stamps in having the service indicator and branch code printed in gravure.

SECTION ZB
Postage Due Stamps
1970-94. Gravure and Lithography

General Notes

Introduction. These stamps had two functions: to collect amounts payable to the postman by the addressee on mail which is unstamped or underfranked and for the collection of customs charges (including purchase tax or value added tax) on mail from abroad. For this reason the old inscription "POSTAGE DUE" was superseded by "TO PAY". This accounts for the need for a £5 value (introduced in 1973) needed for the collection of postage due from time to time when incoming overseas parcels were underpaid as a result of the wrong setting of a meter franking machine in a business firm. They were more frequently used to collect postage due on parcels returned to sender from abroad, often at air mail rates.

Changed Method of Calculating Postage Due. Following changes in the method of collecting money due on unpaid or underpaid mail the use of postage due stamps was restricted from April 1995 to mail addressed to business customers and to Customs/V.A.T. charges levied by the Royal Mail on behalf of the Customs and Excise. This use ceased on 28 January 2000.

Printers. Decimal Postage Due stamps were printed in gravure by Harrison & Sons until the 1982 issue and by Questa in lithography from 1994.

Paper and gum. Like the Machin definitive issues, original printings were on ordinary coated paper with PVA gum followed in 1973/74 by fluorescent coated paper with PVA gum and from 1974 on the same paper but with PVAD gum. In June/August 1980 the 10p. and 20p. values were issued, on phosphorised (fluorescent coated) paper with PVAD gum, which had been used in error.

Perforation. From 1970 to 1982 the stamps were perforated 14×15. Perforation Types A (T) and RE have been used (see Appendix 1). An elliptical perforation hole on each vertical edge was introduced as a security feature from 1994 in the issue printed by Questa.

Dates of issue. Actual dates of issue are quoted for each value on its first appearance but as no official dates were announced for the changes in paper and gum the earliest reported dates to the nearest month are given.

Sheet markings. These are described at the end of each issue and are similar to the postage sheet markings illustrated in Volume 4 Part 1.

Z3   Z4

(Des. Jeffery Matthews)
1970-76. Chalky paper. Perf. 14×15. Gravure

A. Original coated paper. PVA gum

Z48	D77	**Z3**	15.2.71	½p. turquoise-blue	15	2·50
Z49	—		15.2.71	1p. deep reddish purple	40	30
Z50	—		15.2.71	2p. myrtle-green	40	30
Z51	—		15.2.71	3p. ultramarine	70	30
Z52	D81		15.2.71	4p. yellow-brown	25	15
Z53	—		15.2.71	5p. violet	70	35
Z54	—	**Z4**	17.6.70	10p. carmine	80	30
Z55			17.6.70	20p. olive-brown	1·25	60
Z56	—		17.6.70	50p. ultramarine	2·50	75
Z57	—		17.6.70	£1 black	5·50	1·00

Cylinder Numbers (Blocks of Six)
Perforation Type A (T)

Value	Cyl. No.	No dot
½p.	2	1·75
1p.	1	3·00
2p.	1	3·00
3p.	2	5·00
4p.	3	2·00
5p.	4	9·00
5p.	8	£500
10p.	2	5·50
20p.	2	10·00
50p.	1	20·00
£1	2	32·00

B. Fluorescent coated paper. PVA gum

Z58	—	**Z3**	10.74	1p. deep reddish purple	60	
Z59			10.74	3p. ultramarine	3·00	
Z60	—		2.74	5p. violet	3·00	
Z61	—	**Z4**	12.74	10p. carmine	60·00	
Z62	—		10.74	20p. olive-brown	65·00	
				a. Bent frame	75·00	
Z63	D89		2.4.73	£5 orange-yellow and black	36·00	1·50

Cylinder Numbers (Blocks of Six)
Perforation Type A (T)

Value	Cyl. No.	No dot
1p.	1	4·25
3p.	2	18·00
5p.	8	18·00
10p.	2	£600
20p.	1	£850*
£5	1A (black) - 2B (orange-yellow)	£200

C. Fluorescent coated paper. PVAD gum

Z64	D78	**Z3**	12.74	1p. deep reddish purple	15	15
Z65	D79		12.74	2p. myrtle-green	20	15
Z66	D80		6.75	3p. ultramarine	20	15
Z67	—		1.78	4p. yellow-brown	60	40
Z68	D82		1.76	5p. violet	25	15
Z69	D83		21.8.74	7p. red-brown	35	1·00
Z70	D84	**Z4**	3.75	10p. carmine	30	30

ZB Postage Due Stamps

			a. Cylinder crack (horiz. pair)	7·00	
Z71	D85	18.6.75	11p. slate-green	50	1·00
Z72	D86	2.5.74	20p. olive-brown	60	25
			a. Bent frame	3·50	
Z73	D87	12.74	50p. ultramarine	2·00	1·25
Z74	D88	3.75	£1 black	4·00	1·00
Z75	—	11.78	£5 orange-yellow and black	50·00	3·50

Z62a, Z72a
Frame bent at upper left
20p. (Cyl. 1, R. 2/3)

Z70a
Cylinder crack, later printing
10p. (Cyl. 2. R. 1/2—3)

Cylinder Numbers (Blocks of Six)
Perforation Type A (T)

Value	Cyl. No.	No dot
1p.	1	1·25
	2	2·00
2p.	1	1·60
	2	1·75
3p.	2	1·60
	3	18·00
4p.	3	15·00
	4	4·25
5p.	8	2·00
7p.	1A	2·50
10p.	2	14·00*
11p.	1A	4·00
20p.	1	7·00
	2	5·00
50p.	1	12·00
	2	18·00†
£1	1	21·00
	2	26·00
£5	1A (black - 2B (orange-yellow)	£275

Perforation as Type A (T) but with left margin perforated through

Value	Cyl. No.	No dot
1p.	2	1·25
2p.	1	1·60
4p.	3	5·00
5p.	4	4·00
7p.	1A	5·00
10p.	2	£160
£1	2	21·00
£5	1A (black)- 2B (orange-yellow)	£300

The 10p. Cyl. 2, 20p. Cyl. 1 and 50p. Cyl. 1 also exist Perf. as Type A (T) but with right margin perforated through.

†There are two separate cylinder numbers and the price quoted is for a block from the upper or lower left of the sheet.

D. Phosphorised (fluorescent coated) paper. PVAD gum

Z76 —	**Z4**	6·80	10p. carmine		30
Z77 —		6·80	20p. olive-brown		1·25

Cylinder Numbers (Blocks of Six)
Perforation Type A (T)

Value	Cyl. No.	No dot
10p.	1	3·50
20p.	2	15·00

Nos. Z76/7 occurred as a result of the use of the wrong paper. The phosphor additive is the "yellow" type which gives a response under short and long wave ultraviolet light.

CYLINDER VARIETIES
Listed Flaws

Postage Due Stamps

Sheet Details

Sheet sizes: 200 (20×10). Single pane sheet-fed

Sheet markings:
Cylinder numbers: 7p. and 11p. In top margin above vertical row 2, unboxed
£5. In top margin above vertical rows 2/3, boxed
Others: In top margin above vertical row 3, unboxed (10p. has an additional fainter cyl. No. 2 above vertical row 4) and the 50p. cyl. No. 2 has an additional cyl. number in the left margin opposite row 8)
Guide holes: None
Marginal arrows: At top, bottom and sides
Colour register marks: £5. Crossed circle type in each corner of the sheet
Others: None
Coloured crosses: £5. Opposite rows 5/6, at both sides
Others: Opposite rows 6/7, at both sides
Additional coloured crosses: Additional temporary crosses were engraved on the cylinders and used for PVAD printings made on narrower paper to assist in trimming as follows:
10p. Opposite rows 6/7 at both sides and nearer to stamps and another additional cross opposite row 3 at right
20p. Opposite row 7 at left and rows 6/7 at right
50p. As 10p. but without the cross opposite row 3 at right
Sheet values: Above and below vertical rows 5/6 and 15/16 reading from left to right in top margin and from right to left (upside down) in bottom margin
Sold out: ½p. 7.83; 1p. 1.83; 2p. and 3p. 6.84; 5p. 11.82; 11p. 11.83; £1 1.84
Withdrawn: 4p., 7p., 10p., 20p., 50p., £5, 20 August 1984

Z5   Z6

(Des. Sedley Place Design Limited)

1982 (9 June). Perf 14×15. PVAD gum. Gravure

A. Chalky fluorescent coated paper

Z78	D90 **Z5**	1p. lake	10	30
Z79	D91	2p. bright blue	30	30
		a. Retouched frame	3·25	
Z80	D92	3p. deep mauve	15	30
Z81	D93	4p. deep blue	15	25
Z82	D94	5p. sepia	20	25
Z83	D95 **Z6**	10p. light brown	30	40
Z84	D96	20p. olive-green	50	60
Z85	D97	25p. deep greenish blue	80	90
Z86	D98	50p. grey-black	1·75	1·75
		a. Retouch to top of Y	4·50	
Z87	D99	£1 red	3·25	1·25
Z88	D100	£2 turquoise-blue	7·00	4·25
Z89	D101	£5 dull orange	14·00	2·25

B. Phosphorised (advanced coated) paper (1.92)

Z90 — **Z5**	2p. bright blue	£125

This printing was from cylinder 4 and was only discovered in 1998.

Cylinder Numbers (Blocks of Six)
Perforation Type RE
Single pane cylinders. (No dot panes only). Chambon press Prices are for blocks of 8 with gutter from upper pane or blocks of 6 from lower pane.

A. Chalky Fluorescent Coated Paper

Value	Cyl. No.	Block of 8	Block of 6
1p.	4	1·75	1·40
2p.	4	2·50	1·90
3p.	4	1·90	1·50
4p.	5	1·75	1·40
5p.	9	1·75	1·40
10p.	4	3·00	2·25
20p.	3	4·50	3·75
25p.	1	7·50	6·00
50p.	3	16·00	12·00
£1	3	26·00	20·00
£2	1	55·00	42·00
£5	3	£110	85·00

B. Phosphorised (Advanced Coated) Paper

Value	Cyl. No.	Block of 6
2p.	4	—

The above are with sheets orientated with "To Pay" reading from left to right (1p. to 5p.) or at left reading down (others).

The 10p. value exists with a 3 hole extension in the left margin with the stamp orientated to left and "To Pay" reading down. The cylinder was 4 and it is believed that a reserve perforator comb was used on the Chambon press. *Price for upper block of 8 with gutter £275 and lower block of 6, £120.*

CYLINDER VARIETIES
Listed Flaws

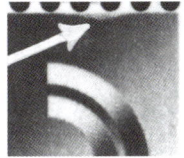

Z79a
Retouched frame at upper left
(Cyl. 4, pane position R. 1/7)
This does not exist on No. Z90

Z86a
Retouch to top of Y
(Cyl. 3, pane position R. 6/10)

Sheet Details

Sheet sizes: 200 (2 identical panes 10×10 separated by a gutter margin). Single pane reel-fed

Sheet markings:
Cylinder numbers: Bottom margin below R. 10/9 and R. 10/19, boxed
Marginal arrows: At each corner of pane and central between horizontal rows 5/6 at both sides
Sheet values: Above and below vertical rows 5/6 and 15/16 reading from left to right in top margin and from right to left (upside down) in bottom margin
Trimming line: In the colour of the stamp between each pane
SOLD OUT: 1p. November 1994, 2p. January 1994, others withdrawn 14 February 1995

Z7

(Des. Sedley Place Design Limited from photographs by David Burton and electronic imagery by Tapestry)

1994 (15 February). Perf. 15 × 14 and one elliptical perf. hole on each vertical edge. Non-fluorescent coated paper. PVA gum

Z91	D102	**Z7**	1p. red, yellow and black	10	75
Z92	D103		2p. magenta, purple and black	10	75
Z93	D104		5p. yellow, red-brown and black	15	50
Z94	D105		10p. yellow, emerald and black	30	75
Z95	D106		20p. blue-green, violet and black	75	1·50
Z96	D107		25p. cerise, rosine and black	1·50	2·00
Z97	D108		£1 violet, magenta and black	7·00	10·00
Z98	D109		£1.20 greenish blue, blue-green and black	8·00	12·00
Z99	D110		£5 greenish black, blue-green and black	30·00	20·00

Early use. The 2p. is known cancelled from Plymouth, Devon, 10 February 1994.
Perforation: As Type L(P) with all margins perforated through except for the margin at right which is imperforate on some panes. These are from the right of a double pane before being separated into post office counter sheets. The gutter between the panes was perforated through.

Sheet Details
Sheet size: 200 (10 × 20). Single pane sheet-fed

Sheet markings:
Plate numbers: None
Marginal arrows: "W" shaped, at top, bottom and sides
Sheet values: Printed four times in the sheet opposite rows 4/6 and 14/16 at left reading up and opposite rows 5/7 and 15/17 at right reading down
Imprint: In top margin above rows 2/5 "The House of Questa" and in bottom margin below rows 6/9 from left to right (upside down)
Traffic lights: None
Withdrawn: 31 May 2000

Presentation Packs

ZPP1 No. 36 (3.11.71) (Sold at £2·00, later at £2·01½) Nos. Z48/57	20·00

In September 1974 the 7p. was added to this pack and the price increased to £2·08½.

ZPP2 No. 93 (30.3.77) (Sold at £2·23½) With 11p. added	10·00

The text was revised on Pack No. 93. As fresh supplies of the above packs were made up, stamps on FCP/PVA and FCP/PVAD were included as available.

For Postage Due stamps sold in slip-in wallet at foreign Philatelic Exhibitions, see note after No. UPP3 at the end of Section UC in Part 1 of this catalogue.

ZPP3 No. 135 (9.6.82) (Sold at £9·40) Nos. Z78/89	48·00

The presentation pack contains an illustrated brochure describing the history of the usage of postage due stamps in Britain and abroad.

ZPP4 No. 32 (15.2.94) (Sold at £8·20) Nos. Z91/99	60·00

Nos. Z54/7 also exist on black card printed in white: "The British Post Office/Special Labels to be issued /17 June 1970/ Decimal Currency To Pay Labels – Four values /10p, 20p. 50p. and £1 / Designed by / Jeffery Matthews MSIA / Printed by Harrison & Sons Ltd". The actual stamps were affixed and embedded in plastic on both sides.

The card was supplied with press releases to certain national newspapers but not to the philatelic press. This practice was not repeated for other postage dues because the colours did not remain fast under the plastic.
Withdrawn: No. ZPP1, September 1976; No. ZPP2, September 1983: No. ZPP3 sold out, May 1994; No. ZPP4. 31 May 2000

First Day Cover

ZFDC1 (15.2.94)	Nine values as ZPP4	22·00

The price is for a plain cover with the Royal Mail pictorial "FIRST DAY OF ISSUE" postmark of London. E.C.3 showing "TO PAY" in a scroll.

APPENDIX J
Post Office Booklets of Stamps

B. £1 and £2 No value indicated, Folded Booklets (2000)

£1 Booklet

FH44/A
No Value Indicated (2nd) and (1st) class

Cover. Printed in scarlet, lemon deep blue and green by Questa.
Composition. One pane of four: Pane UIPQ19 (2nd and 1st (3) *se-tenant* vertically with printed labels (4) showing postcode enquiries and phone number. Centre band 2nd and two bands 1st all with (blue fluor). Printed in gravure by Questa.

Type FH44

FH44	(27.4.00)	6·00
a.	Containing pane No. UIPQ21 (17.4.01)	7·50

On pane UIMP3 the second printed label is inscribed "postcodes"

Withdrawn: 1 January 2003

£2 Booklet

FW12
No Value Indicated (2nd) and (1st) class

Cover. Printed in scarlet, lemon deep blue and green by Questa.
Composition. One pane of eight: Pane UIPQ20 (2nd (2) centre band *se-tenant* vertically with 1st (6) two bands all with (blue fluor). Printed in gravure by Questa.

Type FW12

FW12 (27.4.00)	7·00

Withdrawn: 1 January 2003

D. Barcode NVI Booklets (1989–2000)

General Notes

The first barcode booklets containing Machin stamps with no value indicated were issued on 22 August 1989.

By the beginning of 1990 barcode booklets were available nationwide and had replaced the previous folded counter booklets at Post Offices.

The £1 and £2 folded booklets continued to be sold from automatic vending machines. These ceased production due to declining sales and were withdrawn on 1 March 2003.

Dates of Issue. The dates quoted for those booklets showing the flour change from yellow to blue are those of the first day of availability from the Philatelic Bureau.

Prices. Since it is necessary to examine the contents, prices are for booklets that have been opened carefully. Glue spots designed to prevent scuffing were employed and these spots will cause damage to the covers when opened – this cannot be avoided.

Varnished Covers. Printed in scarlet, lemon and black these were printed with varnished covers late in 1988. Another important feature is the bar and letter codes on the outside back cover.

Barcodes. The first group of figures, e.g. 5 014721, appears on all booklets as this represents the country of origin (50 = United Kingdom) followed by (14721 = Royal Mail Stamps, the producer's code). The second group of figures is quoted in the listings as it represents product, series and control codes.

Walsall phosphor pane layouts. Notes describing the phosphor layouts **A**, **B** and **C** are given in Sections UI. Diagrams are shown above UWB5.

Layout	Pane of four description
A	Split bands 3·5mm wide on each stamp and clear of vert. perfs
B	Solid band centre over the perfs and 3·5mm at left and right edges
C	Solid band centre and bands cover the vert. perfs at left and right of the pane

Errors in Make-up. These are not, at present, listed and collectors should take expert advice before purchase. Some panes are attached by peelable adhesive while the early Harrison panes would show any attempt at fraud since these were well affixed to the cover. Other attempts at moving panes from their original covers can be checked under ultraviolet light.

Illustrations. The illustrations of the covers are reduced unless otherwise stated.

Panes of 4 2nd Class stamps

HA1

Des. Design House Consultants. Small Format

Appendix J Booklets

Cover. As Type HA1, with stamp printed in bright blue by Walsall
Barcode: 100142
Composition. One pane of four: Pane UIPW1 (4 × 2nd. (bright blue) centre band) imperforate on three edges, printed in lithography by Walsall

Type HA1

HA1	(22.8.89)	7·00

No. HA1 was initially sold at 56p which was increased to 60p. from 2.10.89.
Quantity Issued: 2,063,500
Withdrawn: 21 August 1990

Contents changed and printed by Harrison, cover by Walsall
Cover. As Type HA1, with stamp printed in bright blue by Walsall
Barcode: 100142
Composition. One pane of four. Pane UIPH3 (4 × 2nd. (bright blue) centre band) imperforate on three edges, printed in gravure by Harrison

Type HA1

HA2	(28.11.89)	24·00

No. HA2 was sold at 60p.
Quantity Issued: 2,184,050
Withdrawn: 14 September 1990

Type HA3
Multicoloured Crown on White Background

Cover. As Type HA3, with stamp printed in deep blue by Walsall
Barcode: 100203
Composition. One pane of four: Pane UIPW3 (4 × 2nd. (deep blue) centre band) with horizontal edges imperforate, printed in lithography by Walsall

Type HA3

HA3	Round tab (7.8.90)	3·75
a.	Round tab without shoulder cut (4.91)	3·75

No. HA3 was initially sold at 60p., which was increased to 68p., from 17.9.90. No. HA3a was sold at 68p., and was increased to 72p. from 16.9.91.
Withdrawn: No. HA3, 6 August 1991 and HA3a, 30 April 1992

Contents Changed
Cover. As Type HA3, with stamp printed in bright blue by Walsall
Barcode: 100272
Composition. One pane of four: Pane UIPW8 (4 × 2nd. (bright blue) centre band) with horizontal edges imperforate, printed in lithography by Walsall

Type HA3

HA4	Barcode printed in black (6.8.91)	3·50
a.	Barcode printed in blue (22.9.92)	3·50

No. HA4 was initially sold at 68p., which was increased to 72p. from 16.9.91. No. HA4a was sold at 72p.
Withdrawn: No. HA4, 5 August 1992 and HA4a, 21 September 1993

HA5
Olympic Symbols

Cover. As Type HA5. with stamps printed in bright blue by Walsall
Barcode: 100272
Composition. One pane of four: Pane UIPW8 (4 × 2nd. (bright blue) centre band) with horizontal edges imperforate, printed in lithography by Walsall

Type HA5

HA5	(21.1.92)	7·00

No. HA5 was sold at 72p.
Withdrawn: 20 January 1993

As before, but cover as Type HA3 and contents changed
Cover. As Type HA3, with stamp printed in bright blue by Walsall
Barcode: 100272
Composition. One pane of four: Pane UIPW13 (4 × 2nd. (bright blue) centre band (yellow fluor)) and two elliptical perf. holes on each vertical edge. Printed in lithography by Walsall

Type HA3

HA6	Freepost address at left (6.4.93)	4·00
a.	Freepost address at right (6.12.94)	4·00

No. HA6 was initially sold at 72p., which was increased to 76p. from 1.11.93. No. HA6a was sold at 76p.
Withdrawn: No. HA6, 5 April 1994; No. HA6a, 5 December 1995

As before, but cover printed by Harrison
Cover. As Type HA3, with stamp printed in bright blue by Harrison
Barcode: 100272
Composition. One pane of four: Pane UIPH9 (4 × 2nd. (bright blue) centre phosphor band (yellow fluor)) and two elliptical perf. holes on each vertical edge. Printed in gravure by Harrison

Type HA3

HA7	(7.9.93)	4·00

No. HA7 was initially sold at 72p., which was increased to 76p. from 1.11.93.
Withdrawn: 28 April 1995

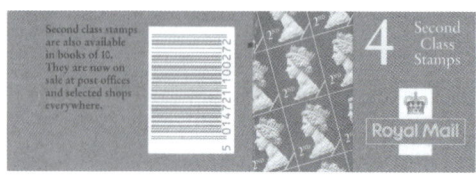

Type HA8

Cover. As Type HA8, with stamps printed in bright blue by Harrison
Barcode: 100272
Composition. As for No. HA7

Type HA8

HA8	Containing pane No. UIPH9 (yellow fluor) (10.1.95)	4·00
a.	Containing pane No. UIPH11 (blue fluor, 4 mm band) (18.7.95)	4·00
b.	Containing pane No. UIPH13 (blue fluor, 4·75 mm band) (11.11.95)	7·00

Nos. HA8/b were sold at 76p.
Withdrawn: No. HA8, 30 November 1995; No. HA8a, 17 July 1996; No. HA8b was sold out soon after issue.

As before, but cover printed by Walsall and contents changed
Cover. As Type HA8, with stamps printed in bright blue by Walsall
Barcode: 100272
Composition. One pane of four: Pane UIPW23 (4 × 2nd. (bright blue) centre phosphor band (blue fluor)) and two elliptical perf. holes on each vertical edge. Printed in lithography by Walsall

Type HA8

HA9	(12.12.95)	4·00

No. HA9 was sold at 76p.
Withdrawn: 11 December 1996

HA10
Olympic symbols

Cover. As Type HA10, with stamps printed in bright blue by Walsall
Barcode: 100272
Composition. One pane of four: Pane UIPW23 (4 × 2nd. (bright blue) centre phosphor band (blue fluor)) and two elliptical perf. holes on each vertical edge. Printed in lithography by Walsall

Type HA10

HA10	(6.2.96)	4·00

No. HA10 was sold at 76p.
Withdrawn: 5 February 1997

NOTE. From No. HA11 onwards the printer of each booklet is identified by a small capital letter below the barcode on the outside back cover.

HA11
"Second Class Stamps" ranged left and without white diagonal line on stamps

Cover. As Type HA11, with stamps printed in bright blue by Walsall
Barcode: 100272
Composition. One pane of four. Pane UIPW23 (4 × 2nd. (bright blue) centre phosphor band (blue fluor)) and two elliptical perf. holes on each vertical edge. Printed in lithography by Walsall

Type HA11

HA11	(4.2.97)	4·00

No. HA11 was sold at 80p.
Withdrawn: 3 February 1998

As before, but stamps printed in gravure
Cover. As Type HA11. with stamps printed in bright blue by Walsall
Barcode: 100272
Composition. One pane of four Pane UIPW27 (4 × 2nd. (bright blue) centre phosphor band (blue fluor)) and two elliptical perf. holes on each vertical edge. Printed in gravure by Walsall

Type HA12

HA12	Imprint at right below validity notice (26.8.97)	3·75
a.	Revised validity notice and imprint at left (5.5.98)	3·75
b.	New website address and phone no. (14.3.00)	3·75

No. HA12 was sold at 80p. and No. HA12a was initially sold at 80p. and 76p. from 26.4.99.
Withdrawn: No. HA12, 25 August 1998; No. HA12a, 30 August 2000.

Panes of 4 1st Class stamps

Cover. As Type HA1, with stamp printed in brownish black by Walsall
Barcode: 100128
Composition. One pane of four Pane UIPW2 (4 × 1st. (brownish black) two bands) imperforate on three edges, printed in lithography by Walsall

Type HA1

HB1	(22.8.89)	8·50

No. HB1 was initially sold al 76p., which was increased to 80p. from 2.10.89.
Quantity Issued: 3,037,150
Withdrawn: 21 August 1990

Contents changed and printed by Harrison, cover by Walsall
Cover. As Type HA1, with stamp printed in brownish black by Walsall
Barcode: 100128
Composition. One pane of four: Pane UIPH4 (4 × 1st. (brownish black) phosphorised (advanced coated) paper) imperforate on three edges, printed in gravure by Harrison

Type HA1

HB2	(5.12.89)	40·00

No. HB2 was sold at 80p.
Quantity Issued: 3,005,450
Withdrawn: 11 September 1990

Cover as Type HB3 and contents printed by Walsall
Cover. As Type HB3, with stamp printed in bright orange-red by Walsall
Barcode: 100180
Composition. One pane of four: Pane UIPW4 (4 × 1st. (bright orange-red) phosphorised (advanced coated) paper/PVA gum) with horizontal edges imperforate, printed in lithography by Walsall

Type HA3

HB3	Round tab (7.8.90)	4·00
	a. Containing pane No. UIPW5 (perf. 13)	12·00
	b. Round tab without shoulder cut (4.91)	4·50
	c. Revised "London" address inside back cover (6.8.91)	4·00
	d. Barcode printed in blue (22.9.92)	4·00
	e. Containing pane No. UIPW11 (PVAD gum) (16.3.93)	4·00

No. HB3 was initially sold at 80p., which was increased to 88p. from 17.9.90. Nos. HB3b/c were initially sold at 88p., which was increased to 96p. from 16.9.91. Nos. HB3d/e were sold at 96p.

Withdrawn or sold out:
HB3	6.8.91
HB3b	30.4.92
HB3c	5.8.92
HB3d	21.9.93
HB3e	15.3.94

No. HB3a was sold out soon after issue.

As before but cover as type HA5
Cover. As Type HA5, with stamp printed in bright orange-red by Walsall
Barcode: 100180
Composition. One pane of four: Pane UIPW4 (4 × 1st. (bright orange-red) phosphorised (advanced coated) paper/PVA gum) with horizontal edges imperforate, printed in lithography by Walsall

Type HA5

HB4	(21.1.92)	4·00

No. HB4 was sold at 96p.
Withdrawn: (21 January 1992)

Cover and contents changed, printed by Harrison
Cover. As Type HA3, with stamp printed in bright orange-red by Harrison
Barcode: 100180
Composition. One pane of four: Pane UIPH7 (4 × 1st. (bright orange-red) non-fluorescent coated paper/PVAD gum) and two elliptical perf. holes on each vertical edge. Printed in gravure by Harrison

Type HA3

HB5	(6.4.93)	5·50

No. HB5 was initially sold at 96p., which was increased to £1 from 1 November 1993.
Withdrawn: 5 April 1994

As before, but contents changed, printed by Walsall
Cover. As Type HA3, with stamp printed in bright orange-red by Walsall
Barcode: 100180
Composition. One pane of four: Pane UIPW15 (4 × 1st. (bright orange-red) two phosphor bands (yellow fluor)) layout A and two elliptical perf. holes on each vertical edge. Printed in lithography by Walsall

Type HB3

HB6	Freepost address at right (17.8.93)	4·00
	a. Freepost address at left (1.11.93)	4·00
	b. Containing pane No. UIPW17 (layout B) (22.4.94)	4·00
	c. Containing pane No. UIPW19 (layout C) (7.10.94)	4·00

No. HB6 was initially sold at 96p., which was increased to £1 from 1.11.93. Nos. HB6a/c were sold at £1.

For notes on the phosphor layouts see above No. UWB5 in Section UI. Nos. HB6b/c show the freepost address at right.
Withdrawn: No. HB6, 16 August 1994; No. HB6a, 28 April 1995; Nos. HB6b/c were sold out soon after issue.

Cover as Type HA3, printed by Questa and contents changed
Cover. As Type HA3, with stamp printed in bright orange-red by Questa
Barcode: 100180
Composition. One pane of four se-tenant with label: Pane UIPQ9 (4 × 1st (bright orange-red) two bands (yellow fluor)) and two elliptical perf. holes on each vertical edge. Printed in lithography by Questa.

Type HA3

Tercentenary of the Bank of England

HB7	Pane of four with se-tenant label at left (27.7.94)	9·50

No. HB7 was sold at £1
Quantity Issued: 1,830,000
Withdrawn: 26 July 1995

Cover as Type HA8, printed by Walsall and contents changed
Cover. As Type HA8, with stamps printed in bright orange-red by Walsall
Barcode: 100180
Composition. As for No. HB6c, pane UIPW19 (yellow fluor, layout C)

Type HA8

HB8	Containing pane No. UIPW19 (yellow fluor) (10.1.95)	4·00
	a. Containing pane No. UIPW21 (blue fluor, layout C) (18.7.95)	4·00
	b. Miscut pane No. UIPW19A (yellow fluor)	—

Nos. HB81a were sold at £1, which was increased to £1·04 from 8.7.96.
Withdrawn: No. HB8, 30 November 1995 and HB8a, 17 July 1996

As before, but contents changed
Cover. As Type HA8, with stamps printed in bright orange-red by Walsall
Barcode: 100180
Composition. One pane of four se-tenant with label: Pane UIPW20 (4 × 1st (bright orange-red) two bands (yellow fluor)) and two elliptical perf. holes on each vertical edge. Printed in lithography by Walsall

Type HA8

Birth Centenary of R. J. Mitchell (designer of Spitfire)

HB9	Pane of four with se-tenant label at right (16.5.95)	6·00

No. HB9 was sold at £1.
Quantity Issued: 39,980,000
Withdrawn: 15 May 1996

HB10
Olympic Symbols

Cover. As Type HB10, with stamps printed in bright orange-red by Walsall
Barcode: 100180
Composition. One pane of four: Pane UIPW24 (4 × 1st (bright orange-red) two bands (blue fluor)) layout B with two elliptical perf. holes on each vertical edge. Printed in lithography by Walsall

HB10	(6.2.96)	6·00
	a. Without diagonal white line across corners of stamps on front cover (8.96)	£120

No. HB10 initially sold at £1, which was increased to £1·04 from 8.7.96.
No. HB10a was not offered by the Philatelic Bureau.
Withdrawn: No. HB10, 5 February 1997

As before, but cover changed back to HA8 and contents changed
Cover. As Type HA8, inscribed "Commemorative Label Inside" and stamps printed in orange-red by Walsall
Barcode: 100180
Composition. One pane of four *se-tenant* with label: Pane UIPW25 (4 × 1st (bright orange-red) two bands (blue fluor)) and two elliptical perf. holes on each vertical edge. Printed in lithography by Walsall

Type HA8
Queen's 70th Birthday

HB11	Pane of four with *se-tenant* label at right (16.4.96)	6·00

No. HB11 was sold at £1 which was increased to £1·04 from 8.7.96.
Quantity Issued: 4,480,000
Withdrawn. 15 April 1997

Note. From No. HB12 onwards the printer of each booklet is identified by a small capital letter below the barcode on the outside back cover.

HB12
"First Class Stamps" ranged left and without white diagonal line on stamps

Cover. As Type HB12, with stamps printed in bright orange-red by Walsall
Barcode: 100180
Composition. One pane of four: Pane UIPW24 (4 × 1st (bright orange-red) two bands (blue fluor)) layout B with two elliptical perf. holes on each vertical edge. Printed in lithography by Walsall

Type HB12

HB12	(4.2.97)	3·50

No. HB12 was sold at £1.04.
Withdrawn: 3 February 1998

Contents Changed
Cover. As Type HB12, inscribed "Special Label Inside" on yellow tab at right and printed by Walsall
Barcode: 100180
Composition. One pane of four *se-tenant* with label: Pane UIPW26 (4 × 1st (bright orange-red) two bands (blue fluor)) and two elliptical perf. holes on each vertical edge. Printed in lithography by Walsall

Type HB12
Hong Kong '97 International Stamp Exhibition

HB13	"Special Label Inside" at right (12.2.97)	6·00

No. HB13 was sold at £1·04.
Quantity Issued: 230,000
Withdrawn: 11 February 1998

Contents changed and stamps printed in gravure
Cover. As Type HB12, with stamps printed in bright orange-red by Walsall
Barcode: 100180
Composition. One pane of four: Pane UIPW28 (4 × 1st (bright orange-red) two bands (blue fluor)) and two elliptical perf. holes on each vertical edge. Printed in gravure by Walsall

Type HB12

HB14	(26.8.97)	4·00
	a. Revised validity notice and imprint at left (5.5.98)	4·00
	b. As a but 1st class rate no longer valid to Europe (16.3.99)	4·00
	c. New website address and phone no. (14.3.00)	4·00

No. HB14c was initially sold at £1·04, which was increased to £1·08 From 27.4.00.

Nos. HB14/b were sold at £1·04.
Withdrawn: HB14, 25 August 1998; No. HB14a, 15 March 2000; No. HB14b, 30 August 2000

Contents Changed
Cover. As Type HB12, inscribed "Commemorative Label Inside" on yellow tab at right and printed by Walsall
Barcode: 100180
Composition. One pane of four *se-tenant* with label: Pane UIPW29 (4 × 1st (bright orange-red) two bands (blue fluor)) and two elliptical perf. holes on each vertical edge. Printed in lithography by Walsall

Type HB12
Commonwealth Heads of Government Meeting

HB15	"Commemorative Label Inside" at right (21.10.97)	11·00

No. HB15 was sold at £1·04.
Quantity Issued: 980,000
Withdrawn: 21 October 1998

Contents changed and printed by Walsall in lithography
Cover. As Type HB12, inscribed "Commemorative Label Inside" on yellow tab at right and printed by Walsall.
Barcode: 100180
Composition. One pane of four *se-tenant* with label: Pane UIPW30 (4 × 1st (bright orange-red) two bands (blue fluor)) and two elliptical perf. holes on each vertical edge. Printed in lithography by Walsall

Type HB12
50th Birthday of HRH Prince Charles

HB16	"Commemorative Label Inside" at right (14.11.98)	7·00

No. HB16 was sold at £1·04.
Quantity Issued: 230,000
Sold out: October 1999

Contents changed and printed by Walsall in gravure
Cover. As Type HB12, with stamps printed in bright orange-red by Walsall
Barcode: 100180

Composition. One pane of four *se-tenant* with label: Pane UIPW32 (4×1st (bright orange-red) two bands (blue fluor)) and two elliptical perf. holes on each vertical edge. Printed in gravure by Walsall

Type HB12

50th Anniversary of the Berlin Airlift

HB17	"Commemorative Label Inside" at right (12.5.99)	8·00

No. HB17 was sold at £1·04. which was increased to £1·08 from 27.4.00.
Quantity Issued: 3,980,000 probably withdrawn early 2000

As before, but Rugby World Cup 1999 label
Cover. As Type HB12, with stamps printed in bright orange-red by Walsall
Barcode: 100180
Composition. One pane of four *se-tenant* with label: Pane UIPW34 (4×1st (bright orange-red) two bands (blue fluor)) and two elliptical perf. holes on each vertical edge. Printed in gravure by Walsall

Type HB12

Rugby World Cup 1999, Wales

HB18	"Commemorative Label Inside" at right (1.10.99)	4·50

No. HB18 was sold at £1·04 which was increased to £1·08 from 27.4.00.
Quantity Issued: 480,000.
Withdrawn: 1 October 2000

Type HB19

The Stamp Show 2000, Earls Court, London

HB19
The Stamp Show 2000, Earls Court, London. 22–28 May 2000

Cover. As Type HB19, with Millennium stamps printed in olive-brown by Walsall.
Barcode: 100180
Composition. One pane of four *se-tenant* with label: Pane UIPW36 (4×1st (olive-brown) two bands (blue fluor)) with two elliptical perf. holes on each vertical edge. Printed in gravure by Walsall.

HB19	"Postman Pat Label Inside" at right (21.3.00)	6·00

No. HB19 was initially sold at £1·04, which was increased to £1·08 from 27.4.00.

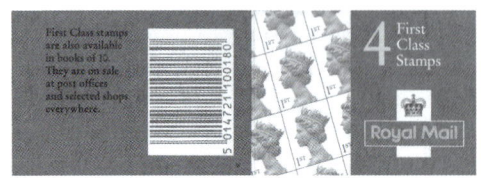

HB20
Opening of The National Botanic Garden of Wales

Cover. As Type HB20, with Millennium stamps printed in olive-brown by Walsall.
Barcode: 100180

Composition. One pane of four: *se-tenant* with label: Pane UIPW37 (4×1st (olive-brown). Two bands (blue fluor)) with two elliptical perf. holes on each vertical edge and printed in gravure by Walsall.

Type HB20

The National Botanic Garden of Wales

HB20	"Botanic Garden Label Inside" at right (4.4.00)	6·00

No. HB20 was initially sold at £1·04, which was increased to £1·08 from 27.4.00.

Panes of 8 (1st) plus pane of 2 Millennium Commemoratives

£2·60 Booklets

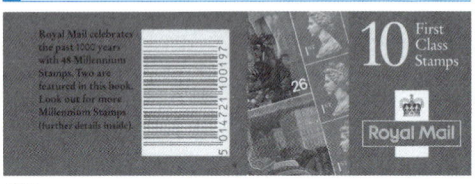

HBA1

Cover. As Type HBA1, with Machin and stamps of the 4th and 5th Millennium issues, printed by Walsall
Barcode: 100197
Composition. Two panes including one of eight 1st class and one pane of two 26p. *se-tenant*: Pane UIPW33 (8×1st (bright orange-red) two bands (blue fluor)) and two elliptical perf. holes on each vertical edge. One pane of two Millennium stamps *se-tenant*: Pane WP1239 (2×26p. two bands (blue fluor)). Printed in gravure by Walsall

Type HBA1

Millennium, Settlers' and Workers' stamps

HBA1	Containing 2 panes affixed by selvedge at left (12.5.99)	10·00

No. HBA1 was sold at £2·60. which was increased to £2·68 from 28.4.00.
Probably sold out by June 2000.

Type HBA2

Cover. As Type HBA2, with Machin and stamps of the Farmers' Tale issue, printed by Walsall
Barcode: 100197
Composition. Two panes including one of eight 1st class and one pane of two 26p.: Pane UIPW33 (8×1st (bright orange-red) two bands (blue fluor)) and two elliptical perf. holes on each vertical edge. One pane of two Farmers' Tale stamps. Pane WP1269 (2×26p. two bands (blue fluor)). Printed in gravure by Walsall

Type HBA2

Millennium. Farmers' Tale stamps

HBA2	Containing 2 panes affixed by selvedge at left (21.9.99)	10·00

No. HBA2 was sold at £2·60.

HBA3

Cover. As Type HBA3, with Machin and Millennium issues. printed by Walsall.
Barcode: 100197
Composition. Two panes including one of eight 1st class and one pane of two 1st class Millennium special issues *se-tenant*: Pane UIPW35B (8×1st (olive-brown), two bands (blue fluor)) with two elliptical perf. holes on each vertical edge. One pane of two Millennium stamps *se-tenant*: Pane WP1290 (2×1st Two bands (blue fluor)). Printed in gravure by Walsall.

Type HBA3

Millennium stamps, Above and Beyond: Life on Earth

HBA3	Containing 2 panes affixed by selvedge at left (26.5.00)	12·00

No. HBA3 was sold at £2·70.
Withdrawn: 20 September 2000

HBA4

Cover. As Type HBA4, with Machin and Millennium issues. printed by Walsall.
Barcode: 100197
Composition. Two panes including one of eight 1st class and one pane of two 1st class Millennium special issues *se-tenant* ;Pane UIPW35B (8×1st (olive-brown). Two bands (blue fluor)) with two elliptical perf. holes on each vertical edge. One pane of two Millennium stamps *se-tenant*: Pane WP1320 (2×1st Two bands (blue fluor)). Printed in gravure by Walsall.

Type HBA4

Millennium stamps, Stone and Soil: Tree and Leaf

HBA4	Containing 2 panes affixed by selvedge at left (5.9.00)	12·00

Panes of 10 2nd Class stamps

Cover. As Type HA1, with stamp printed in bright blue by Harrison
Barcode: 100159
Composition. One pane of ten: Pane UIPH1 (10×2nd. (bright blue) centre band) with horizontal edge imperforate

Type HA1

HC1	(22.8.89)	11·00
	a. Inside cover with new rates (2.10.89)	12·00

No. HC1 was initially sold at £1·40, which was increased to £1·50 from 2.10.89. No. HC1a was sold at £1·50.
Quantity Issued: Nos. HC1 and HC2 3,725,000; HC1a, 3,449,650
Withdrawn: HC1 21 August 1990; HC1a 14 September 1990

As before, but cover printed by Questa
Barcode: 100159
Composition. One pane of ten: Pane UIPQ1 (10×2nd. short centre band) printed in lithography by Questa

Type HA1

HC2	(19.9.89)	10·00

No. HC2 was initially sold at £1·40, which was increased to £1·50 from 2.10.89.
Withdrawn: 14 September 1990

Cover as Type HA3 printed by Harrison
Cover. As Type HA3 with stamp printed in deep blue by Harrison
Barcode: 100210
Composition. One pane of ten: Pane UIPH5 (10×2nd. (deep blue) centre band) with horizontal edges imperforate.

Type HA3

HC3	(7.8.90)	12·00

No. HC3 was initially sold at £1·50, which was increased to £1·70 from 17.9.90.

As before, but cover printed by Questa
Barcode: 100210
Composition. One pane of ten: Pane UIPQ3 (10×2nd. (deep blue) short centre band) printed in lithography by Questa

Type HA3

HC4	(7.8.90)	15·00

No. HC4 was initially sold at £1·50, which was increased to £1·70 from 17.9.90.

As before, but cover printed by Walsall
Barcode: 100210
Composition. One pane of ten: Pane UIPW6 (10×2nd. (deep blue) centre band) printed in lithography by Walsall, with horizontal edges imperforate

Type HA3

HC5	Round tab (7.8.90)	8·50
	a. Round tab without shoulder cut (4.91)	8·50

No. HC5 was initially sold at £1·50, which was increased to £1·70 from 17.9.90. No. HC5a was initially sold at £1·70, which was increased to £1·80 from 16.9.91.
Withdrawn: HC3 6 August 1991, HC4 6 August 1991, HC5 6 August 1991, HC5a 30 April 1992
Contents Changed–stamps printed Questa
Cover. As Type HA3, with stamp printed in bright blue by Questa
Barcode: 100265
Composition. One pane of ten: Pane UIPQ1 (10×2nd. (bright blue) short centre band) printed in lithography by Questa

Type HA3

HC6	Barcode printed in black (6.8.91)	8·00
	a. Barcode printed in blue (22.9.92)	8·00

No. HC6 was initially sold at £1·70, which was increased to £1·80 from 16.9.91. No. HC6a was sold at £1·80.
Withdrawn: No. HC6, 5 August 1992 and HC6a, 21 September 1993

As before, but cover printed by Walsall
Cover. As Type HA3, with stamps printed in bright blue by Walsall
Barcode: 100265
Composition. One pane of ten: Pane UIPW9 (10 × 2nd. (bright blue) centre band/PVA gum) with horizontal edges imperforate, printed in lithography by Walsall

Type HA3

HC7	Barcode printed in black (6.8.91)	7·50
a.	Barcode printed in blue (22.9.92)	7·50
b.	Containing pane No. UIPW12 (PVAD gum) (16.3.93)	12·00

No. HC7 was initially sold at £1·70, which was increased to £1·80 from 16.9.91. Nos. HC7a/b were sold at £1·80 but No. HC7b was increased to £1·90 from 1.11.93.
Withdrawn: HC7 5 August 1992, HC7a 21 September 1993, HC7b 15 March 1994

As before, but cover as Type HA5
Cover. as Type HA5, with stamp printed in bright blue by Walsall
Barcode: 100265
Composition. One pane of ten: Pane UIPW9 (10 × 2nd. (bright blue) centre band) with horizontal edges imperforate, printed in lithography by Walsall

Type HA5

HC8	(21.1.92)	6·00

No. HC8 was sold at £1·80.
Withdrawn: 20 January 1993

As before, but cover printed by Questa
Cover. As Type HA5, with stamp printed in bright blue by Questa
Barcode: 100265
Composition. One pane of ten: Pane UIPQ1 (10 × 2nd. (bright blue) short centre band) printed in lithography by Questa

Type HA5

HC9	(31.3.92)	8·50

No. HC9 was sold at £1·80.
Withdrawn: 30 March 1993

Cover as Type HA3 printed by Harrison
Cover. As Type HA3, with stamp printed in bright blue by Harrison
Barcode: 100265
Composition. One pane of ten: Pane UIPH1 (10 × 2nd. (bright blue) centre band) with horizontal edges imperforate, printed in gravure by Harrison

Type HA3

HC10	(22.9.92)	8·00

No. HC10 was sold at £1·80.
Withdrawn: 21 September 1993

As before, but contents changed, printed by Questa
Cover. As Type HA3, with stamp printed in bright blue by Questa
Barcode: 100265
Composition. One pane of ten: Pane UIPQ6 (10 × 2nd. (bright blue) short centre band (yellow fluor)) and two elliptical perf. holes on each vertical edge. Printed in lithography by Questa

Type HA3

HC11	Questa imprint at left (vert) (6.4.93)	7·75
a.	Questa imprint at right (horiz) (17.8.93)	7·75
b.	Containing pane No. UIPQ8 (cont. band) (19.5.94)	7·75
c.	As b but 3 line Postcode notice (4.10.94)	7·75

Nos. HC11/a were initially sold at £1·80, which was increased to £1·90 from 1.11.93. No. HC11c was sold at £1·90 and was available from August, but was not sold by the Philatelic Bureau until 4 October 1994.
Withdrawn: No. HC11, 5 April 1994, Nos. HC11a/b, 28 April 1995, No. HC11c, 3 October 1995

As before, but cover printed by Walsall
Cover. As Type HA3, with stamp printed in bright blue by Walsall
Barcode: 100265
Composition. One pane of ten: Pane UIPW16 (10 × 2nd. (bright blue) centre band (yellow fluor)) and two elliptical perf. holes on each vertical edge. Printed in lithography by Walsall

Type HA3

HC12	(1.11.93)	7·75

No. HC12 was sold at £1·90.
The Philatelic Bureau date of issue was 22 February 1994.
Sold out: November 1995

Cover as Type HA8, printed by Questa and contents changed
Cover. As Type HA8, with stamps printed in bright blue by Questa
Barcode: 100265
Composition. One pane of ten: As for No. HC11b

Type HA8

HC13	Containing pane No. UIPQ8 (yellow fluor) (10.1.95)	7·75
a.	Containing pane No. UIPQ14 (blue fluor) (18.7.95)	7·75

Nos. HC13/a were initially sold at £1·90, which was increased to £2 from 8.7.96.
Withdrawn: No. HC13, 30 November 1995, No. HC13a, 17 July 1996

As before, but cover printed by Harrison and contents changed
Cover. As Type HA8, with stamps printed in bright blue by Harrison
Barcode: 100265
Composition. One pane of ten: Pane UIPH14 (10 × 2nd. (bright blue) centre hand (blue fluor)) and two elliptical perf. holes on each vertical edge. Printed in gravure by Harrison

Type HA8

HC14	(12.12.95)	6·00

No. HC14 was initially sold at £1·90, which was increased to £2 from 8.7.96.
Withdrawn: 11 December 1996

As before, but cover as Type HA10
Cover. As Type HA10, with stamps printed in bright blue by Harrison
Barcode: 100265
Composition. One pane of ten: Pane UIPH14 (10 × 2nd. (bright blue) centre band (blue floor)) and two elliptical perf. holes on each vertical edge. Printed in gravure by Harrison

Type HA10

Olympic symbols

HC15	(6.2.96)	6·50

No. HC15 was initially sold at £1·90, which was increased to £2 from 8.7.96.
Withdrawn: 5 February 1997

As before, but contents changed, printed by Questa
Cover. As Type HA10, with stamps printed in bright blue by Questa
Barcode: 100265
Composition. One pane of ten: Pane UIPQ14 (10 × 2nd. (bright blue) centre band (blue fluor)) and two elliptical perf. holes on each vertical edge. Printed in lithography by Questa

Type HA10

Olympic symbols

HC16	(6.2.96)	9·00

No. HC16 was initially sold at £1·90, which was increased to £2 from 8.7.96.
Withdrawn: 5 February 1997
Note. From No. HC17 onwards the printer of each booklet is identified by a small capital letter below the barcode on the outside back cover.

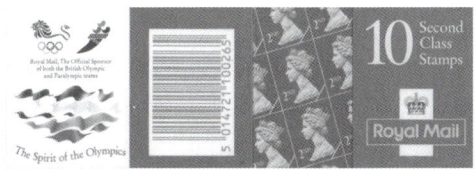

HC17
"Second Class Stamps" ranged left

Cover. As Type HC17, with stamps printed in bright blue by Harrison. Printer's initial on back cover
Barcode: 100265
Composition. One pane of ten: Pane UIPH14 (10 × 2nd. (bright blue) centre band (blue fluor)) and two elliptical perf. holes on each vertical edge. Printed in gravure by Harrison

Type HC17

Olympic symbols

HC17	(6.8.96)	6·50

No. HC17 was sold at £2.
Withdrawn: 5 August 1997

As before, but printed by Questa in lithography
Cover. As Type HC17, but stamps without white diagonal lines and printed in bright blue by Questa
Barcode: 100265
Composition. One pane of ten: Pane UIPQ14 (10 × 2nd. (bright blue) centre band (blue fluor)) and two elliptical perf. holes on each vertical edge. Printed in lithography by Questa

Type HC17

Olympic symbols

HC18	(6.8.96)	8·75

No. HC18 was sold at £2.
Withdrawn: 5 August 1997

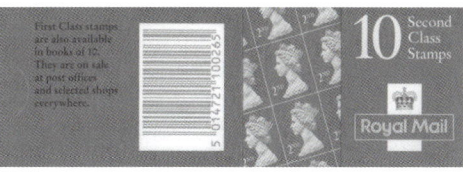

HC19
Without white diagonal lines on stamps

Cover. As Type HC19, with stamps printed in bright blue by Harrison
Barcode: 100265
Composition. One pane of ten: Pane UIPHI4 (10 × 2nd. (bright blue) centre band (blue fluor)) and two elliptical perf. holes on each vertical edge. Printed in gravure by Harrison

Type HC19

HC19	(4.2.97)	6·50
	a. Containing pane No. UIPH14A (PVA gum (bluish)) (4.97)	25·00
	b. Containing pane No. UIPH15 (29.4.97)	6·50

Panes UIPH14A and 15 were printed by chemically etched and computer engraved cylinders respectively.
Nos. HC19/a/b were all sold at £2.
Withdrawn: No. HC19, 3 February 1998: HC19b, 28 April 1998 and HC19a was sold out soon after issue.

As before, but printed by Questa in lithography
Cover. As Type HC19, with stamps printed in bright blue by Questa
Barcode: 100265
Composition. As for No. HC16

Type HC19

HC20	Horizontal imprint at left (4.2.97)	7·00
	a. Revised validity notice and vertical imprint (5.5.98)	7·00

Nos. HC20/a were initially sold at £2, but No. HC20a was sold at £1·90 from 26.4.99.
Withdrawn: No. HC20, 3 February 1998 and HC20a, 15 March 2000

As before, but printed by De La Rue in gravure
Cover. As Type HC19, with stamps printed in bright blue by De La Rue. "D" instead of "H" on outside back cover
Barcode: 100265
Composition. One pane of ten: As for HC19b

Type HC19

HC21	Printer's imprint "D" on reverse (5.5.98)	6·00

No. HC21 was initially sold at £2, which was decreased to £1·90 from 26.4.99.

As before, but printed by Questa in gravure
Cover. As Type HC19, with stamps printed in bright blue by Questa
Barcode: 100265
Composition. One pane of ten: Pane UIPQ16 (10 × 2nd. (bright blue) centre band (blue fluor)) and two elliptical perf. holes on each vertical edge. Printed in gravure by Questa

Type HC19

HC22	Printer's imprint "Q" on reverse (1.12.98)	10·00
	a. New website address and phone no (14.3.00)	10·00

Appendix J Booklets

No. HC22 was initially sold at £2, which was decreased to £1·90 from 26.4.99.
No. HC22a was sold at £1.90.
Withdrawn: 30 August 2000

Panes of 10 1st Class stamps

Cover. As Type HA1, with stamp printed in brownish black by Harrison
Barcode: 100135
Composition. One pane of ten: Pane UIPH2 (10 × 1st. (brownish black) phosphorised (advanced coated) paper) with horizontal edges imperforate

Type HA1

HD1	(22.8.89)	15·00
	a. Inside cover with new rates (2.10.89)	13·00

No. HD1 was initially sold at £1·90, which was increased to £2 from 2.10.89. No. HD1 a was sold at £2.
Quantity Issued: Nos. HD1 and HD2, 4,214,850; HD1a, 5,162,550
Withdrawn: HD1 21 August 1990, HD1a 14 September 1990

As before, but cover printed by Questa
Barcode: 100135
Composition. One pane of ten: Pane UIPQ2 (10 × 1st. (brownish black) phosphorised (advanced coated) paper) printed in lithography by Questa

Type HA1

HD2	(19.9.89)	20·00

No. HD2 was initially sold at £1·90, which was increased to £2 from 2.10.89.
Withdrawn: 18 September 1990

Cover as Type HA3 printed by Harrison
Barcode: 100197
Composition. One pane of ten: Pane UIPI16 (10 × 1st. (bright orange-red) phosphorised (advanced coated) paper) with horizontal edges imperforate

Type HA3

HD3	(7.8.90)	10·00
	a. Revised "London" address inside back cover (6.8.91)	10·00
	b. Barcode printed in blue (22.9.92)	10·00

No. HD3 was, initially sold at £2, which was increased to £2·20 from 17.9.90. No. HD3a was initially sold at £2·20, which was increased to £2·40 from 16.9.91. No. HD3b was sold at £2·40.
Withdrawn: HD3 6 August 1991, HD3b 21 September 1993, HD3a 5 August 1992

As before, but cover printed by Questa
Barcode: 100197
Composition. One pane of ten: Pane UIPQ4 (10 × 1st. (bright orange-red) phosphorised (advanced coated) paper/PVAD gum. HD4 or pane UIPQ5 with PVA gum, HD4a/b) printed in lithography by Questa

Type HA3

HD4	(7.8.90)	10·00
	a. Revised "London" address inside back cover (6.8.91)	10·00
	b. Barcode printed in blue (22.9.92)	10·00

No. HD4 was initially sold at £2, which was increased to £2·20 from 17.9.90. No. HD4a was initially sold at £220. which was increased to £2·40 from 16.9.91. No. HD46 was sold at £2·40.
Withdrawn: HD4 6 August 1991, HD4a 5 August 1992, HD4b 21 September 1993

As before, but cover printed by Walsall
Barcode: 100197
Composition. One pane of ten: Pane UIPW7 (bright orange-red) phosphorised (advanced coated) paper printed in lithography by Walsall, with horizontal edges imperforate

Type HA3

HD5	Round tab (7.8.90)	10·00
	a. Round tab without shoulder cut (4.91)	10·00
	b. Revised "London" address inside back cover (6.8.91)	10·00
	c. Barcode printed in blue (22.9.92)	10·00

No. HD5 was initially sold at £2, which was increased to £2·20 from 17.9.90. Nos. HD5a/b were initially sold at £2·20. which was increased to £2·40 from 16 September 1991. No. HD5c was sold at £2·40.
Withdrawn: HD5 6 August 1991, HD5a 30 April 1992, HD5b 5 August 1992, HD5c 21 September 1993

As before, but cover as Type HA5 printed by Harrison
Cover. As Type HA5, with stamp printed in bright orange-red by Harrison
Barcode: 100197
Composition. One pane of ten: Pane UIPH6 (10 × 1st. (bright orange-red) phosphorised (advanced coated) paper with horizontal edges imperforate, printed in gravure by Harrison

Type HA5

HD6	(21.1.92)	10·00

No. HD6 was sold at £2·40.
Withdrawn: 20 January 1993

As before, but cover printed by Walsall
Cover. As Type HA5, with stamp printed in bright orange-red by Walsall
Barcode: 100197
Composition. One pane of ten: Pane UIPW7 (10 × 1st. (bright orange-red) phosphorised (advanced coated) paper/PVA gum with horizontal edges imperforate, printed in lithography by Walsall

Type HA5

HD7	(21.1.92)	10·00

No. HD7 was sold at £2·40.
Withdrawn: 20 January 1993

HD8

Des. Newell and Sorrell

Cover. As Type HD8 with stamp printed in bright orange-red by Walsall
Barcode: 100197
Composition. One pane of ten: Pane UIPW (10 × 1st. (bright orange-red) phosphorised advanced coated) paper/PVAD gum with horizontal edges imperforate. Printed in lithography by Walsall

Type HD8

HD8	Rupert posting letter (9.2.93)	10·00

No. HD8 was initially sold at £2·40, which was increased to £2·50 from 1.11.93.
Withdrawn: 8 February 1994

Changed back to cover as Type HA3, contents changed
Cover. As Type HA3, with stamp printed in bright orange-red by Harrison
Barcode: 100197
Composition. One pane of ten: Pane UIPH8 (10×1st. (bright orange-red) phosphorised (non-fluorescent coated) paper and two elliptical perf. holes on each vertical edge. Printed in gravure by Harrison

Type HA3

HD9	Harrison imprint at left (vert) (6.4.93)	12·00
a.	Harrison imprint at right (horiz) (17.8.93) .	12·00

Nos. HD9/a were initially sold at £2·40, which was increased to £2·50 from 1.11.93.
Withdrawn: No. HD9, 5 April 1994, No. HD9a. 16 August 1994

As before, but cover printed by Walsall
Cover. As Type HA3, with stamp printed in bright orange-red by Walsall
Barcode: 100197
Composition. One pane of ten: Pane UIPW14 (10×1st. (bright orange-red) two phosphor bands (yellow fluor)) and two elliptical perf. holes on each vertical edge. Printed in lithography by Walsall

Type HA3

HD10	Walsall imprint at left (vert) (6.4.93)	10·00
a.	Walsall imprint at right (horiz) (17.8.93)	10·50

Nos. HD10/a were initially sold at £2·40, which was increased to £2·50 from 1.11.93.
Withdrawn: No. HD10, 5 April 1994, No. HD10a, 16 August 1994

As before, but cover printed by Questa
Cover. As Type HA3, with stamp printed in bright orange-red by Questa
Barcode: 100197
Composition. One pane of ten: Pane UIPQ7 (10×1st. (bright orange-red) Type II (thick value) two phosphor bands (yellow fluor)) and two elliptical perf. holes on each vertical edge. Printed in lithography by Questa

Type HA3

HD11	Two line postcode notice on inside left (1.11.93)	10·00
a.	As HD 11 but three line notice (4.10.94)	10·00
b.	Containing pane No. UIPQ13 Type I (thin value) (4.10.94)	10·00

Nos. HD11/b were sold at £2·50.
Withdrawn: No. HD11, 28 April 95, Nos. HD11a/b, 3 October 1995

Change back to cover as Type HD8 but contents changed, printed by Walsall
Cover. As Type HD8, with stamp printed in bright orange-red by Walsall
Barcode: 100197
Composition. One pane of ten: Pane UIPW14 (10×1st. (bright orange-red) two 3·5 mm phosphor bands (yellow fluor)) and two elliptical perf. holes on each vertical edge. Printed in lithography by Walsall

Type HD8, but without price on back cover

HD12	(1.11.93)	10·00
a.	Containing pane No. UIPW18 (7·5 mm bands) (4.7.94)	10·00

Nos. HD12/a were sold at £2·50
Withdrawn: No. HD12, 28 April 1995. No. HD12a was sold out soon after issue.

Type HD13
Inscribed "FREE POSTCARDS"

Cover. As Type HD13, with stamp printed in bright orange-red by Walsall
Barcode: 100197
Composition. As for No. HD12 but with an additional page describing the Greetings Stamps postcard offer

Type HD13

Free Postcards

HD13	"FREE POSTCARDS" at right (22.2.94)	10·00
a.	Miscut pane No. UIPW14A (yellow fluor)	—

No. HD13 was sold at £2·50.
Withdrawn: 28 April 1995

As before, but cover changed back as Type HD8 with Kite Offer Cover.
As Type HD8, with stamp printed in bright orange-red by Walsall
Barcode: 100197
Composition. As for No. HD12a

Type HD8

Win a kite offer

HD14	"Better luck next time" inside back cover (1.7.94)	10·00
HD15	"You've Won!" inside back cover (1.7.94)	10·00

Nos. HD14/15 each sold at £2·50 and were initially only available from branches of W. H. Smith and Son. They were issued in connection with a competition in which the prizes were Paddington Bear kites. The booklets were not available from Royal Mail philatelic outlets until 4 October 1994.
Withdrawn: 3 October 1995

HD16
Stampers (woodblock rubber stamp) offer

Cover. As Type HD16, inscribed "ORDER YOURS INSIDE" on yellow tab at right and printed by Walsall
Barcode: 100197
Composition. As for No. HD12a

Type HD16

HD16	"DO NOT OPEN UNTIL" (padlock) (20.9.94)	10·00
HD17	"KEEP IN TOUCH" (globe and letters) (20.9.94)	10·00
HD18	"HAPPY BIRTHDAY" (balloons and letter) (20.9.94)	10·00
HD19	"What's Happenin'?" (20.9.94)	10·00

Nos. HD16/19 were sold at £2·50 each.
Sold out: November 1994

Cover as Type HA8, printed by Harrison and contents changed
Cover. As Type HA8, with stamps printed in bright orange-red by Harrison
Barcode: 100197
Composition. As for No. HD9

Type HA8

HD20	(10.1.95)	12·00

As before, but cover printed by Questa
Cover. As Type HA8, with stamps printed in orange-red by Questa
Barcode: 100197
Composition. As for No. HD11b

Type HA8

HD21	Containing pane No. UIPQ13 (yellow fluor) (10.1.95)	10·00
a.	Containing pane No. UIPQ15 (blue fluor) (18.7.95)	10·00

As before, but cover printed by Walsall
Cover. As Type HA8. with stamps printed in bright orange-red by Walsall
Barcode: 100197
Composition. As for No. HD12a

Type HA8

HD22	Containing pane No. UIPW18 (yellow fluor) (10.1.95)	10·00
a.	Containing pane No. UIPW22 (blue fluor) (22.8.95)	10·50

Nos. HD20/22a were initially sold at £2·50 each, which was increased to £2·60 from 8.7.96.
Withdrawn: Nos. HD20/22, 30 November 1995, No. HD21a, 17 July 1996, No. HD22a, 31 July 1996

Type HD23
Thorntons "Sun Chocolates" Offer

Cover. As Type HD23, inscribed "DETAILS INSIDE" on yellow tab at right and printed by Walsall
Barcode: 100197
Composition. As for No. HD12a
Type HD23, Thorntons Chocolates Offer

HD23	"DETAILS INSIDE" at right (14.2.95)R	10·00

No. HD23 was sold at £2·50.
Withdrawn: 13 February 1996

Change back to cover as Type HA8, contents changed, printed by Harrison
Cover. As Type HA8, with stamps printed in bright orange-red by Harrison
Barcode: 100197
Composition. One pane of ten: Pane UIPH10 (10 × 1st. (bright orange-red) two bands (yellow fluor)) and two elliptical perf. holes on each vertical edge. Printed in gravure by Harrison

Type HA8

HD24	(4.4.95)	10·00
a.	Containing pane No. UIPH12 (blue fluor) (18.7.95)	10·00

Nos. HD24a were initially sold at £2·50 each, which was increased to £2·60 from 8.7.96.
Withdrawn: No. HD24. 30 November 1995, No. HD24a, 17 July 1996

As before, but cover printed by Walsall
Cover. As Type HA8, with stamps printed in orange-red and inscribed "WHSmith Special Offer" on yellow tab at right, printed by Walsall
Barcode: 100197
Composition. As for No. HD12a

Type HA8

WHSmith Stationery offer

HD25	"WHSmith Special Offer" at right (24.4.95)	9·00

No. HD25 was sold at £2·50 and was initially only available from WHSmith branches and offered 50p. off the purchase of own brand stationery. The booklet did not become available from the Philatelic Bureau until 3 October 1995. The price was increased to £2·60 from 8.7.96.
Withdrawn: 2 October 1996

As before, but cover printed by Questa
Cover. As Type HA8, with stamps printed in orange-red and inscribed "Sainsbury's Promotion" on yellow tab at right, printed by Questa
Barcode: 100197
Composition. As for HD11b

Type HA8

Sainsbury's Promotion

HD26	"Sainsbury's Promotion" at right (26.6.95)	9·00

No. HD26, sold at £2·50 and initially only available from Sainsbury's branches, offered the chance to win a year's free shopping. The booklet was not placed on philatelic sale until 4 September 1995. The price was increased to £2·60 from 8.7.96.
Withdrawn: 3 September 1996

HD27
Ceramic Figures

Cover. As Type HD27, printed by Harrison
Barcode: 100197
Composition. As for No. HD24a

Type HD27

HD27	Benjy Bear and Harry Hedgehog offer (4.9.95)	9·00
	a. Black square on cover	9·00

No. HD27/a were initially sold at £2·50 each, which was increased to £2·60 on 8.7.96.

In order to monitor this offer booklets sold through retail outlets, No. HD27a, were printed with a small black square on the outside back Cover. Those booklets sold from post offices did not have this mark.
Withdrawn: 3 September 1996

Cover as Type HA10, printed by Walsall and contents changed
Cover. As Type HA10, with stamps printed in bright orange-red by Walsall
Barcode: 100197
Composition. As for No. HD22a

Type HA10

Olympic symbols

HD28	(6.2.96)	8·00

No. HD28 was initially sold at £2·50, which was increased to £2·60 from 8.7.90.
Withdrawn: 5 February 1997

HD29

Cover. As Type HD29, printed by Harrison
Barcode: 100197
Composition. As for No. HD24a

Type HD29

Walt Disney World

HD29	"DETAILS INSIDE" on yellow tab at right (19.2.96)	8·00

No. HD29 with a scratchcard was initially sold at £2·50, which was increased to £2·60 from 8.7.96.
Withdrawn: 18 February 1997

Changed back to cover as Type HA10, printed by Harrison
Cover. As Type HA10, with stamps printed in bright orange-red by Harrison
Barcode: 100197
Composition. As for No. HD24a

Type HA10

Olympic symbols

HD30 (19.3.96)	10·00

No. HD30 was initially sold at £2·50, which was increased to £2·60 from 8.7.96.
Withdrawn: 18 March 1997

Type HD31
Woman lighting Olympic torch

Cover. As Type HD31, with shot put scratchcard printed by Harrison Barcode 100197
Composition. As for No. HD24a

Type HD31

Olympic Games

HD31	Shot Put (13.5.96)	8·00
HD32	Hurdles (13.5.96)	8·00
HD33	Archery (13.5.96)	8·00

Nos. HD31/33 each show a scratchcard on reverse based on different Olympic events. Prices are for covers with unused scratchcards.

Nos. HD31/33 were initially sold at £2·50 each, which was increased to £2·60 from 8.7.96.
Withdrawn: 12 May 1997

> **NOTE**. From No. HD34 onwards the printer of each booklet is identified by a small capital letter below the barcode on the outside back cover.

HD34
"First Class Stamps" ranged left and without white diagonal line on stamps
Cover. As Type HD34, with stamps printed in bright orange-red and inscribed "WHSmith Offer Inside" on yellow tab at right, printed by Walsall
Barcode: 100197
Composition. As for No. HD22a

WHSmith Leisure Guide Offer

HD34	"WHSmith Offer Inside" at right (15.7.96)	8·00

No. HD34 was sold at £2·60 and was initially only available from branches of WHSmith and Sons. It was issued in connection with a special offer of AA/OS Leisure Guides. The booklets were not available from Royal Mail philatelic outlets until 17 September 1996.
Withdrawn: 14 July 1997

HD35
"First Class Stamps" ranged left with white diagonal lines

Cover. As Type HD35, with stamps printed in bright orange-red by Harrison
Barcode: 100197
Composition. As for No. HD24a

Type HD35

Olympic symbols

HD35	(6.8.96)	10·00

No. HD35 was sold at £2·60.
Withdrawn: 5 August 1997

As before, but printed in lithography by Walsall
Cover. As Type HD34, but without inside special offer, printed by Walsall
Barcode: 100197
Composition. As lot No. HD22a

Type HD34

HD36	(6.8.96)	8·00

No. HD36 was sold at £2·60.
Withdrawn: 5 August 1997

Type HD37
Send-a-Cake Offer Cover.

Cover. As Type HD37, printed by Walsall
Composition. As for No. HD22a

Type HD37.

"Send-a-cake" Offer

HD37	(9.9.96)	8·00
a. Black square on outside back cover		8·00

No. HD37 was sold at £2·60.
To monitor this offer booklets sold through retail outlets. No. HD37a. were printed with a small black square on the outside back cover below the barcode "5". Those booklets sold from post offices did not have this mark.
Withdrawn: No. HD37a, 8 September 1997

As before, but ASDA Greetings card voucher offer
Cover. As Type HD34, with stamps printed in bright orange-red and inscribed "Offer Inside" on yellow tab at right and printed by Walsall
Barcode: 100197
Composition. As for No. HD22a

Type HD34

ASDA Voucher for Greetings Cards

HD38	"Offer Inside" at right (7.10.96)	8·R00

No. HD38 was sold at £2·60 and was initially only available from ASDA stores with an offer of £1 off the cost of four single greetings cards, until 31.12.96. The booklet was not placed on philatelic sale until 13.1.97.
Withdrawn: 12 January 1998

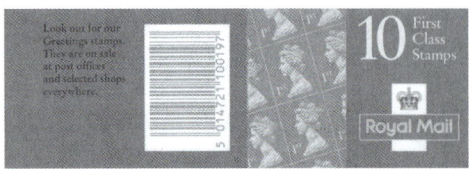

HD39
(1st) Class stamps in bright orange-red

Cover. As Type HD39, with stamps printed in bright orange-red by Harrison
Barcode: 100197
Composition. As for No. HD24a

Type HD39

HD39	(4.2.97)	8·00
a. Containing pane No. UIPH12A (PVA gum (bluish)) (4.97)		25·00
b. Containing pane No. UIPH16 (computer engraved cyl.) (8.11.97)		8·00

Nos. HD39/a/b were sold at £2·60.
Withdrawn: No. HD39, 3 February 1998; HD39b, 30 April 1999 and HD39a was sold out soon after issue.

As before, but printed by Walsall in lithography
Cover. As Type HD39, with stamps printed in bright orange-red by Walsall
Barcode: 100197
Composition. As for No. HD22a

Type HD39

HD40	(4.2.97)	8·00

No. HD40 was sold at £2·60
Withdrawn: 3 February 1998

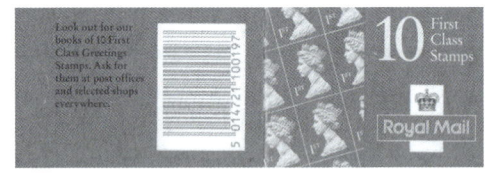

HD41
Royal Golden Wedding (21 April–15 September 1997) (1st) Class stamps in gold

Cover. As Type HD41, with stamps printed in gold by Harrison
Barcode: 100197
Composition. One pane of ten: Pane UIPH15 (10 × 1st (gold) two bands (blue fluor)) and two elliptical perf. holes on each vertical edge. Printed in gravure by Harrison

Type HD41

HD41	(21.4.97)	9·00

No. HD41 was sold at £2·60.
Withdrawn: 20 April 1998

As before, but printed by Walsall
Cover. As Type HD41, with stamps printed in gold by Walsall
Barcode: 100197
Composition. One pane of ten: Pane WP1132 (10 × 1st (gold) two bands (blue fluor)) and two elliptical perf. holes on each vertical edge. Printed in gravure by Walsall.

Type HD41

HD42	(21.4.97)	8·50

No. HD42 was sold at £2·60.
Withdrawn: 20 April 1998

HD43
Holiday Promotion (1st) Class stamps in gold

Cover. As Type HD43, with stamps printed in gold by Harrison
Composition. As for No. HD41

Type HD43

Holiday Promotion Offer

HD43	"OPEN FOR DETAILS" at right (15.9.97)	8·00

No. HD43 was sold at £2·60.
Withdrawn: 14 September 1998

Change back to cover as Type HD39, contents changed, printed by Walsall
Cover. As Type HD39, with stamps printed in bright orange-red by Walsall
Barcode: 100197
Composition. One pane often: Pane UIPW30 (10 × 1st (bright orange-red) two bands (blue fluor)) and two elliptical perf. holes on each vertical edge. Printed in gravure by Walsall

Type HD39

HD44	Horizontal imprint (8.11.97)	7·75
	a. Revised validity notice and vert. imprint (5.5.98)	7·75
	b. As a but 1st class rate no longer valid to Europe (16.3.99)	7·75

Nos. HD44/a were sold at £2·60 and increased to £2·70 from 27.4.00
Withdrawn: No. HD44, 7 November 1998; HD44a, 15 March 2000; HD44b, 30 August 2000

HD45
Win a Holiday to Disney Offer

Cover. As Type HD45, printed by De La Rue
Barcode: 100197
Composition. One pane of ten: Pane UIPH16 (10 × 1st (bright orange-red) two bands (blue fluor)) and two elliptical perf. holes on each vertical edge. Printed in gravure by De La Rue

Type HD45

Disney's Animal Kingdom Scratchcard

HD45	"See reverse for Scratch and Win" at right (2.2.98)	8·00

"D" appears on the back cover replacing "H" of Harrison. No. HD45 was sold at £2·60.
Withdrawn: 1 February 1999

Type HD46
Win a Peugeot 106 Offer

Cover. As Type HD46, printed by De La Rue
Barcode: 100197
Composition. As for No. HD45

Type HD46

Win a Peugeot 106

HD46	"WIN A PEUGEOT 106" at right (27.4.98)	8·00

These booklets were not available from Royal Mail philatelic outlets until 23 June 1998. No. HD46 was sold at £2·60.
Withdrawn: 22 June 1999

Change back to Type HD39 but printed by De La Rue
Cover. As Type HD39, with stamps printed in bright-orange-red by De La Rue
Barcode: 100197
Composition. One pane of ten: Pane UIPH16 (10 × 1st. (bright orange-red) two bands (blue fluor)) and two elliptical perf. holes on each vertical edge. Printed in gravure by De La Rue

Type HD39

HD47	Printer's imprint "D" on reverse (5.5.98)	7·75

No. HD47 was sold at £2·60. Available earlier than the Bureau date, first reported on 19 March 1998.

HD48
Win a JVC Camcorder Offer

Cover. As Type HD48, printed by De La Rue
Barcode: 100197
Composition. As for No. HD47

Type HD48

Win a JVC Camcorder

HD48	JVC Camcorder design (1.7.98)	8·00

No. HD48 was inscribed "WIN A JVC CAMCORDER" on yellow tab at right. These booklets were not available from Royal Mail philatelic outlets until 27 August 1998.
No. HD48 was sold at £2·60.
Withdrawn: 26 August 1999

HD49
"Create a Card" Promotion

Cover: As Type HD49, printed by De La Rue
Barcode: 100197
Composition. As for No. HD47

Type HD49

"Create a Card" Promotion

HD49	"Make their post memorable" (3.8.98)	8·00

No. HD49 was inscribed "See inside for offer details" on yellow tab at right.
No. HD49 was sold at £2·60. This booklet was not placed on philatelic sale until 7 September 1998.
Withdrawn: 6 September 1999

Change back to Type HD39 but printed by Questa in lithography

Cover. As Type HD39, with stamps printed in bright orange-red by Questa
Barcode: 100197
Composition. One pane of ten: Pane UIPQ15b (10 × 1st. (bright orange-red) Type I (thin value) two phosphor band, (blue fluor)) and two elliptical perf. holes on each vertical edge. Printed in lithography by Questa.

Type HD39

HD50	Printer's imprint "Q" on reverse (7.9.98)	8·00

No HD50 was sold at £2·60.
Withdrawn: 6 September 1999

As before, but printed in gravure by Questa

Cover. As Type HD39. with stamps printed in bright orange-red by Questa
Barcode: 100197
Composition. One pane of ten: Pane UIPQ17 (10 × 1st. (bright orange-red) two bands (blue fluor)) and two elliptical perf. holes on each vertical edge. Printed in photogravure by Questa

Type HD39

HD51	Printer's imprint "Q" on reverse (1.12.98)	14·00
a.	As last, but 1st class rate no longer valid to Europe (16.3.99)	14·75

No. HD51 was sold at £2·60.
Withdrawn: 30 August 2000

Pane of 10 1st class stamps

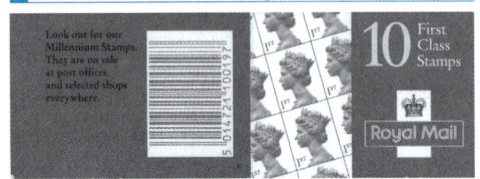

HD52
Printer's Initial on reverse

Cover. As Type HD52, with Millennium stamps printed in olive-brown by Questa.
Barcode: 100197
Composition. One pane of ten: Pane UIPPQ18 (10×1st (olive-brown) two bands (blue fluor)) and two elliptical perf. holes on each vertical edge. Printed in gravure by Questa.

Type HD52

HD52	Printer's imprint "Q" on reverse (6.1.00)	8·00
a.	New website address and phone no. (14.3.00)	8·00

Nos. HD52/a were initally sold at £2·60 which was increased to £2·70 from 27.4.00.

As before, but cover printed by Walsall

Cover. As Type HD52, with Millennium stamps printed in olive-brown by Walsall.
Barcode: 100197
Composition. One pane of ten: Pane UIPW35 (10×1st (olive-brown) two bands (blue fluor)) and two elliptical perf. holes on each vertical edge. Printed in gravure by Walsall.

Type HD52

HD53	Printer's imprint "W" on reverse (6.1.00)	8·00
a.	New website address and phone no. (14.3.00)	8·00

Nos. HD53/a were initally sold at £2·60 which was increased to £2·70 from 27.4.00.
Withdrawn: 28 April 1995

Panes of 4 (E) European Air Mail stamps

Type HF1
"European Airmail Stamps" ranged left

Cover. As Type HF1, printed in scarlet, lemon, blue, deep blue and black by Walsall
Barcode: 104744
Composition. One pane of four: Pane UEAP1 (4 × (E) two bands (blue fluor)) and two elliptical perf. holes on each vertical edge. Printed in gravure by Walsall

Type HF1

HF1	"For items up to 20g" at right (19.1.99)	4·50
a.	New website address and phone no. (27.4.00)	4·50

With four airmail labels affixed to inside cover.
No. HF1 was initially sold at £1·20 each, which was increased to £1·36 from 25.10.99.
For other covers inscribed "European Airmail Stamps" see Nos. GGA1/2 in the Barcode Machin Booklet Section C.
Nos. HF1a was initally sold at £1·44.

E. Barcode Penny Black Anniversary Booklets (1990)

These booklets all have laminated covers, printed in scarlet, yellow and black. The panes either consist of four or ten stamps and booklet covers show the stamp printed in bright blue (15p.) or brownish black (20p.).
For other booklets containing Penny Black Anniversary stamps see, Nos. FB56 (50p.), FH19/20 (£1) and DX11 (£5 London Life prestige booklet). See *G.B. Specialised Vol. 4, Part 1*.

60p. Booklet

JA1

Des. Design House Consultants

Cover. As Type JA1, with stamp printed in bright blue by Walsall
Barcode: 100142
Composition. One pane of four: Pane WP808 (4×15p. centre band) imperforate on three edges, printed in lithography by Walsall

Type JA1

JA1	(30.1.90)		7·00
	a.	Queen Victoria's head in cream	7·00

Withdrawn: 29 January 1991

80p. Booklets

Cover. As Type JA1, with stamp printed in brownish black and cream by Walsall
Barcode: 100128
Composition. One pane of four: Pane WP809 (4×20p. phosphorised (advanced coated) paper) imperforate on three edges and printed in lithography by Walsall

Type JA1

JB1 (30.1.90)	10·00

Withdrawn: 29 January 1991

As before, but cover printed by Walsall and pane by Harrison
Barcode: 100128
Composition. One pane of four: Pane WP803 (4×20p. phosphorised (advanced coated) paper) imperforate on three edges and printed in gravure by Harrison

Type JA1

JB2	(17.4.90)		8·00
	a.	Cream omitted (Queen Victoria's head)	9·00

Withdrawn: 16 April 1991

£1·50 Booklets

JC1
Des. Design House Consultants

Cover. As Type JC1, with stamp printed in bright blue by Harrison
Barcode: 100159
Composition. One pane of ten: Pane WP799 (10×15p. centre band) with horizontal edges imperforate

Type JC1

JC1	(30.1.90)	10·00

Withdrawn: 29 January 1991

As before, but cover printed by Questa
Barcode: 100159
Composition. One pane of ten: Pane WP811 (10×15p. short centre band) printed in lithography by Questa

Type JC1

JC2	(17.4.90)	20·00

Withdrawn: 16 April 1991

As before, but cover printed by Walsall
Barcode: 100159
Composition. One pane of ten: Pane WP811 (10×15p. centre band) imperforate on three edges and printed in lithography by Walsall

Type JC1

JC3	(12.6.90)		12·00
	a.	Incorrect rate panel	12·00

The wrong rates panel used in booklet No. JC3a shows the UK letters and cards rate to 60g. instead of 200g. in booklet No. JC3

£2 Booklets

Cover. As Type JC1, with stamp printed in brownish black and cream by Harrison
Barcode: 100135
Composition. One pane of ten: Pane WP800 (10×20p. phosphorised (advanced coated) paper) with horizontal edges imperforate

Type JC1

JD1	(30.1.90)	11·00

Withdrawn: 29 January 1991

As before, but cover with stamp printed in brownish black by Questa
Barcode: 100135
Composition. One pane of ten: Pane WP814 (10×20p. phosphorised (advanced coated) paper) printed in lithography by Questa

Type JC1

JD2	(17.4.90)	22·00

Withdrawn: 16 April 1991

As before, but with stamp printed in brownish black and cream by Walsall
Barcode: 100135
Composition. One pane of ten: Pane WP814 (10×20p. phosphorised (advanced coated) paper) imperforate on three edges and printed in lithography by Walsall

Type JC1

JD3	(12.6.90)	16·00

Withdrawn: 11 June 1991

F. Barcode Greetings Stamp Booklets (1990–98)

£2 1990. Greetings Booklet (stamps inscribed 20p.)

KX1
(Actual size 184 × 69 mm)

Des. Michael Peters and Partners Limited

Cover. As Type KX1, with smile shaped cut out to show stamps inside. Printed in scarlet, yellow and black on surfaced card
Barcode: 100173
Composition. One pane of ten not attached by selvedge: Pane UMP17 (10 × 20p. Nos. UM7/16, with two bands) with margins all round and folded between rows 3/4. Separate sheet (3 × 4) of greetings labels with margins all round

Type KX1

KX1 "Smile" design cut out showing stamps inside (6.2.90) 30·00

Withdrawn: 5 February 1991

1991. Pane of 10 1st Class Greetings stamps

KX2
(Actual size 184×69 mm)

(Des. Tony Meeuwissen)

Cover. As Type KX2 printed scarlet, lemon, blue and black by Harrison
Barcode: 100241
Composition. One pane of ten: Pane UMP28 (10×1st. Nos. UM18/27, with two bands). Margins top and bottom and narrow gutter margin between stamps and a panel of greetings labels (3×4) on fluorescent coated paper. Attached by the selvedge

Type KX2

KX2 "Good Luck" charms design (5.2.91) 15·00

No. KX2 was initially sold at £2·20, which was increased to £2·40 from 16.9.91
Withdrawn: 4 February 1992

1991. Pane of 10 1st Class Greetings stamps

KX3
(Actual size 184×69 mm)

Des. Michael Peters and Partners Limited

Cover. As Type KX3 printed in scarlet, lemon, blue and black by Harrison
Barcode: 100258
Composition. One pane of ten: Pane UMP39 (10×1st Nos. UM29/38, with two bands). Margins top and bottom and narrow margin between stamps and a panel of greetings labels (3×4) on fluorescent coated paper. Attached by the selvedge

Type KX3

KX3	"Laughing pillar box" design (26.3.91)	12·00
a.	Additional European destinations inside cover (3.3.92)	12·00

No. KX3 was initially sold at £2·20, which was increased to £2·40 from 16.9.91. No. KX3a was initially sold at £2·40. which was increased to £2·50 from 1.11.93.
Withdrawn: No. KX3, 25 March 1993, No. KX3a, 29 March 1996

1992. Pane of 10 1st Class Greetings stamps

KX4
(Actual size 185×69 mm)

Des. Trickett and Webb Limited

Cover. As Type KX4 printed in scarlet, lemon, blue and black by Harrison
Barcode: 100319
Composition. One pane of ten: Pane UMP50 (10×1st. Nos. UM40/49, with two bands). Margins top and bottom and narrow gutter margin between stamps and a panel of greetings labels (3×4) on fluorescent coated paper. Attached by the selvedge

Type KX4

KX4 "Memories" pressed flowers design (28.1.92) 13·00

No. KX4 was initially sold at £2·40, which was increased to £2·50 from 1.11.93.
Withdrawn: 30 June 1997

1993. Pane of 10 1st Class Greetings stamps

KX5
(Actual size 185×60 mm)

Des. Newell and Sorrell

Cover. As Type KX5 printed in scarlet, lemon, blue, green. rosine and black by Harrison
Barcode: 100791
Composition. One pane of ten: Pane UMP61 (10×1st. Nos. UM51/60, with two side phosphor bands). Narrow gutter margin between stamps and block of twenty labels (5×4) on non-fluorescent coated paper. Folded five times and attached by the common gutter margin

Type KX5

KX5	"Gift Giving" Rupert and Children's Characters design (2.2.93)	11·00
a.	Inside back cover reads Thomson for Thompson (bottom line at left) (15.6.93)	11·00
b.	As KX5a but designer's name at right changed from Sorell to Sorrell (17.8.93)	11·00

Nos. KX5/a,b were initially sold at £2·40, which was increased to £2·50 from 1.1 1.93.
Withdrawn: No. KX5, October 1994, No. KX5a/b, 29 March 1996

1994. Pane of 10 1st Class Greetings stamps

KX6
(Actual size 185 × 60 mm)

Des. Newell and Sorrell

Cover. As Type KX6 printed in scarlet, lemon, blue, green, rosine and black by Harrison
Barcode: 101033
Composition. One pane of ten: Pane UMP73 (10 × 1st. Nos. UM63/72, with two side phosphor bands (yellow fluor)). Narrow gutter margin between stamps and block of twenty labels (5 × 4) on non-fluorescent coated paper. Folded five times and attached by the common gutter margin

Type KX6

KX6	"Messages" Rupert, Paddington Bear and the Ice Dragon (1.2.94)	13·00

No. KX6 was initially sold at £2·50 which was increased to £2·60 from 8.7.96.
Quantitiy Sold: 5,414,100
Sold out: February 1998

1995. Pane of 10 1st Class Greetings stamps

KX7
(Actual size 185 × 60 mm)

Des. Newell and Sorrell

Cover. As Type KX7 printed in scarlet, lemon, blue, new blue, green. rosine and black by Walsall
Barcode: 102313
Composition. One pane of ten: Pane UMP84 (10 × 1st Nos. UM74/83, with two side phosphor bands (yellow fluor)). Narrow gutter margin between stamps and block of twenty labels (5 × 4) on non-fluorescent coated paper. Folded five times and attached by the common gutter margin

Type KX7

KX7	Clown holding letter with "Pull Open" on yellow strip (21.3.95) 2,023,125 (1.01.BPB)	11·50
	a. Containing pane No. UMP95 (blue fluor) without inscription (5.2.96)	12·00

Nos. KX7/a were initially sold at £2·50 which was increased to £2·60 from 8.7.96 and £2·70 from 27.4.00.
Withdrawn: Nos. KX7/a 1 November 2000

1996. Pane of 10 1st Class Greetings stamps

Type KX8
(Actual size 185 × 60 mm)
Des. Michael Wolff

Cover. As Type KX8 printed in scarlet, lemon, new blue, green and black by Walsall
Barcode: 102511
Composition. One pane of ten: Pane UMP106 (10 × 1st Nos. UM96/105, on "all over" phosphor (blue fluor)). From 11.11.96 Pane UMP117 phosphor bands. Narrow gutter margin between stamps and block of twenty labels (5 × 4) on non-fluorescent coated paper. Folded five times and attached by the common gutter margin

Type KX8

KX8	"MORE! LOVE" cartoon design (26.2.96) 4,466,250 (all ptgs)(1.01.BPB)	10·00
	a. Containing pane No. UMP117 (short wave bands) (11.11.96)	38·00
	b. Containing pane No. UMP117a (long wave bands) (9.98)	38·00

No. KX8 was initially sold at £2·50, which was increased to £2·60 from 8.7.96. No. KX8a was sold at £2·60 which was increased to £2·70 from 23.4.00.
No. KX8a shows a redesigned inside front cover which omits references to 1996 dates and it was sold by the Bureau from 25.11.96.
Withdrawn: 1 November 2000

1997. Pane of 10 1st Class Greetings stamps

KX9
(Actual size 185 × 60 min.)
Des. Tutssels

Cover. As Type KX10 printed in scarlet, lemon, new blue, green and black by Walsall
Barcode: 102849
Composition. One pane of ten: Pane UMP128 (10 × 1st. UM118/27, with two side phosphor bands (blue fluor)). Narrow gutter margin between stamps and block of twenty labels (5 × 4) on non-fluorescent coated paper. Folded five times and attached by the common gutter margin

Type KX9

KX9	*Gentiana acaulis* design (6.1.97) 12, 210, 350 (all ptgs)(1.01 BPB)	11·25
	a. Containing pane No. UMP128a (long wave phos.)	11·25
	b. As a but 1st class rate no longer valid to Europe (16.3.99)	11·25

Nos KX9/b were sold at £2·60 which eas increased to £2·70 from 27.4.00
Withdrawn: 1 November 2000

1997. Pane of 10 1st Class Greetings stamps

KX10
(Actual size 185 × 60 mm)
Des. Tutssels

Cover. As Type KX10 printed in scarlet, lemon, new blue, green and black by Walsall
Barcode: 102849
Composition. As for No. KX9/9a

Type KX10

Win a Beautiful Bouquet Instantly?

KX10   *Gentiana acaulis* design (3.2.97)   12·00

No. KX10 was printed with a scratch card on the inside back cover inscribed "Open now—See if you've won" on a yellow tab at right.
No. KX10 was sold at £2·60.
Number sold was included with that given for No. KX9.
Withdrawn: 4 January 1999

1998. Pane of 10 1st Class Greetings stamps

KX11
(Actual size 185 × 60 mm)

Des. Tutssels

Cover. As Type KX11 printed in scarlet, lemon, new blue, green and black by Walsall
Barcode: 102849
Composition. As for No. KX9a

Type KX11

"Send Some 1st Class Chocolates"

KX11   Chocolate Box inscribed "Just to Say" (5.1.98)   12·00

No. KX11 was printed with a chocolate box offer from ChocExpress on reverse. Inscribed "See reverse for special offer" on yellow tab at right.
No. KX11 was sold at £2·60.
Withdrawn: 4 January 1999

1998. Pane of 10 1st Class Greetings stamps

KX12
(Actual size 185 × 60 mm)

Cover. As Type KX12 printed in scarlet, lemon, new blue, green and black by Walsall
Barcode: 102849
Composition. One pane of ten: Pane UMP128a two side phosphor bands (blue fluor)). Narrow gutter margin between stamps and block of twenty labels (5 × 4) on non-fluorescent coated paper. Folded five times and attached by the common gutter margin

Type KX12

"Create a Card" Promotion

KX12   "Make their post memorable" (3.8.98*)   12·00

No. KX12 was inscribed "See inside for offer details" on yellow tab at right.
No. KX12 was sold at £2·60.
*No. KX12 was issued in the Midlands postal region on 3.8.98 and the rest of the country including philatelic outlets on 7.9.98.
Withdrawn: 6 September 1999

H. Self-adhesive Barcode Booklets containing No Value Indicated stamps

General Notes

These barcode booklets containing Machin stamps as Types **SA4/5** in Section UJ, replaced the stocks of gummed booklets which were withdrawn on 31 March 2001. They were issued with the self-adhesive sheets which had been issued on 4 September 2000 in certain areas as a trial.
Booklets containing panes of 6 and 12 stamps were retail booklets sold over the counter. Booklets containing 10 stamps were intended for vending machines.
Booklet No. HE1 issued on 19 October 1993 will be relisted as MG1 in this section of booklets containing self-adhesive.

The following booklets were printed by Questa or Walsall

Pane of 6 2nd class stamps (Bright blue)

MA1

Cover. As Type MA1, with Machin stamps printed in bright blue by Walsall.
Barcode: 112275
Composition. One pane of six: Pane UJPW2 (bright blue) centre band (blue fluor)) and two elliptical perf. holes on each vertical edge. Printed in gravure by Walsall.

Type MA1

MA1   (29.1.01)   4·00
  a. "www.royalmail.com" outside back cover
     (1.8.01)   4·00

No. MA1/a were sold at £1·14

Pane of 6 1st class stamps (Bright orange-red)

Cover. As Type MA1, with Machin stamps printed in bright orange-red by Walsall.
Barcode: 112268
Composition. One pane of six: Pane UJPW3 (bright orange-red) two bands (blue fluor)) and two elliptical perf. holes on each vertical edge. Printed in gravure by Walsall.

Type MA1

MB1	(29.1.01)	6·00
a.	"www.royalmail.com" outside back cover (1.8.01)	6·00

Nos. MB1/a were sold at £1·62

Death Centenary of Queen Victoria

MB2

Cover. As Type MB2, with Machin stamps and portrait of Queen Victoria by Walsall.
Barcode: 112268 (printed in black)
Composition. One pane of six and label at left: Pane UJPW4 (61st bright orange-red)) two bands (blue fluor)) and two elliptical perf. holes on each vertical edge and die-cut perf. label at left printed in gold, grey and black. Printed in gravure by Walsall.

Type MA2

MB2	(29.1.01)	14·00

No. MB2 was sold at £1·62

Panes of 6 1st class stamps (gold)

MB3

Cover. As Type MB3, with gold laminated cover by Questa.
Barcode: 112268
Composition. One pane of six: Pane UJPQ5 (6×1st (gold) two bands (blue fluor)) and two elliptical perf. holes on each vertical edge. Printed in gravure by Questa.

Type MB3

MB3	(5.6.02)	5·00

No. MB3 Was sold at £1·62 and shows a single notch at the top right hand edge to facilitate identification by the blind.

As before but printed by Walsall

Cover. As Type MB3, printed in gold by Walsall.
Barcode: 112268
Composition. One pane of six: Pane UJPW6 (6×1st (gold) two bands (blue fluor)) and two elliptical perf. holes on each vertical edge. Printed in gravure by Walsall with matrix removed.

Type MB3

MB4	(5.04) Walsall imprint 29mm at left	5·00

No. MB4 was initially sold at £1·68.
Type MB4 shows the Walsall imprint as 34mm at left. There was no actual date of issue.

MB4a

Cover. As Type MB4a, printed in gold by Walsall
Barcode: 112268
Composition. One pane of six: Pane UJPW10 (6×1st (gold) two bands (blue fluor)) and two elliptical perf. holes on each vertical edge. Printed in gravure by Walsall with matrix removed. Self adhesive Smilers advertisement at left.

Type MB4a

MB4a	Inside Cover with first Smilers advertisement (27.1.05)	4·25
aa.	Imprint 29mm (6.04)	5·00
ab.	Second Smilers advertisement (26.7.05)	4·75
b.	Back cover with added text about new pricing structure (25.4.06)	5·50
c.	Inside cover with "To find correct postcodes for your mail" notice (5.6.07)	4·25
d.	Inside cover with commemorative inscription for Machin Anniversary (5.6.07)	4·25
e.	Inside cover with Harry Potter advert "STAMPS MAKE MAGICAL GIFTS"(28.8.07)	4·25
f.	Inside cover with English and Welsh language postcode text (20.9.07)	4·25
g.	Inside cover with *Carry On* stamps advertisement (10.6.08)	4·25

No. MB4a was initially sold at £1·68, which was increased to £1·80 from 7.4.05. This booklet was produced to see if other Royal Mail products could be advertised via the retail stamp booklets.

There is no advert on the inside front cover facing pane No. UJPW6. No. MB4b was sold at £1·92
No. MB4c/d was initially sold at £2·04 which was increased to £2·16 From 7.4.08.
No. MB4e was initially sold at £2·04, which was increased to £2·16 From 7.4.08.
No. MB4f was initially sold at £2·04 which was increased to £2·16 from 7.4.08.No.
MB4g was initially sold at £2·16, which was increased to £2·34 From 6.4.09.

A notch at top right of cover, was for identification by the blind.

Pane of 6 1st class stamps (Bright orange-red)

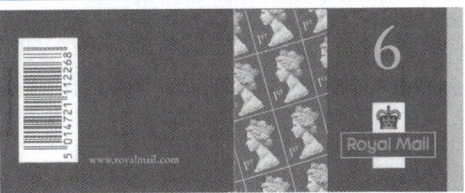

MB5

Appendix J Booklets

Cover. As Type MB5, with Machin stamps printed in bright orange-red by Questa.
Barcode: 112268
Composition. One pane of six: Pane UJPQ6 (6×1st (bright orange-red) two bands (blue fluor)) and two elliptical perf. holes on each vertical edge. Printed in gravure by Questa with matrix intact.

Type MB5

MB5	(4.7.02)	5·00

No. MB5 was initially sold at £1·62 which was increased to £1·68 from 8.5.03.

Panes of 6 1st class stamps (gold)

MB6
"The Real Network" added below logo

Cover. As Type MB6, printed in gold by Walsall
Barcode: 112268
Composition. One pane of six: Pane UJPW6 (6×1st (gold) two bands (blue fluor)) and two elliptical perf. holes on each vertical edge. Printed in gravure by Walsall with matrix removed.

Type MB6

MB6	(27.3.03)	5·00

No. MB6 was initially sold at £1·62 which was increased to £1·68 From 8.5.03.

MB7
("Supporting London 2012")

Cover. As Type MB7, printed in gold by Walsall
Barcode: 112268
Composition. One pane of six: Pane UJPW9 (6×1st (gold) two bands (blue fluor)) and two elliptical perf. holes on each vertical edge. Printed in gravure by Walsall with matrix removed.

Type MB7

MB7	Supporting London 2012 (15.6.04)	9·00

No. MB7 was sold at £1·68. A notch at the top right of cover was for identification by the blind.

Pane of 6 1st class "Security" Machins (gold)

Cover. As type MB3 printed in gold by Walsall
Barcode: 112268
Composition. One pane of six: UJPW23 (6×1st (gold) two bands (blue fluor) U-shaped slits and two elliptical perf. holes on each vertical edge. self-adhesive and printed in gravure by Walsall with matrix removed

Type MB3

MB8	Validation notice on reverse (31.3.09)	4·75

No. MB8 was initially sold at £2·16, which was increased to £2·34 from 6.4.09.

Pane of 10 2nd class stamps

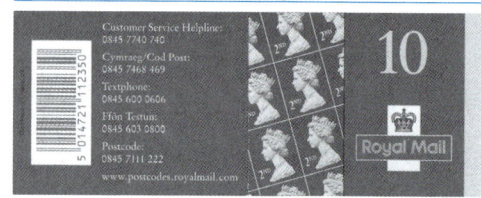

MC1

Cover. As Type MC1, with Machin stamps printed in bright blue by Questa.
Barcode: 112350
Composition. One pane of ten: Pane UIPQ5 (10×2nd (bright blue) centre band (blue fluor)) and two elliptical perf. holes on each vertical edge. Printed in gravure by Questa.

Type MC1

MC1	(29.1.01)	7·50

No. MC1 was sold at £1·90.

Pane of 10 1st class stamps

MD1

Cover. As Type MD1, with Machin stamps printed in bright orange-red by Questa
Barcode: 112243
Composition. One pane of ten: Pane UJPQ3 (10×1st (bright orange-red) two bands (blue fluor)) and two elliptical perf. holes on each vertical edge. Printed in gravure by Questa.

Type MD1

MD1	(29.1.01)	10·00

No. MD1 was sold at £2·70.

Panes of 12 2nd class stamps

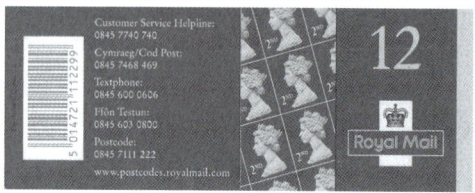

ME1

Cover. As Type ME1, with Machin stamps printed in bright blue by Questa
Barcode: 112299
Composition. One pane of twelve: Pane UJPQ2 (12×2nd (bright blue) centre band (blue fluor)) and two elliptical perf. holes on each vertical edge. Printed in gravure by Questa.

Appendix J Booklets

Type ME1

| ME1 | (29.1.01) | 8·00 |

a. "www.royalmail.com" outside back cover
(1.8.01) 8·00

Nos. ME1/1a were sold at £2·28.

ME2

Cover. As Type ME2, printed in bright blue by Questa.
Barcode: 112299
Composition. One pane of twelve: Pane UJPQ7 (12×2nd (bright blue) centre band (blue fluor)) and two elliptical perf. holes on each vertical edge. Printed in gravure by Questa.

Type ME2

| ME2 | (4.7.02) | 8·00 |

No. ME2 was initially sold at £2·28, which was increased to £2·40 from 8.5.03.

ME3
"The Real Network"

Cover. As Type ME3, printed in bright blue by Walsall.
Barcode: 112299
Composition. One pane of twelve: Pane UJPW8 (12×2nd (bright blue) centre band (blue fluor)) and two elliptical perf. holes on each vertical edge. Printed in gravure by Walsall with matrix removed.

Type ME3

| ME3 | (27.3.03) | 8·00 |

No. ME3 was initially sold at £2·28, which was increased to £2·40 from 8.5.03.and £2·52 in 2004.

Type ME4

Cover. As Type ME4, printed in bright blue by Walsall.
Barcode: 112299
Composition. One pane of twelve: Pane UJPW8 (12×2nd (bright blue) centre band (blue fluor)) and two elliptical perf. holes on each vertical edge. Printed in gravure by Walsall with matrix removed.

Type ME4

| ME4 | (15.6.04) | 10·00 |

No. ME4 was initially sold at £2·52.

Type ME4a

| ME4a. | Back cover with added text about new pricing structure (25.4.06) | 10·00 |

No. ME4a was sold at £2·76.

Pane of 12 2nd class stamps

Type ME4b

| ME4b. | Back cover with text about validity (5.6.07) | 7·00 |

No. ME4b was initially sold at £2·88, which was increased to £3·24 from 7.4.08.

Pane of 12 2nd class "Security" Machins

Covers. type ME2 printed by Walsall
Barcode:112299
Composition. One pane of UJPW27 (12×2nd one band (blue fluor)). U-shaped slits and two elliptical perf. holes on each vertical edge.

Type ME2

| ME5 | Validation notice on reverse (31.3.09) | 7·00 |

No. ME5 was intitially sold at £3·24, which was increased to £3·60 from 6.4.09.

Panes of 12 1st class stamps

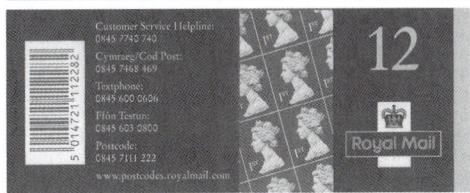

Type MF1

Cover. As Type MF1, with Machin stamps printed in bright orange-red by Questa.
Barcode: 112282
Composition. One pane of twelve: Pane UJPQ4 (12×1st (bright orange-red) two bands (blue fluor)) and two elliptical perf. holes on each vertical edge. Printed in gravure by Questa.

Appendix J Booklets

Type MF1

MF1 (29.1.01)	12·00
a. "www.royalmail.com" outside back cover (1.8.01)	12·00

Nos. MF1/1a were sold at £3·24.

As before but printed in gravure by Walsall.
Cover. As Type MF1, with Machin stamps printed in bright orange-red by Walsall.
Barcode: 112282
Composition. One pane of twelve: Pane UJPW5 (12×1st (bright orange-red) two bands (blue fluor)) and two elliptical perf. holes on each vertical edge. Printed in gravure by Walsall.

Type MF1

MF2 (29.1.01)	12·00
a. "www.royalmail.com" outside back cover (1.8.01)	12·00

Nos. MF2/2a were sold at £3·24.

MF3

Cover. As Type MF3, with gold laminated cover by Walsall.
Barcode: 112282
Composition. One pane of twelve: Pane UJPW7 (12×1st (gold) two bands (blue fluor)) and two elliptical perf. holes on each vertical edge. Printed in gravure by Walsall.

Type MF3

MF3 (5.6.02)	12·00
MF3a. Back cover with added text about new pricing structure (25.4.06)	10·00

No. MF3a was sold at £3·84
Withdrawn: 5 June 2007

MF3b

Cover. As Type MF3A printed in gold by Walsall.
Barcode: 112282
Composition. One pane of twelve: Pane UJPW7 (12×1st (gold) two bands (blue fluor)) and two elliptical perf. holes on each vertical edge. Printed in gravure by Walsall with matrix removed.

Type MF3B

MF3b. Back cover with text about validity (5.6.07)	12·00

No. MF3b was initially sold at £4·08, which was increased to £4·32 from 7.4.08

MF4
"The Real Network"

Cover. As Type MF4 printed in gold by Walsall.
Barcode: 112282
Composition. One pane of twelve: Pane UJPW7 (12×1st (gold) two bands (blue fluor)) and two elliptical perf. holes on each vertical edge. Printed in gravure by Walsall with matrix removed.

Type MF4

MF4 (27.3.03)	12·00

No. MF4 was initially sold at £3·24 which was increased to £3·36 from 8.5.03.

Pane of 12 1st class "Security" Machins

Cover. As Type MB3 printed by Walsall
Barcode:112282
Composition. One pane of 12: Pane UJPW28 (12× 1st (gold) two band (blue fluor)) U-shaped slits and two elliptical perf. holes on each vertical edge.

TYPE MB3

MF5	Validation notice on reverse (31.3.09)	9·50

No. MF5 was initially sold at £4·32, which was increased to £4·68 from 6.4.09

Pane of 20 1st Class Self-adhesive stamps

MG1
(Actual size 232 × 76 mm)

Cover. Printed in scarlet, yellow, black and deep ullramarine on matt card by Walsall. Folded twice between rows 3/4 and 6/7
Barcode: 100968
Composition. One pane of twenty: Pane UJPW1 (20×1st. (bright orange-red) two fluorescent bands with one elliptical perf. hole on each vertical edge. Printed in lithography by Walsall

Type MG1

MG1 (19.10.93)	20·00

No. MG1 contains self-adhesive stamps and was initially sold at £4·80 which was increased to £5 from 1.11.93.
Withdrawn: 28 April 1995

Panes of 6 E (European) Class stamps

Printed by Walsall

MH1

Cover. As Type MH1, printed in deep blue by Walsall
Barcode: 112824
Composition. One pane of six: Pane UJWEP1 (6×E (deep blue) two bands (blue fluor)) and two elliptical perf. holes on each vertical edge. Printed in gravure by Walsall with matrix removed.

Type MH1

MH1	(4.7.02)	12·00

No. MH1 was initially sold at £2·22, which was increased to £2·28 from 8.5.03..

MH2
"The Real Network"

Cover. As Type MH2, printed in deep blue by Walsall
Barcode: 112824
Composition. As for MH1

Type MH2

MH2	"The Real Network" below logo (28.5.03)	12·00

No. MH2 was initially sold at £2·28, which was increased to £2·40 from 1.4.04.

Panes of 4 Europe stamps

MI1
"The Real Network"

Cover. As Type MI1, printed in new blue by Walsall
Barcode: 116495
Composition. One pane of four: Pane UJPWEP2 (4×Europe (new blue and rosine) two bands (blue fluor)) and two elliptical perf. holes on each vertical edge. Printed in gravure by Walsall with matrix removed.

Type MI1

MI1	(27.3.03) With 4 airmail labels	8·50

No. MI1 was sold at £2·08.

MI2

Cover. As Type MI2, printed in ultramarine by Walsall
Barcode: 116495
Composition. One pane of four: Pane UJPWEP5 (4×Europe (new blue and rosine) two bands (blue fluor)) and two elliptical perf. holes on each vertical edge. Printed in gravure by Walsall with matrix removed.

Type MI2

MI2	(15.6.04) With 4 airmail labels	9·00

No. MI2 was sold at £2·78.

Panes of 4 Worldwide stamps

MJ1
"The Real Network"

Cover. As Type MJ1, printed in rosine by Walsall.
Barcode: 116501
Composition. One pane of four: Pane UJPWEP3 (4×Worldwide (rosine and new blue) two bands (blue fluor)) and two elliptical perf. holes on each vertical edge. Printed in gravure by Walsall with matrix removed.

Type MJ1

MJ1	(27.3.03) With 4 airmail labels	12·00

No. MJ1 was sold at £4·48

Type MJ2

Cover. As Type MJ2, printed in red by Walsall
Barcode: 116501
Composition. One pane of four: Pane UJPWEP6 (4×Worldwide (rosine and new blue) two bands (blue fluor)) and two elliptical perf. holes on each vertical edge. Printed in gravure by Walsall with matrix removed.

Appendix J Booklets

Type MJ2

MJ2	(15.6.04) With 4 airmail labels	16·00

Pane of 4 Worldwide Postcard Airmail stamps

MJA1

Cover. As Type MJA1, printed in grey-black by Walsall with multicoloured emblem.
Barcode: 118482
Composition. One pane of four: Pane UJPWEP4 (4×Worldwide Postcard self-adhesive stamps (grey-black, rosine and ultramarine) two bands (blue fluor)) and two elliptical perf. holes on each vertical edge. Printed in gravure by Walsall with matrix removed.

Type MJA1

MJA1	(1.4.04) With 4 airmail labels at right	5·00

No. MJA1 was sold at £1.72

I. Self-adhesive Barcode Booklets containing stamps with face values)

£2·52 Booklets

NA1

Cover. As Type NA1, printed in deep olive-grey by Walsall
Barcode: 112831
Composition. One pane of six: Pane UJWMP1 (6×42p. (deep olive-grey) two bands (blue fluor)) and two elliptical perf. holes on each vertical edge. Printed in gravure by Walsall with the matrix removed.

Type NA1

NA1	(4.7.02)	25·00

NA2
"The Real Network"

Cover. As Type NA2, printed in deep olive-grey by Walsall.
Barcode: 112831
Composition. One pane of six: Pane UJWMP1 (6×42p. (deep olive-grey) two bands (blue fluor)) and two elliptical perf. holes on each vertical edge. Printed in gravure by Walsall with the matrix removed.

Type NA2

NA2	"The Real Network" below logo (28.5.03)	25·00

£4·08 Booklets

Cover. As Type NA1, printed in deep olive-grey by Walsall
Barcode: 112848
Composition. One pane of six: Pane UJWMP2 (6×68p. (grey-brown) two bands (blue fluor)) and two elliptical perf. holes on each vertical edge. Printed in gravure by Walsall with the matrix removed.

Type NB1

NB1	(4.7.02)	28·00

NB2
"The Real Network"

Cover. As Type NB2, printed in grey-brown by Walsall.
Barcode: 112848
Composition. One pane of six: Pane UJWMP2 (6×68p. (grey-brown) two bands (blue fluor)) and two elliptical perf. holes on each vertical edge. Printed in gravure by Walsall with the matrix removed.

Type NB2

NB2	"The Real Network" below logo (28.5.03)	28·00

J. Self-adhesive Barcode Booklets containing No Value Indicated Special and Definitive stamps

2001 £3·24 Cats and Dogs 1st Class stamps

PM1

Cover. As Type PM1, printed by Walsall.
Barcode: 112282
Composition. One pane of twelve: Pane WP1369 (10×1st Nos. 1359/68, 2×1st (bright orange-red) two bands (blue fluor)). Printed in gravure by Walsall.

Type PM1 Cats and Dogs

PM1	"12 First class stamps" (13.2.01)	35·00

No. PM1 was sold at £3·24.

Appendix J *Booklets*

Panes of 4 1st class Machins and 2 special stamps

Type PM2

Cover. As Type PM2, with Machin and Submarine special stamps printed by Questa.
Barcode: 112268
Composition. Pane of 2×(1st) and 4×(1st) Machin bright orange-red. Pane No. WP1384 self-adhesive. Printed in gravure.

Type PM2 Submarine stamps

PM2	(17.4.01)	£100

No. PM2 was sold at £1·62.
Sold out: December 2001.

PM3

Cover. As Type PM3, with Machin and Punch and Judy special stamps, printed by Questa.
Barcode: 112268
Composition. Pane of 2×(1st) and 4×(1st) Machin bright orange-red. Pane No. WP1414 self-adhesive. Printed in gravure.

Type PM3 Punch and Judy

PM3	(4.9.01)	20·00

No. PM3 was sold at £1·62

PM4

Cover. As Type PM4, with Machin and Flags special stamps printed by Questa.
Barcode: 112268
Composition. Pane of 2×(1st) and 4×(1st) Machin bright orange-red, Pane No. WP1391 self-adhesive. Printed in gravure.

Type PM4 Flags stamps

PM4	(22.10.01)	24·00

No. PM4 was sold at £1·62

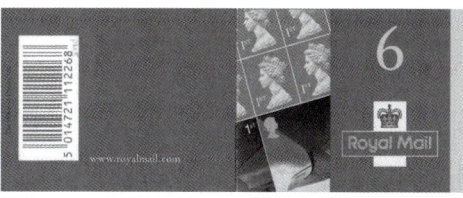

PM5

Cover. As Type PM5, with Machin and Concorde special stamps printed by Questa.
Barcode: 112268
Composition. Pane of 2×(1st) and 4×(1st) Machin bright orange-red. Pane No.WP1476 self-adhesive. Printed in gravure.

Type PM5 Airliners

PM5	(2.5.02)	15·00

No. MB5 was sold at £1·62.

PM6

Cover. As Type PM6, with Machin and World Cup Football Championship, special stamps printed by Walsall
Barcode: 112268
Composition. Pane of 2×(1st) and 4×(1st) Machin bright orange-red. Pane No. WP1481 self-adhesive. Printed in gravure.

Type PM6 World Cup Football Championship

PM6	(21.5.02)	15·00

No. PM6 was sold at £1·62.

PM7

Cover. As Type PM7, with Machin and Tower Bridge special stamps, printed by Questa.
Barcode: 112268
Composition. Pane of 2×(1st) and 4×(1st) Machin gold with surplus self-adhesive paper removed. Pane No. WP1498 self-adhesive. Printed in gravure.

Type PM7 Bridges of London

PM7	(10.9.02)	15·00

No. PM7 was sold at £1·62 And shows (when closed) a single notch at top right edge to facilitate identification by the blind.

Appendix J Booklets

PM8

Cover. As Type PM8, printed in gold with Machin and "Hello" greeting stamps printed by Questa.
Barcode: 112268
Composition. Pane of 2x(1st) and 4x(1st) Machin (gold) with surplus sel-adhesive paper removed. Pane No. UMP140 self-adhesive. Printed in gravure.

Type PM8 "Occasions" Greeting stamps

PM8   (4.3.03)   16·00

No. PM8 was sold at £1·62 (£1·68 from 8.5.03) and shows a notch at top right-hand edge to facilitate identification by the blind.
Withdrawn: 3 March 2004

Type PM9

Cover. As Type PM9, printed in gold with Machin and Extreme Endeavours special stamps. Printed by De La Rue.
Barcode: 112268
Composition. Pane of 2x(1st) and 4x(1st) Machin gold with surplus self-adhesive paper removed. Pane No. WP1554 self-adhesive. Printed in gravure.

Type PM9 Extreme Endeavours

PM9   (29.4.03)   15·00

No. PM9 was initially sold at £1·62, which was increased to £1·68 from 8.5.03. A notch at top right of the cover, when closed, was to facilitate identification by the blind.

PM10

Cover. As Type PM10, printed in gold with Machin and A British Journey: Scotland special stamps. Printed by De La Rue.
Barcode: 112268
Composition. Pane of 2x(1st) and 4x(1st) Machin gold with surplus self-adhesive paper removed. Pane No. WP1586 self-adhesive Printed in gravure.

Type PM10 A British Journey: Scotland

PM10   (15.7.03)   15·00

No. PM10 was sold at £1·68. A notch at top right of the cover, when closed, was to facilitate identification by the blind.

PM11

Cover. As Type PM11, printed in gold with Machin and Meccano Constructor Biplane special stamps. Printed by De La Rue.
Barcode: 112268
Composition. Pane of 2x(1st) and 4x(1st) Machin gold with surplus self-adhesive paper removed. Pane No. WP1601 self-adhesive. Printed in gravure

Type PM11 Classic Transport Toys

PM11   (18.9.03)   15·00

No. PM11 was sold at £1·68 A notch at top right of the cover, was for identification by the blind.

PM12

Cover. As Type PM12, printed in gold with Machin and A British Journey: Northern Ireland special stamps. Printed by De La Rue
Barcode: 112268
Composition. Pane of 2x(1st) and 4x(1st) Machin gold with surplus self-adhesive paper removed. Pane No. WP1645 self-adhesive. Printed in gravure

Type PM12 A British Journey: N. Ireland

PM12   (16.3.04)   15·00

No. PM12 was sold at £1·68 A notch at top right edge of the cover was for identification by the blind. For similar booklet with Scottish issue, see No. PM10.

PM13

Cover. As Type PM13, printed in gold with Machin and Ocean Liners special stamps. Printed by De La Rue
Barcode: 112268
Composition. Pane of 2x(1st) and 4x(1st) Machin gold with surplus self-adhesive paper removed. Pane No. WP1656 self-adhesive. Printed in gravure.

Type PM13 Ocean Liners

PM13   (13.4.04)   15·00

No. PM13 was sold at £1·68 A notch at top right of the cover, was for identification by the blind.

Appendix J Booklets

PM14

Cover. As Type PM14, printed in gold with Machin and A British Journey: Wales special stamps. Printed by De La Rue.
Barcode: 112268
Composition. Pane of 2×(1st) and 4×(1st) Machin gold with surplus self-adhesive paper removed. Pane No. WP1677 self-adhesive. Printed in gravure.

Type PM14 A British Journey: Wales

PM14 (15.6.04) 15·00

No. PM14 was sold at £1·68 A notch at top right of the cover, when closed, was for identification by the blind.

PM15

Cover. As Type PM15, Beside the Seaside. Red cover with multicoloured emblem. Printed by Walsall.
Barcode: 112268
Composition. Pane of 2×(1st) with surplus paper and 4×(1st) Machin gold with surplus self-adhesive paper removed. Pane No. WP2045 self-adhesive. Printed in gravure.

Type PM15 Beside the Seaside

PM15 (13.05.08) 6·00

No. PM12 was sold at £2·16 A notch at top right of the cover, was for identification by the blind.

PM16

Cover. As Type PM16, British Design Classics (1st issue). Red cover with multicoloured emblem. Printed by Walsall.
Barcode: 124681
Composition. Pane of 2×(1st) Telephone Kiosk stamps and Rotemaster Bus with surplus paper and 4×(1st) Machin gold, U-shaped cuts, iridescent overprint with surplus self-adhesive paper removed. Pane No. WP2129. Printed in gravure.

Type PM16 British Design Classics (Telephone Kiosk & Routemaster Bus)

PM16 (10.3.09) 5·00

No. PM16 was initially sold at £2·16 (£2·34 from 6.4.09) A notch at top right of the cover, was for identification by the blind.

As before but containing changed British Design Classics stamps
Cover. As type PM16, British Design Classics (2nd issue). Red cover with multicoloured emblem. Printed by Walsall
Barcode: 124681
Composition. Pane of 2×(1st) (Mini) with surplus paper and 4×1st Machin gold, U-shaped cuts, iridescent overprint with surplus self-adhesive paper removed. Pane No. WP2131. Printed in gravure

Type PM16 British design classics (Mini)

PM17 (21.4.09) 5·00

No PM17 was intially sold at £2·34. A notch at top right of the cover was for identification by the blind.

As before but containing 50th Anniversary of NAFAS stamps
Cover. As type PM16, 50th Anniversary of NAFAS. Red cover with multicoloured emblem. Printed by Walsall
Barcode: 124681
Composition. Pane of 2×(1st) (*Iris Latifolia* and *Tulipa*) with surplus paper and 4×(1st) Machin gold, U-shaped cuts, iridescent overprint with surplus self-adhesive paper removed Pane No. UMP177. Printed in gravure

Type PM16 50th anniv. of NAFAS

PM18 (21.5.09) 5·00

As before but containing changed British Design Classics stamps
Cover. As type PM16, British Design Classics (3rd issue). Red cover with multicoloured emblem. Printed by Walsall
Barcode: 124681
Composition. Pane of 2×(1st) (concorde) with surplus paper and 4×1st Machin gold, U-shaped cuts, iridescent overprint with surplus self-adhesive paper removed. Pane No.WP2168 self-adhesive. Printed in gravure

Type PM16 British Design Classics (Concorde)

PM19 (18.08.09) 5·00

As before but containinng changed British Design Classics
Cover. As type PM16 British Design Classics (4th issue) Red cover with multicoloured emblem. Printed by Walsall
Barcode: 124681
Composition. Pane of 2×(1st) (Mini Skirt) with surplus paper and 4×(1st) Machin gold, U-shaped cuts, iridescent overprint with surplus self-adhesive paper removed Pane. No. WP2187. Printed in gravure

Type PM16 British Design Classics (Mini skirt)

PM20 (17.9.09) 5·00

K. Self-adhesive Barcode Booklets containing No Value Indicated "Smilers" stamps in definitive size (2005 – 2088)

Panes of 6 1st class "Smilers" stamps 20×23mm

QA1

Cover. As Type QA1 printed in gold by Walsall.
Barcode: 120300
Composition. One pane of six: Pane UMP158 (6×1st) two bands (blue fluor). Self-adhesive and printed in gravure by Walsall with matrix removed. Smilers advertisement at left.

Type QA1

QA1	Baby and Robin Smilers advertisement (4.10.05)	12·00

No. QA1 was initially sold at £1·80 which was increased to £1·92 from 3.4.06.

QA2

Cover. As Type QA2 printed in gold by Walsall.
Barcode: 120300
Composition. One pane of six: Pane UMP158 (6×1st) two bands (blue fluor). Self-adhesive and printed in gravure by Walsall with matrix removed. Smilers advertisement at left.

Type QA2

QA2	Baby and Robin Smilers advertisement (17.7.06)	15·00

No. QA2 was sold at £1·92.

QA3

Cover. As Type QA3 printed in gold by Walsall.
Barcode: 120300
Composition. One pane of six: Pane UMP165 (6×1st) two bands (blue fluor). Self-adhesive and printed in gravure by Walsall with matrix removed. "New Baby" yellow stamp Smilers advertisement at left.

Type QA3

QA3	Baby 'add a smile' advertisement at left (17.10.06)	10·00

No. QA3 was initially sold at £1·92, which was increased to £2·04 from 2.4.07.
Withdrawn: 16 October 2007

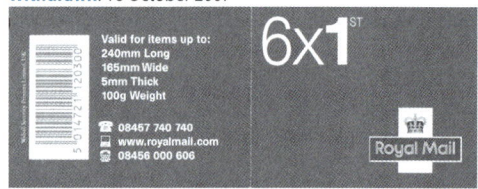

QA4
With "Valid for Items" but without inscription "New Stamps"

Cover. As Type QA4, printed in gold by Walsall.
Barcode: 120300
Composition. One pane of six: Pane UMP174 (6×1st) two bands (blue fluor). Self-adhesive and printed in gravure by Walsall with matrix removed. Child and Smilers advertisement at left.

Type QA4

QA4	Child 'Add a special moment' advertisement at left (28.2.08)	10·00

No. QA4 was initially sold at £2·04, which was increased to £2·16 from 7.4.08.

L. Self-adhesive Barcode Booklets containing stamps with value indicator at upper left

Pane of 4 2nd class stamps inscribed "Large"

RA1

Cover. As Type RA1, printed in blue by Walsall.
Barcode: 120645
Composition. One pane of four: Pane UJP15 (4×2nd) two bands (blue fluor). Self-adhesive and printed in gravure by Walsall with matrix removed.

Type RA1

RA1	Back cover with letter sizes and weight (15.8.06)	6·00

No. RA1 was initially sold at £1·48 which was increased to £1·60 from 2.4.07. Two notches at top right were for identification by the blind.

Pane of 4 2nd class "Security" Machins inscribed "Large"

Cover. As Type RA1, printed in blue by Walsall.
Barcode: 120645
Composition. One pane of four: Pane UJPW29 (4×2nd) two bands (blue fluor) U-shaped slits and two elliptical perf. holes on each vertical edge. Self-adhesive and printed in gravure by Walsall with matrix removed

Appendix J Booklets

Type RA1

	RA2 Validation notice on reverse (31.3.09)	3·50

No. RA2 was initially sold at £1.68, which was increased to £1·88 from 6.4.09. Two 11mm. wide notches at top right were for identification by the blind.

Pane of 4 1st class stamps inscribed "Large"

RB1

Cover. As Type RB1, printed in gold by Walsall
Barcode: 120638
Composition. One pane of four: Pane UJPW16 (4×1st) two bands (blue fluor). Self-adhesive and printed in gravure by Walsall with matrix removed.

Type RB1

RB1	Back cover with letter sizes and weight (15.8.06)	6·50

No. RB1 was initially sold at £1.76 which was increased to £1.92 from 2.4.07. A single notch at top right was for identification by the blind.

Pane of 4 1st class "Security" Machins inscribed "Large"

Cover. As Type RB1, printed in gold by Walsall
Barcode: 120638
Composition. One pane of four: Pane UJPW30 (4×1st) two bands (blue fluor) U-shaped slits and two elliptical perf. holes on each vertical edge. Self-adhesive and printed in gravure by Walsall with matrix removed.

Type RB1

	RB2 Validation notice on reverse (31.3.09)	5·00

No. RA2 was initially sold at £2.08, which was increased to £2·44 from 6.4.09. A single 11mm. wide notch at top right were for identification by the blind.

Pane of 6 1st class stamps

RC1

Cover. As Type RC1, printed in gold by Walsall.
Barcode: 112268
Composition. One pane of six: Pane UJPW16 (6×1st) two bands (blue fluor). Self-adhesive and printed in gravure by Walsall with matrix removed.

Type RC1

RC1	Back cover with letter sizes and weight (12.9.06)	7·00
	a. 'don't just send a stamp' advertisement inside left cover (2.10.06)	7·00
	b. "To find the correct postcodes for your mail" notice inside left cover (1.2.07)	7·00

No. RC1 was initially sold at £1·92 which was increased to £2·04 from 2.4.07. A single notch at top right was for identification by the blind.
No. RC1a was initially sold at £1·92 which was increased to £2·04 from 2.4.07.
No. RC1b was initially sold at £1·.92 which was increased to £2·04 from 2.4.07.
Withdrawn: 1 October 2007

Panes of 12 2nd class stamps

RD1

Cover. As Type RD1, printed in blue by Walsall.
Barcode: 112299
Composition. One pane of twelve: Pane UJPW2 (12×2nd) two bands (blue fluor). Self-adhesive and printed in gravure by Walsall with matrix removed.

Type RD1

RD1	Back cover with letter sizes and weight (12.9.06)	8·00

No. RD1 was initially sold at £2·76 which was increased to £2·88 from 2.4.07. Two notches at top right were for identification by the blind.

RE1

Cover. As Type RE1, printed in gold by Walsall.
Barcode: 112282
Composition. One pane of twelve: Pane UJPW14 (12×1st) two bands (blue fluor). Self-adhesive and printed in gravure by Walsall with matrix removed.

Type RE1

RE1	Back cover with letter sizes and weight (12.9.06)	12·00

No. RE1 was initially sold at £3·84, which was increased to £4·08 from 2.4.07. A single notch at top right were for identification by the blind.

M. Self-adhesive Barcode Booklet containing No value Indicated "Smilers" stamps in definitive size, with Definitive stamps

The following booklets were printed by Walsall

Panes of 6 1st class stamps including one "Smiler" stamp

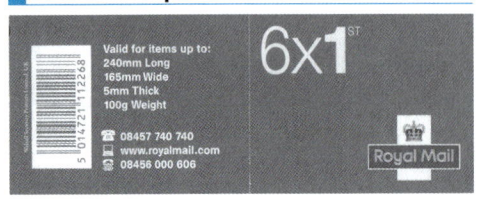

SA1

Cover. As Type SA1, printed in gold by Walsall.
Barcode: 112268
Composition. One pane of six: Pane UJPW18 (5×1st. No. UJW10 (gold), No. UM166 with two phosphor bands (blue fluor)). Self-adhesive and printed in gravure by Walsall with matrix removed.

Type SA1

SA1	Back cover with letter sizes and weight (16.7.07)	30·00

No. SA1 was sold at £1.92; the cover had a single notch at top right which was for identification by the blind.
Sold out: August 2007

Contents changed
Cover. As Type SA1, printed in gold by Walsall.
Barcode: 112268
Composition. One Pane of six: Pane UJPW24 (2×(1st) No. UM167 with labels, 4×(1st) UJW8 (gold), with two phosphor bands (blue fluor)). Self-adhesive and printed in gravure by Walsall with matrix removed.

Type SA2

SA2	Back cover with letter sizes and weight (15.1.07)	20·00

No. SA2 was initially sold at £2·04, which was increased to £2·16 from 7.4.08. A single notch at top right was for identification by the blind.

STANLEY GIBBONS
GREAT BRITAIN SPECIALIST DEPARTMENT

We invite collectors and specialists to have access to one of the finest selections of GB stock in the world by registering to receive our renowned free monthly colour brochure of between 500-550 specialist items from across the whole GB collecting spectrum, from pre-stamp postal history through to modern QE II errors.

Please contact Mark Facey on 020 7557 4424 or Michael Barrell on 020 7557 4448 or email mfacey@stanleygibbons.co.uk or mbarrell@stanleygibbons.co.uk to register.

Stanley Gibbons Limited, 399 Strand, London WC2R 0LX
Tel: 020 7836 8444   Fax: 020 7836 7342
To view all our stock 24 hours a day visit www.stanleygibbons.com

Questionnaire

Dear Catalogue User,

As a collector and Stanley Gibbons catalogue user for many years myself, I am only too aware of the need to provide you with the information you seek in an accurate, timely and easily accessible manner. Naturally, I have my own views on where changes could be made, but one thing I learned long ago is that we all have different opinions and requirements.

I would therefore be most grateful if you would complete the form below and return it to me (or send your answers on a separate sheet if you prefer not to cut the page out of your catalogue).

Very many thanks for your help.

Yours sincerely,

Hugh Jefferies,
Editor.

GB Specialised Stamp Catalogue - Queen Elizabeth II Volume 4 Part 2

1. Level of detail
   Do you feel that the level of detail in this catalogue is:
   a. too specialised ○
   b. about right ○
   c. inadequate ○

2. Frequency of issue
   How often would you purchase a new edition of this catalogue?
   a. Annually ○
   b. Every two years ○
   c. Every three to five years ○
   d. Less frequently ○

3. Design and Quality
   Did you like the new layout of this catalogue?
   a. Yes ○
   b. No ○

4. How would you describe the layout and appearance of this catalogue?
   a. Excellent ○
   b. Good ○
   c. Adequate ○
   d. Poor ○

5. How important to you are the prices given in the catalogue:
   a. Important ○
   b. Quite important ○
   c. Of little interest ○
   d. Of no interest ○

6. Would you be interested in an online version of this catalogue?
   a. Yes ○
   b. No ○

7. What changes would you suggest to improve the catalogue? E.g. Which other indices would you like to see included?
   ....
   ....
   ....
   ....
   ....

8. Which other areas do you collect?
   ....
   ....
   ....
   ....

9. Would you like us to let you know when the next edition of this catalogue is due to be published?
   a. Yes ○
   b. No ○
   If so please give your contact details below.
   Name:...
   Address:...
   ....
   ....
   ....
   Email:...
   Telephone:..

10. Which other Stanley Gibbons Catalogues are you interested in?
    a. ....
    b. ....
    c. ....

Many thanks for your comments.

Please complete and return it to: Lorraine Holcombe
Stanley Gibbons Limited, 7 Parkside, Ringwood, Hampshire BH24 3SH, United Kingdom
or email: lholcombe@stanleygibbons.co.uk to request a soft copy.